D0821294

BLOOD, SWEAT, AND TEARS

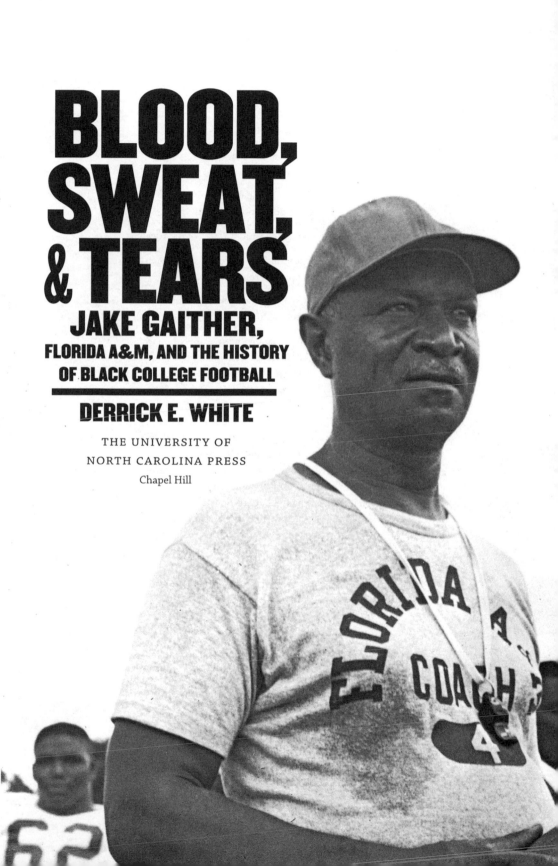

BLOOD, SWEAT, & TEARS

JAKE GAITHER, FLORIDA A&M, AND THE HISTORY OF BLACK COLLEGE FOOTBALL

DERRICK E. WHITE

THE UNIVERSITY OF
NORTH CAROLINA PRESS
Chapel Hill

Set in Chaparral and Champion types
by Tseng Information Systems, Inc.

Manufactured in the United States of America

The University of North Carolina Press has been a
member of the Green Press Initiative since 2003.

Cover photo: Coach Jake Gaither going over plays with his FAMU football
team, 1953 (Florida Photographic Collection, floridamemory.com)

Library of Congress Cataloging-in-Publication Data
Names: White, Derrick E., author.
Title: Blood, sweat, and tears : Jake Gaither, Florida A&M, and the
history of Black college football / by Derrick E. White.
Description: Chapel Hill : The University of North Carolina Press, [2019] |
Includes bibliographical references and index.
Identifiers: LCCN 2019004399 | ISBN 9781469652443 (cloth : alk. paper) |
ISBN 9781469652450 (ebook)
Subjects: LCSH: Gaither, Jake, 1903–1994. | Football coaches—United States—
Biography. | Florida Agricultural and Mechanical University—Football. |
African American universities and colleges—Sports. | Football—Social aspects—
United States. | College sports—United States—History—20th century.
Classification: LCC GV939.G3 W47 2019 | DDC 796.332092 [B] —dc23
LC record available at https://lccn.loc.gov/2019004399

*This work is dedicated
to my late uncle Larry Underwood,
whose stories about HBCU sports
inspired this project.*

CONTENTS

ILLUSTRATIONS AND TABLES

ILLUSTRATIONS

TABLES

ABBREVIATIONS AND ACRONYMS IN THE TEXT

AFL American Football League

AME African Methodist Episcopal

AP Associated Press

CIAA Colored Intercollegiate Athletic Association

FAMU Florida A&M University

FSU Florida State University

HBCU historically black college and university

ICC Inter Civic Council

KC Knoxville College

LSU Louisiana State University

MAA Midwestern Athletic Association

NAACP National Association for the Advancement of Colored People

NAIA National Association of Intercollegiate Athletics

NCAA National Collegiate Athletic Association

NFL National Football League

OBC Orange Blossom Classic

PWI predominately white institution

SEC Southeastern Conference

SIAC Southern Intercollegiate Athletic Conference

SWAC Southwestern Athletic Conference

TSU Tennessee State University

UF University of Florida

UPI United Press International

BLOOD, SWEAT, AND TEARS

INTRODUCTION

Jake and Sadie Gaither caught the elevator to their box seats on the fourth floor of Doak Campbell Stadium. The elderly couple sat quietly alone, as they had arrived two hours early to beat the traffic to the game. As the time got closer to kick-off, Jake Gaither pulled out his binoculars and pressed them to the glass, watching the players loosen up for the game.[1]

On the first weekend in October 1979, the Florida A&M (FAMU) Rattlers hosted the University of Miami Hurricanes. Although Division I college football had been fully integrated for at least a decade, the leading predominately white programs had judiciously avoided playing the powerful HBCU (historically Black college and university) teams such as FAMU, Grambling, Southern, or Tennessee State. Through sheer persistence and a little luck, FAMU had managed not only to get the Hurricanes on the schedule but to play them at home in Tallahassee.

Jake Gaither, more than most, understood the game's significance. He rubbed his thinning grey hair, feeling the two golf-ball-size indentions behind his left ear, a reminder of how much he had physically overcome to build a successful program. He had survived two brain tumors, a broken leg, and the whims of Jim Crow to build the most dominant program in Black college football. Gaither had been a coach at FAMU more than three decades. He was an assistant beginning in 1937 and was the head coach in 1945 until he retired in 1969. In his twenty-five years as head coach, he won 203 games against 36 losses and 4 ties. His teams captured seven national titles and twenty-three conference titles while producing three dozen All-Americans. He had ushered FAMU into the golden age of Black college football. However, he never had the opportunity to play the University of Florida (UF), Florida State University (FSU), or Miami, the three leading

For the sake of consistency, I have chosen to use FAMU as the abbreviation for Florida A&M. Over the course of the school's history, it has had several names, with Florida A&M College or FAMC being the most common before the 1960s. I have not used FAMC (or Famcee) unless it is directly quoted in a primary source.

formerly segregated football programs in the state. The highlight of his career, in terms of race relations, was beating the University of Tampa in his penultimate game in 1969. The victory's significance was muted when Tampa ended its football program in 1974. Even when FAMU, under coach Rudy Hubbard, captured the first I-AA national championship in 1978, the team was often overshadowed by the state's larger, and now desegregated, programs. The game against Miami was finally a chance to prove what many people had suspected for decades: FAMU was the best program in the state.

The game's racial significance was obvious, despite both teams' attempts to downplay the implications. One Rattler player stated, "Sure it's a big game but look around, most of the people going to school here [FAMU] are from Miami. It's not because we're black and they're white."[2] Other Rattler players told reporters that they believed Miami's white players would be scared and intimidated in front of the Rattlers' home crowd.[3]

The racial dynamics eclipsed each program's trajectory. FAMU entered the game as the more highly decorated program. Jake Gaither's teams were so dominant that in most years the final regular season game—the Orange Blossom Classic (OBC)—was a de facto national title game. The teams slumped after Gaither's retirement, but head coach Rudy Hubbard had restored the Rattlers to greatness by the late 1970s. Relying on a strong running game, Hubbard led the Rattlers to a Black college national championship in 1977, and the school won the first-ever Division I-AA playoff in 1978. Heading into the game against Miami, the Rattlers had won 27 of 28 games. On the other hand, the University of Miami had struggled through most of the 1970s. The school even threatened to end football after the 1978 season. Instead, the school hired Howard Schnellenberger, a former assistant coach to University of Alabama's Paul "Bear" Bryant and the offensive coordinator for Don Shula's successful Miami Dolphins teams. The gruff-voiced, pipe-smoking Schnellenberger eschewed the run-oriented offenses favored by most teams in college football for a passing offense modeled on professional football. He publicly rejected the University of Miami's legacy as "suntan-U" and told local fans and alumni at his opening press conference that he planned to win a national championship in five years.[4]

The divergent fortunes of the two programs meant that prognosticators and observers were split on who would win. Most national college football observers believed that Miami's status as a Division I program would mean an easy victory.[5] Others, including prognosticator Jimmy "the Greek" Snyder, thought that FAMU was the favorite.[6] The in-state reporters were aware of Miami's struggles and leaned in favor of FAMU.[7] For instance, five of seven sportswriters picked the Rattlers to win.[8] Gaither was unsure if FAMU could beat one of the state's traditional football powers. "I'm a realist," he said. "I face facts, I know that in order for us [FAMU] to win we have to play way over our heads."[9]

Everyone recognized that it was a big game. Schnellenberger reminded his players that the game was FAMU's "Super Bowl." Hubbard believed the game was "important, but not crucial," as the Rattlers were "already a good team."[10] FAMU alumni and fans streamed into the state capital, occupying every hotel room for nearly fifty miles.

The crowd was electric as kickoff approached. Gaither sat on the edge of his seat as the two teams stormed out of the tunnel. Miami players in their recognizable white pants, orange jerseys, and white helmets with the orange and green U emblem had a businesslike approach to the game. The players followed Schnellenberger's stoic leadership that emphasized offensive execution and defensive domination. The FAMU players had donned all-white uniforms and solid orange helmets. The Rattlers' home crowd and their world-renowned band, the Marching 100, inspired the players to be "boisterous, brash, and loud."[11]

After the opening kickoff, Miami's defense stymied the Rattlers in the game's opening drive. On the Hurricanes' first offensive possession, they settled for a 47-yard field goal to take a 3–0 lead. After stopping the FAMU offense for the second straight drive, Miami appeared to be headed for a formidable two-score lead. The 'Canes started with the ball near midfield and drove it inside the 20-yard line, when the Rattlers intercepted Miami quarterback Mike Rodrigue's pass in the end zone. The Rattlers quickly capitalized on their momentum, putting together an 80-yard drive, finished by a 38-yard run by backup quarterback Eric Truvillion, who had entered the game only because of an equipment malfunction to starting quarterback Sammy Knight's uniform. The Rattler players mobbed Truvillion in the back of the end zone, and the home fans erupted, furiously pumping their orange and green pom-poms.

The University of Miami answered with a 22-yard field goal to cut the lead to 7 to 6. Miami scored a quick touchdown after a rare interception by Miami's Jim Burt, a defensive lineman. With the Rattlers trailing 13 to 7, Hubbard and the coaching staff became more aggressive in their play-calling. Needing a spark, Hubbard inserted Pete Taylor, the former starting quarterback, who was still nursing a knee injury. The statuesque six-foot six-inch Taylor dropped back to pass on the first play of the drive and fired a 20-yard strike to tight end Calvin Forte. The completion was one of two the Rattlers executed the entire afternoon. When Taylor limped backed to the line of scrimmage, Hubbard put starting quarterback Sammy Knight back into the game. Knight converted a pair of fourth downs on the drive, including one on his only completion of the day. As the Marching 100 made their way down the stands to the field in preparation for another magnificent halftime performance, Knight scampered in for a touchdown on the last drive of the first half. The Rattlers' extra-point attempt failed, and the two teams headed to intermission tied at 13.

The two head coaches led their teams back to the field for the second half. Schnellenberger, dressed in a polo shirt and a mesh Miami baseball hat, paced the sidelines urging his men to play better over the next thirty minutes. The business-dressed Hubbard encouraged his young men to seize their opportunity. The third quarter was a defensive struggle, as both teams failed to score. The Rattlers made mistakes that marred most of the fourth quarter. In the opening minutes of the quarter, placekicker Vince Coleman missed a 30-yard field goal. The Rattlers got a key defensive stop when defensive lineman Harrell Oliver plowed through the Miami center to sack Rodrigue on the third down. On the ensuing possession, Knight executed a perfect triple-option pitch to running back Melvin McFayden, who sprinted for a touchdown. The touchdown run did not count, as he had stepped out-of-bounds near the 20-yard line. The Rattlers moved the ball inside the 5-yard line, only to have Knight fumble and Miami recover.

The Hurricanes began to orchestrate a drive to take the lead, when FAMU free safety Thomas Lane decked Miami receiver Larry Brodsky, causing a fumble that Lane also recovered. Hubbard told reporters after the game, "If Thomas Lane and Harrell Oliver had hit any harder, they would have killed somebody." The play was sweet justice for Lane, who grew up in Coral Gables minutes from the Miami campus but was not recruited by the Hurricanes. Seven plays later with under four minutes left in the fourth quarter, Vince Coleman atoned for his earlier miss by connecting on a 34-yard field goal to give the Rattlers a 16 to 13 lead.[12]

Starting from its own 20-yard line and needing a touchdown to win or a field goal to salvage a tie, Miami put together a well-executed drive relying on Rodrigue's passing ability. The Tallahassee native drove the Hurricanes for the winning score. However, the game looked to be over when Miami's Pat Walker fumbled inside the FAMU 5-yard line. Rattler players began celebrating until officials ruled that a Miami player had outfought four Rattlers for the ball in a pile of bodies.

Miami had the ball at the FAMU 3-yard line with little over a minute left in the game. FAMU's defense needed a goal line stand to preserve a tie. On first and goal, Miami ran a toss sweep wide left, and the Rattlers tackled Lorenzo "Smokey" Roan for no gain. On second down, defensive end Tony Hayes batted down Rodrigue's pass whose wide receiver was wide open for a touchdown in the right corner of the end zone. On third down, senior defensive tackle Algie Hendrieth knocked down another pass intended for an open receiver at the goal line. On fourth down with thirty seconds remaining, Schnellenberger was faced with a decision: go for the win or settle for the tie. (There was no overtime in college football until 1996.) He quickly sent the field-goal team onto the field. When the field goal unit trotted out, the mostly partisan Rattler crowd of 35,000 celebrated a potential tie with Miami and a moral victory. Sophomore kicker Dan Miller lined up to attempt a 20-yard field goal, his shortest of the day. It sailed just wide of the left upright.[13]

The Rattler sideline erupted and the Marching 100 danced, while the Hurricane players stood shocked. After FAMU ran out the final seconds of the clock, Hubbard hugged his quarterback, Sammy Knight, and led his team in prayer. The players put Hubbard on their shoulders, "and there, riding in a sea of orange helmets and raised black fists, he disappeared down the field, a man in search of another corner to stampede around." FAMU's famous band, fueled by a crisp horn section and a pulsating drum line, provided the soundtrack for the postgame festivities, as Rattler fans celebrated inside and outside the stadium for the next hour.[14]

The Miami players cried and cursed, refusing to give FAMU the respect it deserved even after the game. Miami's Rodrigue told reporters, "They have a good defense, good athletes, but they're not real sophisticated." The losing quarterback failed to credit the Rattler defense for holding his offense to 271 yards and one touchdown. The FAMU offense was equally impressive. The Rattlers' rushers often followed All-American lineman Tyrone McGriff's blocking on their way to shredding the Hurricanes' tenth-ranked defense for 296 yards rushing. A Miami assistant coach admitted, "They were a lot better on offense than I thought they'd be." In the postgame analysis, the media criticized Schnellenberger's decision to go for the tie, calling it a "chicken move." The school paper also suggested that the Miami coach should have substituted starting quarterback Rodrigue for redshirt freshman (and future National Football League [NFL] Hall of Famer) Jim Kelly.[15]

Lost in FAMU's joyous victory was the end of its football dynasty. Instead of a sign of bigger things to come, the win was the coda to four decades of football success. The very next season Miami beat FAMU in the rematch 49 to 0. Nonetheless, the 1979 game provided a glimpse of the possibilities of a strong Black college football program. The material inequalities borne by segregation and the realities of integration made recruiting the best players to Black college campuses increasingly distant and difficult. In an interview with *Sports Illustrated*, Hubbard argued that the limited resources available to FAMU were a product of racism. "What happens at Florida A. & M. parallels the plight of blacks in general, people not getting due recognition and yet performing. I don't care what anybody says; it's a form of racism. It's not going to keep us from executing, but it's a problem that hits us directly in the face." The most obvious example for Hubbard was the stark difference in FAMU's Bragg Stadium compared with FSU's Doak Campbell Stadium. "You can see it by the kind of stadium we have. Bragg Stadium at A&M is state-appropriated and so is Doak Campbell, but there is a lot of difference between the two." FSU's stadium seated 34,213 more people than Bragg, whose capacity was 13,200. These inequalities were even apparent as the FAMU players reveled in their triumph while awaiting the team bus to return them to their campus across town to change clothes.[16]

While Sadie yelled and screamed at every big play, Jake Gaither quietly watched the Rattlers pull off the win.[17] The legendary coach did not anticipate that FAMU's success would be the first and last for Black college football. While Black colleges continued to meet and defeat predominately white institutions (PWIs) on the gridiron, the opportunities for HBCUs to face their traditional in-state power did not immediately materialize. Traditional powers did not want to risk losing to a Black college until its talent and material advantages were lopsided in their favor. Most of these matchups would not take place until the twenty-first century. For example, FAMU would not play UF until 2003 and has yet to play FSU. Other leading HBCU football programs have had a similar experience. The University of Tennessee has never played Tennessee State (TSU). Louisiana State University (LSU) has never played Grambling or Southern, although it has played the other eight football programs in the state.[18] Black colleges in Maryland, Texas, North Carolina, and Alabama have had similar experiences.

Discrimination and fear explain the absence of these matchups. Opportunities at the onset of desegregation were minimal because of discrimination against Black colleges. There was also fear. College football coaches of the 1960s, 1970s, and 1980s knew that HBCUs had tremendous talent and coaching. They were well aware of the golden age of Black college football, in which hundreds of players from HBCUs made their mark at the professional level. Coaches were cognizant of the players' speed at FAMU, the size and athleticism at Grambling, and offensive creativity at TSU. Traditional southern football powers wanted to make sure these types of players played for them before competing against HBCUs. Traditional southern football programs knew about the coaching innovations introduced by Gaither, Grambling's Eddie Robinson, TSU's John Merritt, and others as well. The combination of players and coaching threatened the presumed superiority of southern PWIs. Rather than play at the height of their equal competitiveness, southern PWIs waited until integration relegated HBCUs to the lower levels of college football. As Gaither recognized, FAMU's victory over Miami was one of potent possibility that was never fully realized after integration.

Blood, Sweat, and Tears tells the history of HBCU football by examining how the Florida A&M University Rattlers, under the leadership of Alonzo "Jake" Gaither, were transformed into one of the greatest programs in the three decades after World War II. Through FAMU and Gaither, one can see the development of Black college football before World War II and the emergence of a golden age. This history is about the institutions—educational, athletic, and media—that buttressed the game. Therefore, this work builds on the insights of scholars of other Black institutions that have toiled behind the veil of segregation, like schools, churches, and fraternal organizations, by revealing the importance of HBCU football to African American culture and communities. More than an extracurricular activity, Black college football was a conduit between HBCUs and Black communities. Before professional football became a realistic option, athletic college men (and women) added the title of "coach" alongside "teacher" and "preacher" as employment options in the early twentieth century. In fact, Gaither and other leading athletic mentors acknowledged that a great coach was a combination of teacher and preacher. To appreciate coach Gaither and FAMU football is to understand one of the most critical sources of Black pride and producers of Black manhood in the twentieth century.

Beyond simply reviving the vital, too-little-told story of HBCU football, this book also puts the story of these programs in context. Crucial to any understanding of HBCU football before World War II is the fact that it was the product of what I call sporting congregations—a network of athletes, administrators, coaches, sportswriters, and fans. Social historians of African American life have provided a language and a theoretical frame with which to comprehend the broader implications of sporting communities. Notably, historian Earl Lewis has described how African Americans in Norfolk, Virginia, "modified the political language so that segregation became congregation," thereby creating "a certain degree of autonomy and, by extension, power."[19] Although white supremacy circumscribed the extent of that potential power, the rise of Black college sports offers remarkable evidence of how much sporting congregations could achieve.

The early years of Black college football highlight the cultural ethos of self-determination. African American communities in the immediate generations after emancipation faced an internal tension between integration and self-determination. In the midst of slavery, Black freedmen and freedwomen wondered if it was "possible to claim their African heritage and their right to American citizenship."[20] This discord manifested itself in bifurcated cultural and political processes. Politically, African Americans desired all the rights guaranteed to white citizens; thus, they demanded political integration. Culturally, however, postemancipation African Americans preferred autonomy.[21] African Americans' massive withdrawal from white religious institutions after the end of the Civil War exemplifies this need for autonomy. Newly freed African American men and women sought a religious assembly that affirmed their faith and heard their testimony.[22] African American communities' educational goals reflected this combination of political integration and cultural autonomy as well. Communities understood that inclusion was essential in receiving equitable material resources—educational funding, classroom materials, and teacher salaries. Simultaneously, communities wanted cultural autonomy in the classroom, believing that African American teachers and administrators, if given the opportunity, would provide better intellectual, cultural, and spiritual support for Black students. Many understood that cultural autonomy ensured that Black communities' human resources in the classrooms would train the future.

African Americans also considered this tension between integration and self-determination in their sporting needs. Many Black athletes and sports commentators believed that sports reflected a unique opportunity to engage Western culture's democratic ethos. These African American sports assimilationists thought that the fields, courts, and arenas were the metaphorical level playing fields made real. Other Black sports enthusiasts treasured the cultural autonomy (and the associated economic opportunities) provided by segregated athletic spaces. Segregation did not directly lead to a sporting congregation. Instead, it was a product of the faith in Black-controlled athletics for the betterment of the university and the community. Hence, college sports, with its attention to academics and personal development, reflected the African American ethos of cultural autonomy. On the other hand, professional sports, with its associated salaries, echoed the desire for political integration (at least for the players). This simplified framework helps explain the fierce defense by HBCU coaches of their segregated programs while promoting HBCU players for the NFL. In the broader context, African American congregations, both religious and secular, personify the autonomous assertion of Black humanity that reverberates the desire for freedom rights in a sea of white supremacy.[23] Thus, the networks of sporting congregations are but one of many areas fashioned in African Americans' interests.

The scholarship on race and sports has failed to account for sporting congregations. One reason is the celebration by many early African American sports advocates of Black players at PWIs. Edwin B. Henderson, described by scholars as the "father of black sport history," believed that Black athletic success could change racial prejudice.[24] Historian Patrick Miller has described Henderson's and others' belief in the ability of sports to alter race relations as "muscular assimilation." From such a perspective, the significance of Black athletes stemmed from their participation in integrated athletics at the college, professional, and Olympic levels. While Henderson was a devoted chronicler of Black college sports, the athletic achievements at HBCUs were an ill fit for his vision of the broader social role of integration. To understand the more widespread experiences of individuals who played in and supported the vast majority of Black college athletic programs, historians must look to HBCUs for their evidence, which demonstrates how Black colleges organized for success in spite of inequitable resources and the contributions of the programs and players to Black communities. As African American novelist Ralph Ellison wrote in his review of Gunnar Myrdal's seminal work on American race relations, *An American Dilemma*, "But can a people (its faith in an idealized American Creed notwithstanding) live and develop for over three hundred years simply by *reacting*? Are American Negroes simply the creation of white men, or have they at least helped to create themselves out of what they found around them? Men have made a way of life in caves and upon cliffs; why cannot Negroes have made a life upon the horns of the white man's dilemma?" Black college football was founded on the contradictions of the level playing field of sports but made Black folks' "lives more meaningful."[25]

As time passed, HBCU football programs used the sporting congregation to usher in the golden age of Black college football. In the three decades after World War II, HBCUs transformed sporting congregations into dominant football programs. The golden age had several attributes: great coaches, elite players, and sustained success. However, great Black coaches truly defined this era. For instance, there are eleven Black coaches in the College Football Hall of Fame as of 2018; all coached at HBCUs, and eight had their best years between 1945 and 1975.[26] These coaches, such as Gaither, Eddie Robinson, and John Merritt, symbolize the best of HBCU football. They were innovative strategists and inspirational leaders who coached some of the best Black football players ever. Just as important as the HBCU players who reached the Hall of Fame, many athletic alumni became leaders in their communities. The golden age of HBCU football was also defined by sustained winning by numerous programs, including those at FAMU, Grambling, Southern, TSU, Morgan State, and Prairie View. Fans Black and white watched these teams compete in the various HBCU football classics. The "classic" epitomizes Black college football, and it varies in type. It can be a rivalry game, such as the Bayou Classic featuring Grambling and Southern; it can be a host school with variable opponents, such as the OBC featuring FAMU; or it can be an event in a city, such as the Circle City Classic held in Indianapolis.[27] During the golden age, these games were regularly played before more than 40,000 fans and often determined the national champion. In addition, desegregation in the 1960s meant that these elite programs played against PWIs and won more than they lost. The opportunities to play leading white teams, especially before widespread racial desegregation, showed that Black college programs were as good as or better than many white programs.

In order to understand the specifics of sporting congregations and the golden age of Black college football, *Blood, Sweat, and Tears* weaves together Gaither's biography with FAMU's football program history. Gaither's early life in the mountains of Kentucky and Tennessee and his education, secondary and postsecondary, at Knoxville College (KC) from 1919 to 1927 coincides with the formation of conferences in HBCU football. During his twenty-five years as head football coach at FAMU, Gaither led one of the most dominant football programs of the 1950s and 1960s amid the civil rights movement and the integration of southern higher education. More-over, Gaither's retirement years—after 1969 as head football coach and after 1973 as athletic director—allow one to observe the changes caused by integration to Black college football through his eyes.

The question remains: why are Gaither and FAMU more emblematic of Black college football than the other leading coaches and programs, such as Eddie Robinson and Grambling, Cleveland Abbott and Tuskegee, or John Merritt and TSU? Five reasons separate Gaither and FAMU from other programs. First, Gaither represents the first generation of Black coaches who earned their degrees from Black colleges. The leading coaches in Black college football before 1930 were primarily racial pioneers from predomi-nately white colleges. This separates Gaither from Abbott, a graduate of South Dakota State, and Tuskegee, the first great Black college football dy-nasty. Second, through Gaither, we can identify the differences between public and private Black college athletic programs. As a graduate of KC and a leading coach at FAMU, Gaither straddles the private/public divide. He came of age when private schools such as Howard, Talladega, and Tuske-gee dominated HBCU football, and he coached when the championship was controlled by FAMU, Southern, Grambling, and TSU. This history separates Gaither from a contemporary such as John Merritt, a graduate of Kentucky State. Third, FAMU under Gaither dominated at the peak of the struggle for civil rights. Between 1950 and 1965, FAMU won or shared six Black college national titles. The only school with a comparable record at this time was Prairie View under Billy Nicks, which won five titles. Grambling, widely considered the best Black college football program in history, won only one title (1955) in this period. Robinson and Grambling transitioned to integrated football better than any program, winning eight Black college titles between 1967 and 1992. FAMU's winning during the height of the civil rights movement allows for the examination of the assumptions of Black inequality built into legal arguments for integration. Fourth, FAMU developed the OBC into the premier Black college bowl game, which under Gaither often became the de facto national championship game. No other "classic" compared to the OBC, in part because of its longevity and signifi-cance to the Black college football landscape. The Bayou Classic, featur-ing Grambling and Southern, became the highest-attended game by the 1970s. However, it, at best, determined the Southwestern Athletic Con-ference (SWAC) champion. Moreover, the rivalry was only regularly played after 1960. In fact, when Eddie Robinson and Grambling won their first national title in 1955, they defeated FAMU under the lights at the OBC in

Miami. These factors position Gaither and FAMU as the best HBCU during the racial reorganization that was the civil rights movement. Finally, one can see, after Gaither's retirement in 1969, the effects of trying to replace a legend during the height of integration. John Merritt (1962–83) at TSU and Eddie Robinson (1941–97) were forces of nature that steered their programs through the choppy and unforgiving waters of athletic integration in the 1970s. A brief sketch of the trajectory of Gaither's career, FAMU's football program, and the development of Black college football will shed light on both how they are interlinked and how they will unfold in the pages that follow.

The narrative begins with the emergence of a sporting congregation. The first chapter examines the process in which the game became organized from the late nineteenth century through the 1930s. Black college football developed parallel to its white counterpart. When segregation forcibly excluded Blacks, they created their own schools, churches, and professional societies to meet their needs, what scholars have called "parallel institutions."[28] The chapter uses Gaither's early biography, including his playing days at KC and his first coaching jobs, to examine how the pieces of the sporting congregation came together to support Black college football.

For most of the first three decades of the twentieth century, FAMU was not very good at football. Ironically, during the Great Depression, FAMU marshaled resources in the makings of a successful football program. In particular, FAMU began its OBC in 1933, hired William Bell as head coach in 1936, and hired Gaither as an assistant coach in 1937. The Rattlers' coaching staff improved the talent on the field and, more importantly, began to develop the high school coaching in the state. Chapter 2 explores how and why FAMU was able to achieve such success during a period of economic stagnation. At the outbreak of World War II, FAMU was in the discussion as one of the better programs in the country.

Yet, World War II almost wrecked FAMU's program, as the third chapter details. All colleges struggled with maintaining their athletic programs during the war. FAMU, however, faced another issue: the near-death of Gaither. In the spring of 1942, Gaither was diagnosed with two cancerous brain tumors. In the fall, the Rattlers won their second national title in five seasons. The football team's future, despite Gaither's illness, looked bright. The optimism quickly ended as the war called nearly every man on campus, including head coach Bill Bell, to boot camps. In nine months FAMU went from having two of the best coaches in the country to none. For FAMU and other HBCU football programs, World War II meant survival.

What followed was the golden age of Black college football. Chapter 4 describes Gaither's triumphant return to coaching after brain surgery. While the school's enrollment increased, he expanded FAMU's sporting congregation, using a coaching clinic and the OBC to build a dynasty. Empirically, *Blood, Sweat, and Tears* shows how FAMU's athletic department in conjunction with its physical education program functioned to staff a vast majority of the coaching positions in Black high schools in Florida, thus providing tangible webs of connections between the state's leading university for African Americans and the schools that prepared its future students.

Black college football and the FAMU program next had to reckon with the coming of the civil rights movement. FAMU was the best football program in the 1950s, and Gaither had become a leader in the Tallahassee community. He had garnered the respect of Blacks and whites alike. The civil rights movement, beginning with *Brown v. Board of Education* (1954) and including the bus boycotts of the mid-1950s and the sit-ins of the early 1960s, undermined Gaither's reputation with activists. At times, Gaither appeared to support his football program over desegregation.[29] I suggest that Gaither's opposition to desegregation not only was an attempt to hold on to his powerful football program but also showed an understanding of how integration would perpetuate PWI athletic dominance at the expense of HBCUs. Also, Gaither had an acute understanding of the ways structural racism worked in his attempt to build a stadium at FAMU. As chapter 5 reveals, the civil rights movement and its logic of integration coupled with structural racism embedded in public education put coaches in a no-win situation. Nonetheless, Gaither prepared his players for an integrated world that devalued the HBCU experience.

The golden age made an impact on the integration of professional football. Chapter 6 chronicles the war between the American Football League (AFL) and the NFL and the subsequent new opportunities for HBCU players. For FAMU, speedster Bob Hayes brought Olympic glory in 1964, and a year later, as a member of the Dallas Cowboys, he joined Gale Sayers and Dick Butkus as the best rookies in the NFL.

The growing number of successful Black college players in pro football coincided with the integration of PWIs. Chapter 7 analyzes the effects of FAMU's struggles on the field during the opening years of athletic desegregation and amid the growing Black Power movement. Gaither and other HBCU coaches pursued playing PWIs as a means to counter the expected effects of desegregation. Black college coaches wanted to prove to the media, fans, and recruits that HBCUs were equal on the field and should not suffer the same fate as the Negro League baseball teams that folded shortly after Jackie Robinson integrated the Major Leagues. In particular, Gaither believed that open competition would show potential recruits that FAMU was the best team in Florida. The Black Power movement exacerbated the team's struggles on the field with desegregation. Black Power advocates quickly depicted HBCUs generally and Gaither individually as an obstacle to liberation. Although the revolt of the Black athlete did not affect Gaither directly, it created an environment in which young people deemed his cautious approach to civil rights and his Black middle-class sensibilities out of touch.

The year 1969 marked Gaither's last season. The clear highlight was the first game between an HBCU and a PWI in Florida, when FAMU defeated the University of Tampa. While the victory on the field had been one of Gaither's most important, off the field, the federal government ordered the end of the dual education system—state-sponsored Black and white schools—in the South. Chapter 8 unpacks the consequences, as Black high schools, which had functioned as a vital cog in HBCU sporting congregations, were officially ended, as the federal government forced recalcitrant districts to abide by *Brown v. Board of Education*. Gaither's retirement marked the end of FAMU's participation in the golden age of Black college football.

What followed was the erosion of the golden age of Black college football. The epilogue explores the broad changes brought on by integration and the role of television to show how the structural deficiencies of HBCU football undermined attempts of Black colleges to compete consistently in the desegregated world of college football. The human resources that made up the sporting congregation could not compete in a world of multimillion-dollar athletic budgets fueled by structural racism and Black athletic bodies. While FAMU initially faltered, other programs such as Grambling and TSU competed at a high level into the 1970s. Under coach Rudy Hubbard, FAMU had a renaissance in the late 1970s, winning the first I-AA national championship in 1978 and defeating the University of Miami in 1979. This success was unsustainable, and the golden age would come to an end for all HBCU football programs. Black college programs could no longer win at the prodigious rates of the 1950s and 1960s. The best players in Tallahassee played for FSU and not FAMU, for LSU and not Grambling.

The golden age of Black college football represents a counternarrative for race and college sports. Rather than simply lauding the racial pioneers that desegregated college football, *Blood, Sweat, and Tears* offers another perspective that allows for critical reassessment of the assumptions of athletic integration. In particular, FAMU's football program undermines the notion that segregated institutions were inferior and suggests that athletic integration has produced as many losses as victories.

THE COLOR LINE OF SCRIMMAGE AND SPORTING CONGREGATIONS

The 1926 season was the finest for the Knoxville College (KC) Bulldogs in their first two decades of play. Founded in 1875 by the United Presbyterian Church, KC, an HBCU, didn't play its first games until the opening years of the twentieth century, as students took the lead in recruiting classmates, planning practices, and arranging games. In the beginning, most of the Bulldogs' early opponents were local. They played against Morristown College, a Methodist-sponsored HBCU in East Tennessee, local Black high schools, and occasionally Fisk (Nashville), Livingstone (Salisbury, N.C.), and Swift Junior College (Rogersville, Tenn.).[1] Though America's participation in World War I forced KC, like many colleges, to discontinue intercollegiate athletics, after the armistice, KC restarted its football team and joined the Southern Intercollegiate Athletic Conference (SIAC) in 1924. Conference affiliation normalized KC's schedule with those of other Black institutions of higher learning, setting the stage for the Bulldogs' great season.

All-conference fullback Raymond Fowles led the 1926 team, but teammates remembered that the true leader was Alonzo "Jake" Gaither, a six-year starter at left end.[2] KC quarterback Claude Cowan recalled that Gaither had "always been an emotional guy. He always shook up guys. Although I was captain of the team, we all looked to Jake for guidance. We looked to him for his judgment more than his playing ability."[3] Teammates described Gaither, a two-way player, as "a tough, forceful competitor."[4] He had arrived at KC in 1919 as a sixteen-year-old high school freshman. By his junior year of high school he was playing varsity, and as a high school senior he was a starter.[5]

Any chance KC had at a SIAC title depended on beating the Tuskegee Golden Tigers, coached by Cleveland "Cleve" Abbott, a racial pioneer and star athlete at South Dakota State. Abbott had originally been offered the coaching job by Tuskegee's founder, Booker T. Washington, before his death in 1915. Abbott eventually accepted the position in 1923, leading the team to undefeated seasons in 1924 and 1925 and claiming back-to-back national titles.[6] In 1926, All-American halfback Ben Stevenson led Tuskegee's explosive offense, making them the team to beat.[7]

The Bulldogs, unlike many of the HBCU football programs in the 1920s, still had a white coach.[8] Under Carl Moore, "a Pittsburgh man," the team adopted the slogan "Trounce Tuskegee" and believed that they had developed the plan they would need to stop the big, strong, and fast Stevenson.[9] Although the *Pittsburgh Courier* praised KC, remarking that the team had "upset pre-game predictions by their marvelous playing and successful ground gaining ability," KC's solid play was still not enough to defeat Tuskegee that year.[10] Even so, the 24 to 3 loss to the best team in Black college football was still a moral victory and set the tone for a season in which the Bulldogs rebounded to win 5 games in a row. Over Christmas break, the team left the cold of East Tennessee for a scrimmage against FAMU in Pensacola. Though the score of the game has been lost, it was momentous in other ways. Alongside his teammates, Jake Gaither swayed in the Jim Crow railcar on the way to Florida. Little did he realize that he was riding into his future.[11]

From 1892 through the 1930s, the opening generations of HBCU football witnessed the creation of a Black sporting congregation that linked campuses, in the form of coaches, administrators, and players, with Black communities through the Black press and the creation of fans. The athletic interactions between campus and community fueled the game's growth and development behind the color line. Black college football merged racial uplift with popular interest to become a significant part of Black culture. All the while, HBCU football reinforced an ethos of self-determination. The threads of the Black sporting congregation were not unique to African American colleges, but like other parts of Black culture influenced by the mainstream, such as jazz or the church, Black sporting congregations developed because of and in spite of segregation. Significantly, Black sporting congregations reflected themes of equality and autonomy shaped by slavery, emancipation, and Reconstruction.

These sporting congregations emerged at a time when racism was spreading to infect every crevice of Black life. Historian Rayford Logan has described the decades between the end of Reconstruction and World War I as the nadir of Black life, as segregation expanded across the South, legalized by the Supreme Court decision in *Plessy v. Ferguson* in 1896.[12] During the nadir, political leaders deemed reconciliation between the North and the South more important than African Americans' citizenship rights. Aided by the benign neglect of northern and western states, southern states eroded Black political rights in an orgy of violence and malicious intent.

In response to their political marginalization, Black Americans leaned on an ethos of independence and self-determination. "Underpinning the specific aspirations," according to historian Eric Foner, "lay a broader theme: a desire for independence from white control, for autonomy both as individuals and as members of a community being transformed by emancipation."[13] Newly freed men and women built institutions—churches, orphanages, and most notably, schools. When white supremacy constrained Black political rights, Black communities relied on their churches, schools, and fraternal organizations to organize their communities to fight for their freedom rights.[14]

The rising tide of white supremacy pushed Blacks out of many integrated institutional spaces. In response, they formed their own cultural, professional, and political institutions. These groups functioned as the seedbed that allowed Black communities to survive the harshest edges of American racism and to launch a counteroffensive to secure citizenship rights. In the assessment of historian Earl Lewis: segregation became congregation.[15] Sport and Black colleges, separately and together, reflected these themes of segregation and autonomy in the formation of a sporting congregation. As African American communities sought to survive the nadir, Black colleges built a sporting congregation with players, coaches, Black communities, media outlets, and athletic conferences as its foundation.

HISTORICALLY BLACK COLLEGES AND UNIVERSITIES

The wellspring for late-nineteenth- and early-twentieth-century Black cultural and professional organizations was HBCUs. The men and women who created, staffed, and graduated from HBCUs provided a steady supply of leadership and membership and reflected the aspirations of Black communities that had marshaled monetary, social, and political resources to build a network of secondary schools, colleges, and universities. Behind these efforts was a desire "to control and sustain schools for themselves and their children."[16] To reach this goal, Black communities accepted assistance from white-controlled individuals and institutions, including Christian missionaries, the federal government, and private philanthropists.

These bodies did not alter the educational aspirations of Black communities, though they did try to control the details. In spite of the desires of outside forces, Black communities shaped and reshaped these agencies' plans to their own will.

There were three founding waves of HBCUs. The first schools were founded before the Civil War. As some northern whites agonized over the validity and morality of slavery, several religious denominations, such as the Quakers and the Methodists, founded schools to educate free Blacks. The Quakers founded Cheney State University (1837) and Lincoln University (1854) in Pennsylvania, while the Methodists founded Wilberforce University (1856) in Ohio.[17] These northern HBCUs were built upon the abolitionist movement. Next, a significant number of private colleges were founded after the Civil War by northern Christian missionaries, often with the help of the Freedmen's Bureau. Attempting to help Blacks transition from slavery to freedom, most church-sponsored schools for African Americans began as parochial, teaching biblical lessons alongside the fundamentals. Soon, church leaders realized that the educational needs of the newly freed exceeded the time constraints of parochial schools. The demand for Black agricultural labor limited the school year in the South to four or five months between the harvest and planting seasons. The missionaries also maintained negative views of African American character and morality and came to believe that boarding schools provided the best means of eradicating illiteracy and countering the supposed moral depravity of their students. Church-supported Black colleges emerged from these boarding schools.[18] Finally, there were the colleges started or enhanced due to the Morrill Act, signed by Abraham Lincoln in 1862 to establish land-grant colleges nationwide. Although Black colleges in Mississippi, Virginia, South Carolina, and Kentucky used the first Morrill Act, the vast majority of HBCUs were products of its successor, the 1890 Morrill Act.

The paradox of Black education during the nadir can be seen in the 1890 Morrill Act's contradictory aspirations to voice support for integration while accepting southern segregationist customs where necessary. Its language stated "that no money shall be paid out under this act to any State or Territory for the support and maintenance of a college where a distinction of race or color is made in the admission of students, but the establishment and maintenance of such colleges separately for white and colored students will be held to be in compliance with the provisions of this act if the funds received in such State or Territory be equitably divided as herein set forth."[19] Six years before the *Plessy v. Ferguson* decision, then, the authors of the Morrill Act accepted segregation as a form of race management.

One key distinction between the missionary-initiated Black colleges and those begun under the auspices of the Morrill Act would be public versus private status. Of the HBCUs founded between 1890 and 1900, three-fourths were public, a complete reversal of the pre-1890 pattern. The public versus private split would shape the trajectory of football at HBCUs, as private schools dominated the opening generations, while public Black colleges would become a force in the mid-twentieth century. Regardless of the specific circumstances of their founding, virtually all HBCUs emerged from the third and final founding wave with a similar mission: to provide higher education for African Americans with the goal of race leadership. HBCU graduates set out to fulfill what W. E. B. Du Bois later described as the "social regeneration of the Negro" and to "help in the solution of problems of race contact and co-operation."[20]

The trajectories of KC and FAMU, founded in the second and third waves, respectively, reveal how the missions and functions of HBCUs transformed between emancipation and the nadir. KC's origins follow the parochial school-to-college trajectory. In 1863, the Reverend Joseph G. McKee arrived in Nashville to begin his missionary work, meeting with African American elders and seeking their support for a parochial school. With African American blessings, financial support, and commitment, McKee opened a school in a Baptist church basement. By 1874, however, the school was being squeezed out for students by other denominations, most notably Fisk University, which was sponsored by the American Missionary Association and the United Church of Christ, and Roger Williams, sponsored by the American Baptist Association. The Presbyterian missionaries decided to move their school to Knoxville in 1875, seeking a less competitive environment to fulfill their Christian educational aims. Once the school relocated to east Tennessee, it transitioned to a boarding school in 1877 and later became a college. At the beginning of the twentieth century, KC filled several educational roles: a secondary-level boarding school, a normal school that trained teachers, a liberal arts college, and a fledgling medical school.[21] KC would later receive money from the Morrill Act, after it agreed to offer "practical" agricultural education. KC's physical plant rapidly expanded from one building on 3 acres in 1877 to twenty-one buildings and 100 acres in 1918.[22] For African Americans, the college was the crown jewel of east Tennessee, but it lacked the influence of Black Nashville's institutions of higher education—Fisk, Meharry Medical College, and TSU. In time, TSU, the lone public HBCU, would surpass the other private Black colleges in the state in terms of enrollment. TSU's late founding but rapid growth represented the increasing importance and role of public HBCUs in many southern states, including Florida.[23]

Although FAMU was founded in 1887, it benefited tremendously from the second Morrill Act. Florida A&M University, originally named the State Normal College for Colored Students, opened in the fall of 1887. The State Board of Education, controlled by Democrats who had "redeemed" the state, named Thomas De Saille Tucker, a graduate of Oberlin College and a Pensacola lawyer, the first president of the Normal College for Colored Students. The school used a $7,500 grant from the second Morrill Act to move to the former Highwood plantation of ex-governor William D. Duval, which sat on a hilltop overlooking Tallahassee.[24]

Early graduates and students of the State Normal College for Colored Students stood as a light in an ever-darkening cave of segregation, racial hostility, and political disenfranchisement. Florida colleges were founded before the U.S. Supreme Court case *Plessy v. Ferguson* established "separate, but equal" as the law of the land, but the state copied the segregation policies emerging across the South in the 1870s and 1880s.[25] In addition, Florida was mired in racial violence, experiencing the highest rate of lynching in the United States. The 1890s witnessed particularly gruesome examples of racial violence. An eyewitness described the torrid details of an 1895 lynching of three men in Lafayette County, ninety miles southeast of Tallahassee. "They were scalped, their eyelids and their noses cut off, the flesh cut from their jaws, their bodies scraped and their privates cut out. The blood flowed in streams from their ghastly wounds and their screams rent the air only to be silenced by the tearing out of their tongues by the roots."[26] Amid pervasive violence, Black Floridians lost their citizenship rights through a network of new laws, including poll taxes (1887), a secret ballot that required literacy (1895), and the white primary (1897). FAMU graduates, through their service, were expected to work to change Black folks' lived experiences.

The question of whether a vocational or a liberal arts curriculum at HBCUs better served the needs of Black communities has been a persistent flashpoint for debate through the years, with the differences between Booker T. Washington and W. E. B. Du Bois anchoring the opposing sides of this argument.[27] The exigencies facing Black communities were too vast for one type of curriculum to be completely effective. Most HBCUs, including KC and FAMU, provided students with a curriculum that taught both liberal arts and vocational education. While vocational education addressed the practical needs of African American communities, teachers, especially Black teachers, employed a liberal arts curriculum that attempted to teach equality.[28] As suggested by Du Bois's observation that "an educated Negro" was "a dangerous Negro," white southerners sought to limit what they saw as the corruptive power of a liberal education.[29] To counter these revolutionary ideals and to promote a compliant labor force, southern states insisted on the teaching of industrial or vocational education. This approach received support from Black leadership. Most notably, Booker T. Washington promoted vocational training as mutually beneficial to Blacks and for an industrializing New South. In his 1895 Atlanta Compromise Speech, he called on African Americans to surrender their immediate claims for social and political equality until they had amassed enough economic capital to warrant first-class citizenship.[30] Southern states threw their support behind Washington and industrial education. At FAMU, for example, Superintendent of Public Instruction William N. Sheats would fire the school's first president for "an obvious inattention to agricultural and industrial education."[31] Although vocational education would take hold at FAMU, its predominately Black teaching faculty was subversive with what historian Jelani Favors calls an "unwritten second curriculum," which "defined the bond between teacher and student, inspiring youths to develop a 'linked sense of fate' with the race."[32] On the other hand, KC's curriculum was predominately liberal arts, but most of its faculty were white. Thus, the message of equality was translated through a liberal arts curriculum. The students, in turn, formed a tight-knit community. No matter the type of curriculum, a Black college community, or "communitas," formed with race and racial equality at its center.[33] Ultimately, sports, especially football, would be a major contributor to the identity of Black colleges. Even though the game on the field was played with the same rules as in predominately white institutions, its meanings and implications were racialized.

COLLEGE FOOTBALL AND SPORTING
CONGREGATIONS IN BLACK AND WHITE

The component parts of Black sporting congregations were assembled from across the landscape of college football, repurposed in light of segregation, and deployed in service of African Americans' desires for equality and autonomy. Although the same notes appear, Black colleges and communities improvise, making the chords and composition all their own. The result is a game that is both familiar and different.

There are five key components in the creation of the sporting congregation that emerges from HBCU football: students, coaches, media, community, and reformers. These factors are present at PWIs and HBCUs, but it is the surrounding culture that reveals the differences. As scholar Michael Oriard has written, "The 'meaning' of football in America is thus to confront a plurality of meanings."[34] For HBCUs, football is the athletic representation of Black culture that holds forth the possibility of broader equality.

STUDENTS TAKE THE LEAD

Before nearly all HBCUs were founded, PWIs had already begun playing football. Rutgers and Princeton played the first football game in 1869. However, the game itself resembled soccer, as Rutgers "dribbled" in six goals to Princeton's four. In the opening decade of college football, the sport created a "college community" on campuses and was an identifying characteristic of white upper-class men. The rules of the game became more structured and the play on the field more competitive after Harvard, Princeton, Columbia, and Yale formed the Intercollegiate Football Association in 1876.[35] For white elites in the nineteenth century, college football came to symbolize industry and manhood. Players had to work as a unit, but each had a different role. Unlike baseball, football was bound by time and by structure—a gridiron. It was a game for the modern man. Historian Julie Des Jardins writes, "Football was a uniquely American phenomenon . . . in both mindset and purpose, because it brought out the penchant for planning in the nation's men. . . . Football [was] work—industrial *and* corporate work and hence modern work; highly organized, disciplined, productive, and specialized work, and hence work with moral and pecuniary value."[36] The best teams were "well-oiled machines" and worked like "clock-work." For a generation of elite college-educated white men born after the Civil War, the game also had the benefit of providing a taste of the strenuous life that offset what Theodore Roosevelt saw as "a life of slothful ease."[37] Football, especially in New England, epitomized elitism, modern work, and manhood in the late nineteenth century.

At these elite colleges, African Americans were often an ill fit for college football in the early years. Slowly over the course of the last decade of the nineteenth century, African Americans appeared on the gridiron for schools in the East and the Midwest. Scholars have identified about a dozen Black football players at white colleges before 1900 and about twice that many before 1914. In 1889, Amherst College's William Jackson broke college football's color line. A year later William Henry Lewis joined Jackson on the Amherst squad. Lewis would later play for Harvard University, while attending law school in 1892 and 1893, where he became the first Black collegiate football star.[38] Pioneering Black players faced various forms of racism from players on the field, from fans in the stands, and from coaches on the sidelines. For instance, the 1903 Dartmouth–Princeton game became a national story because of the ways the color line was enforced on and off the field. Princeton had the reputation as one of the most racist institutions in the Northeast. While Harvard, Yale, Cornell, and Dartmouth had small numbers of Black students at the beginning of the twentieth century, Princeton remained all-white. Matthew Bullock, a budding star at left end, led the Dartmouth team. To counter the Dartmouth star's play, Princeton's players planned to "do up" Bullock. On the game's first play, Princeton players shouted, "Remember what you are to do with the nigger." On the third play of the game, Bullock's shoulder was dislocated. As he lay on the ground writhing in pain, a player shouted to anyone who would listen, "We'll teach you not to bring niggers down to play against us."[39] After the game, the Princeton Inn, not officially affiliated with the college, refused the team and Bullock admittance. The violence of football in the nineteenth and early twentieth centuries caused broken bones and occasionally even death. Racial animus made the mass pile of bodies even more dangerous for the handful of Black athletes.[40]

HBCU football began more than two decades later and was student-led as well. The first Black college football game, for example, was a low-scoring 4 to 0 Biddle College win over Livingstone College on December 27, 1892. Students, led by future university president William J. Trent, organized the Livingstone team in the fall of 1892, buying footballs from Spalding's sporting goods, sewing padding into some old clothes, and practicing. Biddle College had begun practicing football in 1890, calling the team "The Bull Pen" and studying the game through various publications. The Biddle University players made the forty-mile trip from Charlotte to Salisbury for the game over the Christmas break. According to the newspaper report, "The snow hindered the playing of the game."[41]

During Jim Crow, Black men were a living contradiction. Segregation dictated that Black men were less than men. The constant barrage of violence, labor discrimination, scientific racism, racial stereotypes, and expectations of racial deference all functioned to strip away any notion of manhood. However, mainstream expectations of masculinity were still prevalent. Middle-class African Americans, in particular, asserted their manhood, despite Jim Crow, in familiar ways: patriarchal authority, self-employment, education, and sport. Any claim to Black manhood meant success in at least one of these areas. The college gridiron was a site of recovery for Black middle-class manhood, along with the pulpit, the classroom, and the lodge.[42] African American participation in Black college football was a small relief from the daily humiliations of Jim Crow. HBCU football stood at the nexus of Black manhood because it provided patriarchal authority, education, and sport in one package. Thus, Black college football embodied a version of Black manhood that tied student-athletes to the ideology of racial uplift and, eventually, to the mantle of racial leadership. As football players at HBCUs, young men were preparing for a life of leadership. The gap between the start of football at PWIs and HBCUs, however, meant that Black colleges were heavily influenced by the growing importance of coaches.

COACHES

Although students had taken the lead in organizing football at elite PWIs, coaches had begun to take over by the 1890s. College football was blossoming, becoming the organized game akin to the modern version. The driving force behind the game's transformation from a sport resembling rugby or soccer to the most popular sport on late-nineteenth-century college campuses was Yale's Walter C. Camp. Described by many as the "father of American football," he almost single-handedly shaped the direction of football by changing rules and creating a coaching philosophy.[43] Camp played for Yale from 1875 to 1882 as an undergraduate and briefly as a medical student. As a student, he convinced the Intercollegiate Football Association to change the rules, including adding the position of quarterback and the yard-to-gain rule that separated the game from both rugby and soccer. More important, he coached the Yale team after his playing days were over. Coaches in this era did not stalk the sidelines or call plays but, rather, led the teams through organized practices and worked with the team captain to develop game-day strategies. With Camp as a player and as a coach, Yale became a juggernaut, winning thirteen national titles between 1875 and 1900.[44]

Yale's success, on the field and at the turnstile, led many aspiring teams to hire former Yale players as coaches. Camp and his protégés spread the gospel of scientific football. Former Yale players would go on to coach at the University of Chicago, Stanford, the University of Pennsylvania, and other leading schools.[45] Southern colleges got over their opposition to

Table 1. *A partial list of racial pioneers who coached at* HBCUS

NAME	SCHOOL	ALMA MATER
John Hope	Atlanta Baptist College (Morehouse), 1899	Brown University
C. C. Cook	Howard University, 1894	Cornell University
Samuel H. Archer	Atlanta Baptist College (Morehouse), 1905	Colgate University
Charles Winter Wood	Tuskegee University, 1905	Beloit College
George Sampson	Florida A&M University, 1906	Case Western
Matthew Bullock	Atlanta Baptist College (Morehouse), 1908	Dartmouth College
William Henry Bullock	Lincoln University, 1916	Dartmouth College
Harry R. Jefferson	Wilberforce University, 1923	Ohio University
Cleveland Abbott	Tuskegee University, 1923	South Dakota State University
Samuel B. Taylor	Virginia State University, 1924	Northwestern University

Yankeedom and contacted coaches and former players on eastern teams. Elite students, professors, and observers from New England became "football missionaries" who spread the gospel of the pigskin to the South and West.[46] Still, the small number of African American players at northern and eastern colleges suggests a strange quandary for the development of Black college football. Who brought the game to HBCUs?

Similar to Camp's disciples who spread the gospel of football, racial pioneers at northern colleges became the ambassadors of the game for Black colleges.[47] Thus, the development of Black college football was, in part, reliant on the migration of former players at white colleges to HBCUs. Racial pioneers at PWIs (see table 1) brought an understanding of the game and its rules but also experience as players, coaches, and observers. John Hope, who had graduated from Brown before teaching and coaching at Morehouse, explained the importance of sports at HBCUs in a letter to his wife: "I try to put games into prominence among our people." He added, "Sports teach them how to contest without losing self-respect. It is a means of acquiring bravery and gentility."[48]

Former racial pioneers at northern PWIs relocated to HBCUs for several reasons. First, Black college graduates faced limited job opportunities because of segregation and racism. Two careers that educated Blacks obtained amid the racial hostility were teaching and preaching. According to the 1910 census, in the Black population there were more than 29,000 teachers and 17,000 clergy members, but only about 900 physicians and 800 lawyers.[49] W. E. B. Du Bois determined that approximately 53 percent of Black college graduates were teachers by 1910, whereas only 10 percent of graduates were in law or medicine.[50]

Second, the end of the nineteenth century witnessed a massive shift from white teachers to African American educators in Black schools. At the end of 1865, 90 percent of the teachers for the newly emancipated Black population were whites.[51] The calculus of white supremacy, segregation, and Black self-determination led African American parents and communities to ask for Black teachers in their grammar schools, secondary schools, and colleges. African American communities, especially Black-led religious denominations, pressured private HBCUs to change the racial composition of the faculty members and the administration. For instance, Biddle College (now Johnson C. Smith) appointed its first Black professor in 1886 and by 1891 had a Black president. Was it a coincidence that Biddle played in the first Black college football game one year after the arrival of its Black president and majority-Black faculty?

Finally, sporting migration was occasionally bidirectional. Some Black players who integrated northern colleges had prior relationships with HBCUs. A few Black athletes at northern colleges were the products of secondary education at HBCUs, as many Black colleges included secondary, normal, industrial, or seminary schools. HBCUs instructed Black teens into adulthood. Hence, some early Black college football players had attended Black colleges before arriving at northeastern colleges. Harvard's William Henry Lewis went to Virginia Normal and Industrial (now Virginia State College) before continuing at Amherst and Harvard. In another case, William Clarence Matthews graduated from Tuskegee, serving as player-coach for football as a teenager, before suiting up for the Harvard Crimson. The educational experience for some Blacks was fluid as they moved between the North and the South. This intersectional migration permitted football to take root at HBCUs.[52]

MEDIA

For PWIs, Walter Camp was essential not only as a coach but as a publicist for the game. America's growing and competitive newspaper and periodical industry served as an instrumental outlet for Camp's belief in scientific football, in which he espoused the importance of tactics, strategies, and intelligence over physical brawn. He regularly published articles in newspapers and periodicals such as *Harper's Weekly* and *Outing*. Camp detailed the rules of the game for novice fans, told stories of the virtues of football, and provided season forecasts and recaps for readers.[53] His *American Football* quickly became the leading authority on the game in the 1890s.[54] He even selected the game's first All-Americans. Camp's promotion of the game in print was translated into popularity at the turnstile. Four thousand fans watched the 1878 Princeton versus Yale game. A decade later, 15,000 fans attended the contest. College football continued its exponential growth in the 1890s. Twenty-five thousand fans attended an injury-marred 1894 Harvard against Yale game in Springfield, Massachusetts. The following year even captains of industry such as Cornelius Vanderbilt had some difficulty getting box seats to big games.[55]

For HBCU football, the mainstream press ignored the "sepia circuit," and the Black press did not devote significant attention to it until the 1920s. In the early twentieth century, the sports pages of the Black press paid little attention to athletics on Black college campuses, instead focusing on racial pioneers at predominately white colleges and on professional sports. Described by scholars as the "father of black sport history," E. B. Henderson primarily told readers of the accolades of Black student-athletes at PWIs.[56] Henderson's belief that athletic integration could encourage social integration led him to emphasize the role of pioneering athletes. "The millions of Americans who have witnessed colored heroes of the gridiron striving to carry their hopes to fruition in victorious contests cannot but grow more tolerant towards a minority element with which their heroes are identified," he wrote.[57] Additionally, professional sports, especially boxing, stimulated the growth of Black newspapers' sports sections.[58] For instance, Frank "Fay" Young became the sports editor at the *Chicago Defender* in 1915 after convincing the owner, Robert Abbott, to publish a special issue on the Jack Johnson–Jess Willard fight in April 1915, which became the paper's biggest seller. Shortly thereafter, Abbott made Young the first Black sports editor in the country.[59]

Beginning in the 1920s, sportswriters and editors from the leading Black newspapers in the South prioritized the coverage of HBCU football. The *Norfolk Journal and Guide* began its "From the Press Box" column in November 1924, written by Willey A. Johnson Jr., a graduate of Shaw University.[60] In 1925, the *Pittsburgh Courier* released its first Black college All-American team, featuring Tuskegee's Ben Stevenson as the most dominant player of the 1920s.[61] William L. Gibson's column, "Hear Me Talkin' To Ya," appeared in the *Baltimore Afro-American* beginning in 1929.[62] By the 1930s, Gibson could declare in the National Association for the Advancement of Colored People (NAACP)'s *Crisis* magazine, "Football in Negro colleges is becoming more scientific and with this change, new school names are being emblazoned among the gridiron greats."[63]

While Johnson and Gibson were influential in the expansion in coverage of football at HBCUs, no one surpassed Eric "Ric" Roberts in promoting Black college football. In 1927, when Roberts was a freshman at Clark College (now Clark Atlanta University), he wrote columns on Black college football for the *Chicago Defender*.[64] A year later, W. A. Scott II hired him as the first sports editor at the *Atlanta Daily World*.[65] In 1934, Roberts and fellow journalists started a group of "armchair experts" who predicted the winners for more than 25 games per year.[66] The journalists dubbed their group the 100% Wrong Club because of the fickle decisions by coaches and players that often determined the outcomes of games. The prognostications came with detailed coverage of HBCU football from every major conference. Roberts and the 100% Wrong Club celebrated Black athletics for its inherent greatness, not for its potential role in integration. He recalled, "When Howard and Lincoln played a football game in front of 20,000 people . . . there was no such thing about Harvard or Yale; they were just something to read about in the paper."[67] The Black press, led by the 100% Wrong Club, promoted its innovative Black coaches, great teams, and impassioned rivalries. Roberts would add, "Our heaven and our glory was . . . not at Harvard, but at Howard and Lincoln and it [moved] south where Morehouse and Atlanta University and Clark and Morris Brown and Tuskegee and Alabama State and finally Florida A&M and other schools west of the Mississippi . . . all joined the passion [of the] black world."[68] The media was essential in connecting college football to broad segments of the Black community.

COMMUNITY

Walter Camp believed that football was the essential game for a modern and industrial society and a means of unifying ethnically diverse whites. His All-American teams were composed of WASPs and immigrants but rarely included Blacks.[69] Thus, college football, despite its elite origins, could connect with broad but different components of white America by interpreting the game through ethnic, regional, and class lenses. Football was not only a language of modern manhood for young men at elite eastern schools such as Yale, Harvard, and Princeton but a vehicle for regional modernization as well. Historians Patrick B. Miller and Andrew Doyle have shown how football became representative of a modern and proficient South. Although it was just a game, football was especially effective in transmitting this message because it echoed southern themes of chivalry and did not challenge the region's racism.[70] While there was a sliver of space for racial pioneers on the gridirons of northern PWIs, there was no room for broader themes of Black culture.

PWI college football's themes of industrialism, racism, and expansion were mostly unappealing to Black communities. However, the game's emphasis on manhood and a level playing field struck a chord with HBCUs and Black communities. As a theme, manhood or manliness runs through much of the discussion about early college football.[71] For the whites, northern and southern, football became tantamount to war for a generation too young to fight in the Civil War. For Blacks, however, notions of manhood countered racial stereotypes that defined African Americans as second-class citizens. Football emboldened young African American men. HBCU football's promotion of manliness merged with middle-class notions of racial uplift. Besides, the idea of a level playing field was framed by the political and social inequalities facing Black communities. The game, even if only between Black teams, exemplified the possibility of equality for Black communities. In contradistinction, the all-white PWI teams signaled the nation's commitment to inequality.

Nothing illustrated HBCU football's connection to Black communities and its distinct cultural ethos better than the creation of Black college football "classics." Traditional rivalry games such as Harvard versus Yale and Ohio State versus Michigan occurred on Thanksgiving weekend. It was no surprise that Black colleges mimicked this big-game model, as it was lucrative for leading PWIs. Beginning with Howard versus Lincoln, Black colleges began to develop their own big-game rivalries.[72] The *Chicago Defender*'s sports editor, Fay Young, called the Howard–Lincoln game "the most important game in the country as far as we are concerned."[73] By the 1920s, rivalry games, often played at neutral sites, dotted the Black college football landscape. Over time, classics have evolved into three categories: "traditional rivalries, host schools with variable opponents, and identifiable events with two different teams."[74] But a classic was and is more than just a rivalry game. It was a community event that featured parties, reunions, parades, and community service. The game represented Black empowerment—at the colleges, in the community, and on the field. Fueled by the growing sports pages in the Black press, the HBCU classic became a recognizable component of Black culture.

A series of crises on and off the field generated athletic reformers among college administrators and faculty. The rule and structural changes to college football, beginning in the 1890s at PWIs and after World War I at HBCUs, shifted the power and control of the game from students to coaches and administrators. In the late nineteenth century, violence and cheating plagued the game at PWIs. Mass momentum plays, such as the "flying wedge," led to numerous injuries that caused observers to question the value of football.[75] Between 1905 and 1909, sixteen people died per year from football injuries.[76] Critics, led by Harvard University president Charles Eliot, abhorred the broken bodies and the corruption of amateur ideals. Theoretically, the amateur athlete played for the fun of the game, not as a job or for pay. The concept of amateurism, then, separated college athletics from the professional sports. Despite this noble notion, college football programs prioritized winning, and recruiting the best players was the surest way to compete for championships. Before athletic scholarships became the norm, many schools used tramp athletes, players who did not even attend the school, to gain a winning advantage. Schools also supplied talented athletes with extra benefits in the form of money or jobs to lure them to campus. Sportswriter Caspar Whitney, for instance, revealed in 1900 that Columbia University's sudden success under its first paid coach was a result of the team playing four "ringers."[77] In 1905, sixty-two white colleges formed the Intercollegiate Athletic Association to regulate player recruitment and eligibility, in addition to establishing a rules committee.[78] In 1910, the association was renamed the National Collegiate Athletic Association (NCAA), while segregation excluded emerging Black college programs from the new organization. Along with rule changes designed to reduce injuries, college football at PWIs survived the first major crises.

Reforms in Black colleges were less about injuries and the deliberate cheating through the use of tramp players or ringers and more about the effects that the varying types of Black colleges had on player eligibility. The growing competition in HBCU football magnified the differences between Black colleges that focused on liberal arts and the ones devoted to industrial education, as well as the distinctions between public and private HBCUs. The gridiron was not an obvious location for the education debate between W. E. B. Du Bois and Booker T. Washington to play out, but ideas about proper education—classical or industrial—merged with questions of athletic eligibility. Because Black colleges were often boarding schools, normal schools, and colleges, talented athletes had the opportunity to play for more than four years of college. For example, Tuskegee's Ben Stevenson (1924–31) played eight seasons. These long tenures, including Jake Gaither's six seasons at KC, were not against the rules, per se, but they led observers to call for reform.

In the fall of 1911, Ernest Jones Marshall, head football coach and chemistry professor at Howard University, mailed letters to every Black college asking them to come together and form an intercollegiate athletic association. Only four schools answered Marshall's clarion call. Disappointed but determined, Marshall organized a meeting in February 1912 with the four respondents: Lincoln University (Pa.), Shaw University (N.C.), Hampton University (Va.), and Virginia Union University. These five colleges, including Howard University, formed the Colored (now Central) Intercollegiate Athletic Association (CIAA) in 1912. CIAA organizers imagined creating a Black version of the NCAA, establishing rules and regulation for the Black colleges, including a four-year eligibility rule.[79] Many HBCUs opposed the CIAA's rules because they eliminated a high number of players, since team rosters contained players from multiple academic levels. The CIAA's plan to limit eligibility to four-year college students would have ended football at many schools. Case in point: Talladega College's (Alabama) secondary school student enrollment to college student ratio was 180 to 1 in 1907. In 1912, Talladega had only 30 students enrolled in its college. Similarly, FAMU had a student population of nearly 350 in 1916, but only 12 of the students were taking college subjects instead of high school, industrial, or normal education classes. KC boasted comparable numbers before Gaither arrived, with only 30 college students out of 327 students in 1916. The marginal difference between secondary and higher education posed unique problems for HBCUs in determining player eligibility.[80]

Nonetheless, other colleges followed the CIAA's lead. In December 1913, presidents John Milton Putnam Metcalf of Talladega College and John Hope of Atlanta Baptist College (Morehouse) called a meeting about player eligibility. Representatives from Jackson State, FAMU, Talladega, Atlanta Baptist, Clark College, Morris Brown, and Fisk came together to form the Southern Intercollegiate Athletic Conference. The representatives set standards for player eligibility by addressing the use of work-study to recruit talented prep players or to entice players to transfer to another school. Although scholarships were not formally allowed, these jobs programs were the beginnings of the practice at HBCUs. Additionally, the attendees wanted to reduce the number of classes missed by athletes, to determine the financial arrangements for games, and to adopt new rules to reduce major injuries. They also created another organization, the Coaches and Officials Conference, to improve coaching techniques and the quality of the officiating.[81] The plans for the athletic conference were interrupted by World War I, but in SIAC's second decade, coaches and athletic directors took control of the sports programs on campuses. W. H. Kindle, secretary-treasurer of SIAC, remembered, "It was this change [coaches and administrators taking the reins of athletics], perhaps, more than any other which was responsible for the application of the mass attack in football, the expansion of football schedules, the beginning of intersectional and post-season games on a large scale, the increased use and development of Negro officials, the rapid expansion of the program to include basketball, track and field events, and tennis."[82] The conference also expanded in 1924 to include TSU and KC.[83]

Other HBCUs followed the lead of the CIAA and SIAC. Six schools led by Prairie View A&M formed the Southwestern Athletic Conference in 1920. Athletic leaders from Kentucky State, West Virginia State, Bluefield State (W.Va.), Wilberforce, and Lincoln (Missouri) formed the Midwest Athletic Conference in 1924.[84] As the 1920s progressed, other HBCUs joined one of these four conferences. Affiliation, rather than independence, was the future of Black college football.[85] The formation of segregated athletic conferences comprised the final piece of the HBCU sporting congregation. These pieces formed the foundation of the golden age of Black college football.

GAITHER ENTERS THE SPORTING CONGREGATION

Jake Gaither spent eight years at KC, starring on the field and in the classroom. A varsity player since a high school junior, Gaither played six solid seasons, and the Bulldogs went 16–12–1. He soon came to believe that football was a crucible for Black leadership. In an article in the school paper titled "Benefits Derived from Football," Gaither admitted, "Because of my love for football it might be impossible for me to be a fair and impartial critic of the game. But I feel justified in giving some of the benefits to be derived from the game, as I . . . both feel and see them." He continued by describing how football developed "physical manhood"; provided moral value, unity, and sportsmanship; and created lasting friendships. "The pal-like confidence and good fellowship that I have enjoyed with the fellows on the gridiron amply compensate for any hardships, bumps, and knocks that I might have received here," he concluded.[86]

Gaither's beliefs in the middle-class principles produced by football merged with his family's values. Alonzo S. Gaither was born on April 11,

1903, in Dayton, Tennessee. Alonzo's father, Jefferson Davis Gaither, was an itinerant minister, and his mother, Florence Gaither, was a teacher. The Gaithers were strict disciplinarians who instilled in their five children a belief in education, honesty, hard work, and faith. Alonzo was the second oldest child and was expected to become a pastor. His father declared, "This son will follow in my steps and become a minister."[87] After a half-dozen moves in Tennessee, Jefferson Davis Gaither became the presiding elder at a small African Methodist Episcopal (AME) church in Middlesboro, Kentucky, a mining town in the foothills of the Cumberland Mountains. Alonzo's parents, believing their son would thrive in a better academic environment, sent him to KC ahead of the ninth grade. Although the school was of a different denomination, it provided the stark discipline that the family valued. It was at KC where classmates gave Alonzo the nickname "Jake."[88] Sports were not part of the decision-making process for Gaither's family. His father only saw Jake play once at KC, believing football was a distraction. During the senior Gaither's lone fan experience, however, he leaped from his seat when Jake "did something spectacular," shouting, "My boy, my boy."[89] Jefferson Gaither was not a convert to the leadership possibilities of sports, but he was a proud father.

At KC, Jake Gaither developed the personality and character traits that would have enabled him to become a minister, as his father wished, or to satisfy his own goal of becoming a lawyer. According to the school yearbook, "He is aspiring for the ministry, a good candidate, a deep and quick thinker." He was a tremendous debater who led KC to several intercollegiate debate wins. It was Gaither's victories in debate that captured the attention of one particular classmate, Sadie Mae Robinson. According to her recollection of that event, "He [Gaither] and Tom Love were debating away. They [other students] said there was no chance for us to win the one on the road, with that freshman [Gaither] on the team. But about midnight the campus bell started ringing, signifying news of a victory in that road debate. And it was like a football celebration—a parade the next day and everything."[90] Jake and Sadie would marry in 1931. He also engaged in protests against the college's strict rules against dances. Gaither's debating ability and protest activities earned him the nickname "The Stormy Petrel."[91]

The gridiron, like the pulpit, prepared Black men for leadership in their communities. Ultimately, the segregated playing fields would become cathedrals with the coaches as the clergy. Still, there was a difference between metaphorical clergymen and actual men of God. Gaither was torn between the two—the gridiron and the pulpit—as he entered his senior year (1926–27). After starting in a 21 to 0 homecoming victory over TSU, Jake received an urgent message from his father.[92] Rev. J. D. Gaither summoned him to a church conference in Johnson City, Tennessee, a small town 100 miles east of Knoxville in the Blue Ridge Mountains because he was seriously ill. For several weeks Jefferson Gaither had battled a streptococcus bacterial infection. When Jake arrived, his father's body was covered with a painful rash. His father asked Jake to read his conference report. Jefferson Gaither weakly told his son that this was his "first report—and perhaps my last." The elder Gaither passed away before the conference concluded.[93] Mourning the passing of the family patriarch, Jake signed the death certificate and arranged for his father's body to be returned to Middlesboro, Kentucky.[94]

Jake Gaither faced a terrible choice. He could satisfy his father's wishes by going into the ministry. His debating ability had earned him admission into the Presbyterian-led Pittsburgh Theological Seminary.[95] He could seek to achieve his own goal of becoming a lawyer and apply to law school. But with his father gone and his mother and three siblings without support, he knew he would have to go to work.

After his father's death, Jake Gaither had little choice but to accept a teaching position at Henderson Institute, a boarding school started and run by the United Presbyterian Church since 1891. The town of Henderson was in the northern section of North Carolina and was the county seat for Vance County, a Reconstruction-era gerrymandered response to African American electoral success. Henderson was home to more than 25,000 county residents, most of whom were African Americans, and tobacco farming dominated the town and the county. The Southern Railway, the Seaboard Railway, and state highway 50 (now Route 1) connected Henderson to the regional centers of Raleigh, Durham, Winston-Salem, Richmond, and Norfolk.[96] Dr. John A. Cotton, a KC alumnus, directed the institute and hired Gaither to teach math and civics. He would also coach all of the school's sports teams—football, basketball, baseball, and track.[97]

Gaither's employment at the Henderson Institute coincided with the growth of southern Black high school sports in the 1920s. In North Carolina, school segregation produced an athletic world that promoted women's basketball as an expression of Black womanhood, and men's sports in the state were a "cornerstone of black male identity."[98] Significantly, Black high schools became enmeshed in the HBCU sporting congregation. Schools like Henderson played Black colleges well into the mid-1930s. As one report noted, "Although, Henderson is a standard high school it often has a place on college schedules."[99] Thus, the prep fields and courts became an accessible space for coaches to fulfill the aims of racial uplift and for players to learn the associated lessons of leadership.[100]

Fresh off graduation and full of confidence, Gaither arrived in Henderson in the summer of 1927. His first football season shattered his youthful self-assurance. Gaither remembered, "I came out of college cocky. . . . I just knew I was the smartest thing in the world."[101] He was sure that he "knew more football than any coach in North Carolina high schools."[102] But, in truth, Gaither knew little beyond offensive and defensive line play, his old position. In particular, Gaither's offense was atrocious. The Henderson Institute Panthers went winless in Gaither's first two seasons, only scoring one touchdown. The losing ate away at Gaither. He needed to learn more about coaching.

To rectify his tactical inadequacies, Gaither studied local college teams and schemed about how he might find a way to work around the humiliations of Jim Crow to attend coaching clinics at a nearby college. Gaither sent a letter to Duke University's football coach Wallace Wade requesting permission to attend his clinic.[103] Although the dictates of segregation forbid Gaither from attending, he was willing "to come and be a janitor and they'd never know I was attending the clinic." He added, "I could [be a] care taker or a janitor and sweep the floors so that I could hear the lecturers."[104] Wade never responded to the letter, and Gaither never forgot the slight.[105]

Wade's pocket veto did not deter Gaither. He looked at coaching clinics in the North. Notably, the Ohio State University summer sports clinic, which started in 1932, proved to be the most influential to Gaither's career.[106] The Ohio State sports clinic was one of many that introduced coaches to graduate training in physical education. The school capitalized on the post–World War I boom in the field. Nationally, physical education advocates and military men were embarrassed by the number of American men found to be "unfit for service." One military general estimated that 50 percent of men drafted were designated 4-F, not acceptable for service.[107] In 1932, Ohio State became just the third university to offer a graduate degree in physical education.[108] Gaither began taking classes in 1931 and would earn a master's degree in 1937.[109] At the Ohio State coaching clinic, he learned from head football coach Sam Willaman and he met William "Big Bill" Bell, a former Ohio State football All-American who was also taking classes.[110] The two became fast friends and were eager to make their mark on Black college football. Bell's accolades as a player at Ohio State had landed him a coaching job at Claflin University, a Methodist-sponsored HBCU in Orangeburg, South Carolina. Gaither needed to translate the coaching strategies he had learned through observation, study, and the coaching clinic into wins at the Henderson Institute.

Gaither's teams found their form starting in 1930 because the Panthers no longer struggled to score points. Henderson opened the 1930 season with a 48 to 0 win over Columbia High School, it routed Dillard High of Goldsboro 52 to 0, and it shut out Booker T. Washington of Rocky Mount 35 to 0.[111] The Henderson Panthers ended the season with a North Carolina state football title. Gaither had led the Panthers to the pinnacle of North Carolina Black high school football in just four seasons. More impressive, and a tribute to Gaither's coaching acumen, were the Henderson basketball and track teams' state championships. In fact, he had never seen a basketball game before coaching at Henderson, because KC didn't have a team until after he had graduated.[112] Gaither not only captured a state title in basketball, but his team finished second in a national high school tournament held at Hampton in 1933 and went to the national tournament again in 1934 in Gary, Indiana.[113]

The dominance of Gaither's teams drew the attention of the Black press and the ire of high school opponents. The *Norfolk Journal and Guide* ran a profile of Gaither, noting that he had won state championships in football, basketball, and track during the 1930 season. Gaither's best players went on to play at North Carolina A&T, Howard, St. Augustine's, and Hampton.[114] When Gaither won his third state football title in 1934, his fellow high school coaches had grown tired of the Panthers' dominance. The North Carolina Negro High School Athletic Association raised eligibility questions. At the association's annual meeting in 1935, coaches proposed to exclude the state's two boarding schools, Henderson Institute and the Mary Potter School in Oxford, North Carolina, from competing for state titles.[115] The accusatory coaches wanted Gaither to admit that Henderson, as a boarding school, had more money, time, and players than the other schools in the state. Gaither countered by suggesting that his fellow coaches were simply not as good.[116] The ugly incident continued to play out in the Black press for months.[117] A former Henderson player wrote, "Coach Gaither does not care . . . about grouping all-stars on his teams—the so-called boarding school advantage—he tells you to 'forget what you did in Podunk, do it here.'" He reiterated that no players received preferences on

St. Paul's College football team, 1935. Gaither, wearing a suit, is on the far left. (Scurlock Studios, Archives Center, National Museum of American History, Smithsonian Institution)

a Gaither team.[118] Despite the support of students, the association suspended Gaither from coaching for a year.[119] Even without Gaither at the helm, Henderson captured another state basketball title.[120]

Gaither's suspension provided an opportunity for him to move into college coaching. In June 1935, St. Paul's Normal and Industrial School (later College) in Lawrenceville, Virginia, announced that it had hired Gaither as an assistant coach. The Tigers were a member of the CIAA Second Division, a level that Gaither later used to describe his school as a junior college.[121] Many saw the hiring of Gaither as a positive for the St. Paul's football program. The Norfolk Journal and Guide's E. B. Rea, who had been documenting the acrimony in the North Carolina high school ranks for more than six months, lauded Gaither and the school for the hire. "Generally misunderstood, among a clannish group, 'Jake' Gaither went about his business in the face of odds and demonstrated just what his exceptional training and ability could do." Rea concluded, "St. Paul's gain is Virginia's gain and North Carolina's loss."[122] Despite the optimism around Gaither's hire, the St. Paul's job was a difficult one. In Gaither's first season as an assistant coach, the Tigers went winless in 8 games.

At the end of 1935, saddled with a 14-game losing streak, St. Paul's head coach resigned and the school named Gaither as the new head coach.[123] In his first season, Gaither ended the losing streak by winning 2 games, including a 111–0 rout of Fayetteville State.[124] The two wins were a dramatic improvement, but losing the remaining games haunted Gaither. He recalled four decades later that St. Paul's was "where I learn[ed] how to lose." Nonetheless, Gaither still believed his time at St. Paul's was "probably the best coaching I've ever done."[125] Gaither's victories at St. Paul's were the first of many notches in his career win column.[126]

The decade Gaither spent at Henderson and St. Paul's shows how he understood the importance of coaching. Neither Henderson nor St. Paul's was a high-powered program when he arrived, but Gaither dramatically improved each one. Here he learned how to coach. The relationship between high school and collegiate coaches, the publicity of the Black press, and the importance of player development on and off the field provided Gaither with a firsthand understanding of program building. He would also learn how weak ties to Black communities could limit a team's capability of winning long term. While Gaither was making his name as a coach, FAMU was trying to establish itself as a contender in Black college football.

2
FLORIDA A&M DEVELOPS
A SPORTING CONGREGATION

n December 1933 on a warm, breezy, and clear evening at Jacksonville's Durkee Field, FAMU played Howard University in front of more than 5,000 fans in the inaugural Orange Blossom Classic (OBC). The game was FAMU's first intersectional game in fifteen years and attracted the largest crowd in the team's history to that date. The FAMU Rattlers' opponent, the Howard University Bison, represented the Black college football elite. The Bison began playing in 1894, and nearly two decades later Howard became a founding member of the CIAA.[1] Private HBCUs like Howard University, Lincoln University, and Tuskegee University dominated the first twenty-five years of HBCU football, fielding the best and most competitive teams. Between 1920, the year that the *Pittsburgh Courier* named its first national champion, and 1932, only one public college—Bluefield State (W.Va.)—won a national title.[2] Tuskegee University ruled the South and Wiley College dominated the Southwest, while Howard University and Lincoln University fought for supremacy in the East. In 1920, Howard University claimed the first national title on Thanksgiving when it defeated Lincoln 42 to 0 in front of 20,000 fans. Under the leadership of former Tufts University star player Edward Morrison, the Bison had outscored opponents 132 to 3 during their title-winning season.[3] The Bison would add two more titles by the 1926 season.

The inaugural OBC, however, demonstrated that something was shifting. Athletic scandals and the Great Depression had wrecked Howard's previously dominant football program. A disagreement between Howard and Lincoln over the eligibility of a Bison star player caused the Washington, D.C., school to withdraw from the CIAA in 1924 and to end the popular Thanksgiving game between the two schools. The football controversy joined the student body's campaigns calling for fewer religious services and less discipline, all of which resulted in Mordecai Johnson being named Howard's first African American president in 1926. Many believed

J. R. E. Lee Jr. at
his desk, 1948.
(Forrest Granger
Collection, Florida
Memory, Florida
State Archives)

that Johnson's arrival would restore the Howard–Lincoln rivalry and boost
Howard's athletic program, as the new president had been a two-year
starter at quarterback at Morehouse College. But Johnson ended financial assistance for housing and meals for the athletes. Forty-five football
players went on strike in 1927 in response. Howard's administration remained resolute in its opposition to the creeping commercialism in college
football, standing fast against athletic inducements and for strict guide-
lines for player eligibility. The change in athletic policy had immediate consequences. Most notably, the Bison were winless in 1929. Howard still had
tremendous name recognition as the "Capstone of Negro Education," but
the football program paled in comparison with that of its title-winning
teams a decade earlier. Howard's downward trajectory met FAMU's ambitions in Jacksonville.[4]

The OBC was the brainchild of J. R. E. Lee Jr., FAMU's business manager
and the president's son. He envisioned "the biggest intersectional contests
Florida has ever witnessed."[5] By hosting a top intersectional opponent annually, FAMU would be able to show off the improving quality of the Rattler
team, highlight the merits of Black colleges, and promote Black tourism.
The plans were audacious. FAMU had been a perennial loser. According to
official records, the Rattlers had won only 11 games in the decade before

the OBC. The game, which would annually become the Rattlers final regular season game, seemed like a questionable venture, given the school's poor record. Lee Jr.'s plan for a game was based on FAMU's newfound commitment to developing a sporting congregation across the state.

The OBC differed from other games then known as "classics." The early classics, such as the Howard University–Lincoln University game or the Turkey Day Classic, featuring Tuskegee and Alabama State in Montgomery, were played on Thanksgiving.[6] Other successful classics were played in conjunction with state fairs, with games being usually held midseason. For example, Southern tussled with Bishop College in the first Louisiana State Fair Classic in October 1922, and the first Texas State Fair Classic was played three years later.[7] The OBC, on the other hand, was modeled after postseason exhibition bowl games, such as the Rose Bowl, which had created national interest through intersectional games that pitted teams from different parts of the country that did not play regularly. The Rose Bowl matched a team from the Pacific Coast Conference (now the Pac-12) against a quality opponent from the East or Midwest. Intersectional games among HBCUs were immediately popular as well. Ten thousand fans attended the first Black college intersectional football classic in Houston, when Prairie View battled Atlanta University in the Southwestern Classic in January 1929.[8] Despite FAMU's mediocre football history, Lee Jr. envisioned that the OBC, played annually on the first Saturday in December, would determine the Black college football national championship.[9] He believed that the OBC location would allow FAMU to overcome a weak gridiron tradition and defy big-game norms.

FAMU's OBC initially showcased Jacksonville's Black community. School officials worked to make the game a community event, highlighting African American tourism in the state. The aptly named "Gateway to Florida" was home to the state's largest Black population, approximately 50,000. The city's Black middle class was essential to the success of the OBC. Jacksonville's African American elite, led by A. L. Lewis, owner of the Afro-American Life Insurance Company, provided an infrastructure of business interests—hotels, entertainment, shopping, dining, and transportation—that could support the game's grand plans. The OBC featured a variety of parties for alumni, community members, and visitors. Those unable to attend the soirées could watch the band lead the parade through the heart of Jacksonville's Black community. The classic also converged with a burgeoning Black tourist industry. Although segregation laws and customs often prevented African Americans from using the state's hundreds of miles of beaches, Jacksonville's Blacks had carved out a beachfront recreational area only twenty miles from downtown where African Americans could enjoy the sun, sand, and surf. Since the average temperature was seventy degrees on the first Saturday in December, the Rattlers had found a winning formula for a lasting tradition.[10]

Lee Jr. publicized the game across the country. He secured special rates on the Atlantic Coast Line for travelers coming from the east and west coasts of Florida, as well as those coming from southern Georgia. FAMU's marching band (not yet the Marching 100) made the trip to Jacksonville. Significantly, FAMU's administration convinced Chester Washington, sports editor of the *Pittsburgh Courier*, to attend the game. The *Courier* devoted as many as four pages per week to sports coverage. Beginning in 1925, Washington helped to choose Black college football All-Americans for the *Courier*. He typically traveled thousands of miles every fall to report on games and to watch players. Getting Washington to Florida for the first time was a major publicity coup for FAMU.[11] Lee Jr.'s biggest feat, however, was simply getting the Howard football team to the game. Since Abraham Lincoln proclaimed the first Thanksgiving Day in 1863, the holiday traditionally fell on the last Thursday of November. In 1933, there were five Thursdays, meaning the Lincoln–Howard game fell on the afternoon of November 30. The Bison only had two days before they played the Rattlers. After its 13 to 7 victory over Lincoln, the Bison football team rushed to the train, "scarcely stopping to change their clothes," to make the nearly 1,000-mile trek to Jacksonville.[12] Lee Jr. chartered a special train to get the Howard team from Atlantic City to New York to catch "the Havana Special" to Jacksonville. When the Bison pulled into town, "the largest number ever assembled to witness a football contest" awaited.[13]

Although sportswriters picked Howard to win, FAMU upset the Bison 9 to 6 in a spirited game.[14] FAMU scored on freshman kicker Alton Williams's first-half field goal, and its lone touchdown came when Joe Mills Braddock intercepted a fourth-quarter pass and "zigzagged" for a 73-yard return. Howard scored a late touchdown but could not overcome the deficit. Chester Washington captured the game's importance. He described the victory as "one of the greatest grid triumphs in the history of Sunshine State elevens." He continued, "It was a great moment of triumph for a team which was rated as the underdog and a great boost for the splendid and progressive institution at Tallahassee." In the end, "Florida's Rattlers defiantly flashed their fangs," while the band played "Florida's Goin' to Shine Tonight" and more than 5,000 fans, most supporting the orange and green Rattlers, reveled in victory.[15]

Starting with the first OBC, FAMU developed the key components of a sporting congregation. The OBC brought media attention and connected the school athletically to Black communities in the state's largest cities. The game's success also stemmed from the slow but nevertheless real improvement of the Black middle class in Florida. In spite of Jim Crow, Rattler alumni were carving out an existence as teachers, farmers, entrepreneurs, and preachers. As the school produced more graduates, FAMU's influence increased. President Lee used the OBC to mingle with organizational leaders across the state.[16] The school's enrollment grew from 484 in 1933 to 623 in 1934.[17] FAMU's growth and prestige would make the OBC among the best athletic and community exhibitions in the country.

By the third OBC in 1935, the game was a certifiable success, garnering rave reviews from the press and averaging more than 6,000 fans per contest. Still, this success could not obscure the fact that FAMU was not yet very good at football. Opponents were interested in making the long trip to Florida because of the $1,500 to $2,000 guarantee and the belief that FAMU would be an easy victory. For the game to separate itself from the other classics, the Rattlers needed to improve on the field. FAMU wanted better players and a big-name coach. FAMU's first three decades of football demonstrate how one school intentionally put together the pieces of a sporting congregation, including hiring Jake Gaither in 1937. FAMU's sporting congregation would eventually produce a national championship.

THE OPENING DECADES OF FOOTBALL AT FAMU

Faculty members George M. Sampson and Jubie B. Bragg were vital in starting the football program at FAMU, while President Nathan B. Young added critical administrative support. Athletics at FAMU followed the design used by other HBCUs in the late nineteenth and early twentieth centuries. Racial pioneers who played football at integrated colleges in the North organized many of the first teams. FAMU, like many HBCUs, relied on faculty members from integrated colleges in the North to teach traditional educational classes such as literature and math as part of the Normal school curriculum and relied on faculty members from HBCUs to teach industrial classes. Therefore, Sampson, Young, and Bragg represented the dual influence of integrated football programs in the North and developing programs at HBCUs.

Sampson was the first to arrive in Tallahassee, hired in 1899 to teach mathematics.[18] He had a splendid academic and athletic career at Western Reserve University in Cleveland (now Case Western Reserve University), where he ran track and was the starting quarterback for three seasons. Sampson earned his B.A. in 1898 and his M.A. in 1899. Once Sampson arrived at FAMU, he organized a football team, teaching the rules and practicing the game. According to Sampson, "I found no athletics directed by the faculty of the school at Tallahassee and in the interests of the male students and partly to satisfy my own urge, I persuaded the boys that football was a great game for real men." Sampson served as coach, player, and tackling dummy and, over the next several years, drew increasing support from students.[19]

Sampson introduced organized football on FAMU's campus, but its growth needed the support from the school's administration. FAMU, like many HBCUs in the nineteenth century, did not initially believe that its students should engage in many extracurricular activities, because of the religious orthodoxy of school founders and the fear of stereotypes that depicted Blacks as lazy.[20] Thomas De Saille Tucker, FAMU's first president, limited extracurricular activities, believing "an idle mind is the devil's workshop."[21] Although students had begun a debate team under Tucker's administration, athletics seemed out of the question before Sampson's arrival. When Superintendent of Public Instruction William N. Sheats refused to support Tucker's reappointment for president in 1901, he nominated Nathan B. Young as a replacement. Young was a graduate of Talladega College, an HBCU in Alabama, and Oberlin College. Before his selection as president, Young had taught at Tuskegee and later served as the head of the Pedagogical Department at Georgia State Industrial College in Savannah.[22] In Sampson's estimation, student "interest in football increased due to the cooperative spirit of all men and the encouragement given by President N. B. Young."[23] It is unclear when Young's interest in sports began. Over the course of his academic and professional life, he had several opportunities to witness Black participation in college sports. He attended Oberlin from 1885 to 1888 and probably was aware of the exploits of Moses Fleetwood Walker, who played for Oberlin in 1881 and was the first and last Black professional baseball player in the Major Leagues before Jackie Robinson. In addition, Oberlin was a leader in the muscular Christianity

1. Alfred Osgood	6. John Hall	11. Frank Robinson	16. Burris Baker
2. Geo. McDaniels	7. Val Orouke	12. George Sampson, Coach	17. William Raiford
3. _____	8. John R. Scott	13. . . . . Burt	18. Arthur Giflislee
4. Joe Thomas	9. Walter Armwood	14. Harvest Calhoun	19. Samuel Coleman
5. Roy Lancaster	10. Leroy Howell	15. George Campbell	20. Bedney Gilbert
			21. J. B. Bragg, Assistant Coach

FAMU football team, 1904. (Meek-Eaton Black Archives Research Center and Museum, Florida A&M University)

movement, which combined physical activity with Christian activism. The movement was best represented by the formation of Young Men's Christian Associations nationwide.[24] Young's tenure at Tuskegee also coincided with the school's first football games. At the time of Young's appointment as president at FAMU, football was sweeping over college campuses as well.

One of Young's first hires was Jubie Bragg, a Tuskegee graduate, to teach wheelwrighting and other industrial subjects. Like Young, Bragg had arrived in Tuskegee just as the team's first intercollegiate games were being played in January 1894. In total, he spent seven years at Tuskegee learning wheelwrighting and blacksmithing and played varsity football for five years.[25] When Bragg reached Tallahassee, he helped Sampson on the college's athletics committee. Under Sampson and Bragg's tutelage, FAMU initially played local high schools for several seasons. The school's first intercollegiate games came in 1906 when the team traveled to Alabama to face Alabama State and Tuskegee. By this time, however, Bragg and Sampson had left Tallahassee. Sampson became a principal of a school in Ohio. Bragg returned to school at Talladega College to earn a liberal arts degree and where he also played on the football team.

Rising interest in intercollegiate football coincided with FAMU's growing enrollment. The school had more than 300 students heading into the 1909 school year. President Young used this enrollment increase to request additional monies from the state legislature for new buildings. The school's expansion signaled a change in status reflected by a name change from the Colored Normal School to the Florida Agricultural and Mechanical College for Negroes in 1909.[26] School spirit surged with the name change and, partly, through football. "With the success that has come to the football team on the gridiron this year a real college spirit has been born and the campus and chapel and dormitory halls have resounded again and again with the songs and yells in praise of the F. A. M. C.," noted the 1910 academic bulletin.[27] Football, and sports generally, became an essential tool for FAMU's self-definition as a college and in the development of a community. "The orange and green have been more prominent this year on lapels and hats and canes than ever before in the history of the institution. In a desire to foster such enthusiasm as has manifested itself, pennants and college pins have been ordered, so . . . there will be new symbols of the college spirit."[28] However, football's growth in popularity exposed inadequate supervision at HBCUs.

In the 1910s, football at FAMU was still primarily student-led. George Sampson and Jubie Bragg were no longer faculty members, leaving an athletic subcommittee to oversee the team. The football team played an erratic schedule, most often competing with in-state teams such as Edward Waters College in Jacksonville.[29] Student-led football suffered in its quality and consistency of play. The lure of revenues, competition, and injuries fueled the push for intervention. As mentioned earlier (chapter 1), these problems began to trouble several college presidents and faculty representatives, who eventually called for reform. FAMU professor J. D. Avent attended the founding SIAC meeting in 1913. Still, between 1913 and 1923 the Rattlers had no regular coach or athletic director. After World War I, however, FAMU created courses in physical education.[30] Besides changes in the curriculum, administrative and faculty changes fueled the growth of FAMU's football program.

In June 1923, the State Board of Education dismissed President Nathan B. Young. Discontent between Young and the board had grown over several years, and when the president failed to submit a budget report on time, the board used his tardiness as grounds for his dismissal.[31] After a student strike against the interim president's policies, the board named John Robert Edward (J. R. E.) Lee Sr. president in May 1924. Also in 1923, Jubie Bragg returned to Tallahassee as dean of mechanical arts after coaching football at several HBCUs.[32] President Lee believed in the expansion of athletics, the need for trained coaches, and the necessity of an athletic director. He declared, "No school in this day can expect to attract promising men or women that does not give organized athletics a foremost place. Where there are no athletics, it is very likely true that only deadheads are attracted. Young men and women of promise desire to be connected with an institution that has spirit and force."[33] Lee's declaration to the board was a rationalization of the role sports could play in creating a sporting congregation.

Although Bragg was the temporary athletic director and part-time coach, President Lee raised the FAMU athletic profile by hiring Frantz "Jazz" Byrd as athletic director and head football coach in 1926. Byrd had been a star player at Lincoln University (Pa.). Described by the Black press as the "Black Red Grange" and as the "Phantom of the Gridiron," Byrd was known for his dazzling long runs. His most famous feat was an 85-yard run to defeat Howard University in 1924. The *Pittsburgh Courier* later named Byrd to its all-time Black football team that included Fritz Pollard of Brown University and Paul Robeson of Rutgers University. Byrd's hiring increased the press coverage of the school's fledgling football team and announced that FAMU intended to be a serious contender in southern football.[34]

Despite Byrd's accolades, during his tenure the football team still couldn't shake its losing record. Although the Rattlers did upset Alabama State during Byrd's first season, his more substantial effect was on the sporting congregation. The student newspaper the *Famcean* expressed student admiration for Byrd: "During his three years at Famcee, Coach Byrd has won the loyalty, respect, and admiration of those under his charge. Through his manly examples of true sportsmanship on and off the field and his efforts to develop a greater team, he has won the admiration of thousands of sports lovers. . . . His policy of clean sports has made him an idol of the grid."[35] The *Chicago Defender*'s expanded coverage of black college sports now regularly included FAMU. Eric "Ric" Roberts of the *Chicago Defender* described Byrd as building the "foundation of a rip-snortin' team which will entertain any team in the country."[36] The gains FAMU made, however, were threatened by the Great Depression.

ESTABLISHING A SPORTING CONGREGATION
DURING THE GREAT DEPRESSION

The Great Depression arrived in Florida several years before Black Tuesday in October 1929. In the mid-1920s, Florida's coastal cities were beset by land speculation. An unregulated financial structure full of corruption financed these land ventures. Between 1921 and 1926, property value in Miami increased 560 percent. However, as quickly as the land boom began, it went bust. Hundreds of banks failed, and hundreds of millions of dollars were lost beginning in 1926. Besides the depression, Florida experienced two of the most devastating hurricanes in American history. In September 1926, a category 4 hurricane swept through Miami and south Florida, ending any hopes of an economic revival. In September 1928, a category 5 hurricane that hit Palm Beach County proved to be the final nail in the coffin for the state's roaring 1920s economy. In total, 157 banks closed across the state between 1928 and 1940. These economic woes affected public universities that depended on government funding. The poor economy coupled with the logic of racism meant FAMU faced an acute economic crisis.[37]

The financial crisis squeezed black colleges' limited resources. The church organizations and philanthropies that supported private HBCUs no longer had the means to do so. The AME Church that had proudly rebuilt Edward Waters College after a 1901 fire could do nothing as a local lumber company seized the property because of a debt.[38] Smaller schools, such as Roger Williams in Nashville, closed their doors. Financial constraints forced other schools to merge, like New Orleans and Straight, which formed Dillard University. Mississippi assumed support from the American Baptist Home Mission Society of Jackson State, a scenario repeated in Georgia and North Carolina.[39] Supporters of philanthropic foundations also gave less during the depression.

Despite these challenges, new opportunities emerged for public HBCUs like FAMU. The loss of jobs led to increasing numbers of African American youth graduating from high school.[40] This small demographic change led to dramatic changes in the percentage of college students at public Black colleges. By the mid-1930s, 43 percent of Black college enrollment was at public HBCUs, a nearly 20 percent increase from the previous decade.[41] FAMU president J. R. E. Lee Sr. used enrollment growth to request more money from state agencies and outside charitable organizations. Even amid the depression, FAMU was able to enlarge its campus, adding thirty-three new buildings during Lee's administration (1924–44).[42] Black college adminis-

Early football game at FAMU, 1930s. (Florida Memory, Florida State Archives)

trators developed plans to minimize the financial obstacles and maximize opportunities.

FAMU athletics also received new funding. In 1933, the school allocated $8,000 for field improvements and another $1,500 to remodel the gymnasium, and it purchased a thirty-passenger bus for $6,800. By 1940, the school used $19,000 from the New Deal to enclose the football field. Before FAMU had enclosed the stadium, the Rattlers played on a field filled with patches of worn-out grass surrounded by wooden bleachers. Although FAMU began to field successful teams in the late 1930s, the school only covered its expenses through the financial success of the OBC. The $1,000 profit from the 1939 OBC, for example, pulled the athletic department out of the red. The New Deal money for stadium improvements helped ease some of the financial pressures, as more attendees of FAMU home games had to pay.[43]

While FAMU moderately enhanced its athletic facilities, UF built a football stadium in the 1929–30 academic year.[44] Lacking anything comparable to the UF's $118,000 stadium to draw in fans, FAMU utilized the OBC as a sports revenue model. HBCU classics, in the short term, would be highly profitable, without the burdensome costs of building a stadium. FAMU's profits from the OBC, however, were a temporary advantage. The lack of a stadium in the school's early years sowed the seeds of a tremendous economic disadvantage later. For now, the Black college football classic was a lucrative survival strategy. Through the OBC and new money allocations, FAMU was, in fact, able to increase its athletic resources during the depression. These resources would fuel FAMU's position among the elite programs during the golden age of Black college football. Still, FAMU's growth contained the virus of structural racism. The state did not subsidize the building of a comparable stadium that could have allowed FAMU to capitalize on its athletic success financially. Nonetheless, stable athletic funds permitted the FAMU football program to recruit better players.

RECRUITING TALENT

Athletic resources were only one piece of an active football program; FAMU still needed players. From the 1910s through the early 1930s, Edward Waters had the best football program in the state. Located in Jacksonville and founded by the AME Church in 1883, the small private school joined the SIAC in 1929. Tuskegee's Cleve Abbott described the 1930 Edward Waters team, which defeated FAMU 20 to 0, as showing "knowledge of the fundamentals" of football. The FAMU team that was winless in the SIAC was, according to Abbott, "handicapped because of a lack of material from which to mold an eleven."[45] FAMU's lack of quality football players became severe when the SIAC called for the end of using high school players on college teams by 1932. Although FAMU had used only a few high school players, the new ruling depleted an already underperforming roster. When the 1932 season had started, FAMU lost sixteen players, or about half the roster, to graduation or the new eligibility rules.[46] The Rattlers were able to withstand the rule changes because of a growing student body. President Lee wanted FAMU "to have no secondary place among the state colleges for Negroes in the entire south."[47] Because of these plans, FAMU's college enrollment increased from 93 in 1925 to 436 in 1933. Moreover, Lee's plans separated FAMU from Edward Waters and Bethune-Cookman concerning the size of the course offerings.[48]

While Lee was expanding FAMU through his building campaign and by increasing the number of students, Jubie Bragg set out to make FAMU the center of the Black athletic universe in Florida. In March 1930, Bragg organized the first high school basketball championship tournament on

FAMU's campus. Twelve boys' and girls' basketball teams from Pensacola to Fort Pierce played in the inaugural tournament. By 1932 the tourney grew to sixty-eight teams. Bragg believed that the tournament was "a vehicle for recruiting good athletes and for building character among young men and women in Florida."[49] Bragg, along with other high school coaches and administrators, established the Florida Interscholastic Athletic Association in 1932, as the institutional basis for Black high school athletics. More important for the future of FAMU football, the best athletes in football, basketball, and track regularly played on FAMU's campus, allowing the football program to recruit the best athletes in the state. This recruiting model was used by other successful Black college programs.[50]

Between FAMU's institutional growth and its role in Black high school athletics, the school slowly gained a virtual monopoly on the state's best athletic talent. By the 1930s, FAMU had established a "Florida first" educational philosophy that was slowly transferred to athletics. Sportswriters recognized that FAMU's educational improvements led to athletic improvements. *Atlanta Daily World* sports editor Ric Roberts wrote, "The All-Florida or 'Florida first' educational motif is sending most of the Florida grown gridders to Famcee. A Famcee graduate is given preference to a Yale or Northwestern man where a state professorship is concerned so the Floridians are staying home at Famcee in droves. Florida will be [an athletic] threat from this date forward because of this."[51] For now, however, the football teams still featured out-of-state players. In 1937, there were only six players from Florida on the team. The coaches targeted "great black all-state players who couldn't get into white colleges."[52] Out-of-state blue-chip players were the core of FAMU's great teams before World War II, but in time, talented in-state players would become the seeds for FAMU's football dynasty, and the growing sporting congregation was the seedbed. The Rattlers needed a coach who could put all the pieces together.

QUALITY COACHING

Transcendent coaches led the best programs of the 1930s. The national champion coaches of the decade included Cleve Abbott (Tuskegee), Harry Graves (Wilberforce), Fred Long (Wiley), Edward Hurt (Morgan State), Arnett "Ace" Mumford (Texas College), and Henry Arthur Kean (Kentucky State). FAMU's desire to have an elite football coach meant the school needed to hire a coach of this caliber. The school's search for quality coaching would eventually bring William Bell and Jake Gaither to Tallahassee.

President Lee showed his commitment to winning football by hiring

Jubie Bragg as athletic director in 1924 and Jazz Byrd as head coach in 1926. However, after Byrd resigned in 1928, the school spent nearly a decade trying to solidify its coaching position. FAMU had four coaches between the 1928 and 1936 seasons.[53] Five years of instability led FAMU to turn to one of its best players: Eugene Bragg, the son of Jubie Bragg and one of the Rattlers' first star players.[54] During his first season in 1934, Eugene Bragg led the Rattlers to a 7 to 6 upset victory over Alabama State on homecoming. The younger Bragg's successful season ended with a win over Virginia State in the second annual OBC, and a winning record. During his second season, FAMU was plagued by injuries, but it defeated Tuskegee for the first time. It appeared that FAMU had finally found the right coach to grow the program, when tragedy struck.[55] On January 24, 1936, Eugene Bragg's appendix ruptured, and he died in an ambulance on the way to the hospital. Bragg's untimely death at only twenty-eight years old forced FAMU to look for its fifth coach in eight years. This time FAMU struck gold. The school hired former Ohio State University All-American William Bell to lead the football program.[56]

William "Big Bill" Bell was a three-time letter winner in football and earned All–Big Ten and honorable mention All-American honors as a senior in 1931. He was one of the most recognizable Black football players at a white college. Black newspapers followed all his exploits on the field in the fall and even covered his summer job.[57] The Black press reported on Ohio State's acceptance of the gentleman's agreement—northern teams' acceptance of southern segregation on the field—when the Buckeyes refused to play Bell against Vanderbilt in 1931.[58] Bell enrolled in graduate classes at Ohio State University and earned a master's degree in 1937. Beginning in 1935, he was the head coach at Claflin University in South Carolina before accepting the head coaching position at FAMU the following season. Bell quickly announced his goals as a coach and professor at FAMU. He wanted "to instill a new era in the football destinies of Florida as well as to develop one of the most well-balanced physical education programs in any Negro college, giving to each sport and to every phase of physical education its proper stimulus and emphasis."[59]

Bell's first season did not feature as many victories as he would have liked. FAMU won only 2 games; the highlight was its second consecutive victory over Tuskegee, the eventual SIAC champion. The team also achieved a "moral victory" by tying the previous season's SIAC champion, Alabama State. When the season ended with a close loss to Prairie View A&M in the OBC, Bell made two changes that dramatically improved FAMU.[60]

First, Bell started a coaching school as a part of FAMU's summer school curriculum. In 1936, FAMU established a Department of Physical Education, and Bell organized a one-credit class to teach the subtler points of football and basketball coaching. The course was aimed at the state's high school coaches, because, as Bell recalled, "there weren't many knowledgeable black high school coaches in Florida."[61] He used his connections at Ohio State to get Floyd Stahl, a coach of multiple sports, including football, baseball, and basketball, to participate in the coaching clinic. Bell led the football instruction, and Stahl coached basketball. The coaching school marked the beginning of FAMU's coaching clinic that improved the coaching in the high schools. Black players in the state would receive superior coaching because of this program.[62] Second, Bell and FAMU hired Jake Gaither as an assistant football coach, head basketball coach, and athletic director. In the summer of 1937, Gaither earned his master's degree from Ohio State University and leaped at the chance to coach at a large HBCU. The FAMU Physical Education Department had four faculty members, two men and two women, with master's degrees in the field: Bell (Ohio State), Gaither (Ohio State), Cecile Harrison (Ohio State), and Lua Bartley (University of Michigan).[63]

The clinic and the hiring of Gaither were the final pieces of the puzzle that allowed FAMU's football program to take off. Retaining Gaither was a risk because he was a more established coach. But the two coaches complemented each other. Bell stressed the fundamentals and was a technician. Gaither "was an artist" and "he liked to get across the goal line," remembered Pete Griffin, a player under Bell and Gaither who later worked as an assistant coach. Gaither, once on a path to the pulpit, also had the "flowing gift for gab."[64] A. L. Kidd, head of FAMU's sports publicity, gave the coaches equal billing. "Florida Wins Opener under Bill Bell–Jake Gaither Rule," read the headline after the duo's first win.[65] Regardless of how the combination was publicized, the tandem paid dividends immediately. The 1937 FAMU team went 6-1-1, winning its first SIAC title and nearly winning a national championship. The Bell-and-Gaither-coached squad won the 1937 OBC with a comeback victory over CIAA representative Hampton University (Va.). More than 8,000 fans attended the classic, which had moved to Orlando. The Rattlers were undefeated after the win over Hampton, but Bell had agreed to play Prairie View A&M in its classic on January 1, 1938, in Houston, where the Rattlers, along with their undefeated record, were crushed by the Prairie View Panthers. After FAMU's 1937 SIAC championship, the team was favored to repeat heading into the 1938 sea-

Table 2. *Key players from FAMU's 1938 national championship team*

FOUR GHOSTS	
Halfback	John D. Harris
Halfback	Thomas Jones
Fullback	Stanley Strachan
Quarterback	Henry Butler

SEVEN ROCKS OF GIBRALTAR	
Right end	James Manson
Right tackle	Pete McCurdy
Right guard	Demant Nollez
Center	Pete Griffin
Left guard	Edward Travis
Left tackle	Murray Neely
Left end	Jesse Mayes

son.[66] The future was bright. Both Bell and Gaither understood their roles in building a winning team, and the duo looked to build on FAMU's first conference title.

FAMU'S SPORTING CONGREGATION PRODUCES A NATIONAL CHAMPIONSHIP

During the 1938 season, the team continued the previous season's success by orchestrating a perfect season. "The Men in Orange" started the season with shutout victories over North Carolina A&T and Clark (Atlanta). FAMU's championship aspirations depended on a victory against an undefeated Morris Brown in October. Morris Brown students and alumni planned to "burn Florida's 'Men in Orange' in effigy in the largest bonfire ever seen in [Atlanta]," as part of the schools homecoming festivities.[67] Morris Brown was known for its powerful offense; however, FAMU countered with one of the best and fastest backfields of the 1930s. Led by Thomas Jones at halfback, Henry Butler at quarterback, Stanley Strachan, and John D. "Grose" Harris, collectively known as the "Four Ghosts," the Rattlers scored 16 points. The five-foot five-inch Jones was a nightmare for the Morris Brown Wolverines, as he scored 10 points, including a 64-yard touchdown run. More important, the Rattler defense, known as the "Seven Rocks of Gibraltar," held Morris Brown scoreless. The victory cleared a path to a SIAC title. FAMU finished conference play undefeated, unscored upon, and untied. To win a national championship, FAMU had to defeat Kentucky State University in the annual OBC.[68]

Henry A. Kean coached the Kentucky State Thorobreds, and in the previous season he had led the team to its third national championship in four years. Sportswriters believed the winner of the game would be the 1938 national champion. After five years, the OBC would determine the Black college football national champion. The 1938 season was one of Kean's best coaching jobs. Prior to the season, he had graduated eleven players, including five All-Americans off the title-winning 1937 team. Despite the personnel losses, Kentucky State continued to win, including an 86 to 0 victory over Mississippi Industrial College. In a mid-October clash against Texas College (Tyler) at the Cotton Bowl in Dallas, Kentucky State was thoroughly beaten 33 to 6. The loss was Kentucky State's first in two years. *Atlanta Daily World* sports columnist Lucius Jones captured the magnitude of the upset. "Not since the stunning knockout of the sensational Brown Bomber, Joe Louis, by the Hitler-inspired Black Uhlan, Max Schmeling, has such consternation been caused in the colored sports firmament as was produced by those unbelievable words and figures above [Texas College 33, Kentucky State 6]." Kean righted the ship and won the remainder of the games heading into the OBC.[69]

FAMU's remarkable 1938 season even caught the attention of Florida's white press, which was starved for football success. UF was mired in a series of losing seasons. Although the 1920s saw UF have nine winning seasons, the 1930s were an utter disappointment to fans and alumni. Between 1930 and 1938, UF had only three winning seasons. More critical, UF won only once against archrival University of Georgia. FAMU's sudden success began to offset UF's ineptitude. Russell Kay, secretary of the Florida Press Association and author of the syndicated column "Too Late to Classify," believed the Rattlers brought football honor to the state with their recent performances. "While the Florida Gators have given a more or less sluggish performance this season, allowing themselves to be kicked and cuffed around with only an occasional warning snap of their jaws, Florida is not without football honors, for her practically unknown and unsung Rattlers have been gliding throughout the southeast, striking with deadly result at every foe, to secure for the second successive year the coveted title of Southern Conference Champions." Bell's ability to mold the "raw material" into winning football, despite being "handicapped by [a] lack of funds," impressed Kay. The columnist also viewed the OBC as an example of "Florida negroes . . . play[ing] their part in advertising and publicizing Florida to the nation."[70]

The 1938 OBC against Kentucky State was what J. R. E. Lee Jr. had imagined when he started the game in 1933: the national title game. More than 8,000 fans, including 1,200 whites, attended, expecting a close game between the evenly matched teams. Kentucky State used its flanker formation, a passing offense, to take an early lead on FAMU. The Thorobreds were the first team to score on FAMU all season when they connected on a 38-yard touchdown pass. In response, Bell called his first timeout of the season. The players were embarrassed and vowed, "Over our dead bodies will they pass again."[71] FAMU answered with a dazzling 16-yard run by All-American Strachan. What made the difference in the game was a safety in the second quarter. A magnificent 60-yard punt pinned Kentucky State inside the 1-yard line. FAMU earned the automatic safety (2 points) when Kentucky State had an incomplete pass in the end zone. FAMU's defense held on in the second half, including three goal-line stands, to win 9 to 7.[72]

FAMU had won its first national title. At the football banquet, President Lee "pointed to the element of general cooperation on the part of every cog in the institution's machinery, which was the one single factor that contributed more than anything else in accelerating the athletic program . . . in its history-making achievement."[73] The football program's financial stability, player recruitment, and quality coaching formed the nexus of FAMU's sporting congregation and the beginnings of a football dynasty. However, FAMU's budding program would face new threats as an emerging conflict in Europe threatened to upend everything.

3
A DOUBLE-V CAMPAIGN
ON THE FIELD AND OFF

Gaither's first debilitating headache came at the worst possible time.

The Rattlers' basketball team was fighting for its first SIAC tournament championship. More than 3,000 fans squeezed into Tuskegee's Logan Hall gymnasium to watch FAMU battle its hosts for the trophy. The cracker-box gym was hot, and the game was nip and tuck. It was a fitting end to a competitive basketball season in the SIAC.

It was a surprising season for Gaither. When he started coaching at the Henderson Institute, he had never even seen a basketball game, and now he was close to a conference title. His philosophy of tight defense and fast-break offense, developed on the hardwoods of North Carolina, was now being applied on one of the more significant stages in HBCU basketball. The Rattlers started the season with 3 losses in their first 6 games. However, Gaither had the Rattlers playing their best basketball by midseason. FAMU won twelve consecutive games in February, clinching the regular season conference with a sweep of Tuskegee.[1] Sportswriters praised Gaither as the "most technical mentor in the SIAC"; he was blessed with an "ultra-incisive mind" and was "essentially a scholar, an erudite exponent of his task, a man seeming, at times, to possess occult powers due to his phenomenal pre-science."[2] A tournament title would be the final proof of the "contentious" Gaither's basketball coaching ability.[3]

The SIAC tournament did not disappoint fans who wanted to see a FAMU and Tuskegee rematch. To win the title, the Rattlers needed to beat the "law of averages" in defeating the Golden Tigers for the third time, and they hoped that the "fourth game jinx" of fatigue would not slow them down. Logan gym was "seething like a madhouse" as Tuskegee took early leads of 12 to 6, 15 to 8, and 16 to 9. Yet Gaither's players showed their grit, clawing their way back to tie the game at halftime.

With three and half minutes remaining and FAMU trailing 47 to 43, Gaither's head began to pound. His balance was unsteady and he was nauseous. He had never experienced a headache like this before. Through the pain and the confusion, Gaither called a play for Leon "Sunshade" Watts, the Rattlers all-conference forward who scored from the post, and he was fouled on the play. Watts made the free throw, bringing FAMU behind by one point, 47 to 46. To prevent Tuskegee from holding the ball and "freezing" the final minutes on the clock, Gaither called for tight man-to-man defense. The gamble backfired as a Tiger swooped in for an easy layup, plus he was fouled. The bucket and free throw gave the Golden Tigers a 50 to 46 lead with under two minutes to play.

Fans stood nearly on the floor as the Rattlers whipped passes looking for a good shot. The left-handed Wilbert Smith made an "overhead flipper" to cut the lead to 2 points. Gaither again implored his players for aggressive defense, needing a steal and a score to tie the game. After a loose ball "fracas," FAMU's Elwood "Duck" Britt got free for a long pass. He made a layup and was fouled. The crowd exploded in disbelief. Britt calmly made the free throw. The Rattlers led 51 to 50 with under a minute to play. Tuskegee missed a quick shot, and Watt made another field goal. The Rattlers' lead looked safe at 53 to 50 with forty-five seconds remaining. The Tigers added another 2 points, but FAMU held on to win a "dream tournament."[4]

The headache dampened Gaither's celebration. Sadie fought through the crowd to find her husband in a daze. "Jake, you're sick," she said.[5] His pain increased in frequency and intensity throughout March. The initial diagnosis of an ear infection failed to explain his increasingly paralyzing symptoms. His balance suffered; his appetite was nonexistent. The stocky 200-pound Gaither lost 20 pounds. Doctors diagnosed Gaither with Mèniére's disease, because of the hearing loss and vertigo. "You don't have to worry about a brain tumor," said one doctor.[6]

If the debilitating headaches were not enough to worry about, Gaither and his star forward Elwood Britt received their draft numbers for induction in April.[7] Gaither was 760 out of 1,830. His headaches and age (thirtynine) lowered the odds that he would see action. Two decades younger, Britt served three years in the navy. His absence highlighted a bigger problem: FAMU's athletic programs needed a plan for World War II. Key athletes and coaches were expected to report for duty, while Gaither had to survive his illness. Gaither and FAMU alike would have to find a way to make it through the war.[8]

Winning the 1938 football Black college national title transformed the OBC into one of the premier Black college football events, and the game regularly began to determine the Black college champion.[9] Black newspapers picked the national title winner based on the best record and strongest schedule. As mentioned earlier, the *Pittsburgh Courier* bestowed the first title on Howard in 1920. Beginning in 1935, the *Atlanta Daily World* in conjunction with the 100% Wrong Club also named a national champion. With FAMU as a national title contender, the OBC had attracted nearly 50,000 fans in its first eight years. Subsequently, the game drew attention from across the color line. The Tallahassee Junior Chamber of Commerce proposed the game be moved to the state capital, rather than Jacksonville or Orlando.[10] The British Pathé newsreel filmed the 1940 game between FAMU and Wilberforce. The eight-minute clip included the Rattler marching band and marked the first time that Black college football was filmed for a national and international audience.[11] The OBC was becoming the leading HBCU classic.

The escalating war fought with football for column space in the Black press. Before the defending champion Rattlers reported to preseason camp, Germany invaded Poland on September 1, 1939. Two days later, the British and the French declared war on Germany. The war's outbreak overshadowed FAMU's twenty-one returning lettermen, including future FAMU coaches Edward Oglesby, Hansel Tookes, and Pete Griffin.[12] Coach Bell and Gaither knew that it would be difficult to match the previous season's dominance. The German-Soviet Non-Aggression Pact was signed days before the first game, leading the NAACP's *Crisis* to declare the treaty the "Great Betrayal."[13] The Rattlers couldn't recapture the magic of the previous season. FAMU stumbled to start the season with a scoreless tie with North Carolina A&T and a three-point loss to Alabama State. The coaching staff corrected the poor start, and FAMU shut out Tuskegee 20 to 0. A second loss came at the hands of Lane College of Jackson, Tennessee, which eliminated the Rattlers for the national title race. Despite not defending its national championship, FAMU won its second SIAC title. FAMU closed out the season with a dominant 42 to 0 rout of Wiley College.[14] The season's end also marked the end of Bill Bell's first group of players. Led by Hank Butler, Stan Strachan, Pete Griffin, and others, the Rattlers lost only 2 SIAC games their final three seasons and won a national title in 1938. According to sportswriter Ric Roberts, this group "put Florida on the football map."[15]

Across the ocean, the war escalated. Germany invaded France, Belgium, Luxembourg, and the Netherlands in early May 1940. The Nazi war machine forced France into an armistice and crippled the British in the process. Germany's military success in May–June 1940 ended a cornerstone of American foreign policy, which relied on its traditional allies and the oceans to avoid entanglements. President Franklin D. Roosevelt responded to Nazi aggression by committing billions of dollars to modernize the American military in preparation for war by asking Congress for 50,000 new planes. Jim Crow kept African Americans out of wartime industries, but they protested their second-class citizenship. The cover of the July 1940 *Crisis* featured a heavy bomber over an image of a southern California aircraft factory. "For Whites Only" was stamped diagonally in all-capital letters over the picture. The caption below read, "WARPLANES — Negro American may not build them, repair them, or fly them, but they must help pay for them."[16]

While embers of war and the hum of war production seemed a long way from the Black college gridiron, FAMU coach Bill Bell refused to stick to sports. In an open letter to President Roosevelt, Bell explained that his travels for athletics had taken him across the country, where he "discussed [the war's] far reaching effects upon our nation as well as its effects on the Negro, with many of my people in all walks of life — citizens as you know who are not able to share in full or enjoy the true democratic privileges of our free and beautiful America." He described African Americans as "loyal to America," yet they were "forgotten men" by the American military and the war industry. "We, like other sincere citizens, will grant the last drop of our blood to continue democracy and the American way of life," Bell concluded. The war provided Black athletes a chance to demonstrate their manhood on an international stage. War and football were headed to an inevitable collision.[17]

War news interrupted preseason drills for a second consecutive year. In mid-September, President Roosevelt signed the Selective Training and Service Act of 1940. The law initiated the first peacetime draft in American history, which conscripted all males aged twenty-one to thirty-five. The NAACP pushed elected officials to attach a nondiscrimination clause to the bill, but that effort failed. Still, Black men signed up for a segregated military.[18] Bell's letter was prescient; athletes such as heavyweight champion Joe Louis publicly registered in the first month.[19] Despite these high-profile examples, many Blacks heard the echoes of disappointment from World War I. "Negroes received very little of the democracy for which they fought either while they were fighting or afterward," reminded Chas. H. Thompson, editor of the *Journal of Negro Education*.[20] Despite their reservations, 265 black men in Tallahassee registered on the first day.[21]

The expectations for the Rattler football team were low after only three lettermen returned. Still, the coaching staff had developed a winning culture and expected to compete for the conference title and possibly more. In the first big game of the season, FAMU launched a "Blitzkrieg" in defeating favorite North Carolina A&T before an estimated crowd of 10,000 in Greensboro. The media again took notice of FAMU.[22] Bell and Gaither had recruited tremendous size in their backfield. Led by 205-pound Macon "Bodybuilder" Williams, the backfield averaged 188 pounds. Bell's young and powerful backs wore down the competition, beating Lane 7 to 6, nipping Morris Brown 20 to 13, and squeaking by Xavier. The Rattlers tied Kentucky State and North Carolina Central but were upset by Alabama State. Heading into the eighth annual OBC, there was a logjam at the top of the rankings. FAMU, Wilberforce, Morgan State, and Morris Brown were all prepared to claim a national title.[23] The OBC was a defensive showdown, as nearly 8,000 fans witnessed FAMU and Wilberforce battle to a 0–0 tie. The tie led to confusion about who was the national champion. Without a playoff, sportswriters relied on the widely used Dickinson Rating System, a mathematical equation developed by University of Illinois professor Frank G. Dickinson that weighed wins and losses based on the strength of the opponent.[24] According to the equation, FAMU claimed the title before the OBC, based on its strength of schedule.[25] Lucius "Melancholy" Jones of the *Atlanta Daily World* and J. C. Chunn in the *New York Amsterdam News* named Morris Brown as the title winners after the Wolverines easily defeated the Kentucky State Thorobreds.[26] However, Ric Roberts, also of the *Atlanta Daily World*, declared Morgan State the champion.[27] After Morris Brown beat Wilberforce on New Year's Day, the Wolverines' backers were vindicated.[28] Despite the Rattlers' exciting football season and chase for the national title, the growing international conflict in Europe overshadowed FAMU's success.

In a December presidential radio broadcast, Roosevelt called Detroit's conversion to wartime production the "Arsenal for Democracy." For African Americans who remembered the disappointments of racial democracy and the terror after World War I, the thoughts of the United States entering a war for European democracy while Blacks remained second-class citizens was profoundly hypocritical. The very idea of an American democracy, which kept African Americans (and others) as second-class citizens, was dubious indeed. "The U.S. may be the ARSENAL of democracy," wrote the *Pittsburgh Courier*'s George Schuyler, "but it is certainly not the HOME of democracy." He pointed out that an elected government without African Americans having the right to vote was empty rhetoric. He concluded, "There can be no real democracy when millions are terrorized by a . . . dictatorship blessed by the government. And it is useless to say that Negroes are not terrorized. When citizens fear to act like free people then they are terrorized."[29] For black Americans, the primary battle for democracy was at home, not on the battlefields of Europe.

In January 1941, A. Philip Randolph, head of the Brotherhood of Sleeping Car Porters, the largest and most influential Black labor union in the country, called on Black citizens to march on Washington, D.C., to protest against racial segregation and discrimination in the military and the defense industry. His threat to bring 100,000 disaffected citizens to the nation's capital spurred the president to action. In June, President Roosevelt issued Executive Order No. 8802, which barred racial and religious discrimination in the defense industry. The proposed march and the new law were the opening salvo in the three-decade struggle for civil rights.[30]

As the season progressed, football took a backseat to the war. FAMU defeated Tuskegee in the ninth annual OBC one day before the Japanese bombed Pearl Harbor, initiating the full participation of the United States in World War II. With America's official entry into the war, African Americans again asked, "Should I sacrifice to live 'half-American'?"[31] In answering the rhetorical question that had troubled African Americans in every war, the *Pittsburgh Courier* called for a "Double-V Campaign," victory for democracy at home and abroad.[32]

Clouds of war and confusion hung over the end of FAMU's 1941 football season. FAMU again claimed a disputed national title after Morris Brown lost to Langston on New Year's Day. This time Lucius Jones agreed, declaring, "Florida gets the 1941 national football honors."[33] Despite the Rattlers' contested championship, the team's annual banquet was a somber affair. Athletic director Jubie Bragg encouraged players to "take the right attitude toward your government." President Lee added, "I hope you will go triumphantly and gladly remembering what your athletic career has done not only for the Negro as a whole, the State of Florida, and the institution, but what it has done for you."[34] On the night of the banquet, the Rattlers deferred on selecting captains because of the uncertainty of the next season and the reality that many players would not be in football camp but in military training camps.[35] With the United States officially in World War II, it was unclear if FAMU would even field a team. Two months later, Gaither experienced his painful headaches at the SIAC basketball tournament. The future of FAMU football was in doubt.

A NEAR-DEATH EXPERIENCE

Jake Gaither's treatment for Mèniére's disease failed to alleviate his symptoms. His headaches continued, and he was now rail-thin at 135 pounds. After six months of declining health, his wife, Sadie, called Earl Odom, a former teammate of Jake's at KC, a longtime friend, and an internal medicine doctor at Meharry Medical School in Nashville. Odom traveled to Tallahassee hoping to provide an alternative diagnosis for Jake's illness. After talking to Sadie, Odom had a good idea about a medical opinion before he saw Jake in the hospital. Following a few tests, Odom quickly determined that Jake had a brain tumor. The only hope for saving Jake's life would be a complicated and expensive surgery. There was not a hospital or a doctor in Tallahassee that could perform the operation. Many white Tallahasseeans traveled nearly thirty-five miles to the John D. Archbold Hospital in Thomasville, Georgia, for surgeries.[36] African Americans received treatment at the segregated Florida A&M Hospital, founded in 1911, but it was not equipped for such a complicated and intricate surgery. Odom recommended that Sadie rush her husband to Nashville by ambulance.[37]

Nashville was the best medical center in the South, and like the rest of the region, its medical facilities were segregated. That two medical schools, Meharry and Vanderbilt, were founded one year apart, in 1875 and 1876, and were separated by less than five miles was emblematic of the realities of Jim Crow health care. In the first decade of the twentieth century, reformers sought to standardize medical education, attempting to stop quackery. Beginning in 1908, Dr. Abraham Flexner, under the auspices of the Carnegie Foundation, visited all 155 medical schools. His 1910 report called for the professionalization of medical school education, suggesting all schools require a bachelor's degree before admission. He recommended closure for schools with poorly designed curriculums. In particular, Flexner was tough on Black medical schools, suggesting the closure of five of the seven schools. He wrote, "The Negro only needs good schools rather than many schools."[38] Meharry and Howard University were the only Black medical schools to survive, as funding quickly dried up for the other five schools. While Meharry simply had been happy to escape Flexner's judgment, the report praised Vanderbilt as the best medical school in Tennessee. According to the report, "If our analysis is correct, the institution to which the responsibility for medical education in Tennessee should just now be left [is] Vanderbilt University."[39] The glowing evaluation transformed Vanderbilt into a leading medical center in the South for whites, and philanthropists targeted it for support. The school received, for example, $15 million from the Rockefeller Foundation between 1920 and 1934.[40] Together, Meharry and Vanderbilt provided the best medical facilities in the South—separate and unequal.[41]

One area of expertise at Vanderbilt was neurosurgery. Barney Brooks, a 1912 graduate of Johns Hopkins medical school, became the first professor of surgery at Vanderbilt in 1925 and chaired the department until he died in 1952. In 1926, Brooks recommended Cobb Pilcher, a Vanderbilt graduate and the son of a prominent Nashville grocer, to Harvey Cushing, professor of surgery at Harvard. Brooks described Pilcher as an "exceptional man and I should be more than pleased to have him work with you." Brooks added that Pilcher had displayed "exceptional ability."[42] With Brooks's recommendation, the twenty-two-year-old Pilcher studied under Cushing, the most experienced brain tumor surgeon in the nation. Pilcher returned to Vanderbilt medical center in 1933, developing a practice in neurosurgery with patients from across the entire region. In 1939, Vanderbilt founded the Division of Neurological Surgery under his leadership. Pilcher's presence and Vanderbilt's reputation for neurological surgery were just one reason why Odom had Jake Gaither transported to Nashville.[43]

Another reason was Pilcher's relative liberalism regarding race relations. During Pilcher's undergraduate and medical education at Vanderbilt in the 1920s and 1930s, he had the opportunity to study with Alfred Blalock, who was conducting pioneering research on blue babies syndrome, a heart defect caused by the decreased ability of blood to carry oxygen, resulting in oxygen deficiency in different body parts. Assisting Blalock in his research was Vivien Thomas, an African American surgical technician. Pilcher's close contact with Thomas and seeing Blalock's reliance on Thomas provided a brief example of racial moderation in the Jim Crow South. Having witnessed this connection, Pilcher developed a working relationship with Black doctors at Meharry, even participating in the 1946 annual convention of the National Medical Association, the national organization of African American physicians founded in 1895. He further displayed his racial liberalism during his treatment of Gaither.[44]

Pilcher met with Earl Odom and Sadie Gaither to inform them of the surgical options. He explained that the central problem facing brain surgery was finding the tumors. There were two choices: He could remove Jake's skull and identify the tumors visually. Or he could use ventriculography, a process that removed the cerebrospinal fluid and replaced it with air to take an X-ray. Although the second choice was less invasive, it also had potential danger, as increased intracranial pressure could lead to death. Ventriculography was a relatively new neurological process introduced by Walter Dandy in 1919. The inventor believed that the new X-ray technique had the most potential in neurosurgery, asserting, "By far the greatest field of usefulness of ventriculography was in the localization of brain tumors."[45] Regardless of the dangers posed by ventriculography, Sadie chose it because it was less invasive. When Pilcher looked at the X-ray, the white spots showed him that Jake had two brain tumors.[46]

Despite prevailing cultural norms, Pilcher continually demonstrated genuine concern for Jake Gaither's life and a progressive attitude toward race. The Gaithers were also worried about the cost of the surgery. Pilcher explained to the family and to Odom that the brain surgery typically cost thousands of dollars. Pulling the neurosurgeon aside, Odom said that the Gaithers could not afford the cost of the surgery. In a show of goodwill, Pilcher agreed to a drastically reduced payment of $100. The neurosurgeon rationalized, "When I'm operating on a rich man, I charge him a rich man's fee. When I am operating on a poor man, I charge him a poor man's fee. And I try to give them both the same service."[47] Pilcher removed the two tumors, but was doubtful about Jake's recovery. The surgery had left him blind and delirious for weeks. The pain was intense. "Every sinew, every bone [was] aching."[48] After several months, Sadie planned to move Jake to Columbus, Ohio, so his brother could help him in his recovery. FAMU students raised $400 to help with transportation costs, but Jake was too weak to travel by car or in a segregated train car. A Pullman car would have been ideal, but Blacks were not allowed in these luxury train cars. Pilcher helped the Gaithers again, arranging for Jake to travel to Columbus in a Pullman car as his "patient."[49] Jake continued his recovery in Columbus during the fall of 1942, while FAMU prepared for the first season of college football with the United States engaged in World War II.

COLLEGE FOOTBALL DURING WORLD WAR II

The onset of World War II posed problems for the 1942 college football season. The draft and college-age volunteers meant manpower shortages at all levels of football. As such, teams nationwide lost players and coaches to the war. The Southeastern Conference (SEC) lost more than 225 players and coaches, including legendary University of Tennessee coach Bob Neyland and Paul "Bear" Bryant, then an up-and-coming line coach at Vanderbilt University.[50] Just before the football season started, the Office of Defense Transportation barred the use of special buses or train charters for football games to conserve transportation for war needs.[51] Teams responded to this wartime sacrifice by moving games to nearby big cities.[52] As the U.S. military initiated its first air assaults of Europe in August 1942, college football teams prepared for an uncertain and undermanned 1942 season.

The wartime manpower and travel restrictions were particularly hard on HBCUs. Black college football teams had slightly smaller, less-experienced rosters. FAMU entered the 1942 season with only thirty players, of whom only ten had varsity playing experience.[53] The Rattlers' roster was similar in size to UF's in this era of single platoon football (two-way players); UF had thirty-six players on its 1942 roster.[54] Coach Bell was confident despite the smaller roster and the team's inexperience. He fully expected FAMU to finish in the top three in football and basketball. Bell stated, "We get more out of the limited material we have had than most coaches. For instance, we floated our entire varsity athletic program this year with only 36 athletes for sports, including both basketball and football. We don't have a large number of men anyway and even if the material is depleted some this year, we still think we can get as much or more out of it as the next coach."[55] Other HBCU football programs failed to share Bell's confidence. Travel restrictions left only half of the SIAC playing a full 9-game football schedule. Other HBCUs, such as Bishop College in Texas and Livingston College in North Carolina, stopped football for the duration of the war.[56]

The Rattlers had a tremendous season amid the disorder caused by the war. Despite the loss of coach Gaither, who was replaced by a sociology professor Jim Taylor, the Rattlers were among the favorites to win the SIAC championship.[57] The Rattlers relied on the tricky double wingback offense that used the deception of ball fakes to open running lanes. The offense was a success, as the Rattlers entered the OBC undefeated.[58] The 1942 OBC was a "dream game" pitting Black college football's only two undefeated teams. The game was a classic matchup of offense versus defense, as the Texas College Steers' offense averaged an HBCU best 40.8 points per game, while the Rattler defense held opponents to 2.85 points per game.[59] The OBC returned to Jacksonville after being held in Orlando and Tampa previous seasons. A smaller than usual crowd of 5,000, limited by federal travel restrictions and the unease of the first year of war, saw the Black college national championship game. The Steers led at halftime after a 51-yard touchdown run. Reports described that FAMU was "outclassed" the entire first half. Coach Bell gave a fiery and inspiring speech during intermission, and the Rattlers came out for the second half ready to play. Bell made several key substitutions in the game, switching from an inside power running game led by All-American Macon "Body Builder" Williams to an outside running attack using the team's speedy "scat backs" Oscar Tanner and James Thompson. Led by the "two speedy youngsters," FAMU scored two touchdowns in a come-from-behind 12 to 6 victory, making FAMU the 1942 Black college football champion.[60]

FAMU's jubilation was short lived. America's expanding participation in World War II tempered the Rattlers' celebration of its undefeated season and its third Black college national title in five seasons. For African Americans, the war was a two-front war against fascism and Jim Crow. Although a substantial number of Blacks chose to become conscientious objectors, most notably future civil rights activist and strategist Bayard Rustin, many African Americans waged a Double-V Campaign in uniform. Despite nearly a 35 percent delinquency rate among Black draftees, between November 1942 and December 1943, the number of Blacks in the army increased by approximately 480 percent, from 97,725 to 467,883.[61] The expansion in Black military participation affected FAMU's football team and the campus, briefly interrupting the beginnings of the school's football dynasty. By April 1943, twenty-eight players from the title team reported for active duty in the U.S. Army. The mass exodus left only three returning players for the following season. By spring 1943 more than 300 men from FAMU's student body had departed campus for the military, leaving only 68 men on the entire campus.[62]

FAMU's football program took a more significant setback when coach Bill Bell took a leave of absence to join the war effort in March 1943. Bell stated, "Most of my boys are in the service or expect to be at any time now and I wanted to be with them."[63] As he had suggested in his open letter three years earlier, Bell saw military service as a vehicle to alter America's standing race relations and as a demonstration of African American patriotism. On March 23, 1943, Bell enlisted at Camp Blanding, near Starke, Florida, as a private.[64] His decision stood at the intersection of racial uplift, black manhood, and football, symbolizing the racial sacrifice expected of Black male leadership. As an editorial about Blacks and war proclaimed, "Let us pray that the Hand of God will shape his destiny so that he can be a 'man amongst men' not only in the theaters of war, but an equal participant in all the joys, benefits and results that may come out of war."[65]

Besides Bell's belief in the importance of African American military service, two incidents during the season might have solidified his decision to volunteer. For the homecoming game, FAMU President Lee instituted a three-way segregation policy that separated blacks, whites, and soldiers attending the game, with the military police enforcing the segregation laws among soldiers. When a white member of the military police (MP) tried to force a black soldier out of the civilian section, students "razzed" the officer, who in response "unfastened the flap on his holster." Realizing he was outnumbered, the white MP retreated to avoid an incident. The MP returned with a "heavily armed detachment of soldiers" near the end of the game. The show of force and the rudeness of the white soldiers "left a bad taste in the mouths" of many Black fans. According to the Tallahassee Civic League, a local civil rights organization, the military's show of force against its Black citizens in the name of segregation was "a hell of a show." The near-riot was only a prelude to a case in January 1943 where white soldiers shot a Black girl in the back. As the injured girl, May Frances Cofield, struggled to survive, Tallahassee witnessed a rare case of interracial cooperation. Numerous white Tallahassee citizens volunteered for blood transfusions that aided in the young girl's survival. Perhaps these two events, along with his belief about the role of African American service, weighed heavily on Bell in his decision to join the military and in helping America live up to its ideals.[66]

Although the venerable Jubie Bragg had believed FAMU would "carry on," the players' and coach Bell's departures made the Rattlers' defense of their championship extremely difficult in the 1943 season. The school promoted assistant coach Herman "Buck" Neilson to be the head coach. Neilson spent a decade as an assistant at Hampton University and a year as an assistant at Lincoln University before joining the Rattlers coaching staff in 1941. Neilson also benefited from the dramatic return of Jake Gaither after a year of rehabilitation. Gaither's part-time assistance failed to offset the fact that only five varsity athletes returned for the 1943 season.[67]

The larger question troubling college football was whether schools should even play the 1943 season, given the war effort. There was little consensus among college administrators, Black or white. Colleges nationwide suffered from the Office of Defense Transportation's travel restrictions that limited team travel and from a draft that inducted approximately

250,000 men per month in 1942 and 1943.[68] Attendance for the 1942 season declined by 19 percent, and officials expected steeper declines for the 1943 season.[69] In the spring of 1943, colleges began to announce the cancellation of their football seasons. Schools big and small canceled their seasons, including Harvard University and UF.[70]

Black college football faced these challenges plus rising racial tension. The SIAC lost seven coaches to the military, including FAMU's Bell, as well as hundreds of players.[71] The problem of declining numbers of men paled in comparison with the racial tensions that worsened in the summer of 1943 due to the gap between war aims and racial realities. That summer, race riots gripped Mobile, Detroit, Los Angeles, and Harlem. In each case, a combination of the government's efforts to desegregate the defense industry, housing strains caused by the migration of workers to cities, economic competition between Black and white workers, and rumors of sexual assault or Black insurrection fueled racial tensions that resulted in race riots.[72] The calculus of racism, segregation, and economic competition made Detroit and other cities "a racial tinder box waiting to explode."[73]

Racial tensions exploded in the summer of 1943 with the lynching of Cellos Harrison in Marianna, Florida. Convicted on a dubious murder charge in neighboring Jackson County, Harrison was kidnapped from the jail and beat to death by local whites. The kidnappers were never found; thus, Harrison's death happened at the hands of "persons unknown."[74] The lynching occurred sixty-five miles from Tallahassee and was a stark reminder to FAMU students, faculty members, and administrators about the broader goal of the war effort for Blacks. After the tension-filled summer set against the backdrop of the 1941 Atlantic Charter signed by President Roosevelt and British prime minister Winston Churchill that outlined the war's democratic aims, Blacks were a "disillusioned people" and wondered if the "Freedom from Fear" applied in America.[75] Amid this context of player and coach limitations and rising racial tension, FAMU set out to defend its national title.

In 1943 and 1944, college teams white and Black added military teams filled with current and former players to their schedules to offset travel restrictions and the loss of opponents. Given the similar connection between war and football, it was no surprise that the U.S. military made football a part of the training regiment, such as the navy's V-5 preflight program. The V-5 program instructors and graduates, for example, consisted of legendary coaches such as Ohio State University's Woody Hayes, University of Alabama's Paul "Bear" Bryant, the Chicago Bears' George Halas, University of Missouri's Don Faurot, and University of Maryland's Jim Tatum. Teams such as the Iowa Pre-Flight Seahawks and one from the naval air station in Jacksonville played college teams, and in 1943, five military teams, in addition to West Point and the naval academy, finished in the top-twenty Associated Press (AP) poll.[76] Though some service football teams were integrated, most were segregated.[77] Although the military did not initially form teams among its Black soldiers, a team emerged by the fall of 1942 composed of the Service Battalion at Fort Benning. Numerous ex-college stars filled the Fort Benning Panthers roster, including FAMU's Macon "Body Builder" Williams. The Panthers played other service teams, but also FAMU, Tuskegee, and Morris Brown in 1943.[78]

The war years were uneven for FAMU. The 1943 season was its worst in over a decade. FAMU was routed 50 to 0 by Morgan State before 14,000 fans in Washington, D.C. According to longtime sports reporter Ric Roberts, "The hapless Floridas [sic], outmanned and outsmarted, were a sad sight."[79] FAMU's usually prolific offenses were held to 31 points for the entire season.[80] The Rattlers improved in the 1944 season. Led by Neilson and Gaither, who was back on the sidelines, FAMU started the season 4 and 0 but finished 7 and 3. Fans began to return to the games as well. Ten thousand fans watched FAMU defeat Virginia State in the twelfth OBC in Tampa.[81]

The winning record and fan support signaled that FAMU had survived the war on the field, and Gaither had managed to beat death. FAMU saw its enrollment grow by 15 percent over 1943, and as the war wound down, school officials concluded that a similar increase would follow the next year.[82] The Allied powers D-Day invasion marked the beginning of the end of German power in Europe, meaning more men would return to campus the following year, along with the return of coach Bill Bell. The return of Jake Gaither to the sidelines and the 1944 SIAC championship team meant that FAMU's football program had survived World War II off and on the field. The school's endurance through the difficult war years set the stage for the development of a football dynasty.

FAMU's was not the only football program preparing for the war's end. TSU president Walter S. Davis decided that athletics was a means to improve the school as well. He made two significant hires, showing the sepia sports world that he meant business. First, he hired Jessie Abbott, Tuskegee's women's track and field coach and Cleve Abbott's daughter, to lead TSU's women's track and field program. In hiring Jessie Abbott, TSU began the process of becoming a leader in Black women's athletics.[83] In the fall of 1944, Davis made his most significant hire to date, luring legendary coach Henry Arthur Kean away from Kentucky State to become the football and basketball coach as well as athletic director. Davis simply offered Kean more money than Kentucky State could afford. Davis announced, "He is a great coach, and we are expecting Tennessee to regain the high place it once held in the college football world."[84] Meanwhile, Grambling State College (now University) and Southern University sought to control the Southwestern Athletic Conference. Southern, led by Arnett "Ace" Mumford, looked to build on its three SWAC titles before the war. Grambling hired Eddie Robinson in 1941, and his squad went undefeated and unscored upon in his second season. At the end of World War II, Robinson set out to make Grambling a formidable program.[85] Eddie Hurt's Morgan State Bears dominated the East.

The war years made it difficult to determine a national champion, but with armistice, the best programs looked for football supremacy. The two and a half decades after World War II would become the golden age of Black college football.

4
THE GOLDEN AGE OF
BLACK COLLEGE FOOTBALL
BEGINS

The pollen from southern live oak trees fills the Tallahassee air every spring and summer. Pods resembling green worms hang amid Spanish moss from the iconic trees' unfurling branches. As the temperature warms, the pods erupt, and breezes carry the pollen throughout the city. Unbearable as this seasonal ritual was for allergy sufferers, few in the FAMU community could have guessed that the annual nuisance of sneezing and watery eyes would shape its football future.

The June 1945 coaching clinic was designed for "the purpose of improving instructional techniques among Negro coaches and officials."[1] The summer session also marked the triumphant return of Lt. William "Big Bill" Bell to Tallahassee. His participation at the coaching clinic signaled to many that he was returning as FAMU's head football coach. But Bell surprised the university community and the sports world when he announced his resignation as FAMU's head football coach and his intention to lead the athletic department and football team at North Carolina A&T. He explained to the administration and the media that his six-year-old son's violent asthma attacks were the reason for his departure. Shortly after Bell's announcement, Herman "Buck" Neilson, who had served as football coach while Bell was in the military, shocked the Rattlers' community a second time when he resigned citing similar reasons. Neilson's wife could not bear the pollen and had only been living in Tallahassee for half of the year. In the late summer, Neilson accepted the head coaching position at Hampton. The groundbreaking coaching clinic that sought to improve the black coaching ranks ended with FAMU losing two football coaches.[2]

Just a month before the start of the 1945 football season, FAMU was without a head coach. Meanwhile, the school was in a state of flux in its own right. After shepherding the school through the depression, President Lee had died in early 1944. Interim president Jubie Bragg named a still-ailing Gaither as the athletic director. Now Gaither had to find a new coach, and time was running out.

FAMU's new president, William H. Gray, then sent a telegram that changed both Gaither's life and the Rattlers' football program. "Since it is now August," the communication read, "and we can't get anybody else to coach the football, it looks like you will have to take over."[3] At Gray's request, Gaither agreed to become the interim head coach. Gaither's wife, Sadie, worried about his ability to withstand the rigors of head coaching, given his ongoing recovery from surgery. As Sadie recalled, "I really let him have it, but it didn't do any good."[4]

The years after World War II were a crucial time in college football. There was a tremendous reshuffling of teams, coaches, and players. During the depression, the FAMU athletic department had positioned itself to be a leader in the postwar Black athletic world. Although FAMU had won two national titles, the school's position in the upper echelon of HBCU football was not guaranteed, especially after Bell's departure. Having survived two brain tumors, Gaither seized his opportunity. He wove together the strands of the sporting congregation—coaching, recruiting, the Black press, community, and player development—ushering in the golden age of Black college football. Gaither developed the leading coaching clinic that improved his coaching and enhanced recruiting. The postwar Black press promoted Black college football and exalted Gaither's coaching prowess. Black Miamians made the "Magic City" home of the OBC, signaling the strength of the Black sporting community. Gaither's coaching philosophy promoted both winning and character development. He imbued his players with the responsibility of racial uplift.

Gaither was not alone in leading young men and developing a leading team. Programs like those at Grambling, TSU, and Southern University also produced dominant teams and players. Thus, for two and a half decades, Black college football was nearly equal to or better than its white counterparts. Black coaches and players individually broke barriers, but it was far more difficult for teams to get the same opportunities. In the decades before athletic desegregation, FAMU was on a par with and in many cases better than many of the state's PWI teams. Gaither's promotion to head coach in 1945 marked the beginning of a football regime built on his ability to operationalize the sporting congregation during the days of Jim Crow segregation. In time, FAMU's football success would be the envy of PWI football programs throughout the state, and many nationwide.

JAKE TAKES OVER

After Gaither named former Rattler Pete Griffin as his assistant coach, Gaither's first task was to fill out the Rattlers' roster, as he hoped to add veterans ready to resume their athletic careers. With 15 million veterans returning to civilian life, recruiting war veterans was an essential task for football coaches across the country. Two-thirds of returning servicemen took advantage of the Servicemen's Readjustment Act of 1944, better known as the G.I. Bill, which provided veterans with considerable benefits that catapulted many into the middle class. One million black veterans benefited from the bill by returning to college and vocational schools. Black colleges that had traditionally struggled for enrollments during the war were now over capacity. FAMU was no different from its contemporary Black colleges, as it saw its postwar enrollment double from nearly 900 in 1940 to more than 1,800 in 1949.[5] Some veterans had played football in college before the war or had played on military teams during the war. Coaches now openly recruited these men. Although there had been some disagreements among the major conferences about the eligibility of such players, the consensus was that veterans should be allowed to attend the school of their choice without punishment for one season.[6] Because Gaither was hired so late in the season, FAMU did not actively recruit a large number of veterans. Fortunately, FAMU was not losing any players from the previous season's forty-four-man squad, including its starting quarterback, Leroy "The Brain" Cromartie, and end Nathaniel "Traz" Powell.

In Gaither's first season as FAMU's head coach, the Rattlers faced their toughest schedule to that point in the school's history. Besides the traditional SIAC battles against Tuskegee and Morris Brown, the Rattlers were slated to play intersectional opponents Wilberforce (Ohio) and TSU. Despite the uncertainty that had dominated the summer, the Rattlers had a tremendous season that marked the beginning of Gaither's dynasty. The season began with a tough road game at Wilberforce College. For Gaither, the game was deeply personal as well. In his first game as interim head coach after his miraculous recovery from brain surgery, he faced A. D. Gaither, his younger brother, now an assistant coach for Wilberforce. The star of the game was Cromartie, who scored two touchdowns, including a 70-yard interception return for a touchdown. Cromartie's tremendous play gave the Rattlers a 26 to 20 win and Gaither's first of his head coaching career.[7] Gaither's first month as head coach featured wins over Alabama State, Morris Brown, and KC, his alma mater. At midseason, the Rattlers were atop the SIAC standings, holding conference opponents to only 2 points while scoring 81.[8]

The second half of the schedule featured Gaither's first matchup against Henry A. Kean's TSU Tigers. Ten thousand fans squeezed into Jacksonville's Durkee Field and watched the underdog Rattlers avenge the two losses from the previous season. The game was a seesaw affair. FAMU scored first on a Cromartie 30-yard pass. The field general added two more touchdown passes, each longer than 40 yards, to complete Rattlers' scoring. What made the difference in the game was FAMU's ability to convert extra points after its touchdowns. When the Tigers scored a fourth-quarter touchdown, the Rattlers stopped a 2-point conversion to preserve a 20 to 18 victory.[9] According to one reporter, the game was "the Fiercest [sic] fought football game ever played in this gateway city to Florida."[10] The victory pushed the Rattlers to the top of the Black college polls.

FAMU finished the regular season undefeated with wins over Tuskegee, Clark, and Morehouse. The Rattlers' last game of the season was against Louisiana Normal. FAMU won 33 to 12, but the game was significant, since it marked the first coaching matchup between Gaither and legendary coach Eddie Robinson. In 1946, Louisiana Normal would change its name to Grambling College. Few fans watching in 1945 could have anticipated the historic nature of the late-season matchup.

Gaither announced that FAMU's OBC opponent would be the Wiley College Wildcats. The Fred-Long-coached Wildcats were the only other undefeated and untied team in Black college football. In securing the SWAC champions, Gaither again made the OBC a de facto national title game. The classic returned to Tampa's Phillips Field on the banks of the Hillsborough River, and more than 7,000 fans attended the game. Led by All-American candidate Vernon Hicks, the Wildcats' speed and passing attack were too much for the home team to overcome. Wiley jumped out to a 2-touchdown lead in the first half and won handily, 32 to 6. All-American Cromartie threw for 210 yards and a touchdown, but he also tossed a costly interception that the Wildcats returned for a touchdown.[11]

Gaither's first season was a tremendous success, given the uncertainty of FAMU's coaching staff at the beginning of the season. In March 1946, the FAMU administration removed the "interim" from Gaither's title and named him permanent head coach. Then the school made him one of the highest-paid Black coaches in the country. FAMU president William H. Gray declared, "His feat in producing a Conference championship football team that was the runner-up for the National title this year clearly merits the reward that this promotion and salary increase bestow." The announcement made it clear to the Black college football community that FAMU was now Gaither's program.[12]

Gaither would need that job security, given how the 1946 season played out. The season started on a wrong note when SIAC members complained about the eligibility of All-American quarterback Leroy Cromartie. Member schools heard rumors that the Rattlers' star player had played professional baseball for the Indianapolis–Cincinnati Clowns. Syd Pollack, the owner of the Clowns, reported to the *Chicago Defender* that Cromartie participated only in spring training and was not paid. However, the *Defender*'s Fay Young consulted the Howe News Bureau baseball statisticians and discovered that the Rattlers' star quarterback had played in seventeen regular season games. B. T. Harvey, SIAC commissioner, ruled Cromartie ineligible for the 1946 season.[13]

The suspension was a blow to the Rattlers' title hopes. FAMU lost the opening game of the season to Wilberforce, 22 to 14. The Rattlers rebounded to win their next 3 games, but an upset loss to Kentucky State ended any chance of the Rattlers winning a national title. The Rattlers defeated Tuskegee but lost to Southern and to Lincoln in the OBC.[14] The four losses were disappointing, but there was still one more game in which FAMU could redeem its season.

Although the OBC had previously marked the end of the Rattlers' season, Gaither broke with tradition in 1946 by accepting an invitation to play a rematch against Wiley College in the first Angel Bowl in Los Angeles a few days before the New Year. The Angel Bowl Association, led by African American businessman Edgar S. Browne, had sought for several years to bring a major Black college bowl game to southern California.[15] Browne and his associates wanted to take advantage of Los Angeles's Black population, which had grown from approximately 39,000 in 1930 to more than 170,000 by the 1950 census because of the Great Migration to the West.[16] The Angel Bowl Association saw a financial opportunity with the overflow of southern migrants, many of whom had decent-paying jobs as a result of World War II. Still, the association's decision to bring FAMU to Los Angeles was a sign of how highly the Rattlers' football program was now rated. Wiley College was the host team and had agreed to the game a year earlier, reflecting that most of the black migrants to Los Angeles were from Texas, Louisiana, and Mississippi.

The bowl committee made an attractive offer to bring the team 3,000 miles. Browne promised Gaither $1,000 for travel expenses, a percentage of the gate receipts, and tickets to the Rose Bowl on New Year's Day. In practice, Gaither had to pay travel expenses out of the athletic department's budget and even threatened to withhold his team from playing until the Angel Bowl Association repaid the costs. Browne provided no Rose Bowl tickets for FAMU or Wiley. Gaither grew frustrated at the committee's false promises. In the end, FAMU and Wiley battled to a 6 to 6 tie before 12,000 fans. Browne, however, failed to give the players souvenir programs. Gaither's experiences in Los Angeles meant that the OBC would return as the end to the Rattlers' season.[17]

After a season that featured four losses, the most in any single season in Gaither's twenty-five-year career, Gaither would spend the off-season seeking a permanent home for the OBC in Miami and working to develop a stronger coaching clinic that would improve future Rattler players.

THE ORANGE BLOSSOM CLASSIC MOVES TO MIAMI

In the nadir of race relations in the late nineteenth and early twentieth centuries, Black Miami was a diasporic mix of African American and Afro-Caribbean laborers, primarily from the Bahamas. Marginalized politically, Black Miamians also faced residential segregation that limited their housing choices. The most populous section of town was northwest of Henry Flagler's Florida East Coast Railroad, simply known as "Colored Town."[18] By 1930, Colored Town had entered its prime as a location for Black entertainment and social life. The hub of Black life in Miami was "The Avenue," or Second Avenue. Along The Avenue in the 1930s and 1940s stood the Lyric Theater, the main center for Black entertainment, and other nightclubs that held performances by leading Black stars such as Count Basie and Billie Holiday. During this period, residents began referring to the area as "Overtown." According to sociologist Marvin Dunn, the name was derived from Black residents having to go "over" downtown to reach the area. By the post–World War II period, more than 55,000 blacks called Miami home.[19]

A segregated sporting world was vital to Black and white Miamians alike. Throughout most of the 1930s and 1940s, baseball was the king. For whites, spring training baseball dotted the landscapes of central and south Florida. Blacks also enjoyed spring training and winter baseball for Negro League teams. The controversial Ethiopian Clowns, with their stereotypical antics alongside the team's excellent baseball, briefly called Miami home before moving to Cincinnati in 1942.[20] The aftermath of World War II began to chip away at segregated sports across Florida. In February 1946, Jackie

Robinson reported to spring training for the AAA Montreal Royals, marking the beginning of the desegregation of Major League Baseball.[21] Despite baseball's dominance for south Florida sports fans, football slowly became the sport of choice in Miami. In 1935 the city hosted its first Orange Bowl, and by 1939 the annual New Year's Day classic was a major bowl along with the Rose Bowl (Pasadena), the Sugar Bowl (New Orleans), and the Cotton Bowl (Dallas).[22] The city of Miami owned and controlled the Orange Bowl stadium (also known as Burdine Stadium) and enforced segregation through the end of World War II. The Orange Bowl Committee, which was in charge of selecting teams for the annual game, acquiesced to segregation norms by choosing all-white teams.[23] The segregation ordinance eventually posed a problem for the University of Miami, which also used the stadium for its home games. In November 1946, the law forced the University of Miami to cancel a game with Penn State University. The home team asked the visitors to leave their two black players, Wallace Triplett III and Dennie Hoggard, at home for the game. The Hurricanes used the seemingly veiled threat of fearing "unfortunate incidents."[24] Penn State students and faculty lauded the school's decision to cancel the game rather than leave the Black players at home, which had been a custom.[25] As one student wrote to the school newspaper, "The ideals of Democracy are more important than any football game."[26]

Similar problems emerged with the newly formed professional football team, the Miami Seahawks. After World War II, several new professional football leagues started to take advantage of the postwar boom in spectator sports attendance and to challenge the dominance of the NFL. One of the NFL's initial challengers was the All-America Football Conference. In 1945, the Miami Seahawks replaced the Baltimore franchise. Amid the Great Depression, the NFL's decision makers had decided it was no longer acceptable to employ Black players, such as Ray Kemp and Joe Lillard.[27] The All-America conference's need for talented players posed a challenge to the gentleman's agreement in professional football. However, the inclusion of the Miami franchise signaled the continuation of segregated professional football. Wendell Smith, the sports editor for the *Pittsburgh Courier*, aptly described the disappointment of adding the Seahawks: "Any hopes football fans may have had for Negro players in the All-American [sic] Conference . . . died recently when a franchise was awarded to a syndicate in Miami, Fla. The insertion of Miami into the new loop killed all chances for Negro players, for that city is one of the most 'Nazi-fied' of all the cities in the world on matters of racial equality."[28]

Sportswriters were wrong about the integration of the league but right about the effect of the Miami franchise on Black participation. The Cleveland Browns, under head coach Paul Brown, integrated their roster by signing Bill Willis and Marion Motley. Motley and Willis faced death threats ahead of the Browns' penultimate game in Miami, and the team decided it was best to stay home and not break segregation laws or endanger the players' lives.[29] Miami had steadfastly upheld segregated sporting events, a position made simpler with the folding of the Seahawks franchise after its inaugural season. While the sporting public was debating the ethics of segregated sporting events in Miami after World War II, influential FAMU alumni were negotiating with the city to make the Rattlers the first Black team to play in the Orange Bowl.

In the decade between the end of World War II and the emergence of the full-fledged civil rights movement, Black communities secured minor concessions from the Jim Crow power structure through negotiations between Black power brokers and white civic leaders.[30] The move of the OBC to Miami should be seen as part of this process. In December 1946, a small contingent of Blacks representing twelve different organizations met with the city council. The group "requested the [Miami City] Commission to provide space for the negroes [sic] in the Roddy Burdine Stadium." The group explained that they wanted FAMU to "play one game at the Stadium." The commission explained that there was not a "colored section" at the stadium, but when a planned expansion occurred, Blacks would "be given consideration at the time."[31] In the spring of 1947, a committee composed of Rattler alumni such as Dr. G. W. Hawkins, influential local Black leaders such as attorney Lawson E. Thomson, and FAMU president William H. Gray met with city officials to move the OBC to Miami.[32] Behind the scenes, Hollis Rinehart, a Miami lawyer and member of the State Board of Control, assisted in helping FAMU play in the Orange Bowl.[33] The secret negotiations worked, and FAMU announced that the 1947 OBC would be played in the Magic City.[34]

The expansion and importance of the OBC was also a product of an activist Black press. The sports pages after the war saw sports as a vehicle to promote fairness and equality. Sportswriters pushed to end segregation in baseball, football, golf, and youth sports. They lauded the OBC as a means to demonstrate that Black college football could produce events on par with white bowl games. The writers also pushed for equality in the stands. Coverage of the OBC would regularly note the number of white fans, a proxy for the quality of the product on the field. The Black press's coverage made the OBC the leading classic game.[35]

With the OBC moving to Miami, sportswriters stoked expectations for the Rattler football team in the 1947 season. Gaither's team returned four All-Americans on the seventy-two-man squad, including Leroy Cromartie, who came back from suspension.[36] Despite the talent-laden roster, neither Gaither nor Black sportswriters assumed the Rattlers were "unbeatable," as they faced what some called a "suicide schedule."[37] The schedule led to the second of Gaither's eleven 1-loss seasons. After a disappointing 6 to 0 win over in-state rival Bethune-Cookman College, FAMU headed to Raleigh, North Carolina, to play the Shaw Bears. The game was a nightmare for the Rattlers and Leroy Cromartie, who threw seven interceptions in a 19 to 0 loss.[38] Gaither and the Rattlers righted the ship, winning the remainder of their games, including significant victories over Kentucky State, Tuskegee, and Southern. In early November, FAMU announced that the Hampton Institute Pirates would be its Orange Blossom opponent. The Pirates had a successful season, finishing second in the CIAA and holding a no. 4 ranking in the country.[39] This was a classic matchup of HBCU conference powers. However, before sportswriters could begin breaking down the game, they and others mourned the death of Jubie Bragg. Earlier in the season, FAMU honored Bragg and his son, the former coach who died in 1936, by naming the school's football field Bragg Field. More than 2,000 people attended the "Grand Old Man's" funeral, signaling his importance to the development of Black college football, the SIAC, and FAMU.[40]

Bragg's funeral during the week leading up to the OBC could not dampen the excitement for and the importance of the game. The Rattlers were favored to win the game. But the story was the game being in Miami. The *Pittsburgh Courier's* Calvin Adams described the game as the "most colorful of those played to date."[41] The game was scoreless for most of the first half when FAMU quarterback Jim Williams threw a 79-yard touchdown pass to Nathaniel "Traz" Powell for the only score of the game.[42] The main story, however, was the OBC's record crowd. Nearly 20,000 people attended the first classic in Miami, making it the largest crowd in the game's sixteen-year history and the largest ever to see Black college football in the South. More than 6,000 white fans, including Florida's governor Millard Caldwell, attended the game.[43] *Chicago Defender* sportswriter Fay Young summarized the game's success: "If the hospitality and enthusiasm shown . . . is a sample of what Miami had to offer, let us go on record as saying Miami is the one place the classic ought to be held each December. The straw hats, Panamas, summer suits we left behind to always remember that night in December under the moon and stars, the tropical flowers and everybody trying to make us feel 'welcomed.' But we are going back. The Orange Blossom Classic is a fixture in our planning of football jaunts next December. Do you blame us?"[44]

FAMU held the OBC in Miami every season between 1947 and 1979. Moreover, the game, because of the Rattlers' dominance, often became the de facto national title game and the premier Black college bowl game. FAMU's victory in 1947 could not propel the Rattlers to the top of the national rankings. They finished third behind TSU and Shaw, but FAMU claimed its fourth consecutive SIAC title, as a consolation prize.

The successful season reinforced FAMU's growing reputation in Black college football, and the large crowd at the OBC forced white fans to pay attention. The presence of Governor Caldwell suggested that he would support a winner, regardless of race. As a candidate for governor, he had lambasted the State Education Board of Control over UF's poor performance in football, and he had supported the firing of the Gators' coach in 1945. While Gaither was establishing his dynasty, the state's other universities struggled for consistency on the field after World War II. From 1945 to 1947, UF's record was 8–19–1, including 3 blowout losses to archrival University of Georgia. Florida had not defeated Georgia since 1940. The Gators won only 1 game in the SEC in this three-year span and had a 13-game losing streak in the period. The University of Miami was slightly better but also inconsistent. After winning the Orange Bowl in the 1945 season and winning 8 games in 1946, the Hurricanes won only twice in 1947. Head coach Jack Harding resigned after 1947 to become the full-time athletic director. The 1947 season also marked the beginning of FSU football. The Seminoles lost all 5 games in their first season. Despite FAMU finishing third in Black college football, the Rattlers had the best season of any team in Florida.[45] However, winning conference titles no longer satisfied Gaither. He needed and wanted a national title.

CHASING A NATIONAL TITLE

Gaither's amazing recovery and success on the field were still incomplete without a national title. Although he had been an assistant coach on three national title teams, Gaither needed a championship as head coach to warrant consideration as one of the great Black head coaches of the 1940s, such as TSU's Henry Kean, Wiley's Fred Long, Southern's A. W. Mumford, and

ORANGE
BLOSSOM

CLASSIC

FLORIDA A & M
COLLEGE
TALLAHASSEE, FLORIDA

VS.

HAMPTON
INSTITUTE
HAMPTON, VIRGINIA

ORANGE BOWL STADIUM

MIAMI, FLORIDA ★ DEC. 6, 1947 ★ 8 P. M.

Orange Blossom Classic program, 1947. (Courtesy of the author)

Morgan State's Edward Hurt. Over the next several seasons, the Rattlers continued to ascend toward the elite programs in Black college football. Along the way, Gaither secured his place among the ranks of great coaches in Black college football.

A tough regular season schedule or a high-quality opponent in the OBC derailed FAMU's title dreams over the next two seasons. The 1948 Rattlers started the season 8 and 0, with wins over Kentucky State, Morris Brown, and the Shaw Bears, avenging the only loss from the previous season. The last game of the regular season pitted the Rattlers against the undefeated Southern Jaguars; the winner would most likely claim the national title.[46] Southern dominated FAMU in a 37 to 12 victory on the way to its first national title. In the OBC, the Virginia Union Panthers upset Gaither's team 39 to 18 before nearly 16,000 fans.[47] The 1949 season was a mirror of the previous one. The Rattlers headed into the late season matchup against Southern undefeated, only to be routed 31 to 13.[48] In the OBC, Bill Bell's North Carolina A&T Aggies defeated FAMU 20 to 14.[49] After the loss to Bell's Aggies, Gaither was still in the shadow of his former mentor.[50]

Gaither hoped the new decade would change his team's fortunes, as his first five seasons fell short of a national title. Before his season had begun, the Black press featured Gaither as a leading coach in the Southeast. The feature touted Gaither's five consecutive conference titles and his 36-game conference-winning streak.[51] Despite the acclaim, some sportswriters believed that the 1950 season would end FAMU's conference dominance, as the Rattlers were devastated by graduation. The *Atlanta Daily World*'s Marion Jackson noted that this was the first season in a long time that the Rattlers did not start a "'name' backfield, a rockribbed line, or with veterans that can withstand the battering that never-say-die SIAC elevens are planning."[52] Still, the *Pittsburgh Courier* had the Rattlers ranked fifth in its preseason poll.[53]

The Rattlers surprised many with their impressive start to the 1950 season. FAMU's first test was against Morris Brown before 10,000 fans. The Rattlers leaned on their strong running game and a stout defense for a 20 to 0 shutout.[54] The following week FAMU had a rematch of the previous season's OBC in its game against the North Carolina A&T Aggies. Again, a strong running game and a stingy defense led the Rattlers to a 14 to 9 victory. Gaither's win over his former mentor was his first over a CIAA team in three years and put FAMU along with an unbeaten Southern University at the top of the polls.[55] The two undefeated teams headed to a pivotal mid-November clash that seemed to determine the national title. Southern was favored at home heading into the big game. Both defenses dominated the game, and it ended in a 0 to 0 tie. The tie meant that the Rattlers remained on top and guaranteed at least a piece of a national title, Gaither's first as a head coach.[56] Still, FAMU would have to win the OBC, for which Gaither selected Wilberforce University.

Before FAMU and Wilberforce had played in the OBC, the University of Miami defeated the University of Iowa, breaking the color line on the field at the Orange Bowl.[57] The Iowa Hawkeyes played five Black players in their 14 to 6 loss. Bernie Bennett, who scored Iowa's lone touchdown and one of the barrier-breaking players, recalled, "We were aware that we were setting a precedent, but nothing happened during the game that reflected any conflict. There was no special security, and there were no racist remarks. Once the game started, we just played."[58] Still, when Bennett scored a touchdown in the east end zone, Black spectators stood and cheered.[59] The desegregation of football at the Orange Bowl reflected larger trends but also points to the success of the OBC. When FAMU had pushed to play the classic in the Orange Bowl, it opened the door for the University of Miami and the Orange Bowl to host integrated teams.

The Rattlers were favored in the OBC matchup. However, the Green Wave surprised the top-ranked Rattlers, winning 13 to 7 in front of nearly 20,000 fans. Gaither offered no excuses for the loss and said, "It just wasn't in the books for us."[60] This was Gaither's third consecutive loss in the OBC and the most heartbreaking loss in Gaither's early head coaching career.[61] Despite FAMU's disappointing finish to the season, it was a national champion, as the *Pittsburgh Courier* poll did not include the OBC, treating it as a postseason exhibition game.[62] The controversial and unconvincing title was Gaither's first, but he would not be satisfied until he won another, without any doubts this time. In order to win it, he knew he would have to become a better coach.

THE COACHING CLINIC: CATALYST TO A DYNASTY

Gaither's first national title, although disputed, added to his growing reputation as a leading coach in Black college football. FAMU's annual coaching clinic was essential in activating the sporting congregation and in Gaither's ability to form a football dynasty. Ahead of the 1945 clinic, Gaither explained, "For some time we have felt the need of a coaching school of the kind directed by Negro Coaches who have had success in their field over a number of years." He added, "We have in mind inviting two or more outstanding Negro coaches to supplement our staff here at the College in supervising the school."[63] The goal of the clinic was to improve the teaching of football and basketball fundamentals to Black high school and college coaches. For Gaither, the clinic also disabused Black high school coaches of the notion that "everything good came out of the white colleges" and emphasized that "there were good Negro college coaches, too."[64] Participants received physical education college credits upon completion. More important, the clinic enhanced the recruiting pipeline from Black Florida high schools to Tallahassee. Some of the best high school coaches in the state improved their tactics and strategies by learning from the best coaches in America in the steamy hot summers in Tallahassee. Some of Gaither's success should be attributed to the coaching clinic that enhanced his reputation among Black and white coaches, allowed the Rattlers to monopolize recruiting in Florida, helped to develop FAMU's innovative playing style, and demonstrated the school's investment in athletics, especially football. The clinic also became a laboratory of sporting democracy. Coaches, Black and white, swapped strategies and stories. Ultimately, Gaither's coaching clinic contributed to the breaking of racial barriers at PWIs.

THE DESEGREGATION OF THE COACHING CLINIC

The first three coaching clinics brought together leading HBCU coaches. The 1947 weeklong clinic included Southern University's A. W. Mumford, Virginia State College's Harry Jefferson, and Morgan State College's Eddie Hurt, along with the FAMU coaching staff. The following year, and a year after Jackie Robinson had desegregated Major League Baseball, Gaither began to desegregate his coaching clinic, inviting UF head football coach Raymond Wolf and FSU basketball coach Charles A. Armstrong to lecture.[65] FAMU was not the first HBCU to desegregate its coaching clinic. North Carolina Central College secured Duke football coach Wallace Wade in 1946, and by 1948 several other HBCUs had started interracial coaching clinics. Still, Gaither's clinic was among the best and the longest running in the South.[66] Attendees were primarily Florida and Georgia high school coaches earning graduate school credits in physical education. Ralph Long, an assistant coach at David T. Howard High School in Atlanta, attended the 1948 session and described the clinic as "a great success." He noted that HBCUs in Georgia needed a clinic similar to FAMU's, as "the program was packed full of activity from Monday morning until Saturday evening and was highly informative."[67] A typical session during the weeklong camp included "The Modern Approach to Football," "Personnel Requirements for the 'T' and Single Wing Offense," and "Fundamental Pass Plays and Patterns."[68] More than fifty coaches attended the seventh annual clinic in 1951.

Gaither also began to secure higher-profile white coaches not based in Florida, through his connections with the state of Ohio. The first national coach Gaither invited was Chuck Mather, an innovative coach at Washington High School in Massillon, Ohio. At Washington High, Mather followed and upheld the legacy created by Cleveland Browns head coach and former Ohio State University coach Paul Brown by winning six consecutive state high school football titles. Mather was one of the first coaches to use IBM punch cards for statistical analysis. He codified these ideas in *Winning High School Football*, a leading coaching text throughout the country.[69] In 1952, Gaither secured future pro football and college football Hall-of-Famer Sid Gillman, a former assistant at Ohio State and then head coach of the University of Cincinnati. Gillman, arguably, was the mastermind behind modern football. In an era of "three yards and a cloud of dust," he believed in spreading players across the field and throwing the football. Gillman's passing offense was the beginning of the West Coast offense that now dominates professional football. In addition, Gillman, a son of Minneapolis theater owners, also pioneered film study. Mather's and Gillman's participation in the clinic reveals Gaither's belief in football innovation at the coaching clinic.[70] However, Gaither did not rely merely on outside coaches to introduce innovative coaching techniques and strategies. He contributed many of his own.

COACHING INNOVATIONS

Gaither's return to coaching coincided with the development of the T-formation offense. Developed by Stanford University's Clark Shaughnessy and popularized by George Halas's Chicago Bears, the T formation stressed speed and deception instead of the power football used by the single- and double-wing formations.[71] Gaither's 1940s teams used the formation en route to dominating the SIAC.[72] By the 1951 season, Gaither had begun using and teaching at the clinic a spread T-formation offense that relied on a mix of pitch-out and interior running plays and pass plays.[73] In the mid-1950s, Gaither shifted to his version of the split-line T offense. In a formation developed from Don Faurot's offense at the University of Missouri, Gaither spread his linemen farther apart to create better angles for blocks.[74] Gaither's split-line T differed in a few fundamental ways from Faurot's split-T formation. First, Gaither spread his interior linemen farther apart. The guards lined up 4½ feet on each side of the center. In the split-T formation, the interior linemen were a foot on each side of the center. Gaither's line spread 48 feet from end to end, whereas in the split-T, the distance was about 33 feet. This extra space allowed Gaither to use speedy tailbacks. The results were devastating to opponents.[75]

The split-line T offense was not without critics, as some white coaches viewed the experimentation by Gaither and other Black coaches as akin to clowning-type sporting events, such as the Negro Leagues Indianapolis Ethiopian Clowns or basketball's Harlem Globetrotters. At the 1952 OBC, for example, Georgia Tech's football coach Bobby Dodd told the *Atlanta Journal*, "You never have seen such spread formations in all your life. Both teams scattered linemen in one direction and backs in another. The players could run like antelopes and tackled for keeps, but could not punt nor did they have any for the passer."[76] The African American press read Dodd's comments as unfair criticism of Black college coaching expertise. Dodd issued a formal apology after talking with Gaither.[77] Later, University of Alabama head coach Paul "Bear" Bryant did not believe that Gaither's split-line offense would hold up in the upper levels of white football. At a clinic, Bryant announced, "It'll never work, particularly in big-time football." Gaither responded, "I'll take my players and beat yours with it and take your players and beat mine with it."[78] Gaither's ability to tweak the leading offenses expressed his willingness to learn from others but also make innovations.

THE CLINIC AND RECRUITING

Gaither knew he could run the split-line T offense with average speed in the backfield. Nonetheless, Gaither, like all coaches, still sought out elite players to run his offense. The combination of wins on the field and FAMU's successful coaching clinic provided a significant recruiting advantage. The NCAA's decision to allow multiplatoon football during the war enhanced Gaither's edge. When the NCAA had decided to return to single-platoon football, Gaither used his deep talent pool to turn a potential disadvantage into a nearly unstoppable depth superiority.

Gaither controlled in-state athletic talent. The postwar explosion in higher education and the concurrent baby boom increased the number of teachers who were FAMU graduates in classrooms across the state. Gaither would regularly boast that 85 to 90 percent of the Florida high school coaches were FAMU graduates.[79] FAMU's anticipation of increasing requirements for teachers put the athletic program in a position to be dominant. In the mid-1930s, President J. R. E. Lee convinced the State Board of Education that FAMU needed a Department of Health and Physical Education. Lee stated, "The only teachers capable of teaching physical education are those who have been trained in physical education."[80] In the years after World War II, the State Board of Control and the state legislature passed the Minimum Foundation Program, which among its provisions increased the teacher requirements. In the state's enhanced requirements, there was a stipulation that high school coaches have college credit in physical education.[81] FAMU's coaching clinics provided college credits to attendees and allowed Gaither direct contact with most of the state's high school coaches. The coalescence of FAMU's growing enrollment and the state's new teaching requirements lends credence to Gaither's claim that an overwhelming number of the state's Black coaches were Rattler alumni.

Recruiting football players, however, was not as simple as having a network of coaches. Gaither recalled a shift from his first seasons in Tallahassee. When he had arrived at FAMU in 1937, most of the players were from the North. As head coach, Gaither sought to remedy the in-state coaching deficiencies through the coaching clinics. He used the clinics to improve coaching, and he persuaded many of the coaches to use the Rattlers' offensive and defensive systems. Recruits came to Tallahassee familiar with the playbook, easing their transition to college football.[82] Finally, Gaither served as commissioner of the Florida Interscholastic Athletic Association from 1944 to 1949. This position allowed Gaither to foster a relationship with every Black high school in the state.[83]

Gaither dominated in-state recruiting in the 1950s. *Atlanta Daily World* sports columnist Marion E. Jackson noted that Gaither had "a fence around the state and no prep talent that he wants gets out to other colleges." The coaches at Bethune-Cookman, Edward Waters, and Florida Normal (now Florida Memorial) complained about the Rattlers' "farm system." Gaither's control of the talent pool was so dominant that Jackson suggested, "Edward Waters has virtually quit football because of its inability to recruit topflight talent and put players on the field comparable to the highly-beloved Rattlers."[84] Gaither's farm system was not infallible. When an alumnus begged Gaither to take a five-foot ten-inch, 170-pound player from Palmetto, Florida, he agreed. When the player had entered his office, a preoccupied Gaither turned around only to see the top of the young man's head. "Get up off your knees, son. You don't have to do that," Gaither said. It turned out that the player was not on his knees, only a small five feet five inches. Gaither kept the young man, Eddie "Shorty" Shannon, on the team, and then he became the first full-time trainer and equipment man.[85] Despite the occasional poor information, Gaither routinely sent assistant coaches down each coast and had his choice of players.[86] By 1950, fifty-one of sixty-five players were from Florida, and in 1951 only seven of the thirty-nine lettermen hailed from outside Florida.[87]

The growing concerns the NCAA had about big-time college football did not apply to the ways that Gaither and other HBCU coaches were forced to recruit. In 1948 the NCAA adopted the Principles of Conduct of Intercollegiate Athletics, known as the Sanity Code, as a mechanism to enforce a code of conduct and punish violators. The code regulated the recruiting and retention of student-athletes. The NCAA designed the legislation to prohibit extra benefits beyond tuition and fees. Violations of the Sanity Code initially meant expulsion from the NCAA. By 1951, the code was rejected when big-time programs, such as the Universities of Maryland and Virginia, faced expulsion. Observers of Black colleges athletics believed that the new law would have little effect. The *Atlanta Daily World*'s Marion E. Jackson wrote, "We don't see any reason for race colleges to accept or reject the NCAA sanity code. Not a single one of our colleges has enough money or resources to commit a single violation of the code."[88] North Carolina Central basketball coach John McLendon added, "The 'Sanity Code' is not necessary in my estimation for [Black] colleges."[89] HBCUs' lack of revenue and wealthy alumni signaled that recruiting would rely on human relations.

COACHING PHILOSOPHY

Gaither's coaching philosophy, honed in the sweltering Tallahassee summers, promoted character development through athletic success, which reflected his coming of age during the period in which Black college athletics was expected to produce racial leadership and be in service to communities. His style was ministerial. Players were expected to attend church every week. Before games, he led the team in prayer:

> Dear God. You have been so good to us, much better than we deserve. We don't ask You for victory today, but rather the ability to do our best so that every one of these kids gets every full measure. I want my kids to shine like a Lilly in the Valley, Bright and Morning Star. Let them block. Let them tackle. Let them run like they never run before. Dear God, give my kids the strength to perform well. Help them today to do their best. This is my prayer.

The players responded in unison, "We wounded them. They have fallen beneath our feet. They shall not rise. The Lord is my shepherd."[90]

Gaither was a master motivator. Former Rattler Al Frazier noted, "He could get you up for the game even if you came into the dressing room feeling a little low. . . . When he finished, we'd break out of that dressing room[,] and I guess if we had seen some of the opposition at that moment, we would have tackled them right there."[91]

As FAMU's head coach, Gaither demanded that his players be "A-gile, MO-bile, and HOS-tile." Agile players had "good balance and good muscular coordination." He added, "If a boy is agile, he can recoil from a hard block and still get the ball carrier." For a player to be considered mobile, he had to have a "quick reaction time." Colloquially, Gaither sought players who could "cut on a dime and give you a nickel's change." Finally, a player had to be hostile. Football was a hard game and "a football player's gotta be mean."[92] He wanted his players to make opponents wish that they had never been born.[93] Off the field, however, he expected players to conduct themselves respectfully by going to class, staying out of trouble, and giving 110 ten percent in all endeavors.[94]

Gaither insisted that the character development of his players was paramount. He explained that he didn't measure a player "by the number of games he helped me win (oh, that's fine) but I rather measure him by what he is doing ten or fifteen years later."[95] For Gaither, his players becoming respectable men was as important as wins. He later would codify this philosophy into the "Spirit of Excellence."[96] Gaither and his wife were childless; thus calling his players "my boys" spoke to what he saw as his parental obligation. "A coach has a tremendous responsibility," he recalled. "When a parent is willing to turn over to a man their child and say, 'Take my boy and make a man out of him.' That is a very high tribute and along with it goes a great responsibility."[97] Gaither shepherded his players into adulthood with tough love, firm discipline, and a gentle touch. "If he is a ditch digger, I want him to be the best in the town. If he is a doctor, I want him to be the best in the community. If he is a tackle, I want him to be the best in the conference," Gaither preached routinely.[98]

FAMU's recruiting methods and pipeline worked flawlessly. In 1952, for instance, FAMU recruited Willie Galimore from St. Augustine to play basketball. At Excelsior High, the first public school for Blacks in the nation's oldest city, Galimore played football and basketball for Solomon Calhoun. Coach Calhoun was a FAMU graduate and the first player to make the coveted *Pittsburgh Courier* All-American team in 1934 under the tutelage of Jubie Bragg. There is little doubt that Calhoun informed Gaither of Galimore's abundant football talent. By 1953, Galimore was a major part of a speedy backfield in which the 100-yard dash times ranged from 9.7 to 10.3 seconds. (The world record was 9.3). Galimore would become a four-time HBCU All-American and the greatest running back in FAMU history.[99] The Rattlers' wins, coaching clinic, and recruiting pipeline signaled FAMU's concern with and its effective use of the human resources of college football.

FAMU's multisport success needed a significant material investment in the athletic program, especially in football. Gaither, his coaching staff, and the faculty provided considerable human resources to incoming athletes. The coaching clinic combined human and material resources that provided immediate benefits for FAMU. However, the economic and infrastructural resources for Rattler athletics were separate and unequal in the long term. The network of alumni coaches and on-field dominance made Tallahassee the preferred college choice of most Black high school football players. Nonetheless, the material resources, or lack thereof, plagued the FAMU program, making it unable to capitalize on its on-field success and its recruiting pipeline fully. Despite the inequities, Gaither made ends meet with his meager athletic budget through the success of the OBC and the unequal returns from the Race Track Allocation Fund. FAMU received funds from a state tax on horse race betting, which would separate it financially from other HBCUs. Although pari-mutuel betting was illegal in the state, horse racing thrived at the Hialeah track in South Florida. The track's wealthy owner, Joseph Widener, waged a one-person campaign to legalize gambling. Ultimately, the "Hialeah Bill" successfully legalized pari-mutuel betting in 1931 by placing a 15 percent tax on attendance and a 3 percent tax on bets. The revenue collected would be evenly distributed to all sixty-seven counties, big and small.[100] By World War II, more than $6 million would be added annually to the state treasury.[101]

Politicians would soon see gambling revenue as a panacea for a host of ills, including a losing football program at UF.[102] In 1949, the legislature approved a bill that allowed an extra day of racing in which the profits went to a scholarship fund for the three public universities: the University of Florida, Florida State University, and Florida A&M University. The scholarship fund, or "football fund," subsidized athletics at all three state universities.[103] The football fund provided needed financial reinforcement to FAMU's athletic department. Between 1952 and 1962, FAMU received nearly $400,000. However, this was only 12 percent of the money allocated. Despite the unequal distribution, the money provided financial stability for FAMU's athletic department.[104] In 1951, despite finishing third in the final poll and winning the OBC 67 to 6 over North Carolina Central, the Rattlers' football program lost more than $14,500. The following season, FAMU's athletic budget was augmented by the state's Race Track Allocation Fund, which provided an additional $23,000 to the budget. The 1952 OBC generated $20,000 more in profits. Still, the Race Track Allocation Fund allocated monies discriminatingly. While FAMU received only 12 percent of the distributed funds, UF received 56 percent (approximately $130,000) and FSU collected 32 percent (nearly $74,500). The money allowed FAMU to dominate the Black college ranks, but the Rattlers' funding inequality with UF and FSU meant that FAMU was on an unequal plane, with school desegregation looming.[105]

Even with these unequal material resources, many HBCU faculty members and administrators began to question the ethics surrounding college athletics. In 1948, Gordon B. Hancock, dean at Virginia Union University and co-organizer of the interracial Southern Regional Council, loudly criticized Black colleges' overemphasis on football. In an article for the *Atlanta Daily World*, he declared, "College athletics is bidding for the driver's seat in our educational scheme of things." Hancock viewed college football as the grounds for creeping professionalism. He continued, "The professionalization of college football is going apace with only here and there a muffled protest." Football, according to the professor, was too costly in terms of money, energy, and morality. The seeming shift toward professionalism was "bad enough for the well-supported white schools, but it is calamitous for poor struggling Negro schools who are doomed to a 'from-hand-to-mouth-existence.'"[106] Similar complaints about the role of athletics emerged from the FAMU campus. In February 1952, the school held a public forum on the state of its athletics. The "Intercollegiate Athletics—Big Business or Sportsmanship?" forum was a public debate between Wilson Gray, a law school faculty member, and Gaither. Gray argued that sports had become a big business that focused on winning at all costs, the numerous stadium expansions, and the costs of football. Gaither countered, "Is big business bad?" The head coach and athletic director noted the collegiate athletic funding model of successful football supporting other nonrevenue sports. Gaither ended by emphasizing his "spirit of excellence," pointing out the value of college sports for the players themselves.[107]

Hancock's and Gray's criticisms echoed larger scandals in college athletics in the early 1950s. The College of William and Mary engaged in an admissions scam to build up its surprisingly successful football team. Army's football team was besieged by a cheating scandal, basketball players were caught in a point-shaving scandal that forced Adolph Rupp's University of Kentucky basketball team not to play the 1952–53 season, and Clair Bee's Long Island University basketball team was suspended for six seasons for aiding gamblers.[108] These scandals tainted all of college sports, leading reformers to question the purpose of athletics.

Despite inequitable funding and growing criticism, FAMU and other HBCUs devoted their limited resources for two reasons. First, there was a continued belief that on the field, success could be translated into meaningful desegregation at the individual and institutional level. Gaither and the FAMU administration expected their student-athletes to become leaders. Black college sports were a cauldron that produced race men and women. Second, educational leaders understood that the development of a sporting congregation contributed to the broader Black communal ethos embodied by HBCUs. Gaither and others accepted that Black colleges' athletic success was representative of the possibility of Black cooperative success.

THE CREATION OF THE BLOOD, SWEAT, AND TEARS UNITS

Criticisms about the financial and social influence of football also reflected the growing size of rosters in the post–World War II period. The Rattlers' roster nearly doubled in size from the 1930s to the 1950s because of the unlimited substitutions rule implemented during World War II. Prior to 1941, players played both ways (offense and defense) in single-platoon football. Substitutions only occurred because of injury. This kept roster sizes small. In 1941, the NCAA allowed unlimited substitutions and allowed freshmen to play varsity to help teams whose rosters had been reduced during the war. In a 1945 game against Army, University of Michigan coach Fritz Crisler used a two-platoon system (players competed in only offense or defense) in a losing effort. Despite the game's outcome, coaches emulated Crisler's innovation, and teams quickly adopted the two-platoon system. Unlimited substitutions, two-platoon football, and returning players on the G.I. Bill allowed coaches to expand their rosters at all levels, including HBCUs. Many of these roster spots were funded by scholarships, thereby increasing athletic budgets.[109]

Growing rosters created athletic economies of scale, in which larger, mostly public Black colleges had financial advantages over smaller, mainly private schools. The larger student populations and state support for public HBCUs created a shift in their sporting futures over private Black colleges. Church-supported Black colleges, such as Fisk University, Morris Brown College, and Xavier University, often struggled in the wake of the expansion of college football, while traditionally weaker football programs, such as those at Alabama State, Alabama A&M, and South Carolina State, dramatically improved in the 1950s. Unlimited substitutions and two-platoon systems led to increasing dominance by FAMU, Grambling, Southern, and

TSU. Between 1945 and 1970, Wiley College (1945) and Morris Brown College (1951) were the only private HBCUs to win a national title.[110]

In 1950, college rosters were again stretched by war. The Korean War was the first military engagement after President Harry Truman's Executive Order No. 9981, which desegregated the military. Although the Korean War did not drum up the level of patriotic support of World War II, the war took its toll on college football, especially at private schools. Manpower shortages and the increasing cost of football led colleges such as Georgetown University, the University of San Francisco, and St. Louis University to eliminate the sport. Harvard, Yale, and similar schools formed the Ivy League, which deemphasized football.[111] On the Black college football landscape, Le Moyne College in Memphis ended football for the second time in a decade in 1951. The Mad Magicians were hugely successful in the 1930s and early 1940s, but school president Hollis F. Price cited "the mounting costs of athletic equipment and the possibilities of a limited number of male students during the 1951–1952 season."[112] Similarly, Tillotson College in Austin, Texas, ended football for similar reasons. Its president, William H. Jones, cited "heavy deficits," although some sportswriters blamed the SWAC schools for avoiding the small-school "giant killers" who defeated three SWAC teams in 1949, including perennial power Prairie View. Nonetheless, by 1951 Tillotson's foray into major HBCU football was over.[113]

Legendary Tuskegee coach Cleveland Abbott lamented the effect of big-time football on private colleges. Abbott noted, "The change in the rules during the last few years . . . made it mandatory to maintain large squads in order to match strength with opponents." He also identified the increasing cost of equipment, fueled by the introduction of plastic helmets in 1946, and the introduction of spring football practice as adding to football's expenses. Abbott called for the end of spring football in the SIAC, a position supported by several presidents in the SIAC. A difference between the larger schools and the small schools emerged over the use of the platoon system. "It seems that the private colleges no longer can afford to finance the great squad required under the free substitution rule. Neither can it pay the expensive coaching staffs required to teach the platoons," declared Abbott. He concluded that there was an "over emphasis on intercollegiate sports." This was a startling admission from a legendary coach.[114] Separately, the NCAA and the SIAC debated reforms at their conferences in the winter of 1951–52, electing to limit spring football to twenty practices over thirty days. Gaither opposed these reforms, seeing them as backward-looking.[115]

In January 1953, the NCAA ended free substitution and the two-platoon system. Old-time fans rejoiced at a return to "individual heroes," while many coaches and players opposed the new rules.[116] Black coaches weighed in on the new ruling. Smaller private schools applauded the new rules. Talladega College's William A. Twyman stated, "The re-installing of one-platoon football will be a boom to small colleges because the need for large colleges to recruit large squads will be lessened; therefore many good football players will be free to enroll in small colleges or play football for football's sake."[117] Of the coaches opposing the new decision, Gaither was among the most vocal. He stated that the judgment was poorly timed and detrimental to the growth of the game. "In my opinion the quality of play will suffer; injuries will increase; the number of participants will be reduced; and the problem will not be solved . . . . This return to the 'horse and buggy days' of football curtails specialization, a desirable trend in education, industry and business. I cannot reconcile the two points of view."[118] Gaither doubted that returning to a one-platoon system would reverse the balance of power between big teams and small teams. Gaither was not alone in his opposition, as other leading coaches, including Bill Bell (North Carolina A&T), Henry A. Kean (TSU), and A. W. Mumford (Southern) opposed the rule as well.[119]

Gaither's fierce opposition to a one-platoon system also contained seeds of his innovative plans to subvert the single-platoon system. He suggested that instead of returning to a one-platoon system, he could possibly develop a four-platoon system, "a team for each quarter."[120] The new substitution rule stated that a player removed from the game could not return in the same quarter, unless that player was removed before the last four minutes of the second or fourth quarter.[121] Rather than rely on sixty-minute men, Gaither sought to develop three equally talented units who played in the first three quarters, and then a combination would finish the game. The groups were called Blood, Sweat, and Tears, after the team's motto. While three equal units did not fully develop until 1959, it was clear that Gaither had this as a goal when the rule change was announced.[122]

In the decade after World War II, Gaither operationalized the various components of the sporting congregation. Anchored by the coaching clinic and the OBC, FAMU's football program improved coaching in the state's high schools, developed a brutally efficient recruiting pipeline, and connected college athletics to the Black communities in Florida's leading

Gaither leading the team in prayer. (Florida Memory, Florida State Archives)

cities—Jacksonville, Tampa, Orlando, and Miami. The outcome of Gaither's efforts was wins and respect. Between 1945 and 1952, he won nearly 85 percent of his games. He was a master motivator. He was, as one sportswriter described, "the most skilled tactician of psychological warfare." Gaither "injects into his gridders . . . a fanaticism for perfection, a superego for stardom, and the fatherly blend of acknowledgment."[123] For Gaither it was more than motivation; it was the spirit. Gaither's pep talks demanded that players be agile, mobile, and hostile. On most Saturday afternoons, the Rattlers were just that. Beginning with his 1945 season, Gaither was called a pastor over the FAMU sporting congregation.

A chance to win a second national title at the 1952 OBC against Virginia State meant that Gaither could join an elite group of Black coaches with two or more titles. In the buildup to the OBC, Ric Roberts cataloged a list of the great football coaches on the "sepia circuit." At least two national titles were needed to merit inclusion on Roberts's list. The "Fabulous Seven" top coaches were Morgan State's Edward Hurt (7 titles), Tuskegee's Cleveland Abbott (5 titles), Kentucky State and TSU's Henry A. Kean (4 titles), Southern's A. W. Mumford (3 titles), Wiley's Fred Long (2 titles), Virginia State and Hampton's Harry Jefferson (2 titles), and FAMU and North Carolina A&T's Bill Bell (2 titles). Virginia State's Sylvester Hall, Morris Brown's Edward Clemons, and Gaither each had one title and were poised to enter Roberts's illustrious list.[124]

Sylvester "Sal" Hall's Virginia State Trojans had only surrendered 6 points all season in victories over TSU, North Carolina A&T, and others. Morgan State's Eddie Hurt thought Virginia State had "too much defense for Jake."[125] Before more than 35,000 fans, the Rattlers stunned Virginia State, winning 29 to 7. Despite two losses, the Rattlers' upset victory provided Gaither with his second national championship.[126] The title signaled to the country that Gaither was among the elite Black college coaches of all time. The scary part for the Rattlers' opponents was that Gaither was just beginning to win titles. The mid-1950s established Gaither as the best coach in Black college football at the same time that the civil rights movement emerged.

POSTWAR CIVIL RIGHTS IN FLORIDA

In the aftermath of World War II, the cauldron of racial politics, civil rights, and white supremacy swirled nationally, regionally, and locally. Heading into the 1948 election, President Harry S. Truman made civil rights a fundamental component of the Democratic Party platform, including stronger civil rights enforcement; the elimination of poll taxes, literacy tests, and other mechanisms designed to disenfranchise Black voters; and the desegregation of the armed forces.

The emergence of a civil rights agenda put Black college employees in a bind. How would the support for racial justice affect their schools and their jobs? The 1949 Florida governmental session sought to reaffirm segregation and white supremacy by ostensibly cracking down on Communism in the state's colleges. A legislative committee developed a questionnaire that asked faculty members at FAMU, UF, and the recently turned coed FSU if they were Communists, if they supported the violent overthrow of the government, and if they were or had been involved with a subversive organization. The state house questionnaire followed a blueprint created by the U.S. Congress's House Un-American Activities Committee. The Florida questionnaire also had a question about segregation. "Have you ever taught or expressed yourself as being against any provision of the racial segregation laws of Florida?" With this question, the state legislature connected integration and civil rights with Communism, putting FAMU's faculty and administration in a no-win position. Leading FAMU alumni and faculty members asked the house committee for clarification. "The question paramount in our minds," queried J. Leonard Lewis, an alumnus and an attorney for the Jacksonville-based Afro-American Insurance Company, "is what would be the interpretation of the committee of an affirmative answer to the question?" He continued, "No honest person being exposed to [segregation can] honestly say he hasn't expressed himself in opposition to the segregation laws as administered by Florida officials." Florida representative Guy Strayhorn answered, "If many professors answer 'no' to the question they should very properly consider their positions in doubt for lying." He added, "We feel we have a right to know if teachers are teaching contrary to the laws of Florida."[127]

Representative Strayhorn's comments revealed that a purpose of the inquiry was to stop budding civil rights activities in the state. Specifically, several white faculty members at UF had helped six FAMU students, including Virgil Hawkins, to apply for graduate or professional school at UF. Assistant Attorney General James Toney, who prepared the initial questionnaire, suggested that it was "communist tactics to try and break down racial barriers."[128] As historian Jeff Woods and others have noted, white politicians' suggestion that connections existed between Communism and desegregation was a potent weapon in maintaining white supremacy in the late 1940s and 1950s.[129]

The survey results were a factor in FAMU president William H. Gray's resignation in July 1949. Ninety-seven percent of FAMU faculty denounced segregation. Moreover, state officials had been frustrated that Gray refused to crack down on students, faculty, and staff who tested the limits of exclusion through integrated education, equalizing salaries, and interracial socializing.[130] In addition, some Black alumni believed that strengthening FAMU undermined broader goals of integration. Gray had spent five years increasing the school's budget. He managed to get the state legislature to enhance appropriations from $208,000 to $1,599,000, improving, among other things, faculty and staff salaries.[131] A series of articles from Tampa's Black newspaper, the *Florida Sentinel*, suggested that Gray had mismanaged university funds and concluded, "Look for us [the *Sentinel*] to shout somewhere along the line: Dr. Gray has got to go."[132] The *Sentinel* editor and publisher, C. Blythe Andrews, wrote Governor Fuller Warren, stating, "We want him [Gray] removed because we think he is hurting the morale of our college."[133] Although Gray had support from Mary McLeod Bethune, founder of Bethune-Cookman, Gray still resigned, as he was unable to balance the growth of FAMU with the call for desegregation.[134] His resignation was just the beginning of the civil rights movement in Tallahassee.

President Gray's resignation was symptomatic of the unexpected effects of the NAACP's legal campaign to end school segregation. A critical strategy for the civil rights organization was to sue under the idea of equality in "separate but equal." Their belief was that a dual system of education was untenable. The NAACP's lawsuits on behalf of Ada Sipuel to enroll in the University of Oklahoma law school and for Herman Sweatt to enter the University of Texas law school were crucial victories in the desegregation of higher education.

The NAACP's success, however, produced the unintended consequence of furthering segregation in higher education, to the temporary benefit of HBCUs. As the new monies that FAMU received exemplified, southern states responded by dramatically increasing their funding to Black colleges. Walter White, head of the NAACP, observed, "Each time the NAACP wins a court case against a Southern state, new buildings spring up on the campuses of the colored land-grant colleges." After the *Sipuel* and *Sweatt* cases, the NAACP switched its strategy to attack *Plessy v. Ferguson* directly. The NAACP believed that Black people had to be willing to "give up their little kingdoms" at HBCUs.[135] Gaither's successful athletic program stood suspended between segregated educational success and growing calls for desegregation. *Brown v. Board of Education* put the program in the crosshairs.[136]

5
CHAMPIONSHIPS AND CIVIL RIGHTS

t was just before dinner when Gaither knocked on the door of C. Spencer Pompey, principal and head football coach at George Washington Carver High School in Delray Beach. Pompey was not expecting Gaither or his traveling companion A. S. Parks, a FAMU professor. The host invited the two men inside. Hettie, Spencer Pompey's wife, quickly pulled out two extra plates from the cabinet. Southern hospitality dictated that the reasons for the house call would be discussed over dinner. At first glance, Gaither's arrival seemed like a normal recruiting visit. As Pompey recalled, "A high school coach always enjoys having the head coach of the leading state college football team come to his home." But he sensed something was amiss. May was late in the year for a recruiting visit, as the Rattlers had already signed several prep all-stars from the area. Moreover, the absence of Pete Griffin and Hansel Tookes, Gaither's leading assistant coaches, suggested another reason for the visit. As soon as they started eating, Gaither leaned over and asked, "What is going on with the beach situation we have been reading about."[1]

In the early 1950s, African Americans in Delray Beach, located in southern Palm Beach County, had demanded that the city provide either a pool or access to the beach. Amid the emerging civil rights movement, African Americans and Afro-Caribbean residents called for equal access to the city's recreational amenities. Black Delray Beach residents formed the Negro Civic League to represent their interests in this and other civil rights matters. The city council responded in 1950 by trying to find a location outside the Delray Beach city limits.[2] After four years and little progress, the Civic League filed a lawsuit in November 1954, based on the precedent set by *Brown v. Board of Education*.[3] More than five years after the Civic League's original request, Black residents grew frustrated, especially after a teenager, James McBride, drowned on Mother's Day in 1956.[4]

A week after the tragic death, more than sixty Black residents conducted a well-organized campaign to integrate the beach. They were met by a group of nearly seventy white teens.[5] The Delray Beach police quickly intervened, breaking up a potentially violent confrontation.[6] In the aftermath of the protest, the city commission passed a series of ordinances, including one that punished violators of segregation laws with sixty days' hard labor.[7] Sleepy Delray Beach was a tinderbox when Gaither arrived at Pompey's door.

Despite his request for an update, Gaither was already familiar with "the particulars of the situation." Gaither explained to his hosts that he was in town acting as an emissary for Governor LeRoy Collins, and he wanted to meet with the other leaders of the Civic League. Pompey agreed because Gaither's name "was a household word, his integrity was unquestioned, and his presence . . . was welcomed."[8] Pompey called the other members of the Civic League. When they arrived, men such as Leroy Baine, a FAMU graduate and World War II veteran, were "carrying guns," because of the threats they had received after the lawsuit and the beach protest. Gaither realized the seriousness of the situation. As the men talked, one league member kept an "eye on any passing car," with his hand on the holster. Gaither ascertained what issues the Civic League considered nonnegotiable. Notably, he made "no proposals or suggestions to the group." When the Delray commission submitted its proposal to stop the protests the following day, the league debated about the appropriate response. At the meeting, "neither Gaither nor Parks [was] asked for or [gave] any advice."[9] While Gaither was in Delray Beach, two FAMU students, Wilhelmina Jakes and Carrie Patterson, sat down in the "whites only" section of a Tallahassee city bus, marking the beginning of the Tallahassee bus boycott.

Jake Gaither's first decade (1945–54) as head coach established him among the best coaches in Black college football. By 1954, he had won two shared national titles and seven conference titles. His second decade (1955–64) was better than the first. The Rattlers under Gaither would win five national titles, have three undefeated seasons, and lose only 9 games. The Rattlers epitomized the golden age of Black college football; they had the best teams, the best coach, the best classic, and (arguably) the best band. The emerging civil rights movement, however, revealed that its goal of integration had little concern for the future of Black institutions. The desegregationist logic of *Brown v. Board of Education* argued that material inequalities of Black education spaces trumped the educational value of Black teachers, and in this case athletics. As scholar Albert L. Samuels points out, "Advocates of integration . . . look at HBCUs as mere symbols of *Plessy*, with no consideration of the academic substance nor the institutional missions of these institutions."[10] As the activists expanded outside the legal realm to include direct action strategies, the movement uncovered the structural weaknesses plaguing HBCU football.

With public Black colleges dominating the golden age, the game's best coaches—Gaither, Robinson, Mumford, and Merritt—were ill positioned, as state employees, to vocally support the movement. In Gaither's case, he worked, as in Delray Beach, to push for gradual racial changes that would have left Black institutions intact. The civil rights movement put strong Black institutions in a quandary because vocal support for the movement destabilized these very institutions. The leading HBCU coaches tried to thread the needle by scheduling their teams to play against PWIs at the collegiate level. Thus, as Gaither's teams reached their apex, the civil rights movement functioned to undermine their future. This nuanced position was not always appreciated, and it led Black Tallahaseeans to question Gaither's racial loyalty. The civil rights landscape and the appropriate roles for established Black leadership changed quickly after World War II. Old strategies died, and new ones emerged. In the athletic realm, individual and team integration were at odds.

FLORIDA AND *BROWN V. BOARD OF EDUCATION*

President Gray's forced resignation put FAMU in a problematic situation. His departure was a reminder to the FAMU faculty, staff, and supporters that the college had to balance its wishes for institutional success with the realities of segregation. Longtime Dean H. Manning Efferson became acting president, while the State Board of Control and the FAMU search committee sought a new president. In March 1950, the search committee and the Board of Control selected George W. Gore Jr., a dean at Tennessee Agricultural and Industrial State College. Gore had an M.A. degree from Harvard University and a Ph.D. in journalism from Columbia. Gore, like Gray, planned to enhance the college's academic reputation.[11] Gore was also an excellent choice for athletics. He had worked with TSU president Walter S. Davis, who for more than two decades believed in the importance of athletics in enhancing the school's exposure and reputation. Gore followed in his mentor's footsteps by supporting athletics as a key part of the college's mission, announcing shortly after his selection that he would request funds for an athletic field house.[12]

In 1953, the State Board of Control renamed Florida A&M College as Florida A&M University. The name change represented two conflicting interests. FAMU's faculty, students, alumni, and supporters understood the symbolic and financial importance of becoming a university. The title of "university" meant Florida A&M could symbolically shed its vocational and normal school origins while presenting itself as an equal with the white universities in the state. By making FAMU a university, the state argued that the postbaccalaureate degree programs should satisfy the needs of Black students seeking admission to UF. Despite the tension between supporters of FAMU and UF's wish to prevent desegregation, both sides got what they wanted. FAMU gained additional academic legitimacy, while the state could avoid desegregation for another five years.

On May 17, 1954, the Supreme Court handed down its unanimous decision on *Brown v. Board of Education*, ostensibly ending legal racial segregation. The ruling reconfigured the politics of race in the South, strengthening the racist appeals of rabid segregationists and forcing racial moderates to cower. Most Florida communities, however, preferred segregation but recognized *Brown* as the law of the land.[13] White Floridians' initial reactions were initially mild, preferring obstruction, in place of massive resistance strategies used in other southern states.[14] Blacks were more optimistic about the effects of *Brown* on Florida. Gaither, for example, in the 1954 FAMU commencement speech, encouraged students to "regard the law" as a "friend and protector."[15] Black Floridians' hopefulness was also informed by the recognition that the space between law and reality could be quite vast. As James A. Bond, supervisor of Pinellas County's Black schools stated, "The light we now see is not the full blaze of the noonday sun, but only the purple tines of the dawn heralding the coming of the golden sun."[16]

Problems for the Black institutions that nurtured communities in hostile waters lurked behind Blacks' near-unanimous support. The NAACP's Thurgood Marshall noted that a chief strategy in winning the case was to argue that segregation damaged African Americans. He recalled, "I told the staff that we had to try this case just like any other one in which you would try to prove damages to your client."[17] Kenneth and Mamie Clark's doll test reinforced that segregation damaged only Black students, not an entire population, Black and white. Moreover, the NAACP's plan required a tremendous sacrifice by a core constituency: Black teachers. As historian Adam Fairclough notes, the NAACP's shift from ensuring that separate was indeed equal to overturning *Plessy* "did not allow sufficient time to build up grassroots support for this change in tactics."[18] The NAACP's change forced Black teachers to support integration with the possibility of the elimination of Black schools and their own jobs.

As summer led into fall, the 1954 HBCU football season again neared, but with the possibility of desegregation looming in the background. Prominent sports columnist Ric Roberts asked, "What will our coaches do?" regarding desegregation. The column used Booker T. Washington's "Atlanta Compromise" speech as the basis for its commentary, describing the Tuskegee College founder's compromise with white supremacy as a "stopgap" and a "creative spirit of withdrawal." Roberts declared that the time for self-segregation was over. The winds of change would affect Black colleges and their sports, he acknowledged. "Our football traditions may be jolted by the new alignment which seems forthcoming." The sportswriter wondered if the legendary coaches of Black college football, "the revered Eddie Hurt, the marvelous Arnett Mumford, the precise Harry Jefferson, the brooding Cleve Abbott, the grim Billy Nicks, and the brilliant Bill Bell, Sal Hall, Dwight Reed, Jake Gaither, Herman Riddick, Mark Cardwell, Fred Long, the matchless Henry Arthur Kean, Sam Taylor[,] and many more" would be forgotten. Roberts's column anticipated the problems facing Black colleges regarding the possibilities of desegregation. Yet, like many other concerned fans and observers of HBCU athletics, Roberts had few solutions.[19] Black colleges prepared for another season, but the future of their coaches, teams, and traditions remained opaque.

In the aftermath of *Brown*, Gaither had titanic clashes against Mumford's Southern teams and Robinson's powerful Grambling squad. He relied on the running attack led by Willie Galimore and Al Frazier for 1-loss seasons in 1954 and 1955. The Rattlers opened the season with easy victories over Texas College, Benedict, and Morris Brown. The competition improved, but "scintillating runs" by Galimore and Sal Gaitor powered FAMU wins over Prairie View and North Carolina A&T.[20] Undefeated, the Rattlers' championship season hinged on a highly anticipated matchup against Southern University. Mumford's teams had consistently been a thorn in the side of Gaither's best teams. Ric Roberts wrote, "On the basis of yesteryear, Gaither will be tripped by the Cats this week."[21] Twenty thousand fans watched the Jaguars face off against FAMU under the lights. "It was big stuff," reported the *Pittsburgh Courier*'s Robert M. Ratcliffe. "It was two top coaches of the nation throwing out problems for the other to solve. It was eleven stalwart young men on one team matching brawn and skill against the power and intelligence offered by eleven other masters of the gridiron." The competition extended to the schools' bands. On that evening, Mumford's Jaguars had all the answers, winning 59 to 23.[22] "We make no apologies for winning or losing, it's all part of the game," said Gaither.[23] However, his dreams of an undefeated season dissipated under the lights of Baton Rouge.

The success of the OBC encouraged the creation of new classics seeking to challenge the OBC's growing dominance. In 1954, a new game stopped one of the most anticipated matchups. Fans and sportswriters clamored for Gaither to pick Henry A. Kean's TSU Tigers. The "Keanmen" were in the midst of a 26-game winning streak and ranked first in the midseason polls. Plans for the "dream game" were dashed before the season even started, however, when TSU's Midwestern Athletic Association (MAA) and the CIAA agreed to change the annual National Classic into a title game between the conference champions, to be played the same weekend as the OBC. Gaither was incensed upon hearing the news of the agreement because it removed two premier potential opponents for the OBC. As sportswriter Marion E. Jackson noted, "Gaither and the Miami Orange [Blossom Classic] are caught in a crossfire. It is a 'squeeze play' that will be the test of the Rattlers' skill and diplomacy to nip in the bud."[24] With FAMU unable to arrange TSU to play in the OBC, officials chose Maryland State College (now University of Maryland–Eastern Shore) to play in the 1954 OBC.

The selection of Maryland State and the MAA and CIAA title game agreement added to a growing feud between Gaither and Kean. When the press had suggested that Kean's Tigers were avoiding the Rattlers, the TSU coach fired back, "No one can accuse us of backing out of a game with Florida A. & M. We had them on our schedule several years ago and they backed out on us" because of extremely cold weather.[25] Even the choice of Maryland State churned the animosity. As TSU headed toward the National Classic, Kean wanted to avoid playing North Carolina Central, CIAA conference leaders, twice in the same season. He pushed the game organizer to name Maryland State as TSU's opponent. Vernon McCain, coach of Maryland State, understood the prestige and financial benefits of playing in the OBC. He announced that his team would not play TSU and only wanted to play in Miami.[26]

FAMU's loss to Southern took some of the luster out of the 1954 OBC. Still, Maryland State was a strong opponent that was undefeated in the season, with a record of 6 wins and 1 tie. The Hawks also had an impressive 6-season run of success in which the school won 59 of 63 games. Nonetheless, the Rattlers were a touchdown favorite. Coming off the blowout loss to Southern, the Rattlers adopted the mantra "Somebody's got to pay."[27] More than 40,000 fans watched Willie Galimore set an OBC rushing record in the Rattlers 67 to 19 rout of Maryland State. The speedster from St. Augustine rushed for 295 yards and three touchdowns. The dominant victory allowed FAMU to claim a national title after North Carolina Central upset the TSU Tigers. The Tigers loss was devastating off the field as well. Henry A. Kean suffered a heart attack during the game, which led to his retirement. TSU's loss threw the rankings into chaos, as four teams—TSU, FAMU, North Carolina Central, and Prairie View A&M—all claimed the 1954 national title.[28] The disputed title was Gaither's third in five seasons. However, all three were shared titles.[29] Gaither was still looking for the elusive outright national championship. The clearest path was for his team to go undefeated.

In 1955, Gaither had his split-line T offense running on all cylinders, beating Benedict College 80 to 60, Fort Valley State College 49 to 0, and Xavier College 60 to 19.[30] A late Rattlers rally led to a 28 to 28 tie against North Carolina A&T.[31] The following week the Rattlers routed Southern 51 to 0, thrusting the Rattlers back to the top of the polls.[32] An undisputed national title was within reach if Gaither's team could beat an undefeated and upstart Grambling team in the OBC.

The Grambling Tigers had made tremendous strides since World War II, led by head coach Eddie Robinson, who was hired in 1941. Located between Shreveport and Monroe, Louisiana, Grambling was a minor football program that Robinson transformed into a powerhouse. Robinson's first major victory came in 1947 when the Tigers, led by Paul "Tank" Younger, beat Southern. Younger would later become the first player from an HBCU to play in the NFL. Robinson's 1955 team was his best ever. Led by defensive tackle/linebacker Willie Davis, Grambling outscored its first nine opponents 328 to 40. Despite Grambling's impressive record, some at FAMU did not believe the small school from northern Louisiana would generate the type of interest typical of the OBC. FAMU publicist Charles J. Smith III told reporters about the unpopularity of Grambling, saying, "Sponsors wanted a better known opponent."[33] Grambling publicist Collie J. Nicholson aggressively countered this perception, even suggesting that a "comparison between Grambling and Famu [sic] shows that the Rattlers have been more erratic than their Tiger counterparts against top-flight competition." FAMU players also taunted Tiger players before the game. The slighting of Robinson's team provided bulletin-board material for the Tigers. All-American and future pro football Hall of Famer Willie Davis said, "This . . . is more than I can understand." Tiger fullback Howard Scott vowed to make them "gulp humble pie in wholesale lots in Miami."[34]

Most observers expected FAMU, led by All-American running backs Frazier and Galimore, to win. The duo combined for more than 1,750 rushing yards, and they scored twenty-one touchdowns in the season. "The big classic will be one of the power of Grambling against the speed and power Coach [Jake] Gaither has developed in his T formations for the Rattlers," summarized Russ Cowans of the *Chicago Defender.* He predicted, "From this distance it looks very much like Florida will emerge the winner."[35]

The game surprised the prognosticators and fans. More than 40,000 attendees watched FAMU's prolific rushing attack sputter against the Tigers' dominant defense. Grambling won a "spine-tingling thriller" 28 to 21. Willie Davis had 25 tackles, including one that knocked Al Frazier out of his shoes. The game was decided when Galimore fumbled inside the Rattler 30-yard line late in the fourth quarter. After the FAMU turnover, the Tigers scored the decisive touchdown. The 100% Wrong Club and the *Atlanta Daily World* awarded Eddie Robinson and the Grambling Tigers the national championship trophy.[36] Gaither's chance at an undisputed national title was again thwarted under the Orange Bowl lights. In eleven seasons, Gaither's chance at perfection had ended four times in FAMU's bowl game. The OBC, the jewel of Black college bowls, was all too often becoming the source of Gaither's misfortune.

JAKE GAITHER AND THE TALLAHASSEE BUS BOYCOTT

The Thursday before the twenty-third OBC, Rosa Parks's arrest for defying segregation on a Montgomery, Alabama, city bus dramatically altered the civil rights movement in terms of tactics and leadership. The apprehension of Parks, a longtime NAACP member and activist, galvanized the Montgomery Black community. Various community organizations, such as the Women's Political Council and the Brotherhood of Sleeping Car Porters, proposed a one-day boycott of the buses.[37] In the wake of the boycott, Martin Luther King Jr. emerged as a preeminent civil rights spokesperson. After the first day of boycotts, King encouraged more than 5,000 attendees at the first mass meeting to continue economic reprisals. The young preacher from Atlanta delineated that the impetus for the boycott grew out of "American citizens' [desire] to exercise our citizenship to the fullness of its meaning." He wanted Montgomery's Black residents to transform freedom from "thin paper to thick action." King's eloquence in capturing the religious and political philosophy behind the boycott thrust him into the national spotlight. The success of the Montgomery bus boycott, which continued for more than a year, also made nonviolent direct action the principal tactic in the growing civil rights movement. King's leadership style and the tactics used in Montgomery encouraged other communities to confront the daily dehumanization of Jim Crow. Within six months, a bus boycott engulfed Tallahassee.[38]

On Saturday, May 26, 1956, three FAMU students boarded a bus to downtown Tallahassee. Seeing a crowded bus, two students, Wilhelmina Jakes and Carrie Patterson, sat down next to a white female passenger directly behind the bus driver. The driver ordered the students to move to the rear of the bus. Jakes and Patterson refused unless their fares were refunded. The irate driver parked the bus at the nearest gas station and called the police. Minutes later, multiple squad cars surrounded the bus, and the police took the two students into custody. After the campus community heard about the arrest, students quickly organized a rally for their classmates. Students decided to boycott the buses for the remainder of the semester. C. K. Steele, a Baptist minister and head of the local chapter of the NAACP, and other Black leaders began outlining a protest strategy similar to the one in Montgomery. They formed the Inter Civic Council (ICC), modeled on the Montgomery Improvement Association, to coordinate the boycott of Tallahassee buses. The creation of the ICC signaled to local and state politicians that the boycott was locally led and not directed by "outside agitators," such as the NAACP or Communists.[39]

The boycott revealed the hostile underside of the ostensibly moderate race relations in Florida's capital city. Shortly after Jakes was arrested, someone burned a cross in front of her apartment. Both women received threats by phone and mail. The state legislature approved the Florida Legislative Investigative Committee to probe "subversive activities" of civil rights organizations across the state, namely, the NAACP. Governor Collins, a racial moderate, had resisted establishing a "mini-HUAC" in previous legislative sessions, announcing that he would veto any measure, as Black voters had been a vital bloc in Collins's victory eighteen months prior.[40] However, the *Brown* decision and now the bus boycott pushed racial moderates like Collins to align with ultra-segregationists like Florida state senator Charley Johns, who presided over the Florida Legislative Investigative Committee. The Johns committee harassed civil rights activists, the NAACP, suspected Communists, and homosexuals across the state.[41]

The success of the boycott and the backlash from the white community revealed divisions in Tallahassee's Black community. Younger and newer residents, such as the Reverend C. K. Steele, pressed for immediate integration of the buses, refusing the city's compromises. Steele had only been in Tallahassee four years when he was elected to lead the boycott. Economically autonomous African Americans were also strong supporters of the boycott. Most of the ICC board members and elected officers were clergy or self-employed members of the Black community. The group's economic autonomy from whites allowed them to push for more immediate change. This newer leadership group displaced an older leadership core that was often centered at FAMU. This older leadership group, which included Jake Gaither, believed in desegregation but preferred to negotiate with white moderates to preserve the peace. This conciliatory strategy was shaped by the racial violence of previous decades.[42] One week after the boycott had begun, city commissioners called a secret meeting with a select group of Black leaders that included only one member of the ICC. The summit amplified the growing divisions between the leadership groups. Steele, who was not at the meeting, preached a sermon on Judas the following Sunday. Many in the congregation assumed he was targeting the attendees of the secret conference. Although Steele steadfastly denied he was referring to the attendees of the secret meeting, the sermon damaged the reputation of the older leadership generation.[43]

The escalation of the boycott and the rise of a new cadre of Black leadership put FAMU's leadership in a precarious position. Many whites expected the FAMU administration to reprimand the students for breaking the segregation laws and etiquette. The swift formulation of a boycott by the ICC and students left little time for the administration to develop a plan that could accommodate Blacks' increasingly vocal wishes for immediate desegregation and the white legislature's insistence on segregation. At the beginning of the 1956 school year, President Gore reportedly requested that FAMU faculty members and staff stop participating in the boycott, recognizing the financial power the legislature had over the university. Gore stated, "Either you are loyal to the university or loyal to something else out there; cast your lot with this ship or get off. You can't be loyal to both."[44] Behind Gore's implicit threat was a fear that FAMU would receive fewer educational dollars or, worse, that the state would close the school. The ICC tried to create space between its activities and the university. Steele retracted a press release that was critical of Gore's statements. The ICC president stated, "The affairs of the university should be something completely apart from the bus dispute."[45] The divisions amid the Black community were readily apparent, despite Steele's attempts to quell the controversy.

As the most popular Black person in Tallahassee, Jake Gaither was in a position similar to that of President Gore. Gaither had attended the secret

May meeting in which Steele's sermon had labeled attendees as traitors. Because of Steele's sermon and the private accusations of racial disloyalty, Gaither refused, for over a decade, to talk to Episcopal priest David Brooks, who many assumed had informed Steele of the meeting's participants. Gaither had also spent years developing relationships with powerful whites. Leading politicians watched the Rattlers from the stands and occasionally from the sidelines. White spectators often sat in a roped-off section at the 50-yard line during games. The premium seating often irked Black fans and supporters, but Gaither knew that his athletic budget depended on white support. In addition, Gaither's experience with his brain surgeon, Dr. Cobb Pilcher, and the dozens of well-known white coaches who trekked to Tallahassee every summer for the coaching clinic allowed him to see a side of whites that few Blacks ever did. Longtime *Tallahassee Democrat* sportswriter Bill McGrotha believed, "Later generations would see his actions as a little bit 'Uncle Tomism.' Gaither, however, felt that one had to deal with society the way that it was and work within the system for change."[46] Gaither's actions were indicative of the thorny position that the emerging civil rights orthodoxy placed Black institutions in. The unfolding civil rights position implicitly and explicitly opposed these strong institutions that were the products of segregation. For Gaither, this meant undoing his lifework at FAMU.

Players and coaches seemed to accept Gaither's pragmatism. Al Frazier remembered, "If [Gaither] had taken a radical stand, he wouldn't have been able to get a lot of things he got. It was political expediency—Jake was playing a role."[47] Assistant coach Hansel E. Tookes believed that Gaither's position was "the best thing to do."[48] Behind Gaither's pragmatism was the potential opportunity to compete against predominately white teams. Grambling's Eddie Robinson also sought to challenge segregation through pragmatism. He remembered, "I didn't know if I could help lead people as a civil rights activist, but I knew that I could help to groom young black men as intelligent leaders at Grambling. . . . If we could make a big enough impact with football at Grambling, if our plans worked and our goals were met, then the national stage would provide us the opportunity to smash the stereotypes that blacks couldn't be leaders, be they athletes, civil rights activists, corporate leaders, or politicians."[49] Gaither believed that his teams and other leading Black college teams could compete against any white team in the country, but they needed an opportunity and permission from the State Board of Control to do so.

Across the country, Black coaches looked for openings to knock down segregation by showing the quality of Black college teams. Lincoln University in Pennsylvania had the first white player in Black college football, Ralph Oves, in the 1940s and had scheduled athletic contests against white schools since 1927.[50] Legendary basketball coach John McLendon led his North Carolina Central basketball team in a "secret game" against Duke University in 1944. McLendon's Eagles ran Duke medical school, which had defeated the varsity and conference champions earlier in the season, out of a mostly empty gym 88 to 44.[51] Moreover, Black colleges began to schedule games against white schools. In 1954, the McLendon-coached TSU Tigers won the pre-Christmas National Association of Intercollegiate Athletics (NAIA) Tournament in Kansas City against white schools.[52] Eddie Robinson told Tank Younger, the first HBCU player in the NFL, "If you don't make it [in the NFL], there's no telling how long it will be before another black gets a chance. They're going to say they took the best we had and he couldn't make it."[53] In 1954, Xavier University and Fisk University scheduled games against white teams. Gaither listened to McLendon's stories of the "Secret Game" and his team's invitation to the NAIA tournament during the coaches' clinics. The ever-competitive Gaither had to have argued with Frank Broyles, Sid Gilman, FSU's Tom Nugent, and other white coaches who attended the coaches' clinic about whether his Rattlers could match up against the best white schools.[54] Unfortunately for Gaither and most other Black college football coaches, segregation denied their teams the opportunity to compete against white schools in the 1950s.

As Gaither headed into his twelfth season as head coach, he pushed civil rights to the background and focused on winning his first outright title. Although FAMU returned three-time All-Americans Al Frazier and Willie Galimore, Gaither believed that losing six starters "forecasts trouble" for his team.[55] Fueled by the running game of Frazier and Galimore, the Rattlers won their first 6 games. In the opening games, FAMU averaged more than 45 points per game, while allowing only 45 total. The white press and the professional football scouts began to take notice of Galimore's and Frazier's talents. The Florida Sportswriters Association named Galimore "Back-of-the-Week" after his performance against Bethune-Cookman. The St. Augustine speedster returned the opening kickoff for an 87-yard touchdown and ran for 153 yards and another touchdown on six carries.[56]

A series of events allowed FAMU and TSU to resume their rivalry in the OBC. In particular, Gaither believed that TSU's Henry Arthur Kean and others had moved the date of the National Classic in 1954 to com-

Willie Galimore and Jake Gaither, 1953. (Florida Memory, Florida State Archives)

pete against the OBC. However, the game was a failure, as only 2,500 fans showed up.[57] The feud between the two programs thawed after the untimely death of legendary TSU coach Kean in 1955. The following year, TSU hired Howard C. Gentry as head coach, a former Rattler player under Bell and Gaither. These events led to the resumption of the rivalry.[58] The twenty-fourth OBC featured Black college football's two best teams — a true national championship game.

More than 40,000 fans witnessed "one of the wildest and most free scoring encounters in collegiate football history." The seesaw affair saw FAMU's Galimore score four touchdowns but also fumble twice. The game was nip and tuck to the very end. The Rattlers trailed 41 to 39 with less than four minutes remaining in the fourth quarter. If Gaither was going to win his first undisputed national title, he needed his defense to make a play. TSU was desperately trying to run out the clock when the Tigers fumbled deep in their end and the Rattlers recovered it on the 23. Two plays later, FAMU was at the 2-yard line as the clock was ticking under two minutes. Gaither tried to make a late substitution but was called for a penalty, backing the Rattlers to the 7-yard line. On second down, Frazier moved the ball to the 4-yard line; on third down, Galimore slammed the ball to the 2-yard line. It was now fourth down and the clock ticked down to one minute remaining. Senior quarterback Dennis Jefferson tried to sneak the ball into the end zone. There was a pile of bodies followed by an "ominous and echoing silence" in the stadium. The referees untangled the tired men and signaled that the ball was short of the end zone. The TSU Tigers had a "miraculous defensive stand." As the final seconds ticked off the clock, the Tigers' band "started a rock 'n roll war cry with partisans . . . whipping it up mercilessly." Coach Gentry, the pupil, schooled Gaither, the teacher, going undefeated in his first season as head coach. Gaither and his All-American running backs' dreams shriveled inches short of the elusive perfect season.[59]

The Tallahassee bus boycott encircled Gaither's eighth 1-loss season. On November 13, the Supreme Court declared that Alabama's segregation laws on buses were unconstitutional. The ruling immediately affected the protest in Tallahassee. Shortly after the OBC, the ICC ended the seven-month boycott and returned to riding the buses in a "non-segregated manner." The boycott was successful, as the bus company eventually phased out its "safety" seating policy. What was evident in the aftermath of the boycott was that tranquil race relations were forever changed and integration was coming to Florida's capital city.

Despite his apprehensions and a desire to protect his football program, Gaither used football success to contribute to integration. The Chicago Bears drafted Galimore in 1956 after his junior season, and by January 1957 the FAMU All-American running back agreed to a contract. Galimore was the second Rattler ever drafted when the Bears selected him in the fifth round. He had an impressive rookie campaign for the Bears, and he told reporters that playing Black college football did not hamper his adjustment to pro football.

CHAMPIONSHIPS AND CIVIL RIGHTS

Naturally, when I first reported to the Bears, I was a little dubious. . . . After all I was going up against a lot of big name players whose reputations were even bigger. It was enough to make you wonder. . . . I'll say this though, I honestly felt that if I got the opportunity to run I could hold my own. That was the one thing Coach Gaither pounded into us at Florida. He made everyone on the team believe that he was as good if not better than any other player anywhere else in the country. The confidence he instilled in me was one of my biggest assets when I reported to camp. . . . Once I began playing it didn't take long to find out that I had been well trained in college as anybody else in camp. There was a lot to learn and I'm still learning about professional football, but I wasn't held back because of my college training.[60]

Gaither also became the first Black coach to give a report at the American Football Coaches Association. The statement rated Black and white teams in his district and reflected Gaither's growing stature in the coaching community. The association's officers "highly praised" Gaither's account. Gaither's report along with the annual coaching clinic continued to break down segregation in the coaching profession.[61] Athletic integration was coming. Questions remained about how it would be enacted and its effect on FAMU and the rest of Black college football.

UNEQUAL FACILITIES

Despite FAMU's on-field success, its athletic facilities paled in comparison with those of white schools and some Black colleges. After decades of discriminatory funding, in 1955 the state finally appropriated $366,000 to FAMU for stadium construction. The decision to fund FAMU's Bragg Stadium came five years after the legislature appropriated $250,000 to build FSU's Doak Campbell Stadium and $500,000 to add 13,000 seats to UF's stadium.[62] The quick decision to fund Doak Campbell Stadium was a stark reminder of the inequities of segregation. Occasionally, FAMU rented Doak Campbell Stadium to play big games, because Bragg field could not hold more than 10,000 fans.[63] The state legislature appeared to rectify the inequality, but the FAMU appropriation also reflected the state's wish to adhere to "separate but equal" as a way to slow desegregation.[64]

Before FAMU could even celebrate the stadium funding, the state legislature looked to give the monies to FSU. The Board of Control asked Attorney General Richard Ervin whether FAMU's funding could be diverted to

FSU and that both colleges share a stadium. Behind this request was the state legislature's 1955 mandate that UF and FSU play each other in football and other sports.[65] UF had steadfastly refused to play FSU in a home-and-home series in part because of the Seminoles' small stadium, their meager football reputation, and FSU's former status as a women's college. Using FSU's proximity to the capital, President Doak Campbell and other influential supporters saw the money appropriated to FAMU as the solution to their problem and the basis of their dreams for big-time football. FSU athletic director Howard Danford outlined the program's lofty goals. "The SEC is the only logical conference for us to get into from a geographic standpoint. . . . But a lot of it depends on increasing the size of our stadium and the ability of our football team to beat some of the SEC members."[66]

When the news of FSU's plans had come to light, Gaither fired off a letter to Governor Collins. Gaither was "deeply concerned" about the reports, and FAMU was in need of a stadium. "Enlarging Doak S. Campbell Stadium does not solve our problems or meet our needs," wrote Gaither.[67] He noted that "students, alumni, and friends of the Florida A & M University . . . have shown a dislike for playing their games off the campus of the University."[68] Gaither also believed that his team's success had merited a stadium. He reminded the governor that the Associated Negro Press ranked his Rattlers no. 1, and the school's record between 1945 and 1955 was 87–15–4. The Rattlers had lost only 3 games in Tallahassee in the last nineteen years. "All of this has been done with limited facilities," he mentioned. By listing FAMU's numerous accomplishments, Gaither implicitly compared his program to UF's and FSU's. The Gators had only one winning season in that same period and were on their third head coach. FSU, which started football in 1947, had a winning start in its early years but played against lower-level competition such as Randolph Macon College, Stetson, and Sewanee. In 1952, FSU stepped up its competition and won only 1 game. It was clear that in Gaither's implicit comparison of the state-supported programs, FAMU was the best and should be rewarded with appropriate facilities. In the end, Gaither implored, "We have dreamed that a decent home for the Rattlers would be realized under your able leadership for good government in Florida."[69] It seems Governor Collins heeded Gaither's concerns.

Within a week of the reports of the diverting of FAMU's stadium funds, the Leon County Board of Commissioners in a special meeting declared "that it is in the best interest of Florida A. & M. University and of Florida

State University that each of said institutions of higher learning be furnished and equipped with its own stadium and athletic facilities."[70] FAMU kept its funding, but state officials revised the stadium plans. The school's initial request was for a stadium to hold 15,000 fans; it was reduced to 10,000 in the final version. Even after cutting the seating capacity by a third, the Board of Control wanted to reduce the seating to 5,200, as it accused FAMU of "wanting too much for the available money." The board decided to erect just one side of the stadium.[71] Gaither, in a letter to the FAMU president, expressed his disappointment in the new plans. "This type of stadium," Gaither wrote, "is undesirable in both appearance and location." He also noted that there were safety concerns with the continued used of the wooden bleachers.[72] By the Rattlers 1957 season, the final touches were put on FAMU's new stadium that held 10,000 fans.[73] While the Rattlers got the stadium they needed, they did not have the one they deserved. By 1957, UF's Florida Field held 38,000 fans and FSU's capacity was 19,000. The lack of a stadium that was proportionate to the Rattlers' success meant that FAMU did not have a key piece of athletic infrastructure that it needed to flourish in the coming desegregated athletic world. Despite having the most successful football program in the state, FAMU had the worst athletic facilities because of the strictures of segregation. For decades, FAMU's sporting congregation could counteract the limits of its inequitable material resources. However, when the stadium opened in 1957, the glow of new Bragg Stadium was already overshadowed by the more extensive facilities at UF and FSU.

FINALLY UNDEFEATED

On the heels of another 1-loss season, fans criticized Gaither's coaching. They were especially judgmental of the late-game substitution that led to a delay of game penalty in the final minutes of the 1956 OBC.[74] Coming up inches short of the winning touchdown and an outright championship left a bitter taste in fans' mouths. With the loss of eighteen seniors from the team, many, including Gaither, expected the next season to be a rebuilding effort after three consecutive title runs. Gaither told reporters, "Our backs will be slower and we will play more control ball. We will have to be satisfied with shorter gains and increase our efforts on defense."[75] Sportswriters did not believe Gaither's laments, however. The *Atlanta Daily World*'s Marion E. Jackson suggested that Gaither was "hoodwinking" opponents with the story of a ball control offense.[76] Jackson's intuition was right. Gaither's

Gaither in front of construction of football stadium, 1957.
(Florida Memory, Florida State Archives)

team, despite the loss of Galimore and Frazier, was still explosive and looked to win a national title. The Rattlers opened the season with a 74 to 0 rout of Fort Valley State. Jackson viewed the blowout as an example of Gaither's "time-tested witchcraft." He added, "Jake merely bided his time before lifting the lid on his scoring [Pandora's] Box. . . . It appears to these eyes that Jake played possum with his rivals. They thought the Rattler boss was stewing in his own juice, but all the while he was plotting to cook their goose."[77]

The Rattlers ran roughshod over the competition, winning their first 8 games by a combined score of 316 to 20. FAMU finished the regular season undefeated, for the fourth time in five seasons. Gaither selected Maryland State, from among several contenders, for the twenty-fifth OBC. The Rattlers came into the silver anniversary of the OBC as favorites. Sportswriters believed that Gaither would finally "beat the jinx" and win an outright championship. In Gaither's thirteen seasons, he had lost an undefeated regular season five times at the OBC. Despite that history, Gaither was confident as well. "My present squad is the most surprising and well-balanced team I have ever coached."[78]

A crowd of nearly 40,000 that included New York Yankee great Joe DiMaggio witnessed an exceptional game. Maryland State scored in the game's first two minutes on four quick passes. Fans grimaced as the Rattlers fell behind 7 to 0. In the second quarter, the Rattlers responded with their vaunted running game when Louis Johnson ripped off a 90-yard touchdown run. The Rattlers missed the conversion and trailed 7 to 6. Led by the blocking of All-Americans Carl Crowell, Charles Gavin, and Vernon Wilder, FAMU put together a 91-yard touchdown drive to take the lead, 13 to 6 at the half. In the second half, the Rattlers again showed their explosive running game as David Latimer rushed for a 70-yard touchdown. With the score 20 to 7, many fans thought the rout was on, but the Maryland State Hawks responded with a short touchdown pass. Leading by only 6 points, the Rattlers put together a championship-clinching 80-yard drive in the fourth quarter. The Hawks' All-American John Sample tried to keep his team in the game with a long 78-yard touchdown run to cut the score to 27 to 21. But it was not enough.

After thirteen seasons as head coach and 94 victories, Gaither had finally achieved perfection.[79]

DOMINANCE

Gaither turned perfection into dominance. Fueled by his split-line T formation and the speed of All-American running backs, Gaither's program reached its peak. The eight seasons between 1957 and 1964 were particularly impressive, as Gaither's teams won or shared five national titles, determined by the Associated Negro Press, the *Pittsburgh Courier*, or the 100% Wrong Club/*Atlanta Daily World*. Gaither also demonstrated innovative coaching when he used three equal playing units to overcome the one-platoon playing system. As mentioned earlier, one-platoon football returned in 1954 after college football experimented with free substitution during and after World War II.[80] In 1958, college football liberalized some of the rules of one-platoon football by allowing any player, not just starters, to enter a game twice per quarter. Gaither adapted a substitution strategy developed by LSU's Paul Dietzel, a 1956 FAMU coaching clinic instructor, in which he deployed three units on the way to the 1958 national title.[81] Gaither named his three groups Blood, Sweat, and Tears, a team motto since 1945.[82] Although players played both offense and defense, the Blood team was a mostly offensive unit, the Sweat team was Gaither's "shock troops" going both ways, and the Tears team was primarily a defensive unit.[83] These equally dominating personnel groups and the split-line T formation propelled FAMU to new heights.

After going undefeated in 1957, Gaither, President Gore, assistant coach Macon Williams, and All-Americans Jim Williams and Vernon Wilder collected the W. A. Scott Memorial Trophy from the 100% Wrong Club.[84] At the team banquet, Gaither described his first undefeated team as the "most surprising one" he had ever coached.[85] Gaither didn't celebrate long, turning his attention to spring football and "working . . . new men into a smooth working machine" for the next season.[86]

The Rattlers were among the favorites to win the 1958 title, but they lost twice. The *Pittsburgh Courier* described Gaither's squad as "a veteran team," with depth, an "abundance of speed," and "one of the best coaching staffs to be found anywhere."[87] Still, losses to Southern and Prairie View meant that FAMU finished with an 8–2 record and ranked third in the final poll in 1958.[88] One hundred and ten victories against twenty losses did not satiate Gaither's appetite for winning. Nor was he content with six consecutive SIAC titles. The blowout losses to Southern and Prairie View to end the 1958 season stung on the heels of his first perfect season. Gaither and his "boys" wanted perfection again. A key to the Rattlers fulfilling their lofty goals was improving their passing game. Both Southern and Prairie View jumped out to big leads and forced Gaither's prolific split-line T rushing attack to come from behind. In 1958, Mumford's Jaguars average 184 passing yards per game, which, if the college football stats would have been integrated, would have led the country.[89] Billy Nicks's Prairie View Panthers also used a passing attack to defeat Grambling and FAMU on their way to a national title.[90] Gaither told the press corps assembled after a 1959 preseason scrimmage, "We are about as smooth as we expected to be at this stage of the season. Our passing game is coming along and I'm pleased about that."[91] With nineteen returning lettermen, FAMU prepared to reclaim the national title.[92]

The 1959 season was Gaither's best, but he and the team would face tragedy before it was over. As usual, FAMU dominated the opening month of the 1959 season. A close win against Morris Brown was sandwiched between blowouts of Benedict, Wiley, and Bethune-Cookman. Gaither tried to explain the lopsided scores to the press. "We used our first, second, and third units against the [Benedict] Tigers. Each one was a firecracker. . . . I guess it is impossible to try and stop a player from doing what you have trained them to do."[93] The lead-up to the Bethune-Cookman game was marred by an accident, however. During practice, highly regarded freshman Oliver Joyce suffered a critical spinal cord injury, when the five-foot nine-inch, 220-pound Joyce went to tackle future All-American Robert Paremore. The running back's knee violently crashed against Joyce's face mask, snapping his neck backward. Joyce died one day after the Bethune-Cookman game. The team was "shrouded in sadness" as it defeated South Carolina State the following week for homecoming.[94] Gaither and the athletic department raised more than $1,500 for Joyce's mother, and the school covered the funeral and medical bills.[95]

FAMU's undefeated and high-scoring opening month of the 1959 season distinguished it from the state's other leading football programs. Four of Florida's white college football programs were mired in mediocrity that frustrated fans and led to calls for coaching changes. Around Halloween, students hung effigies of UF's Bob Woodruff, FSU's Perry Moss, University of Tampa's Marcelino Huerta, and University of Miami's Andy Gustafson on their campuses. At FSU, nearly 100 students chanted "Go Home Moss" and "We Want a Coach." At Miami, Gustafson's effigy had a sign that read, "Here lies Mickey Mouse Gus / To him, we show no mercy / He ruined a good football team / By using only [quarterback] Fran Curci." In Gainesville, Woodruff's grave read, "Here lies Woodhead / he is no more / passed three times / on second and four." The sign on Tampa's dummy simply read, "Hang Huerta." All four programs suffered bad losses the last weekend in October, and each team had won 50 percent or less of its games.[96] Clemson head coach Frank Howard sent a letter to Gaither: "Congratulations on being the only coach in Florida to escape the noose this week."[97]

Not willing to let his team rest on their laurels, Gaither prepared them to set aside their grief and get ready for the most challenging part of the schedule. The Rattlers not only were undefeated but also led the nation in scoring and total offense. The season was determined once again by the Rattlers' matchup against Southern. FAMU had just a 7–6–1 record against Southern over the previous fourteen meetings, including a blowout loss the past season. Writers and fans recognized this as the most important regular-season game. The game did not disappoint. Before a home crowd of more than 10,000, FAMU scored a late touchdown and won 21 to 14. After the thrilling game, Gaither announced that Prairie View would return for a rematch in the OBC. Once again, the OBC pitted the top two teams in HBCU football.[98]

The rematch between FAMU and Prairie View was a game many longed to see, despite the Panthers' late-season loss to Southern. After the two teams routed a couple of early-season opponents, the *Atlanta Daily World*'s Marion E. Jackson was forecasting "a return engagement" between the Rattlers and the Panthers.[99] As the game approached, organizers expected more than 40,000 fans to attend the game. Gaither's Rattlers knew the importance of the game and the team's proximity to perfection. "We have tried to get our boys ready for this one. They know what this one means to us, and I believe they are going all out to win it," asserted Gaither.[100]

Another undefeated season was tantalizingly close. The Rattlers encircled Gaither one last time before the start of the game. With players hanging onto every word, Gaither admitted, "I'm scared to death." He continued, "Some day mama's gonna die. Some day papa's gonna die. Some day you'll lose your job. And there'll be some days you can't balance that budget. . . . You can't always win. But, today you can win! This is what you've been waiting for . . . the national championship. Last year they humiliated you in the first half, but now we have the better team. This is our chance to prove it." The Rattlers punctuated Gaither's statements with "Hubba, Hubba." He told his offense, "They're bigger and you have to be harder and faster. Every unit, give your top speed every minute." Gaither demanded that his defense "lay the wood on that big slow quarterback. Let him know he's been hit. It's open season on quarterbacks. I want you to hit them high, low, and in the middle. I want you to hit them from the top of their heads to the tip of their toes. I want their toenails to come loose. But I want you to play them cleanly, but as hard as you know how." The team prayed and then ran out of the tunnel to the sounds of the Marching 100 and 43,000 fans yelling, "Strike, Rattlers, Strike."[101]

Gaither's fiery pregame speech worked. The Rattlers' defense held the high-powered Panthers to one touchdown in a 28 to 7 win in the twenty-seventh OBC. The victory was Gaither's 120th win, his first 10-win season, his second undefeated season, and his fifth national title. After his second perfect season, Gaither compared his two perfect seasons. "My 1957 team had more natural talent and better individual players than this year's squad," Gaither told reporters. "But as far as desire and ability to get the job done," he continued, "I would say this is the top team I've ever coached."[102]

The undefeated season and national title guaranteed Gaither would win coach-of-the-year honors. As the 1950s came to an end, sportswriters began debating who were the candidates for coach of the decade. Sportswriter Ric Roberts named the leading coaches of the previous three decades—Tuskegee's Cleveland Abbott (1920s), Morgan State's Edward Hurt (1930s), and TSU's Henry Arthur Kean (1940s)—before outlining the resumes of the contenders for top coach of the 1950s: Jake Gaither, Morris Brown's Edward "Ox" Clemons, Prairie View's Billy Nicks, TSU's Henry Gentry, and Southern's Arnett Mumford. Roberts concluded that Gaither's seventy-three wins, winning 89 percent of his games against high-level competition, made the FAMU leader the best of the decade. "When the stocky-legged, square-jawed A. S. (Big Jake) Gaither played his last game at his post as a sturdy end for dear old KC 30 years ago, there was no way of knowing at the time that he would win indelible glory as a coach. Yet there, he towers—on the brink of claiming this . . . decade of football as his very own."[103] The 100% Wrong Club named Gaither coach of the decade. His next decade, however, was about to be overshadowed by the sit-in movement and the growing civil rights movement.

SIT DOWN AND FIGHT A LITTLE WHILE

Three days after Gaither was honored as coach of the decade, four North Carolina A&T freshmen—Ezell Blair Jr., Franklin McCain, Joseph McNeil, and David Richmond—quietly sat down at the Woolworth's in Greensboro, North Carolina, and loudly asserted their humanity. Gaither's dominating teams ran headlong into a rapidly expanding civil rights movement, where Black college students blitzed segregation. The sit-in movement spread to fifty-five cities and thirteen states in the next three months.[104] On February 13, 1960, FAMU students led by Pricilla and Patricia Stephens and the Reverend C. K. Steele's high-school-aged sons, Charles and Henry, held a "sympathy sit-in" at Woolworth's in Tallahassee. Black students across the South and eventually the country decided to do as the protest song said: "Sit Down and Fight a Little While."[105]

The Stephens sisters, Priscilla and Patricia, were the catalysts of the sit-in movement in Tallahassee.[106] On Saturday, February 13, eight FAMU students and two high school students entered Woolworth's and asked for service. The ten students followed the script of the Greensboro four, right down to their formal dress clothes.[107] The waitress and then the store manager denied the students service. The young activists proceeded to open their textbooks, indicating that they would not leave. All the while, the activists stoically ignored a small group of hecklers yelling, "What are you niggers doing in here?"[108] The inability to bait the activists into a response demonstrated their determined discipline in the confrontation with Jim Crow. Their resolve even earned the support of sympathetic whites, who encouraged them to "just sit there."[109] The activists avoided arrest, and the local Congress of Racial Equality chapter planned another sit-in for the following week.[110] On February 20, seventeen Black activists plus two white activists increased the "sociodrama" of the sit-ins.[111] The protesters had prepared for a stronger, and possibly violent, reaction from either local whites, the police, or both. The waitresses again ignored the activists' requests for service, and the manager quickly closed the lunch counter. A crowd of whites formed behind the protesters, snarling, "I thought I smelled some niggers."[112] Someone called the police, warning, "If you people don't turn them out, we will."[113] The police along with the mayor, Hugh Williams, arrived within the hour and asked the activists to leave. The cops arrested eleven activists who had defied the request to move. The Stephens sisters, Rev. C. K. Steele's two sons, six FAMU students, and Mary Ola Gaines, a forty-three-year-old ICC member who had been active in the bus boycotts four years earlier, were booked at the city jail.[114]

The arrests galvanized student agitation. On March 12, waves of inter-racial groups sat in at Woolworth's and McCrory's. When the police arrested eleven more activists, Patricia Stephens led more than 1,000 students toward downtown. Local law enforcement stood in formation blocking entrance into downtown, while a mob of whites stood waiting to attack with clubs. After a brief standoff, the police, under City Commissioner William T. Mayo's orders, fired tear gas into the crowd. The police arrested thirty-five demonstrators.[115] At the trial, the eleven protesters were convicted and sentenced to either a $300 fine or sixty days in jail. Eight activists, including the Stephens sisters, Henry Steele, and FAMU student government president William Larkins, elected jail over bail.[116] When Martin Luther King Jr. heard of the students' sacrifice, he telegrammed Rev. C. K. Steele: "I assure you that your valiant witness is one of the flowing epics of our time and you are bringing all America nearer the thresh-hold of the world's bright tomorrows."[117] The Tallahassee movement had made history, introducing a new tactic in the civil rights movement—the jail-in.

King's commentary on the significant activism in Tallahassee illumi-nates Jake Gaither's conspicuous absence from the public record on the protests. As one of the most recognizable African Americans in Tallahas-see, Gaither remained publicly silent on the local civil rights protests. Gai-ther's reticence to use his masterful rhetoric for civil rights led some Blacks, even some who supported the football program, to label him an "Uncle Tom."[118] Despite Gaither's admonishments to his players to avoid the pro-tests, some players still found themselves on the front lines of struggle. Fullback Alton White saw his cousin yanked out of a church by her hair after a protest. He remembered thinking, "We got to fight." White soon

Patricia Stephens (Due) is at the far left, and Jake Gaither is in the center
wearing the hat, leaving the March 17, 1960, trial for sit-in demonstrators.
Eight activists were sentenced to sixty days in jail. Five chose jail over bail.
(Florida Memory, Florida State Archives)

joined the sit-in movement, against Gaither's wishes.[119] He attended the
next meeting, led by Patricia Stephens, and engaged in protests throughout the spring and summer. White's participation was rare for a FAMU
athlete, as the vast majority adhered to Gaither's command not to get involved. Despite not lending his powerful voice for the movement, Gaither
still kept close tabs on the protests and the students. A press photographer
captured Gaither leaving the March 17 trial. It is unclear whether he was
lending moral support to the students arrested or looking to see whether
any of his players were involved. Regardless of motive, Gaither paid attention to the trial and the protests.

Gaither's refusal to support the Tallahassee movement publicly reflects
the complicated position that Black college administrators, professors, and
coaches would come to inhabit. It also meant that he missed another opportunity to challenge structural inequities such as facilities and salaries.
Growing up and working in the segregated South, Gaither knew the hu-

miliation of segregation. He knew the fear of entering a white business, the inability to get a decent meal while traveling, or the inability to use the bathroom without exposing "yourself to rattlesnakes and indecent exposure."[120] On the other hand, Dr. Pilcher's lifesaving kindness indicated the possibilities of integration. Gaither's limited support for the movement was a product of his being a state employee and one who needed political help to expand his football program. Even though Gaither was one of the most successful coaches in college football, the Board of Control still determined his employment and salary. Too-vocal support would jeopardize his and his wife's jobs at FAMU. It was common knowledge that FAMU music professor Richard Haley was fired one month after supporting the sit-ins.[121] Moreover, Gaither had also actively courted support from white politicians. Governor Collins spoke at the reception for the twenty-fifth OBC, and he attended the game.[122] Gaither sought these relationships not only for political reasons but for personal ones as well. Biographers and friends have suggested that he enjoyed currying the favor of political whites.[123] Given Gaither's positive relationship with influential whites, the State Board of Control increased his salary from $9,600 to $12,000 per year. Thus, during the early days of the sit-in movement, Florida made Gaither the highest-paid coach in Black college football.[124] Gaither wrote to Governor Collins thanking him for his "active support" for his and his coaching staff's raises.[125] Gaither flattered Florida's politicians for his program to receive the proper state support.

Although the salaries of Gaither and his assistants put them atop Black college football, these wages were still a reminder of their second-class citizenship. At the end of the 1950s, UF and FSU were looking for new coaches. While Gaither had won 120 games in the decade, Florida's other two state-supported football teams had won only 139 games combined in the same time span.[126] Both programs turned to unproven but well-respected assistant coaches to turn around their football fortunes. In December 1959, FSU hired Bill Peterson, a former assistant for Paul Dietzel at LSU. The State Board of Control approved a salary of $14,000 per year.[127] In January 1960, UF announced that it had hired Ray Graves, an assistant under Bobby Dodd at Georgia Tech. The state agreed to pay Graves $17,000 per year.[128] Gaither, through the coaching clinic, was familiar with the coaching abilities of Graves and Peterson.[129] As an assistant coach, Graves admitted that Gaither "had the best [clinic] that could be offered in football here."[130] The close setting of the coaching clinics allowed Gaither to see that white coaches were no better or worse than Black ones. However, in the eyes of the State Board of Control, whiteness, not wins, was sufficient for more money. Broad support for civil rights could have severed the precarious yet inequitable relationship between Gaither and state politicians. Nonetheless, the young activists' jail-in exposed the weakness of Gaither's accommodationist strategy. Although his approach could improve the salary of his assistants, it could not promise African Americans first-class treatment, stop state violence against protesters, or even guarantee equal salaries.

Gaither was also a believer in Black institutions. A product of a segregated world, Gaither rejected the civil rights logic that Black institutions were inferior. Civil rights lawyer and scholar Derrick A. Bell has explained that the prevalent desegregation argument was "blacks must gain access to white schools because 'equal educational opportunity' means integrated school, and because only school integration will make certain that black children will receive the same education as white children."[131] Football provided Gaither an alternative framework to view desegregation. He knew through his coaching clinic that the white coaches were not significantly better than the Black ones. He was aware that Southern University had defeated San Francisco State in the 1948 Fruit Bowl, in one the few cases of an HBCU playing a PWI in football before the 1960s. The game proved that on the level playing field of the gridiron, Black colleges were not inferior.[132] Gaither simply wanted an opportunity for his high-scoring Rattlers to prove their equality against the state's white football programs.

Gaither's belief that Black athletic institutions could compete with white ones reflected a longer African American sports tradition. The Negro Leagues stars and owners perhaps expressed the ambivalence toward athletic integration clearest. Although many African American players had wanted to prove themselves in Major League Baseball, others believed that integration should not come at the expense of the teams. Most notably, Satchel Paige and owner Effa Manley felt that "a Negro Leagues ball club or two should be brought into the Major Leagues as a whole unit."[133] This version of athletic desegregation stood counter to the one where Black athletic talent was individually integrated at the expense of the Black institutions that often helped to produce the talent.

Outside the white lines of the gridiron, changes were all around. During the twenty days of spring football practice, student activists attacked segregation.[134] In April, student activists from across the South, including two from Tallahassee, met in Raleigh, North Carolina, and founded the Student Nonviolent Coordinating Committee. For Gaither, football was a welcome relief from the growing civil rights movement.

FAMU CAN'T OUTRUN THE COLOR LINE

The 1960 and 1961 seasons marked the best offensive football of Gaither's twenty-five-year career and put the Rattlers on the national radar for small college football. *Time* magazine profiled Gaither in the fall of 1960, describing him as the coach of the "nation's top all-Negro football school."[135] By 1960, the integration of professional sports was in full swing as well. Nearly every team in baseball, basketball, and football had at least one African American player. The lone holdout was the NFL's Washington Redskins, who did not integrate until 1962. Also, northern and western colleges, big and small, began to add African American players. Black college teams tried to forestall the loss of Black recruits to predominately white college teams by playing predominately white teams. According to this logic, victories in these games would show that HBCU teams were competitive against white teams. By integrating as a team, Black college football programs could retain their sporting congregation, and its associated power, amid a changing athletic landscape.

Gaither was unusually confident in the weeks before the Rattlers began their title defense. The normally coy Gaither told reporters that his 1960 team was the fastest he'd ever coached. All four of his backfield players, led by returning All-American Clarence Childs, could run the 100-yard dash in under 10 seconds. (The world record was 9.3 seconds). Speed was always a main feature of the split-line T formation; now Gaither arguably had more speed than any team in the country.[136] The Rattlers' speed led to another slate of blowout victories to open the season. FAMU beat Benedict College 68 to 0; next it handed Morris Brown the worst loss in its conference rivalry with a 64 to 0 victory; then it beat cross-state rival Bethune-Cookman 97 to 0; and FAMU ended the first month of games by destroying South Carolina State 80 to 0. After a month of games, FAMU led HBCU football in scoring and was a leader in three NAIA statistical categories.[137] FAMU's early-season success also created a potential crisis in the embryonic NAIA football championship.

The NAIA began as the National Association of Intercollegiate Basketball in 1937 when basketball founder James Naismith and others organized a basketball tournament championship for smaller colleges. The basketball association drew the color line in the tournament until 1948, when legendary coach John Wooden integrated the tournament with his Indiana State Sycamores team. After considerable work from Black college administrators and coaches, the association accepted Central State as its first HBCU member institution in 1951. HBCU basketball coaches and athletic directors—John B. McLendon (North Carolina Central and TSU), Mack Greene (Central State), and Harry Jefferson (Virginia State and Hampton)—also secured the opportunity for one Black college team to compete in the annual basketball tournament in 1953. A year earlier, A. O. Duer, NAIA executive secretary and former Pepperdine University basketball coach, and other executives had renamed the National Association of Intercollegiate Basketball as the National Association of Intercollegiate Athletics and began organizing championship tournaments in track, tennis, golf, and football. By 1955, 45 of the more than 400 NAIA member institutions were HBCUs, and Greene, McLendon, Edward Hurt (Morgan State), A. W. Mumford (Southern), and others held leadership positions in the association.[138] Although only one HBCU basketball team could be in the tournament, the NAIA—when compared with the NCAA, which had no HBCU participation in its basketball tournament, bowl games, or leadership—was a leader in sports integration in the 1950s.[139]

Amid the opening volleys of the civil rights movement, racial tensions plagued the first five NAIA football championship games. Little Rock, Arkansas, hosted the first football championship game in 1956. The nationally televised inaugural Aluminum Bowl had an inauspicious beginning as Montana State and St. Joseph's College (Ind.) played to a scoreless tie in a driving rainstorm. The NAIA anticipated building on its shaky debut, when school desegregation arrived in Little Rock the following year. When the world watched Governor Orval Faubus and white segregationists stop nine African American students from attending Little Rock's Central High in the fall of 1957, the NAIA executive committee "felt the conditions in Little Rock at present time were too unstable" to host the second championship game. With only a month until the game, the committee moved the football championship game to St. Petersburg, Florida, and renamed it the Holiday Bowl.[140]

Racial issues followed the game to Florida when Hillsdale College (Mich.) and Pittsburg State College (Kans.) made the championship game in 1957, as both teams had Black players. Again, the NAIA was unprepared to deal with segregation, as it put together a hastily organized segregated dance for the players and local African American students.[141] According to press reports, Averett Moon, Hillsdale's African American male cheerleader, was more shocking to the 7,000-plus attendees than the integrated game itself. The local press reported that the combination of an integrated game and a Black cheerleader "apparently was the last straw." "While this might appear bigoted to many," a reporter wrote, "the fact remains that St. Petersburg of all the large cities in Florida probably maintains the strongest front against integration."[142] The game exposed differences between "segregationists" and local "business and civic leaders."[143] In the sportswriter's estimation, the championship game's future in St. Petersburg depended on the NAIA drawing the color line. Despite the local press's prediction on the bowl game's future, Richard A. Parker, the Holiday Bowl chairman and a local business leader, suggested the game would return the following season.[144] The NAIA and local leaders renewed the contract for 1958, with the city increasing its financial contribution from $17,000 to $20,000.[145] Notably, the new agreement did not require the NAIA to draw the color line. The game's new selection procedures actually reduced the NAIA's or the city's ability to enforce segregation. An NAIA committee picked the 1956 and 1957 championship participants, but going forward the committee created a four-team playoff. The new format lessened the ability to eliminate teams that had Black players and even created the remote possibility that an HBCU team could be in the playoff and championship game.[146]

The 1958 and 1959 games mostly avoided racial controversies, but FAMU's hot start in 1960 raised new questions. Could a Black college team make the NAIA playoffs? Could one make the NAIA title game in St. Petersburg? Could that team be FAMU? An HBCU football team signaled something different from the individual Black players who had integrated bowl games. Black players on PWI teams had participated in southern bowl games since 1948. Thus, the Holiday Bowl's acceptance of a few African American players on PWI teams was on par with other regional bowl games.[147] A Black college team in the NAIA bowl, however, would have undermined the notion of the athletic superiority of white teams and, by extension, the very schools themselves. In addition, if FAMU played in the NAIA title game, Rattler fans and alumni would have had a precedent to call for FAMU to play either UF, FSU, or the University of Miami. A game against the big three all-white college programs could have confirmed FAMU as the state's best team, as African American fans argued and some white fans suspected and feared.

FAMU's dominant start to the season forced NAIA executives, St. Petersburg officials, and Governor Collins to address these issues.[148] NAIA executive secretary A. O. Duer announced that FAMU was "definitely not under consideration as a playoff entrant." Duer noted that it was not the quality of the Rattlers but, rather, the possibility of them playing for a championship in St. Petersburg. "While we feel that there is a definite place for a Negro school in our championship picture," he told reporters, "we do not feel that St. Petersburg is ready for a ball game that would send a white school against a colored one." The NAIA's denial of FAMU an opportunity to prove itself against a white opponent signaled the end of the championship game in St. Petersburg to many local observers. Duer announced the NAIA's desire to make the playoff "a completely democratic one" soon. He apologized to Gaither in a letter: "I look forward to the time when the NAIA football program will be as integrated and truly representative as are all of the other athletic programs." Gaither, though disappointed, let the NAIA off the hook by focusing on the difficult logistics of playing additional games around its OBC.[149]

The NAIA suddenly reversed course and refused to police the color line for Florida. Duer clarified the NAIA's position, announcing, "If Florida residents were real hot for the Rattlers to play in the Holiday Bowl — and they would be playing a white team — then we would definitely consider it." Duer added, "I am anxious to see the reaction of Florida to such a possibility."[150] The local Black press noted that the game, despite being televised, was a "loser" financially and interest-wise. But a game pitting FAMU against a white school "would provide the shot-in-the-arms [the] Holiday Bowl needs."[151] Before fans and sportswriters could debate the chance of FAMU playing in the game, Governor Collins gave his answer. He ruled the game "off-limits" and insisted "it would not be prudent nor wise to match Florida A&M University with a white football team in a Florida bowl game."[152] Governor Collins denied the Rattlers an opportunity, despite Gaither's support of his racial moderation on civil rights. The governor's stance proved once again that Gaither's support of his civil rights policies was misguided.

The Rattlers had to recover quickly from their disappointing exclusion from the NAIA championship playoff because the game against archrival Southern University was days away. Both teams arrived in Baton Rouge for their mid-November clash undefeated and ranked no. 1 and no. 2 in the Black college polls. Mumford's Southern Jaguars, behind a stout defense, spoiled Gaither's perfect season for the sixth time in fifteen seasons with a 14 to 6 upset victory.[153] FAMU finished the season with the lone loss to Southern, defeating Langston College (Okla.) in the OBC. The Rattlers set a new record with 515 points scored on the season (an average of 51.5 points per game).

FAMU's near-participation in the NAIA playoffs had sportswriters and coaches asking about the quality of HBCU football vis-à-vis white opponents. The final NAIA poll, for instance, ranked FAMU sixth, Southern seventh, and Langston eleventh.[154] The *Pittsburgh Courier*'s Ric Roberts asked, "Is there no more room at the top for Negro College Football? Is the annual $100,000 FAMU-owned Orange Blossom Classic our football's final piece de resistance, within the rigidity of 'race'?" Roberts suggested, "The deadly caste system is what ails America," and he called for an "anti-caste crusade." Roberts pushed for more than the "individual victory" of pioneering athletes such as Joe Louis or Jackie Robinson, suggesting that Black colleges with leading coaches would be valuable in the battle against racial caste.[155] The *Courier*'s Bill Nunn Jr. also reported that two anonymous HBCU coaches attending the NCAA convention in Pittsburgh stated, "We [HBCU football teams] wouldn't be able to defeat all of the major colleges, but there are a lot of schools with major ratings we wouldn't have trouble with."[156] Ulysses McPherson, an assistant at Arkansas AM&N (Pine Bluff) later suggested, "If teams like Grambling, Southern, Florida A&M, Tennessee A&I (State) and Prairie View could meet the better teams in the South and Southwest[,] I'm convinced they would hold their own."[157] Billy Nicks believed his Prairie View team would have beaten at least five teams in the Southwest Conference.[158] Gaither disclosed that white coaches were well aware of the talent on HBCU teams. "I'm not saying how many of the teams we would beat. But I'll tell you this. In conversations I've had with some of the top Southern coaches I've learned that I would have a hard time keeping any of the boys on my first or second team if segregation laws didn't prohibit them from going after them." He added that white southern coaches, off the record, could not wait to recruit the top Black athletes.[159] As of 1961, HBCU coaches still had a monopoly on top Black talent in the South. What many wanted was an opportunity to show the country and future players the quality of their football programs.

In the winter of 1961, the NAIA set out to rectify its racial problems during the organization's annual meeting. The executives unanimously decided to move the football title game from St. Petersburg to Sacramento, California, after another racial controversy. This time segregated living arrangements marred the 1960 title game between Humboldt State (Calif.) and Lenoir-Rhyne (N.C.).[160] With the announcement of the NAIA title game's move to Sacramento, NAIA president A. O. Duer confirmed that the decision was in part based on "racial discrimination against Negro athletes in Florida."[161] The relocation of the game to Sacramento increased the chances that an HBCU would participate. Now for Gaither, all he had to do was be equally dominant offensively and go undefeated to make the NAIA playoff game.

"If you can trust yourself when all men doubt you / But make allowance for their doubting too; / If you can wait and not be tired by waiting," recited Earl Kitchings, athletic director and head coach at Jacksonville's Matthew Gilbert High School, at the FAMU football banquet. In dedicating Rudyard Kipling's "If" to the Rattlers, Kitchings, a former FAMU team captain, highlighted the necessary resolve for the Rattlers to put the 1960 season's disappointing second-place finish in the Black college rankings, and the governor's decision to block FAMU's opportunity at the NAIA championship game, behind them. The chance to play for an NAIA national title reinvigorated Gaither, but he was worried that he had lost too many valuable players to make a run. Perhaps his window of opportunity had closed. However, in the audience that evening was Kitchings's former player, freshman Bob Hayes, who would bring national and international attention to FAMU.[162]

The 1961 off-season was more tumultuous than usual. The athletic department's nonsupport of civil rights became a national story during a contentious personnel decision. In March, the school fired Macon "Bodybuilder" Williams, a longtime assistant coach and former All-American on FAMU's 1942 national title team. Three women charged that Williams entered their home uninvited and molested one of the women and "terrorized the household." Students rallied to support the women and pushed for his dismissal. In an attempt to save his client's job, Williams's lawyer resorted to defaming the women, calling them "trashy" and of "questionable moral character." When this line of argument failed, he claimed that Williams was dismissed because he "consistently opposed student participation in sit-ins and other demonstrations." While the FAMU administration quickly asserted that Williams was dismissed for a "moral issue," his firing revealed the underlying tensions between FAMU's well-respected football program and the activism emerging from the city.[163] Columnist Marion E. Jackson declared, "The struggle of the Negro people is more important than the ambition and frustrations of any man."[164] Gaither was again publicly silent on Williams's case, which furthered student activists' suspicions about Gaither's lack of support for the movement, especially its women leaders.

As the new season quickly approached, Gaither had to figure out how to replace a top assistant coach and key players who had graduated off the best offensive team in school history. He believed, "We won't have a real great team this fall, but we won't embarrass you either."[165] For the first time since the creation of the Blood, Sweat, and Tears units, Gaither worried he did not have enough depth. Gaither did, however, have a secret weapon in redshirt freshman Bob Hayes. In the summer before the 1961 season, Hayes tied the world record, running a 9.3-second 100-yard dash. Gaither moved the speedster to varsity during preseason practice.[166] Per usual, FAMU routed its early opponents and was ranked no. 1. Again, FAMU's hot start put it in the national discussion for the NAIA playoffs.

In order for a Black college team to secure a spot in the playoffs, Black sportswriters had to promote the quality of Black college football teams. This cause was aided by HBCUs scheduling white teams when possible. The *Pittsburgh Courier*'s Ric Roberts was the leading promoter of HBCUs getting their shot at smashing the glass ceiling. He observed that the first step toward "the eventual integration of our football" started with Maryland State facing Southern Connecticut's all-white squad in the twentieth annual Capital Classic in Washington, D.C.[167] He later added that the game was a part of the broader goal of narrowing the "'gap' which separates our brand of football from the brand played by our white intercollegiate contemporaries." The previous season, Southern Connecticut shut out Maryland State 12 to 0, and in 1959 Youngstown State defeated TSU 13 to 12. The losses gave Roberts and others pause about comparing the best Black college teams with white ones. "Can we brush past the Connecticut State Owls, a high ranking NAIA football power, and then aim for Notre Dame, Texas Christian, Georgia Tech, Iowa and/or Missouri?" asked Roberts. He wanted Black college football teams to emulate their basketball teams and no longer settle for being the "best among Negro Colleges."[168] The Maryland State Hawks won 7 to 6, giving many the hope that a Black college team would make the NAIA playoffs.[169]

NAIA pollsters ranked FAMU fifth in a midseason poll.[170] Duer contacted FAMU about the possibility of the Rattlers' participation in the playoffs. Gaither considered the thorny logistics of competing in a playoff game and playing in the lucrative OBC. Gaither declared to the press, "We will play our Miami game [the OBC] of course, but we will play in California, if they want us." Gaither planned to fly his team to California on the Saturday before or after the OBC.[171] Gaither's Rattlers were caught between the segregation policies of Florida and their successful OBC. The Rattlers' increasing marginality was confirmed when the NAIA again failed to select them for the playoffs.[172] Southern University publicity director Bennie Thomas observed that Black college football occupied a "middle ground" trapped by segregation and success. The NAIA and NCAA knew little about Black college teams and their quality, and it was "increasingly obvious that only those who are known are rated."[173] Denied again, the Rattlers still had their most difficult games of the season remaining.

The final month of the season was tougher than the beginning, as the Rattlers had intersectional games against North Carolina A&T, Southern, and Texas Southern.[174] The Rattlers turned an 8 to 6 halftime lead into an impressive 32 to 12 win over the Aggies, fueled by a 52-yard touchdown run by Bob Hayes.[175] The Rattlers avenged their 1960 loss to Southern by thoroughly dominating the Jaguars 46 to 0.[176] The Rattlers sat alone at the top of the Black college polls as the only undefeated team. Gaither's boys solidified their perfect regular season by thumping Texas Southern, 48 to 7. The *Atlanta Daily World* and the 100% Wrong Club crowned FAMU national champions with the W. A. Scott Memorial Trophy.[177] The first week in December, FAMU defeated Jackson State in the OBC to complete another undefeated season. With the opportunity to play for an integrated NAIA title tantalizingly close, the W. A. Scott Memorial Trophy was an incomplete victory.

While the NAIA had denied the Rattlers a chance to compete in an integrated competition, Gaither and his players received individual honors. Coaches nationwide recognized Gaither for his insight and success. More than 500 coaches in the American Football Coaches Association voted him the Small College Coach of the Year. Gaither joined basketball's John McLendon as the only other African American to win the award. Winning the award was an honor, but some believed that had Gaither coached at a major college, he would have won the prize awarded to Paul "Bear" Bryant "hands down."[178] J. R. E. Lee Jr. closed the season by praising Gaither's "uncompromising integrity, unwavering fairness and unswerving defense of the right."[179]

SMALL COLLEGE CHAMPION WITH AN ASTERISK

The space between sport and politics revealed differences among whites on desegregation. The leadership governing Florida's universities exhibited an ambiguous mix of southern progressivism and conservatism, making Gaither's attempts to put his Rattlers on equal footing with UF and FSU tricky. Politicians' attempts to slow desegregation in Tallahassee belied impending racial changes on the athletic front. Major bowl games played in the state, including the Holiday Bowl, hosted integrated teams. When the

Paul "Bear" Bryant (*left*) and Jake Gaither receiving 1961 Coach of the Year awards from Gerald Zarow, vice president of Eastman Kodak. (Courtesy of Bettmann/Corbis)

Big-8 conference signed a contract with the Orange Bowl guaranteeing its champion a spot in the New Year's Day game in 1953, Florida's most prestigious exhibition game would regularly include integrated teams. The 1961 Gator Bowl pitted an integrated Penn State team, led by All-American end Dave Robinson, against Georgia Tech. It was becoming clear to many that segregated athletics was an affront to the idea of a level playing field in sports.[180]

Track and field, not football, provided the first opportunity for FAMU to compete against leading white colleges. At a February track meet in Miami, Bob Hayes ran the 100-yard dash in 9.2 seconds, tying the world record.[181] In addition to his record in the 100-yard dash, Hayes anchored the nation's best 440-yard relay team, which included football All-American Robert Paremore. Hayes's achievements put the FAMU track program in the national spotlight.[182] Track coach (and assistant football coach) Pete Griffin stated, "Invitations have been coming in from all over the country for sprinter Robert Hayes and our 440-yard relay team."[183] One invitation Griffin did not get was for the Florida Relays hosted by UF. The FAMU track team's absence caught the attention of the school newspaper. *Alliga-*

tor sports editor Mike Gora noted, "The Florida Relays . . . was a well-run meet with a sprinkling of top athletes. Teams from all over the eastern half of the United States participated in the event." Gora lamented, "A school just 150 miles from Gainesville was not invited. This uninvited school has the best track team in the state and one of the best in the country. The un-invited school placed well in the NCAA finals last year in several events. Florida didn't qualify anyone for participation [in the NCAA finals]." He asserted, "Track events are between human beings. The color doesn't rub off." Finally he queried, "Why must good athletes or good anything else be sacrificed for the radical Jim Crow southerner?"[184] This was a question that Gaither had been asking for quite some time.

Gora and Gaither received an answer to their rhetorical question when the press announced that Darryl Hill had transferred from the Naval Academy to the University of Maryland. Hill had to sit out the 1962 sea-son, but in 1963 he would be the first African American athlete at Maryland and in the Atlantic Coast Conference. Significant athletic desegregation was on the horizon, and Gaither needed to assess the effects on FAMU. More important, he had to wonder how his Rattlers fit into this chang-ing landscape, especially when the state prevented them from competing against white teams.

The consequences of the changing racial composition of sports on the golden age of HBCU football were compounded by retirements and death. At the end of the 1959 season, Morgan State's Eddie Hurt retired as foot-ball coach (he continued to coach track and field until 1970), because his doctor had asked him to slow down. In his career, Hurt led the Bears to six national titles and eleven undefeated seasons, including six straight from 1932 to 1937.[185] During the summer of 1962, longtime Southern head football coach A. W. "Ace" Mumford died from a heart attack. Archrivals on the field and friends off it, Gaither and Mumford, as much as any pair of coaches, pushed Black college football onto the national radar. After the 1961 game in Tallahassee, Mumford arrived at Gaither's home for a postgame celebration. He admitted that the Rattlers had gotten the better of his Jaguars in the 46 to 0 rout, but he warned, "It won't be the same next season." The conversation indicated the camaraderie among Black col-lege coaches.[186] Hurt's retirement at age fifty-nine and Mumford's death at sixty-three were stark reminders of how fortunate Gaither was to be alive. At age fifty-nine, Gaither recognized that the number of years left for his program to participate on a level playing field and to show the country the Rattlers' greatness was dwindling.

The expectations for the 1962 season were the same as every season since 1938: the W. A. Scott Memorial Trophy and an undefeated season. However, with the team barely missing the NAIA playoffs the previous two seasons, held back by segregation in Florida and institutional bias by the NAIA committee, FAMU added a new goal: small college champion, regardless of race. The Rattlers returned key players off their undefeated 1961 team, including quarterback Jim Tullis and running backs Robert Paremore and Bob Hayes. The team was prepared to become the first team to repeat as champions in fifteen seasons. Still, Gaither wondered if his talented squad could dominate the HBCU terrain and be selected for the NAIA playoffs.

As the season started, the Rattlers continued winning. They routed Benedict, Lincoln (Mo.), Morris Brown, and Bethune-Cookman in the opening month of the season, outscoring their overmatched opponents 200 to 24. The wins pushed the Rattlers' win streak to 16 games. After three and half seasons of dominance in which FAMU went 33 and 1, it appeared that Gaither's boys were finally getting respect from white coaches and sportswriters.[187] The season's first United Press International (UPI) coaches' poll had FAMU ranked first over Southern Mississippi, Fresno State, Delaware, and defending champion Pittsburg (Kans.).[188] The sportswriters of the AP poll had the Rattlers on top as well.[189] FAMU's 20 to 0 win over an always tough TSU team should have solidified FAMU's hold on the top spot in the UPI rankings, but Southern Mississippi closed within 8 points in the poll despite an early-season loss to Memphis.[190] The next week, FAMU held on to the top spot in the UPI poll by a single point, in spite of a 19-game winning streak.[191] The Rattlers shut out Southern 25 to 0, stretching their winning streak to 20 games.[192] Still, the road victory could not stop the inevitable; Southern Mississippi overtook FAMU for first place in the UPI poll.[193] In the AP rankings, an undefeated Wittenberg University (Ohio) tied FAMU for first place.[194] FAMU defeated Texas Southern to finish the season undefeated. Despite four consecutive seasons of superiority on the gridiron and a 21-game winning streak, most white coaches and sportswriters were not willing to give the team and the program the full respect it deserved.

Sportswriter and amateur Black college football historian Ric Roberts called out pollsters for their disrespect of HBCU football. He accused some UPI voters of "subtle" discrimination in their selection of Southern Mississippi because "the Hattiesburg 11 . . . would never be allowed to prove its mettle; even against a team with one non-white aboard." Moreover, he believed Southern Mississippi was misclassified as a small school because it regularly played major programs such as North Carolina State and FSU. Roberts declared, "The placing of any small college ahead of FAMU, this year or last, can be little else than . . . a wish." Moreover, when the NAIA overlooked FAMU for the third consecutive year, the *Courier's* leading college football reporter suggested that Alex Duer "deep down . . . must know that FAMU would be favorable to ruin any small college 11 in the U.S.A." In his estimation, no small college program had the resources or the talent to beat FAMU consistently.[195] Roberts only directed his ire at the NAIA and the UPI, as the AP poll ranked FAMU no. 1 over Wittenberg by a single point.[196]

Although the rankings did not reflect FAMU's supremacy on the gridiron, Gaither leveraged the school's athletic success into small racial changes. Leading up to the thirtieth annual OBC, the FAMU athletic department, administration, and alumni obtained a major concession from the Miami Beach hotels. The growth of the OBC had begun to outstrip available hotels in Overtown, forcing attendees to board in local homes. Miami Beach hotels had quietly moderated their segregation policies for big sporting events, such as the Floyd Patterson versus Ingemar Johansson title fight in 1961.[197] Still, the announcement of an "open door" policy for a gathering between two Black colleges showed the OBC's financial influence, which reportedly generated $250,000 for the city of Miami.[198] The opening of these hotels reveals the effectiveness of private negotiations in limited circumstances between Black and white elites. Though triumphant in gaining access to Miami Beach hotels, Gaither never completely acknowledged the weaknesses of this strategy in assuring broad-based civil rights.[199]

FAMU brought its 21-game win streak into the thirtieth annual OBC in a rematch against Jackson State. Coached by former Kentucky State star John Merritt, the Tigers had won the SWAC title for the second year in a row. Rattler fans felt confident that they would beat the Tigers again and claim another undefeated season. Jackson State had other plans, prevailing 22 to 6 in front of nearly 45,000 fans. Venerable *Afro-American* sports reporter Sam Lacy vividly described the aftermath. "Coach John Merritt's Mississippians, true to his word, grabbed coach Jake Gaither's 'blood' and 'sweat' units and squeezed the 'tears' from both of them and their multitude of followers."[200] The loss was a disappointing end to a wonderful season that witnessed FAMU get tempered support from a national panel of coaches and sportswriters.

The Rattlers met most of their goals for the season while creating opportunities for Black college football nationally. The accolades the Rattlers received from winning the AP small college title seemed to vindicate Gaither's nonconfrontational approach to gaining racial openings. Los Angeles sportswriters called for Gaither to become the next coach of the Los Angeles Rams, while Ohio scribes suggested that FAMU play white teams from the Mid-American Conference such as Bowling Green or Kent State.[201] Still, Gaither's approach had yet to put FAMU in a position to play against a white team. With Darryl Hill's enrollment at the University of Maryland, Gaither needed a chance soon to show Floridians and the nation that the Rattlers were indeed one of the best programs.

Despite the apex of FAMU's football success, the tension between the local civil rights activists and Gaither indicated a strain between African American political and cultural goals. The Stephens sisters' and other activists' use of nonviolent direct action highlighted the lack of African Americans' citizenship rights. Gaither viewed his athletic program as a cultural space—a congregation. He used FAMU football as a counter to broader notions of Black cultural pathology. He knew that, despite segregation, his football team and Black institutions by extension were not inferior. In the early 1960s, both approaches made contributions in improving African Americans' opportunities. In other words, what was the purpose of Black cultural institutions without the political protections of citizenship rights? Are citizenship rights incomplete without the bedrock of Black cultural institutions? In the early 1960s, many civil rights activists pushing for political and social equality failed to account for the possibility that the de-emphasis on Black cultural institutions would be the price of the integration ticket.

Ironically, both approaches worked equally well in Tallahassee in the early 1960s. In spite of the Stephens sisters' sit-ins and jail-ins, Tallahassee was still the only major city in Florida that had not desegregated its downtown lunch counters in late 1962. Activists turned to boycotts to put further pressure on businesses. In December 1962, several store managers met a small group of Congress of Racial Equality activists and agreed to integrate lunchroom facilities in January 1963.[202]

Gaither's use of biracial negotiation also gained an important concession in late 1962. He asked Andy Gustafson, the University of Miami head coach, to include two Black players on the South team for the annual North–South Shrine Bowl game. Gaither's mediations got FAMU's Robert Paremore and Jackson State's Willie Richardson added to the South team. They were the first Blacks to play on the South team and the first from

HBCUs. Richardson caught an 80-yard touchdown with thirty seconds left in the game to give the South the win in the Orange Bowl. The Jackson State star was the game's most valuable player, while Paremore won the sportsmanship award. One newspaper report captured the importance of their accomplishment: "The performances of Richardson and Paremore made a deep impression on the southern teammates, not only because of their playing, but their all-around attitude on and off the field. It could very well mean the end of segregated college athletics in the South."[203]

Gaither's efforts proved to the larger sporting community that Black college football was on par with white teams and players. Gaither's team and personal success produced tremendous results. Despite pushing the doors open, FAMU had yet to receive the opportunity to show its football program to the country. The success of Black college players in professional football planted the seeds of HBCU football's decline.

Jake Gaither addressing the team in the locker room, 1953.
(Florida Memory, Florida State Archives)

Florida governor Claude R. Kirk Jr. and twin sons, Frank and Will, visiting
FAMU football coach Jake Gaither. (Florida Memory, Florida State Archives)

Jake Gaither. (Florida Memory, Florida State Archives)

FAMU running back Robert Paremore. (Florida Memory, Florida State Archives)

Fans watching the FAMU football game at Bragg Memorial Stadium, 1961.
(Florida Memory, Florida State Archives)

FAMU president George Gore (*center*) and Mrs. Gore attending a football game
at Bragg Memorial Stadium. (Florida Memory, Florida State Archives)

No. 22 Bob Hayes running the ball during a FAMU football game, 1962.
(Florida Memory, Florida State Archives)

6
BLACK GOLD

Jake Gaither was fed up. For two seasons, Rattler players had chafed at the outsized attention their teammate Bob Hayes received from the media and fans. Besides setting a new world record in the 100-yard sprint at 9.1 seconds in the spring of 1963, Hayes was also a highly effective part-time player for the FAMU football team. In 1963, Hayes only carried the ball 55 times for 260 yards; he caught 15 passes for 401 yards but tied for the team lead with eleven touchdowns. The publicity surrounding "the Bullet" would grow to astronomical levels once the Dallas Cowboys drafted him after the 1963 season, and after his two gold medal performance at the 1964 Olympics.

Hayes was eager to return to football at the conclusion of the Olympics. Having missed the opening games of the season, he was among the first to the practice field to quickly transition from track to football. Gaither stopped Hayes one day as he left the locker room. "Bobby, I want you to go inside. I don't want you to practice today," Gaither told his star player. Hayes was confused, but he never questioned Gaither and headed back to the locker room. As the other players saw Hayes walking in the opposite direction, starting running back Bobby Felts and others audibly mumbled about "Hollywood" Hayes missing practice again. Gaither ordered the players to huddle around him. "I think you boys should be proud to have Bob Hayes as a member of the team. I heard some of you call him 'Hollywood' because he gets so much exposure. If you guys are jealous of Bobby Hayes, I know how every one of you can get as much publicity as Bob does." The players asked, "How coach?" Gaither responded, "Well, you only have to do one thing—outrun him." The players were crestfallen, knowing that none could beat the fastest man in the world.[1]

Bob Hayes's explosion onto the national and international scene highlighted the growing awareness of the talent in Black college football. Although the mainstream college football media and pollsters often failed to appreciate the quality of FAMU, Grambling, Southern, Prairie View, or TSU, professional football had little choice. Sparked by the competition between the NFL and the AFL, Black college players had an opportunity to shine in professional football.

UNEASY IS THE HEAD THAT WEARS THE CROWN

At the twenty-eighth annual 100% Wrong Club banquet in February 1963, the club's leadership handed out three Pioneer Awards, the organization's highest honor. Members gave a prize to the SIAC, which began celebrating its fiftieth year. A second award went to the University of Miami head football coach Andy Gustafson for including African American players on the South team in the North–South Shrine Bowl. The evening's final honor went to the OBC. The night ended with FAMU receiving its fifth W. A. Scott Memorial Trophy for the 1962 season.[2]

Despite the celebration, all was not well in the SIAC. FAMU's dominance caused consternation for other programs during the SIAC's semicentennial. The Rattlers' upcoming 1963 football schedule contained only three SIAC opponents. FAMU planned to play three MAA teams, two teams from the SWAC, and North Carolina A&T from the CIAA. Sportswriters saw FAMU's schedule as a move to "independent" football status, a position held by leading PWI programs such as Penn State, Notre Dame, Syracuse, FSU, and Miami. No Black college program had contemplated an existence outside conference affiliation, and FAMU's move toward such a status would have been a disaster for the SIAC. In previous seasons, the SIAC, realizing FAMU's role as a founding institution and as the conference's best program, made several compromises to include the Rattlers in the conference standings. Conference officials had counted games against Lincoln (Mo.) and Southern as conference games. Now, member institutions spurned this agreement. Tuskegee's athletic director, Edward Jackson, led the chorus of objections to the SIAC's accommodation to FAMU's scheduling, calling for an end to the policy. The *Atlanta Daily World*'s Marion Jackson understood the ramification of Jackson's claim. The sportswriter wrote, "Barring Florida A. & M. from future championship would open the door for the Lilliputians to win a championship." FAMU had won the SIAC every year since 1952, losing just 1 conference game in eleven seasons. The Rattlers' future relationship with the SIAC was cloudy. Marion Jackson concluded, "Uneasy lies the head that wears the crown!"[3]

The Rattlers looked to repeat as Black college champions and possibly secure a spot in the NAIA playoffs. The graduation of star players like Robert Paremore made the task more difficult. FAMU turned to running backs

Bob Felts, Bob Hayes, and Charlie Ward, along with senior quarterback Jim Tullis, to meet the team's title aspiration. Gaither was optimistic about the team's chances, calling on the Rattlers to be as "explosive as a powder keg with a short fuse."[4] The season started as expected, with victories over Lincoln (Mo.), Benedict (S.C.), and Morris Brown. In the Rattlers' fourth game of the season, they faced new rival TSU, with its recently hired coach John Merritt.

After Merritt had orchestrated Jackson State's upset over FAMU in the 1962 OBC, he decided to take the job at TSU. The move caught many by surprise. Most sportswriters had speculated that Merritt would return to his alma mater, Kentucky State University, to become its head coach. When TSU president Walter Davis fired the entire football staff after the Tigers won only 1 game in 1962, Merritt was on the radar as a replacement. Davis told fans and reporters, "My goal is to re-establish football excellence along with academic excellence."[5] In the spring of 1963, President Davis lured the young, up-and-coming coach who reminded many of TSU's legendary Henry Arthur Kean with a $15,000-per-year salary. That Davis saw many of the late Kean's traits in Merritt was no surprise, since Merritt had played for Kean at Kentucky State and used his coaching philosophy.[6]

Most writers and fans predicted the no. 2–ranked Rattlers would easily defeat the twice-defeated TSU Tigers. Late in the fourth quarter, the game was still closer than many had expected. The Rattlers led 12 to 8 with about four minutes remaining. The Tigers' defense had stymied the Rattlers the entire game and forced another punt. Tiger freshman Nolan Smith caught the punt at his 17-yard line and weaved his way through the FAMU special teams for the game-winning touchdown. After the 14 to 12 upset, Merritt needled Gaither's team in the press after holding Bob Hayes to minus 20 yards rushing. Merritt told reporters, "Hayes is not as good of a football player as they play him up to be." Merritt's consecutive wins over Gaither marked the beginning of an intense rivalry between the coaches. The loss dropped the Rattlers to no. 3 in the small college poll and all but eliminated them from the NAIA playoff.[7]

After the tough loss to TSU, the Rattlers still had intersectional games against North Carolina A&T, Southern, and Texas Southern. The Rattlers rebounded to trounce the undefeated North Carolina A&T Aggies 32 to 0. The following week FAMU held Southern scoreless in a 37 to 0 rout. In the final game before the OBC, the Rattlers traveled to Jacksonville to face Texas Southern. In front of more than 10,000 fans, the Rattlers lost another heartbreaker. In the fourth quarter, Bob Hayes returned a punt 85 yards to tie the game. But with nine seconds left in the game, the Texas Southern Tigers completed a 34-yard touchdown pass to win 20 to 14.[8] The Rattlers had lost 2 games for the first time in five seasons.

The OBC lost some of its usual luster with the Rattlers firmly out of the title picture. Financial jealousy and scheduling logistics also cast "ominous shadows" over the game.[9] Gaither had chosen a SWAC team for the OBC six of the previous ten seasons, signaling the high-quality football being played by Grambling, Jackson State, Prairie View, and Southern. SWAC leaders now wanted a larger percentage of the gate receipts. Per custom and contract, FAMU guaranteed opponents a set amount for the game. For 1963, Gaither pledged $18,000 to the opponent. SWAC officials rejected the guaranteed payout and demanded 37.5 percent of the gate receipts. SWAC officials knew this was the percentage for white bowl games and believed they deserved as much. Gaither told reporters that if the OBC had paid the percentage in 1962, "we would have gone $15,000 in the hole." The *Pittsburgh Courier*'s Bill Nunn Jr. supported FAMU's position, believing the OBC "is a game that has been built and nurtured by Florida A. & M.," and most fans were Rattler supporters. Still, the SWAC refused to budge.[10] As a result, FAMU officials chose Morgan State for the thirty-first OBC.

Television and tragedy created another logistical nightmare for FAMU and the OBC. The NCAA controlled and negotiated all college football television contracts. Beginning in 1957, the NCAA TV Steering Committee chose the teams for the nine nationally and four regionally televised games. The NCAA divided the monies from television contracts among member institutions, with the teams playing in the televised games receiving a larger share. CBS won the television rights for college football with a $10.2 million bid in 1963. For the lucky teams selected to play on TV, there were substantial financial benefits. Miami had scheduled perennial powerhouse University of Alabama for December and signed a contract with CBS for the game to be on national television. The televised game in the Orange Bowl was worth nearly $140,000 in revenue per school.[11] In anticipation of its substantial payday, Miami had asked for FAMU to move the OBC from its regular date, the first Saturday in December, to the following week. FAMU agreed, in part, because of the goodwill created by Miami head coach Andy Gustafson. Moreover, the game took on added significance after Alabama's governor George Wallace stood in the schoolhouse door at the University of Alabama in June 1963, declaring his unwavering support for segregation. The Miami versus Alabama game looked to be one where the South's progressive future would face off against its repressive past. However, the assassination of President John F. Kennedy on November 22, 1963, upended the college football schedule. Most schools canceled their games on Saturday, November 23, including the highly anticipated Army–Navy game. The annual game between the service academies, featuring Navy's All-American and eventual Heisman Trophy winner Roger Staubach, was rescheduled to December 7, pushing Miami versus Alabama off the TV. With Alabama vying for a Sugar Bowl bid, and Miami needing the money from a nationally televised game to fund its athletic aspirations, the two schools rescheduled the game for the same day as the OBC. The University of Miami agreed to compensate FAMU for a smaller than usual OBC crowd. The new game time meant the Orange Bowl stadium hosted a double-header: Miami versus Alabama in the afternoon and the OBC in the evening.[12]

In the OBC, FAMU turned an early fourth quarter 8 to 7 lead into a 30 to 7 rout. Although the crowd was smaller than most years, nearly 31,000 fans still attended the game. Fewer fans meant that the University of Miami would recompense FAMU about $40,000, based on the difference in attendance between the 1962 and 1963 games. The star of the OBC weekend was boxer Cassius Clay (Muhammad Ali), who had been training in Miami for his fight against Sonny Liston in February. According to one reporter, "[Clay] is the most exciting athlete active today and even with the 31st Orange Blossom Classic in progress he maneuvered himself into the headlines."[13]

While FAMU wrapped up another successful season, Prairie View A&M University garnered an opportunity to compete in the NAIA playoffs. The revelation had to have been bittersweet for the longtime Rattler coach. Gaither had spent the previous four seasons trying to maneuver his team into the NAIA playoff picture. FAMU's best teams in 1960 and 1961 were stopped by Florida enforcing the color line in St. Petersburg. The NAIA selection committee failed to pick Gaither's 1962 team, and the 1963 team suffered two losses. So it had to be disappointing for Gaither to watch Billy Nicks's Prairie View Panthers reap the benefits of his prodding. To compete in the NAIA playoffs, Prairie View canceled its "classic" bowl game in Houston. The Panthers, led by All-American quarterback Jim Kearney and end Otis Taylor, traveled to Nebraska to face Kearney State (the University of Nebraska at Kearney). The Panthers trailed 7 to 0 at halftime but scored three unanswered touchdowns after the intermission.[14] The win sent Prairie View to Sacramento for the Camilla Bowl, the NAIA title game, against St. John's University (Minn.). The Panthers held a slim 14 to 13 lead at halftime. But St. John's controlled the second half to win 33 to 27.[15]

FAMU's push to be in NAIA playoffs opened the door for Prairie View. The inclusion of a Black college team was representative of a changing college football landscape in which HBCUs needed to compete against white teams. The Black press made this claim more forcefully in 1963. Sheep Jackson, the sports editor at the *Cleveland Call and Post*, wrote, "Let's see how a match between [FAMU] and a white school would stack up."[16] Following the University of Maryland's lead in breaking the color line in the South, Wake Forest University, Texas Christian University, and other southern schools planned to follow suit. Amid this new athletic environment, Gaither faced new pressures to win. More African American recruits from the South now had the option of playing for newly desegregated programs in the region. Winning a Black college championship was not enough. Gaither needed to show recruits what many fans and sportswriters already knew: FAMU was the best program in the state of Florida and one of the best in the nation, regardless of race.[17]

THE WORLD'S FASTEST MAN

The end of the 1963 football season meant most of the sports attention focused on world-record-holder Bob Hayes's quest for a gold medal at the 1964 Tokyo Olympics. Hayes had arrived in Tallahassee with the goal "to be a professional football player and [to] better the conditions of [his] family."[18] After Hayes was redshirted during his first year of football in 1960, Pete Griffin, assistant football coach and track coach, persuaded Hayes to run track. Three years later, he was the fastest man in the world and favorite for Olympic gold. Hayes opened the track season by tying his world record time in the 100-yard sprint at the Orange Bowl Track and Field meeting in January. He was confident after his tremendous start to the track season, where he set indoor world records for the 60-yard and 70-yard sprint, that he could win three gold medals, in the 100, 200, and 4x100. By May, Hayes had run a record-tying 9.1-second 100-yard (91.44 meters) sprint for the fifth time in two years.[19]

Hayes's success on the track increased the responsibility for the quiet young man from Jacksonville. Not only did he need to defend his title as the world's fastest man, but he also carried the torch for HBCU men's track and field. From Eddie Tolan to Jesse Owens to Mal Whitfield, African

Pete Griffin and Bob Hayes at a track meet at the University of Miami
after Hayes tied the world record, 1962. (AP Photo/Joe Migon)

American men's track and field Olympians overwhelmingly hailed from PWIs. Before Bob Hayes's emergence before the 1964 Olympics, only Lee Calhoun (North Carolina Central), in the 100-meter hurdles, and Ralph Boston (TSU), in the long jump, had represented the United States and HBCUs. (Morgan State's George Rhoden won a gold medal in the 400 meter for Jamaica in the 1952 Olympics.) The lack of success by HBCU trackmen stood in contradistinction to African American women. Tuskegee's Alice Coachman was the first African American woman to win a gold medal at the 1948 Olympics, in the high jump. TSU's track coach Ed Temple sent seven women to the Olympics, including Barbara Jones, Wilma Rudolph, and Willye White. No HBCU men's program had success equal to that of the TSU Tigerbelles' track program. Bob Hayes, Ralph Boston, and Grambling's Richard Stebbins represented HBCUs men's track and field heading into the 1964 Olympics.[20]

In late June, a week before the U.S. Olympic trials, Hayes pulled his hamstring. The injury caused him to miss the first trials in July, jeopardizing his chances of going to Tokyo. Hayes needed a waiver from the national coach to run in the second trial in September in Los Angeles. Yale University's Bob Giegengack was the head U.S. track coach, and Morgan State University's Eddie Hurt was the top assistant. Hurt was also good friends with Gaither, and he reassured Hayes, "Don't worry; you're going to L.A." At the second Olympic trial in Los Angeles, Hayes won the final heat in the 100-yard sprint, ensuring his place on the team for the games in Tokyo in October.[21]

In late July, tragedy befell the FAMU athletic community when Willie Galimore and Bo Farrington, teammates with the Chicago Bears, died in a car accident driving to preseason training camp in Indiana. After a day of relaxation and golf at a nearby country club, Galimore and Farrington watched the U.S. track team face off against the USSR on television. They had hoped to see Bob Hayes run. Disappointed that Hayes had yet to recover from his torn hamstring, the two HBCU graduates—Farrington played for Billy Nicks at Prairie View—hopped into Galimore's new Volkswagen convertible and sped back to training camp, trying to beat the 11:00 P.M. curfew. Missing a warning sign, the car took an L-shaped curve too fast, skidded, and then flipped into a ditch. Both players were thrown from the vehicle and pronounced dead upon arrival at the local hospital. Bears head coach called the accident "the saddest day in Bears history." At Galimore's funeral service on FAMU's campus, Gaither eulogized the fallen Rattler as "the finest athlete I had ever coached." Several thousand students, faculty, and alumni somberly passed through Lee Hall to pay their respects.[22]

The excitement of Hayes's chance at an Olympic gold medal and the sadness of Galimore's untimely death set an anxious mood as another football season began. Although the Rattlers had won their eleventh consecutive SIAC football title in 1963, football observers wondered if FAMU could return to the top of the polls. Heading into his twentieth season, Gaither was confident, believing that he had the "potential of a great team." He had to replace an All-American quarterback, Jim Tullis, and Bob Hayes would not be available to play until after the Olympics. Despite these key losses, the goal was still the same: a small college national championship.[23]

FAMU opened the 1964 season with three straight victories. The Rattlers' defense led the way, unlike previous seasons. With Hayes at the Olympics until late October, FAMU's offense averaged only 28 points per game, declining from the beginning of the decade, when the team averaged more than 50 points per game for the entire season. The opening wins served as a prelude to the rivalry game against John Merritt's TSU Tigers. Both coaches knew that any chance for a national title required a win over the other.

The hotly contested game confirmed a new coaching rivalry. The Rattlers had lost two consecutive games to Merritt-coached teams, making the TSU coach the only one with a winning record against Gaither. Ric Roberts believed that TSU "poses a real threat to the Gaither legend."[24] The centerpiece of the Tigers' prospects was freshmen quarterback Eldridge Dickey, who earned the nickname "The Lord's Prayer" because he always delivered.[25] The FAMU game was the young quarterback's first real test. The Rattlers jumped out to a 15 to 0 lead at halftime. Dickey led the Tigers to two touchdowns in the third quarter. FAMU added a score in the fourth quarter, taking a 22 to 14 lead. After Dickey orchestrated a 74-yard drive, he ran the ball into the end zone for a touchdown, cutting the lead 22 to 20. The FAMU defense stopped the tying 2-point conversion.[26] The Rattlers had the ball and needed to run out the clock to secure the victory, but chaos ensued during the game's final minutes. The Rattlers had the ball deep in their end of the field, and John Eason prepared to punt. As he received the snap, several TSU players broke through the blockers, and it appeared that the Tigers were going to block the kick. Eason improvised and threw a pass to a teammate, who snared the ball centimeters from the turf and ran for a first down. The officials changed their minds at least three times on whether it was a completed pass and a first down, an incomplete pass and TSU's football, or a penalty and rekick. The officials took nearly ten minutes to make a decision, while both teams' coaches and players paced anxiously on the margins of the field. In the end, the officials ruled there was a penalty on the play; FAMU rekicked and held on for the 22 to 20 victory. After the game, Merritt declared that the officials "blew" the call and even accused Gaither of making the officials change the call. While Merritt lambasted the officials and Gaither, the FAMU mentor praised both teams for spirited play and their sportsmanship, describing the game as "one of the best I've seen in a long while." This would be FAMU's only win over a Dickey-led TSU team. The controversial win, however, kept the Rattlers in the hunt for a national title.[27]

Hours after the game ended, millions of Americas gathered around their television sets and watched the closing ceremonies of the 1964 Tokyo Olympics. Nine days earlier, Hayes had coiled into the lane 1 starting block for the 100-meter sprint final. In the quiet moments before the starting gun, Hayes feared the ridicule that came with losing, remembered the efforts that FAMU track coaches Pete Griffin and Dick Hill poured into him, honored Willie Galimore's legacy, and prayed for his best performance. Hayes won by 7 feet, tying the world record and setting a new Olympic record with his 10.0-second race. Tokyo celebrated Hayes as the "World's Fastest Human." After Hayes dined with friends and family, he returned to his room to find a congratulatory telegram from Gaither.[28]

Six days later, Hayes ran the anchor leg as a member of the 4x100 relay team. Injuries to key members put a gold medal in doubt. Still, the team improved each round. In the semifinals they ran an Olympic-record-tying 39.5-second heat, edging out France and Jamaica. In the moments before the relay finals, Hayes gathered the sprinters — Gerry Ashworth, Paul Drayton, and Richard Stebbins — and led them in a prayer he learned from his high school coach and FAMU alumni Earl Kitchings. "God, let us so shine as the golden sun. Give us the necessary endurance to run, give us the speed that we may need, so that we may our opponents exceed." The race was close throughout. When Stebbins handed Hayes the baton for the anchor leg, the Americans were trailing France, Poland, Russia, and Jamaica. Hayes exploded down the backstretch, passing "guys like they were standing still." When he crossed the tape first, he threw the baton high into the air. The U.S. relay team set a new world record with a 39.0-second race. Coaches and experts estimated that Hayes ran the final 100 meters of the relay in 8.6 seconds. Hayes was an Olympic hero.[29]

Hayes returned to the football field an Olympic champion. At FAMU's

Golden Triangle Football Classic in Tampa, Hayes rode in the parade, met the mayor, and received the key to the city. He also helped the Rattlers rout Benedict College 54 to 6.[30] The following week at FAMU's homecoming, Hayes and running back Bobby Felts led the Rattlers to a 46 to 24 comeback win over North Carolina A&T. With Hayes missing the first month of the season, Felts emerged as FAMU's star running back, and against the Aggies, he showed his worth by scoring four touchdowns.[31] Hayes's return to the gridiron rankled the emerging star, but the duo also put FAMU atop the rankings. Another title would be secured if the Rattlers could exorcise their demons in Baton Rouge. But yet again, Southern University ended FAMU's perfect season with a 45 to 20 upset win.[32]

Although FAMU bounced back to defeat Bethune-Cookman and Texas Southern, the Rattlers' only chance at earning a title was by winning the OBC. The natural choice was the defending champions: the Prairie View Panthers. However, the NCAA had banned the Panthers from any bowl game for their participation in the NAIA playoffs the previous season. One reporter noted that Prairie View's probation was a product of the "bitter rivalry going on between" the NCAA and the NAIA "for Negro athletic teams." The NCAA's action was surprising, given its failure to include Black college football teams in any of its sanctioned bowls.[33] Nonetheless, Prairie View's suspension from postseason exhibition games forced Gaither to find another opponent for the thirty-second OBC. The lack of a postseason game meant the Panthers won a national title because of their undefeated regular season.[34] Once more, the Rattlers were denied a title.

In place of the Panthers, FAMU officials picked Eddie Robinson's Grambling Tigers. The Tigers finished the season with 8 wins and 1 loss to Prairie View. Although the game was played on the field, the two coaches were center stage. Ric Roberts summarized the thoughts of many: "The game boils down to a consolation duel between two coaching geniuses."[35] Robinson won the last meeting between the two teams in 1955, and this year Grambling entered the game as one-touchdown favorites. On a rainy Miami evening, the Rattlers routed the Tigers. FAMU turned a slim 14 to 7 halftime lead into a track meet, winning 42 to 15. Senior running back Bobby Felts scored two touchdowns on his way to MVP honors. Bob Hayes caught a 47-yard touchdown pass, proving Grambling's massive defensive linemen were no match for FAMU's speed.[36] Still, the dominating victory was not enough for FAMU to claim a share of the national title.

Although FAMU's Bobby Felts had been a first-team All-American and the team's leading rusher and scorer, Bob Hayes continued to dominate

John Huarte (*second from left*) of Notre Dame and Bobby Hayes (*second from right*) of FAMU were named Most Valuable Players of the North–South Shrine charity game in Miami, December 25, 1964. They are pictured with Shrine Imperial Potentate P. Carlyle Brock (*left*) of Chicago and Potentate Malcolm McAllister (*right*) of Miami. (AP Photo/ Harold Valentine)

the headlines. Felts and Hayes followed in Bob Paremore's footsteps and played in an integrated postseason all-star game. The HBCU stars played for the South team at the Senior Bowl.[37] Hayes had an opportunity to impress his future professional coach, the Dallas Cowboys' Tom Landry. The Cowboys had drafted Hayes as a future pick in the seventh round of the 1963 draft (held in December 1962) and signed a three-year $100,000 contract after the OBC.[38] The North coaches focused on stopping Hayes. "We know [Joe] Namath and Steve Tensi are outstanding passers," said the North team and Detroit Lions head coach George Wilson, "but Hayes worries us most. Hayes has so much speed that he can wreck you in a split second."[39] Wilson's predictions came true, as Namath connected with Hayes for a 53-yard touchdown pass in the fourth quarter to secure a tie in the sixteenth Senior Bowl. Landry was pleased with his new signee and eagerly awaited unleashing his speed on the NFL.[40]

The Cowboys' signing of Hayes was emblematic of the larger trend: professional teams were beginning to draft and sign Black college players. Before 1960, former FAMU star Willie Galimore, playing for the Chicago Bears, was among the NFL's top African American players. He and the New York Giants' Roosevelt Brown, a Morgan State alumnus, were the leading players from HBCUs. In this era, teams often acquired HBCU talent by luck. For instance, the New York Giants decided to draft Hall of Fame offensive lineman Roosevelt Brown in the twenty-seventh round of the 1953 draft because team officials saw a copy of the *Pittsburgh Courier* All-American team.[41]

Professional football opportunities were limited for all players, since there were only ten teams, but chances were exceptionally rare for players from HBCUs. In 1959, there were only fifty Black players in the entire NFL, and the Washington Redskins were still all-white. Only ten of the fifty Black players were products of HBCUs, with FAMU producing three — Galimore, Herm Lee, and Willie McClung.[42]

The 1960 season, however, presented new opportunities in pro football, as the AFL began to play. After the NFL rebuffed his attempt to purchase a franchise, Lamar Hunt, son of millionaire oilman H. L. Hunt, organized other men spurned by the NFL to start a competing league. The NFL reversed course and added two new teams in AFL cities — Dallas and Minneapolis — in an attempt to snuff out the new league before it even started. The Minneapolis franchise ownership group switched from the AFL to the NFL before ever playing a game.[43] Heading into the 1960 season, there were ten new professional football teams, meaning that there were more than 350 new jobs. The number of African American players in the NFL increased to fifty-seven. In addition, another forty-six African American players joined teams in the AFL. The number of players from HBCUs went from ten to twenty-nine.[44] FAMU was still the leader in putting players in the professional ranks.[45]

At the core of the nascent rivalry between the two leagues was the acquisition of talent. Both leagues held collegiate player drafts, with college stars being drafted in both leagues. Professional scouts, however, had to look beyond major colleges to find the best players. Many of those athletes were often found between the lines of the OBC. As Marion E. Jackson wrote, "Many pigskin scouts representing warring tribes annually converge on the Orange Blossom Classic with ink-loaded pens instead of

Hayes signs a professional football contract with the Dallas Cowboys as Jake Gaither and Tex Schramm look on, December 1964. (AP Photo/Harold Waters)

primitive tomahawks."[46] While FAMU had led HBCUs in producing professional players, Jackson noted that more than twenty-five professionals had played in the OBC.[47] Seven members of FAMU's 1961 championship team signed professional contracts, led by All-American center Curtis Miranda.[48] The professional accomplishments of former FAMU and other HBCU players reflected the quality toiling behind the veil of segregation. Slowly mainstream football was becoming aware of the secret HBCUs' athletic hush harbors.

Gaither was also a source of information about Black college players. For instance, Sid Gilman attended FAMU's 1954 coaching clinic, and the following season he was named head coach of the Los Angeles Rams. Gaither supplied scouting reports of players in the SIAC.[49] *Cleveland Call and Post* sports columnist Sheep Jackson described Gaither's role for readers: "Did you know that one of the greenest pastures for the recruiting of Negro professional football talent is at Florida A&M?" He continued, "Hardly a day goes by during the football season when Coach Gaither isn't playing host to pro scouts from the National and American Football Leagues. . . . Both the NFL and AFL are chuck full of Negro gridders from Negro Colleges proving that their coaching is so good and the pro scouts are satisfied in what they see each football season in the Negro colleges on the gridiron."[50]

In addition to relying on coaches for information, the NFL and AFL battle led to an expansion of scouting. By the mid-1960s, professional teams spent more than $100,000 on player scouting, including hiring African American scouts.[51] When former University of Illinois All-American Buddy Young retired from pro football in 1956, the Baltimore Colts hired their former player as a scout and as an assistant director of public relations.[52] Several years later, Emlen Tunnell, an All-Pro defensive back for the New York Giants and the Green Bay Packers, the first African American professional assistant coach, and the first to be inducted into the Pro Football Hall of Fame, became a scout for the Giants and the Packers. Young and Tunnell were primarily responsible for scouting Black colleges in the South.[53] African American scouts helped the teams find HBCU stars. Teams that employed African American scouts had better information than those that did not. Tunnell did not discuss the Black college prospects with the press because he felt "he [had] an edge . . . because the players are unpublicized and unknown."[54]

Hidden diamonds at Black colleges become known commodities over the course of the 1960s.[55] In the 1963 draft, the AFL's Kansas City Chiefs (then the Dallas Texans) drafted Grambling's Buck Buchanan first overall.[56] The following year, NFL teams drafted twenty-three players from Black colleges, including FAMU's Al Denson. The AFL drafted many of the same players, leading to teams from the competing leagues using the African American scouts to get players to sign.

The 1965 draft (held in November 1964) was the climax of the competition between the two leagues over players. Teams from both leagues coveted college stars such as Alabama's Joe Namath, FSU's Fred Biletnikoff, Illinois's Dick Butkus, and Kansas's Gale Sayers. Joe Namath spurned the NFL's St. Louis Cardinals to sign with the AFL's New York Jets for a record $427,000 contract. Biletnikoff chose the AFL's Oakland Raiders over the NFL's Detroit Lions. The NFL signed key players in the draft as well. The NFL's Chicago Bears signed Dick Butkus over the AFL's Denver Broncos. Buddy Young, an NFL executive in 1965, helped the Bears outmaneuver the

Kansas City Chiefs for Gale Sayers's signature by telling the running back that the NFL offered better opportunities for Black players.[57] After missing out on Sayers, the Chiefs needed to sign Prairie View's star wide receiver Otis Taylor, whom the team drafted in the fourth round. Lloyd Wells, a former Prairie View star and sportswriter for the *Houston Informer*, had already persuaded Taylor to sign with the Chiefs before the draft. Wells had befriended Taylor's family through his coverage of the star athlete since junior high school, and the reporter had convinced Taylor to attend Prairie View, his alma mater. In the early 1960s, the Chiefs hired Wells as a part-time scout. Wells's relationship with Taylor and his savvy helped Kansas City sign Taylor. The Philadelphia Eagles had also selected Taylor in the fifteenth round, and the NFL had invited Taylor and other draftees to a regional party in Dallas, as a ploy to keep promising players from signing with AFL teams. Wells tracked Taylor down at a suburban Dallas hotel and ferreted Taylor and a Prairie View teammate, Seth Cartwright, through a hotel window in the in middle of the night. Wells took the two prospects to the Fort Worth airport, where they caught the first plane to Kansas City. The following year, the Kansas City Chiefs hired Wells as the first full-time African American scout in the AFL. Wells's antics marked the height of the league war over prospects.[58]

Although the influx of Black players in professional football showcased increasing desegregation, it also revealed additional layers of discrimination. With more than 100 Black players in both leagues, positional limitations became readily apparent. The most glaring absence was the lack of African American quarterbacks. Talented black quarterbacks were often switched to other positions or cut from teams. After Prairie View had won its second consecutive Black college title in 1965 and the *Pittsburgh Courier* named head coach Billy Nicks coach of the year, Nicks used his acceptance speech to castigate professional football for the lack of Black quarterbacks. With Pittsburgh Steelers coach Buddy Parker sitting in the audience, Nicks declared that African Americans "have a long way to go" to be equal in football. He added, "While we are accepted in most phases of pro football, there are still positions closed to us." He pointed out that the Detroit Lions had signed his quarterback Jim Kearney but planned to make him a running back. "Here is a youngster," Nicks lamented, "who has never taken a handoff in his life. The kid can run and he can throw. He's always been a quarterback. Now they talk about making him running back. It doesn't make sense." He ended by asking, "When will the time arrive for them [professional football teams] to give kids like Kearney an opportunity to show what they can do?" In the mid-1960s, neither the NFL nor the AFL was ready for Black quarterbacks.[59] Kearney exemplified the lack of opportunities for Black quarterbacks but also the kind of talent at Black colleges. The former Prairie View signal caller played twelve years in the NFL as a defensive back, which included a Super Bowl IV championship with the Kansas City Chiefs alongside Emmitt Thomas (Bishop College), Goldie Sellers (Grambling), Willie Mitchell (TSU), Caesar Belser (Arkansas Pine Bluff), Frank Pitts (Southern), Gloster Richardson (Jackson State), Jim Marsalis (TSU), Robert Holmes (Southern), Willie Lanier (Morgan State), Morris Stroud (Clark Atlanta), Buck Buchanan (Grambling), and Otis Taylor (Prairie View). No team relied on more talent from HBCUs than the Chiefs.

The two professional football leagues also fueled the athletic and metropolitan ambitions of emerging cities, especially in the South. Officials in Atlanta, Houston, Miami, and New Orleans all tried to lure professional baseball or football franchises to their city. After a successful 1964 season that established the AFL as a legitimate pro league, it planned to hold its all-star game in New Orleans. The league received assurances from the organizers that African American players would not face any discrimination. When the twenty African Americans players arrived on Bourbon Street, they faced discrimination from taxicab drivers and nightclub owners. "People shouted insults and doors were shut in our faces," said San Diego Charger Dick Westmoreland. Frustrated by their treatment and inspired by civil rights protests nationwide, the players, comprising 40 percent of the all-stars, threatened a boycott. Eight of the African American players were alumni of Black colleges, including Ernie Warlick, spokesperson for the group. AFL commissioner Joe Foss quickly moved the game to Houston. While professional football provided more opportunities than most areas of professional life, the lack of African American quarterbacks and the discrimination in New Orleans reminded many that sports were not a perfect model of race relations.[60]

Many of the players from the golden age of Black college football reaped accolades at the professional level. Bob Hayes's speed made him an immediate star in the NFL. He made the Pro Bowl his rookie season, catching 46 passes for 1,003 yards and twelve touchdowns. Hayes finished fourth in receiving yards and first in receiving touchdowns. Moreover, he symbolized the talent at HBCUs. Professional football's expansion provided new opportunities for Black college players. Notably, there were no players from FAMU on the AFL all-star team. Through the 1950s, FAMU was the leading producer of professional football players. But by the mid-1960s, the Rattlers had fallen behind Grambling State University. The decline in professional players was a testament to Eddie Robinson's acumen at Grambling but also signaled that FAMU was sliding just as desegregation in the South was gaining momentum.[61]

7
DESEGREGATION, DECLINE, AND BLACK POWER

The 1964 season marked Gaither's eleventh 1-loss season in twenty years. He had the highest winning percentage of any active coach in America, Black or white. His former players roamed the sidelines as coaches at high schools across the state. Professional football coaches sought his opinion about HBCU prospects. And recent graduates were increasingly found on professional football rosters. FAMU's consistent and dominant success made its football program the epitome of Black athletic power, but as the Black Power movement made its impact on cultural life, Gaither grew uncomfortable.

The air of rebellion seemed to trouble Gaither most. Speaking to reporters after Tommie Smith and John Carlos protested at the 1968 Olympics, Gaither said, "Nationally and internationally, the trend today is for youth to rebel. The young are dissatisfied with the way the old have handled things." For Gaither, "patience and understanding are necessary on the part of both races to rectify racial problems." Gaither never invoked Blackness, preferring to use the word "Negro." "I am an American and I will support my county," he said. "I enjoy the privileges of being an American," he added.[1]

For some, Gaither's reaction to Black Power solidified the notion that he was an "Uncle Tom." By the late 1960s, young African Americans hurled this charge at the NAACP leadership, HBCU administrators, and nearly any African American who counseled patience and understanding over immediate change. Ironically, Black Powerites, much as they called for Black-controlled institutions, rarely invoked dominant Black college athletic programs like FAMU's, Grambling's, or TSU's as examples of Black Power. This contradiction was not lost on Gaither as he experienced the decline of his program in the wake of desegregation. FAMU struggled on the field just as Southern PWIs found religion and began to recruit African American players. The trickle of Black athletes to white campuses started by Maryland in 1963 turned into a deluge by 1968, as the SEC, led by the University of Kentucky, desegregated the gridiron and weakened HBCUs in the process.

THE RATTLERS' STRUGGLES OF 1965 AND 1966

After two decades of dominance, there were signs that FAMU's gridiron supremacy was beginning to fade. The Rattlers' offensive production had declined by nearly 20 points per game since the 1960 season. It seemed that opponents had deciphered FAMU's split-line T offense. The graduation of running backs Bob Hayes and Bob Felts and the declining production led Gaither to change his offense for the first time in a decade.[2] Beginning in 1965, he added more pro-style plays to his split-line T formation, which reduced the number of running backs from three to two and spread the flanker or end further from the formation. "We feel that we can spring our fast backs better with the pro-type offense," Gaither reasoned. This change was also a nod to the growing influence of professional football on the college game. Gaither wanted to put his players in a position to succeed at the next level. With only three returning starters, Gaither scrapped plans for the Blood, Sweat, and Tears substitution packages, hoping for "two strong units."[3] After finishing in the top ten for two decades, Gaither knew any changes to his offense were risky.[4] Heading into the season, it was unclear if these changes would stop the offense's decline in scoring.

Gaither's changes to his offensive system did not reverse his declining offensive numbers as he had hoped, but FAMU continued to win. In defeating Allen, South Carolina State, Alabama A&M, and Morris Brown, the Rattlers averaged 24 points per game. After FAMU's early wins, the Rattlers faced the heart of their schedule with games against TSU, North Carolina A&T, and Southern. The midseason showdown between FAMU and TSU was defining for both teams. Gaither needed to know whether his offensive changes would be effective against a quality opponent. John Merritt, who had told reporters and alumni he would produce a national championship by 1965, understood that title winners typically had to beat the Rattlers.[5]

Coach John Merritt, quarterback Eldridge Dickey, and the TSU Tigers ended the Rattlers' 1965 title aspirations. The Tigers routed FAMU 45 to 6. It was Gaither's worst lost since 1954. "We just got the hell beat out of us," fumed Gaither after the game. The Rattlers' vaunted rushing attack was held to negative 7 yards. While the TSU defense had been tremendous, Dickey was the star, throwing for 205 yards and two touchdowns.[6]

The Rattlers recovered to beat the Aggies 28 to 14, and in front of a raucous home crowd, they defeated Southern 41 to 38.

With only 2 games left before the OBC, Gaither believed his team had worked itself back into title contention. OBC officials picked the undefeated Morgan State Bears, now coached by Earl Banks, as FAMU's opponent. But before Gaither's squad took on the Bears, Texas Southern upset the Rattlers 34 to 21 in the Jacksonville Classic.[7] The following week, Morgan State thumped FAMU 36 to 7 in front of an unusually small crowd of slightly more than 35,000. It was Gaither's first 3-loss season since his second season in 1946. The subpar season was such uncharted territory that the athletic department sent a press release to sports reporters apologizing for "their worst season in years."[8]

At age sixty-two, Gaither was the last coach of his generation. The winter and spring of 1966 saw several legends of Black college coaching retire or pass away. In January, Prairie View's Billy Nicks ended his thirty-six-year coaching career, which included twenty as the Panthers' head coach.[9] Kentucky State's Sam Taylor and Wiley's Fred Long passed away in April 1966.[10] As FAMU prepared for spring practice, Gaither was one of three active head coaches, including Eddie Robinson and John Merritt, who had won a Black college title. He was also the oldest. With losses to young coaches like Merritt and Banks piling up, questions remained whether FAMU's 3-loss 1965 season was an abnormality or the beginning of a trend.[11]

For the first time in nearly two decades, Gaither's Rattlers were not among the best teams in Black college football. The coaching staff needed to improve a pass defense that surrendered more than 1,500 yards passing and thirteen touchdowns. "We were definitely weak on pass defense," Gaither admitted. He also told reporters that FAMU intended to improve on its below-average 44 percent pass-completion rate.[12] Fewer high-quality players, especially at key positions such as quarterback and the offensive line, limited the team's plans. The coaching staff again abandoned the Blood, Sweat, and Tears units because of the lack of personnel. "We are definitely committed to a two-unit stem of offense and defense," said Gaither.[13]

The 1966 season was similar to the previous one. The Rattler offense failed to produce as it had in years past. In the second game of the season, South Carolina State upset FAMU 8 to 3. It was FAMU's first loss in the SIAC since 1952, ending its 56-game conference-winning streak. It was also the first game since a 0 to 0 tie against Southern in 1950 that FAMU had been held without a touchdown. Three weeks later, TSU went to Tallahassee and shut out the Rattlers 29 to 0. It was Gaither's first home loss in fifteen years. The score could have been much worse, as the Tigers had five touchdowns nullified because of penalties and Dickey threw five interceptions.[14] The Rattlers' third loss of the season came after they blew a 13 to 0 halftime lead to Southern University, losing 17 to 13. Again the offense was inept. The Jaguars held the Rattlers to 65 yards of offense. Even FAMU's famed band, the Marching 100, were blown off the field, according to one report.[15] The Rattlers finished the regular season with more pass attempts than rushing attempts.[16] The golden age of the split-line T was over.

Consecutive 3-loss seasons had the *Pittsburgh Courier*'s Bill Nunn Jr. asking if "the Rattlers are beginning to go downhill as a football power." Gaither quickly retorted, "Definitely not. We are doing nothing now that we haven't been doing in the past." Unanswered in his response was whether the old methods could work in the changing environs of college football. Moreover, rumors abounded that Gaither could no longer keep top athletes academically eligible, as the administration had passed more stringent academic requirements. Gaither declared that he had no problems with the administration. "Sure our kids must get their books. But that is the way it's supposed to be." Gaither told Nunn that, despite his age, he was "a long way from being through."[17]

The Rattlers routed Alabama A&M 43 to 26 in the thirty-fourth OBC to salvage part of the season.[18] The victory over a previously undefeated Alabama A&M quieted some of the questions surrounding Gaither's program. For the first time, the game was nationally televised, but the increased media coverage obscured a low turnout. The attendance for the game was approximately 26,000, a sharp decline from the regular 40,000-plus the game regularly drew. Questions remained: Was this an outlier because of the Rattlers' poor season, or had the classic "reached its peak at the turnstiles?"[19] Consecutive subpar seasons raised concerns about how much longer Gaither could or should lead the Rattlers. Added to the doubts of the alumni, fans, and sportswriters about the future of the FAMU program was the fact that the white colleges in Florida had yet to integrate athletics.

DESEGREGATION OF FOOTBALL IN FLORIDA'S COLLEGES

For some, FAMU's two-year absence from title contention reflected a reduction in talent on the field. It seemed that by the mid-1960s, some of the state's best African American players did not arrive in Tallahassee. In his interview with Bill Nunn Jr. before the 1966 OBC, Gaither admitted that "recruiting [was] becoming more difficult." No longer was FAMU the "first choice" for Florida's African American athletes. Gaither added, "Not only are the big white universities grabbing Negro youngsters in the state, other Negro schools are invading the area. It makes the job of recruiting a lot tougher."[20]

Given the Rattlers' inconsistent quarterback play in 1965 and 1966, the loss of a pair of star high school players to colleges in Ohio stood out. Miami's Carroll Williams was a star quarterback at Xavier University in Ohio. During his career (1964 to 1966) at the Catholic school in Cincinnati, Williams threw for 4,000 yards and thirty-three touchdowns.[21] In 1968, he was the only Black quarterback in professional football, playing for the Montreal Alouettes in the Canadian Football League.[22] In 1966, another star African American quarterback headed to Ohio. St. Petersburg's Steve Jones chose to play football for the University of Toledo Rockets. Although Jones's tenure was not as prolific as Williams's, the Rockets star passed for nearly 1,200 yards his junior season.[23] Sportswriters asked how Gaither had missed the two prep stars. The answer was a troubling sign for the future of FAMU football specifically and Black college football generally, as it pointed to the waning effectiveness of a key part of the sporting congregation—the connections between Black high schools and HBCUs. Williams had desegregated high school athletics in Miami–Dade County, as the first African American student at Archbishop Curley High School. Although Jones did not desegregate athletics in St. Petersburg, he was the only African American on the Dixie Hollis High School team, whose school mascot was a Confederate Rebel. Thus, Jones earned high school accolades with a Confederated flag affixed to his uniform. Moreover, his high school coach's friendship with Toledo's head coach, Frank Lauterbur, led Jones to play for the Rockets. Not being able to recruit two talented players to FAMU occasionally happened, but the fact that these two players had attended desegregated high schools suggested that larger recruiting problems lay in the future. Williams's and Jones' decisions not to attend FAMU reflected the crumbling of the sporting congregation that Gaither had built. The two prep stars were among the first cracks in Gaither's recruiting pipeline. These cracks turned into a blowout when the state's white colleges decided to recruit Black players.[24]

The University of Miami increased the stakes for the Rattlers when the Hurricanes announced that they had signed their first African American player, Ray Bellamy, in December 1966. Unlike Williams and Jones, Ray Bellamy was a part of the FAMU sporting congregation. Bellamy attended a still-segregated Lincoln High School in Palmetto, Florida (north of Sarasota). His coach was the diminutive Eddie Shannon, the Rattlers' first trainer. Still, Bellamy chose to be a racial pioneer at Miami.[25] The slow march of desegregation had established a beachhead in Miami. The signing of Bellamy did not spur UF or FSU to sign African American players. Florida's head coach Ray Graves, who had affixed Confederate battle flags to the Gators' helmets and uniforms in the 1962 Gator Bowl, told Bellamy that UF would not recruit Black players.[26] The remaining segregated colleges in the state would soon follow the Hurricanes' lead and desegregate their athletic rosters. Integrated athletics would affect HBCUs similarly, as it presented Black college athletic programs with similar competitive disadvantages.

UF's reluctance to desegregate would not last long, as teams in the SEC slowly desegregated their rosters. When the University of Kentucky announced that it had signed two African American players in 1966, desegregation had arrived in the SEC. The SEC's legacy of competition, which had stimulated massive stadium building after World War I and led to the creation of athletic scholarships in the 1930s, would eventually include the recruitment of Black athletes. It also appeared that the voters in the final AP poll for the 1966 season had punished an undefeated and all-white University of Alabama football team by ranking the Crimson Tide third behind once-tied integrated teams, the University of Notre Dame and Michigan State University. The surprising poll results prodded SEC teams to recruit Black players.[27] SEC commissioner A. M. Coleman stated, "There's no longer any ban, written or unwritten on Negro athletes."[28] Despite the claim, most of the conference teams were still all-white. The continued lack of African American players was blamed on subpar high school education. Coleman added, "Many schools have expressed keen interest in recruiting Negroes. But, too often, when they find one they are interested in, he is unable to pass the entrance requirements." The ostensibly nonracial explanation for the continuation of all-white teams in the SEC belied the use of testing as a way to evade court-mandated desegregation by schools in the Deep South.[29] Most objective observers recognized that the academic excuse was "lame."[30] Despite the claims of inferior academics as a means to avoid desegregation, the UF and FSU athletic departments agreed on a set of enhanced academic standards that stalled desegregation. Florida assistant coach Hobe Hooser wrote to head coach Ray Graves explaining, "I had prospect questionnaires completed by Negro players in white schools but in all cases they could not meet our scholastic requirement or football ability requirement."[31]

Delays in desegregation were also caused by a search for the "right" player who met the academic requirements and a player who had experience in a desegregated school. Looking for a Jackie Robinson type was, in essence, a delaying tactic, since only sixteen of sixty-seven school districts were desegregated. In other words, only 1.5 percent of Black students in all grade levels attended schools with whites at the end of the 1963–64 school year.[32] The number grew to forty-eight school districts by the 1965–66 school year, setting the stage for UF and FSU to begin to desegregate their football teams.[33] UF began trying to find African American players who played desegregated prep football after the 1967 season. The Gators signed Leonard George, who had attended desegregated Tampa Jesuit High School, and Willie Jackson, who attended desegregated Sarasota High School and Valley Forge Military Academy in 1968.

Added to FAMU's athletic headaches were FSU's growing athletic aspirations. After changing from a women's college to a coeducational institution in 1946, FSU quickly increased its football competition. Against opposition from UF, FSU developed an athletic tradition from scratch. The school started football in 1947. Initially playing schools like Randolph Macon and Sewanee, the Seminoles regularly played top teams in the 1950s, including the University of Georgia in 1955. The state's racetrack allocation pushed FSU to begin offering scholarships and fueled the school's athletic ambitions. As FSU president Doak Campbell noted, "While the scholarships to be awarded from such funds were not designated in the act for any particular purpose, it was generally understood and intended that they were to be used for the assistance of outstanding athletes."[34] FSU also built a 15,000-seat stadium in 1950. FSU coaches and supporters sought regular competition against UF. The initial game between FSU and UF required the intervention of the state legislature, which ensured an annual rivalry game beginning in 1959.[35]

FSU signed its first Black player, Calvin Patterson, in 1968. However, he never played a down for the Seminoles, struggling with injuries and academic troubles. Ashamed of his academic failings, he told friends and family that he would not play in the 1972 season. He concocted a story of being shot during a robbery. Tragically, he accidentally killed himself attempting to provide evidence of the theft.[36] While Patterson struggled to adjust to Tallahassee, the Seminoles second Black player, James Thomas, excelled. Thomas, one of four players signed in 1969, was the first African American to play football for FSU, the school's first Black All-American, and a first-round draft pick of the Pittsburgh Steelers, eventually winning four Super Bowls. FSU's basketball program also aggressively pursued Black players. While the 1967–68 NCAA tournament team had no Black players, the following year coach Hugh Durham added four.[37]

While desegregation provided new opportunities for these players, PWIs had little to no congregation to support Black athletes. Thomas recalls the racism he and his teammates faced from the white students, faculty, and even the coaching staff. For instance, FSU psychology professor Kent Miller wrote in a university-sponsored book, "To the extent that the Negro has to respond to the demands of a white middle-class environment, on the *average* he is less well equipped to meet these demands than is the white."[38] On the other hand, FAMU students refused to welcome Patterson, Thomas, and their Black teammates, seeing Patterson and Thomas not as racial pioneers but as a confrontation to the Rattlers' athletic excellence. Thomas's college experience and Patterson's death were extreme examples of the nonexistent sporting congregation at predominately white colleges.[39]

FSU's failure to nurture Patterson through a difficult time stood in contradistinction to the FAMU sporting congregation. When Bob Hayes was a freshman biding his time on the scout team on the practice field known as the "pit," he was falsely arrested after a teammate, James Vickers, robbed a fellow student. Hayes's father and coach Kitchens believed that the young speedster had nothing to do with the robbery, and each appealed to the Rattlers' head coach. Gaither investigated the incident and decided to help Hayes get released after a week in jail. While in jail, Hayes, who had yet to speak to a lawyer, parent, or school official, signed a confession with the hopes of getting out of jail. Gaither paid for a Hayes's lawyer and pleaded with the judge for leniency. "If you give me this boy for four years," Gaither swore, "I guarantee you he won't get in trouble and he'll make you proud of him." Hayes received ten years' probation instead of jail. At the time, Hayes was just a player on the team, not yet a world-record holder or a gold medalist, and Gaither used his influence to save Hayes's life. After Hayes became an Olympic champion, Gaither asked Governor Haydon Burns for a pardon, which the sprinter received in the summer of 1965. Gaither did this because Hayes was a member of the FAMU sporting congregation who had been wrongly accused.[40]

As previously all-white teams began to recruit African American athletes, Gaither and other Black college coaches promoted their sporting congregation as a valuable component of the college experience. Gaither told the press that players would "find a better social life and more satisfying comradeship." Gaither continued, "The entire faculty is interested in the welfare of the boy. He gets lots of personal attention, and we follow him all the way through life. . . . They can't get this kind of treatment at the white schools."[41] Morgan State's Earl Banks told reporters, "A kid wants to go to college where he can get a good education and have a good social outlet. We provide these things. Any youngster getting a scholarship to Morgan is more than an athlete, he is a student, too."[42] The appeal to the human resources rather than to the material resources reflected an understanding of the social dynamics on desegregated campuses.

Black coaches anticipated the turmoil that Black students faced on the recently desegregated campuses. Morgan State University's head coach Earl Banks was an All-American lineman at the University of Iowa in the 1940s and experienced racism on campus that belied his status as an athletic star. He watched his best friend and teammate transfer to another school because of discrimination.[43] In Tallahassee, FSU's Black Student Union declared, "The prevalent mood among blacks, struggling for dignified and productive existence on this campus, is *severe frustration!*"[44] Still, the eventual desegregation of collegiate sports in Florida and nationwide threatened to ruin Black colleges' recruiting pipelines, leaving the leading programs like FAMU, Morgan State, TSU, and Grambling without the talent to compete against white colleges.

One strategy was for Black colleges to recruit white players. The first white player in Black college football was Lincoln University's Ralph Oves, who was an All-American lineman in the early 1940s.[45] By the mid-1960s, there were a handful of white players on Black college teams. Schools in the Mid-Atlantic CIAA took the lead in desegregating their rosters.[46] When Morgan State arrived at the 1965 OBC, it had its first white player, who was "tickled pink" to be on a bowl team in his first year.[47] In 1968, FAMU and Grambling added their first white players. Eddie Robinson signed Jim Gregory (who later become the subject of the television movie *Grambling's White Tiger*).[48] In turn, Gaither recruited Rufus Brown, an offensive lineman from Stuart, Florida, just north of West Palm Beach. His recruitment suggested potential adjustments to FAMU's sporting congregation. Brown's high school had recently integrated, and his offensive line coach was Louis Rice, a former Rattler in the mid-1950s. Rice was "shocked" when Brown asked for help getting in at FAMU but agreed to contact Gaither on the student's behalf. Gaither's first response was "Can the boy play football for me?" The legendary coach understood the racial implications and did not want him to sit on the bench. Moreover, Brown's goal of becoming a physical education teacher and a coach meshed with FAMU's strengths.[49] Brown admitted to thinking "a lot about going to a Negro school," but it was his only scholarship offer. Brown added, "But I don't think it's going to bother me. When you're on the football field, everyone is the same. It doesn't matter what color you are."[50] FAMU used its proximity to FSU as a selling point, a recruiting strategy that FSU would employ in reverse for decades. Brown told reporters, "I know people at Florida State and that [being at FAMU] wouldn't affect my social life any."[51]

Brown's recruitment shows that despite the integration of high schools and the demotion of Black coaches, FAMU's sporting congregation still had considerable influence. By the end of preseason, FAMU's racial pioneer had earned the nickname "Rap Brown."[52] Despite these breakthroughs, few white players, outside of Oves, made a significant impact. The value of Black college football would not be determined through the adding of a few white players, but in direct competition with white teams.

THE CAMPAIGN TO PLAY A PREDOMINATELY WHITE TEAM

Gaither's consecutive 3-loss seasons came at the worst possible time for the program. The Rattlers' dominance of the 1950s and early 1960s waned during the opening years of the desegregation of Southern college athletic teams. The success of former HBCU players in the AFL and the NFL signaled that there was tremendous talent at Black colleges. Thirty-eight players from Black colleges had made All-Pro teams between 1963 and 1968, including two FAMU Rattlers (Bob Hayes and Al Denson). The accolades earned by former HBCU players at the pro level highlighted the ignored talent in the Black college ranks. The success of African Americans at the professional level and forced desegregation in high schools began to ease the fears of integration for many all-white college programs. As one college representative explained, "People get used to seeing Negro athletes at the professional and high school levels, then they don't give it a second thought when the colleges use them."[53] *Chicago Defender* sports columnist A. S. Doc Young concluded, "Sports [gets] the integration job done."[54] Sports integration came at the expense of the virtual monopoly that HBCUs had on African American talent. To stem the tide, Gaither and other HBCU coaches recognized the urgency to prove themselves against predominately white teams.

By the calculations of many Black college coaches, their programs needed to show potential recruits that HBCUs were still the best destination for college football players, socially and athletically, even after desegregation. HBCU coaches thus countered the implicit assumptions of the civil rights movement, namely, that Black institutions were inferior. The goal for coaches was twofold: win on the field against white programs and persuade recruits that the cultural advantages of HBCUs outweighed the material benefits of white programs. Coaches hoped that wins, cultural pride, and the success of HBCU football stars at the professional level would be enough to keep their programs competitive in the era of desegregation. These plans all hinged on getting to play and defeat white programs on the field.

State officials continued to obstruct FAMU's attempts to play white teams. Although Congress had passed of the Civil Rights Act in 1964 and schools were being desegregated across the state, Florida officials still stopped FAMU from playing a PWI school in either the OBC or the newly established NCAA regional championship. Legally, Gaither had the right to schedule games but still needed state approval. He had asked the State Board of Regents for permission to schedule Xavier University of Ohio, which had integrated its roster and featured Miami's Carroll Williams. Some in the state government supported Gaither's position. Florida secretary of state Tom Adams announced that FAMU's football team "should be allowed to play any school it wants to." He added, "Unless we give only lip service to desegregation there is no explanation for this decision."[55] Adams was strongly supported by Clifton G. Dyson, the first African American on the State Board of Regents. This support notwithstanding, the Board of Regents refused Gaither's request. The director of the regents, Broward Culpepper, explained the executive committee's decision to uphold the "unwritten policy" against FAMU playing a PWI team because it feared racial strife and that an interracial game might "detract from the 'wholesome' aura which should surround athletic events."[56]

The chance for HBCU teams to prove themselves as competitive equals had unexpected risks while spurring new opportunities. The NCAA had put Billy Nicks's team on probation in 1964, banning the Panthers from postseason games for one year for playing in the NAIA-sanctioned Camellia Bowl. The punishment seemed patently unfair, as the NCAA had done little to facilitate competition between HBCUs and PWIs. However, the penalty was tied to the NCAA's plan to limit the NAIA's appeal to small colleges, especially Black colleges. Shortly after Prairie View's punishment had been announced, the NCAA revealed its plans for a College Division. The NCAA's new division benefited Black college football teams seeking opportunities to compete against white teams. The NCAA plans got an additional boost when the primary financial sponsor of the NAIA's Camellia Bowl withdrew its support. The governing body quickly secured the rights in 1964 to the Sacramento-based exhibition game as part of a plan for four regional bowl games in the College Division—the Camellia Bowl for teams on the Pacific Coast; the Pecan Bowl, held in Abilene, Texas, for Midwest teams; the Grantland Rice Bowl, held in Murfreesboro, Tennessee, for Mideast teams; and the Tangerine Bowl, held in Orlando, Florida, for Atlantic Coast teams. With strong Black colleges in three of the four regions (there were no Black colleges in the Pacific Coast region), HBCUs now had competitive opportunities beyond conference titles or the array of postseason classics.

In 1964, the first year of the new NCAA College Division bowl games, no HBCU teams were selected, although the NCAA inquired about naming FAMU to the Tangerine Bowl.[57] Prairie View's probation and the NCAA's snub of HBCUs in its new regional bowl games left Black sportswriters suspicious of the "totalitarian" NCAA. As one report noted, "The NCAA officially 'froze' Prairie View back into the Negro race and, in 1964, indirectly punished the entire Negro collegiate membership."[58] The following season, however, two HBCUs made the regional bowl games. Grambling lost to North Dakota State 20 to 7 in the Pecan Bowl.[59] TSU tied Ball State 14 to 14 in the Grantland Rice Bowl.[60] The results were disappointing to HBCU fans and supporters. The following season, Morgan State was invited to the Tangerine Bowl, and TSU earned another bid to the Grantland Rice Bowl. This time the results were different. Morgan State, led on defense by All-American and future NFL Hall-of-Famer Willie Lanier, defeated West Chester State (Pa.) 14 to 6. *Baltimore Afro-American* sportswriter Sam Lacy understood the win as a "tremendous psychological victory."[61] TSU avenged the previous season's tie in the Grantland Rice Bowl by defeating Muskingum College (Ohio) 34 to 7. TSU's Eldridge Dickey accounted for all five touchdowns in the win.[62] The victories against white teams combined with the tremendous success that Black college players were having in professional football solidified the idea that Black colleges were among the best small college programs in the country.

Unfortunately for FAMU, by 1966 discussions about the best Black college program revolved around Earl Banks's Morgan State Bears and John Merritt's TSU Tigers, and just outside the top two programs were Eddie Robinson's Grambling State Tigers. Consecutive 3-loss seasons in 1965 and 1966 hindered FAMU's chances of earning a bowl bid. As the Rattlers were mired in an unprecedented slide under Gaither, Morgan State was amid an 18-game winning streak, and TSU had not lost in 24 games. In 1966, TSU finished second in the small college poll behind the Don Coryell–coached San Diego State Aztecs. Merritt further solidified TSU among the small college elite by scheduling a home-and-home series with San Diego State in 1967 and 1968.[63] These games were the first regular-season matchups between an HBCU and a PWI. Gaither watched as the upstart programs replaced his Rattlers for national accolades, in pioneering games against PWIs, and at the top of the Black college rankings.

In trying to return FAMU to the Black college elite, Gaither faced three interconnected problems. First, Gaither needed better players. Sportswriters described the Rattlers as "no longer invincible." FAMU's eleven losses from 1960 to 1966 were two more than the Rattlers lost in the entire decade of the 1950s.[64] A return to the top of the polls meant that FAMU needed to stem the flow of athletic talent attending white colleges. FAMU started publicizing the signing of local recruits for the first time, matching some of the recruiting tactics white colleges employed. Although the signees would not have an impact on the team for several years, Gaither adjusted to the changing recruiting landscape.[65]

Second, FAMU and Gaither needed to remind players and fans of the quality of their program against a white opponent. The NCAA's restructuring of its College Division provided this opportunity. Heading into the 1967 season, the Rattlers knew that an undefeated campaign could lead to a Tangerine Bowl invitation to play against a white team. Although Florida's bowl games—the Orange Bowl, the Citrus Bowl, and the Tangerine Bowl—had desegregated, it was unclear if state officials would allow FAMU to play a white team. Rather than leave it up to a winning season and the whims of the Tangerine Bowl selection committee, Gaither began trying to schedule a game against a white team. As the athletic director, he succeeded in arranging for the Rattler basketball team to play against the University of Miami and the University of Tampa, a first in the state's history.[66] Ed Oglesby, FAMU's head basketball coach and an assistant football coach, described the importance of interracial games for the Rattlers' recruiting efforts. Winning games was tied to "how well you recruit." Oglesby told a key recruit in Miami that "he might receive more publicity at an integrated college, but I thought he might be happier at A&M."[67] However, Gaither's attempts at scheduling an in-state football opponent were more difficult, in part due to the Rattlers' reputation. No in-state white coach was willing to risk losing to one of the best Black college football programs in the country. Even with the Rattlers in decline, neither UF, FSU, Tampa, nor Stetson wanted to take them on.

The third issue was Gaither's age. As Gaither headed into his twenty-third season as head coach, sportswriters acknowledged his accolades while simultaneously raising doubts about the program's future. Gaither entered the season only 21 wins from 200 victories, a plateau that only six coaches, three whites and three African Americans—Glenn "Pop" Warner, Amos Alonzo Stagg, Jess Neely, Southern's Ace Mumford, Prairie View's Fred "Pops" Long, and Tuskegee's Cleveland Abbott—had reached. Writers noted, "The Jake Gaither era is reaching the end of the trail," as he battled "the relentless march of time."[68] Gaither also watched more colleagues leave the game. Prior to the 1967 season, J. R. E. Lee Jr. retired after forty-three years. Lee, the school's business manager for thirty-three years and a vice president for ten, had been instrumental in founding and growing the OBC. Lee's retirement had to look like the end of an era. Gaither knew that he could not outrun Father Time. His time to step aside would come soon, but he wanted to leave as a champion.

Change defined the Rattlers' 1967 season. There was pressure to alter the offense after consecutive 3-loss seasons. No longer was the OBC satisfactory; now the Rattlers needed to earn a spot in the Tangerine Bowl. Gaither continued to try to schedule a game against an in-state, predominately white college. SIAC teams challenged the Rattlers for the conference title for the first time in two decades. After two seasons of struggles, by Gaither's impossibly high standards, the Rattlers were poised to return to the national title picture led by quarterback Ken Riley, end John Eason, running back Hubert Ginn, and defensive back Major Hazelton.[69] The Rattlers needed to prove they were back on the field.

A return to national title contention hinged on 3 games on the Rattlers' 1967 schedule: a rematch against Alabama A&M, the 1966 OBC opponent; TSU, which owned a 2-game win streak over FAMU; and Southern, which had won more games against Gaither than any other team. The no. 10-ranked Rattlers opened with shutout victories over Allen and South Carolina State. In the third game of the season against the upstart Alabama A&M Bulldogs, FAMU signaled to sportswriters, fans, and opponents that it was a contender by winning 45 to 36.

Two weeks later, the Rattlers headed to Nashville in a face-off against TSU. John Merritt's Tigers had easily defeated the Rattlers the previous two seasons by a combined score of 74 to 6. Despite the past lopsided results, the Rattlers were confident. The Rattlers were 13-point favorites, as the TSU Tigers entered the game having lost 3 of their first 4 games. The Tigers still had Eldridge "The Lord's Prayer" Dickey at quarterback. For the third consecutive year, Dickey led the Tigers to a rout of the Rattlers. The Tigers jumped out to lead 22 to 0 by halftime. The star quarterback passed for 293 yards and three touchdowns on the way to a 32 to 8 win.[70] FAMU's loss upset the Black college football championship race, as the Rattlers, TSU, Grambling, and Prairie View all had lost by the second week in October. Only Morgan State had made it through the first half of the season unblemished.[71]

As the Rattlers returned to practice, Gaither yelled, "Shake it off, baby!"[72] The Rattlers needed to win the remainder of their games to have any chance at a title. In front of 10,000 home fans, FAMU rallied to defeat Southern. During the game, several players from both teams ran into Gaither on the sideline after the Rattlers' Ken Riley threw an interception. In the scrum, Gaither broke his leg. He admitted that he "just froze" when the players barreled toward the sideline. After the injury, longtime assistant Pete Griffith ran the day-to-day operation until Gaither could return to the field.[73] The Rattlers routed Bethune-Cookman and Texas Southern in the final 2 games of the season. The Rattlers were in title contention once again.

FAMU announced that Eddie Robinson's Grambling State Tigers would be the 1967 OBC opponent. It would be the third meeting between Gaither and Robinson at the classic. Each coach had led his team to one victory in a game now dubbed "the cradle of the pros" for tremendous professional football talent displayed by participating teams. For the 1967 OBC, this moniker had never been truer. Grambling and FAMU had produced the most professional football players in Black college football. Grambling had twenty active players, including future Hall-of-Famers Willie Davis and Buck Buchanan. FAMU had ten active professional players led by future Hall-of-Famer Bob Hayes. Pro scouts, who could no longer afford to exclude Black colleges, made plans to attend the game to see FAMU's Major Hazelton, John Eason, and Ken Riley and Grambling's James "Shack" Harris, Bob Atkins, and Charlie Joiner. OBC organizers expected the quality matchup between 1-loss title contenders to turn around the game's lagging attendance. Observers expected more than 50,000 fans to fill the Orange Bowl. The game almost lived up to expectations. FAMU led three different times, only to watch James Harris lead the Tigers to a 28 to 25 victory. Gaither, however, stayed in Tallahassee nursing his broken leg.[74] The highly anticipated game, however, failed to draw more than 40,000 fans, a troubling sign for Black college classics in an era of desegregation. The Rattlers' 1967 season was a reminder that FAMU was still among the best Black college programs in the country. Nonetheless, trouble lurked below the surface. It was another season without a title, Gaither's injury reminded observers of his age, and the Rattlers had yet to play a predominately white college team on the field. The fissures in FAMU's football dynasty were quickly becoming chasms.

BLACK POWER AND BLACK COLLEGE FOOTBALL

Before the 1968 season, the emergence of a Black Power movement chipped away at Gaither's popularity among activists. In 1966, Stokely Carmichael (later Kwame Ture) introduced the slogan "Black Power" in the sweltering heat of Greenville, Mississippi. The slogan and idea spread like wildfire through the civil rights movement, especially among young activists frustrated with the slow pace of change. At its core, Carmichael's definition of Black Power was one in which Black people controlled their destiny.[75] Carmichael traveled extensively spreading the message of Black Power. In April 1967, the FAMU administration refused to sponsor a Carmichael speech. The young firebrand disseminated his message from the hood of a parked car. FAMU administrators, like many leaders at HBCUs, became the targets of student criticism and activism.[76] The Tallahassee branch of the Student Nonviolent Coordinating Committee called President Gore and FAMU administrators, including Gaither, "Uncle Toms" for denying Carmichael the right to speak on campus.[77] Sports also became a site for Black Power expression and protest.

Black college athletes nationally rebelled against the discipline, rules, and racism in big-time college sports. Over 100 college campuses were affected by conflicts between Black players and mostly white coaches. Few, if any, Black athletes at HBCUs revolted against the likes of Gaither, Robinson, or Merritt. These coaches, despite the turmoil in athletic departments nationally, had an abiding faith in the importance of sports for society. Gaither said sports were "about the last stronghold of discipline" on a college campus.[78] Moreover, he and other coaches viewed athletics as developing the kind of character that contributed to student-athletes being "substantial men." While athletic revolts did not rock HBCU campuses as they did at PWIs, HBCU sports were still the object of scorn.

Harry Edwards emerged as the chief spokesman for the Black athlete in revolt. A former college track star and then professor, he forcefully spoke out on behalf of Black Power athletics. Edwards organized the Olympic Project for Human Rights, which proposed that African American athletes boycott the 1968 Olympic games in Mexico City. Although the boy-

Stokely Carmichael, national head of the Student Nonviolent Coordinating Committee, speaks from the hood of an automobile on the campus of FAMU, April 16, 1967, in Tallahassee. Several hundred students listened as Carmichael spoke of Black Power and the Vietnam War. (AP Photo/stf)

cott never materialized, Tommie Smith and John Carlos used the medal stand to make an iconic statement. Wearing black socks and black gloves and with their fists raised, the two sprinters visually represented the ethos of athletic revolt.

Gaither, who had watched his star pupil win gold four years earlier, was disgusted. He told reporters, "I'm ashamed." He added, "If they are going to represent this country in the Olympics, this is certainly no place to air their displeasure by raising clenched fists. After all, this is our country and we should be patriotic and loyal, and work like everything to get the wrongs corrected. I don't think that we should, under any circumstances, openly declare our disloyalty to America."[79] Young activists quickly condemned his statement, but he refused to back down. His commentary aligned with the dominant white views, confirming for many civil rights and Black Power activists that Gaither opposed the cause of racial equality. Gaither's rejection of the language of Blackness and Black Power protest strategies obscured his institutional approach to racial equality. He refused to accept the integrationists' premise that Black educational spaces were inferior. This method, which emanated from his winning football program, viewed the sporting congregation as important as equal treatment. Nonetheless, Black Powerites like Edwards missed the self-determination in Gaither's nuanced position.

Edwards outlined his philosophy in *The Revolt of the Black Athlete*, which also included his analysis of HBCUs. He spared no athletic institution—professional sports, PWIs, and HBCUs—from withering criticism. For HBCUs, he levied a common critique that financial support from southern states or white philanthropists forced Black college administrators to accept the racial status quo. Edwards argued that the HBCU curriculum functioned to keep Blacks in their place as second-class citizens. "Safe educational programs" allowed by whites included an emphasis on "agriculture, music, and physical education," whereas the "abstract use of intellectual skills were significantly scarce," wrote Edwards. He mocked Black colleges by suggesting that "A&M" stood for Athletics and Music rather than Agricultural and Mechanical. Despite these criticisms, Edwards briefly recognized that HBCUs "provided an avenue to athletic prominence for many black athletes." Edwards failed to credit HBCUs in supporting athletes who didn't make the professional ranks. He lambasted PWIs for the "Mickey Mouse courses" given to Black athletes and the abysmal graduation rates of African American athletes at PWIs, but he did not mention that HBCUs' track record in these areas was considerably better. Black athletes at least graduated with degrees in physical education and became members of the sporting congregation and the Black middle class. It's not clear that Edwards investigated Black colleges beyond parroting colloquial critiques. Edwards's *Revolt* was more concerned with attacking the exploitations at PWIs than with understanding how HBCUs had served community needs for more than a century. An honest evaluation of Black college athletes would have revealed that programs like football at FAMU, basketball at Winston-Salem State, and track and field at TSU embodied the self-determination sought by Black Power.[80]

At the *Pittsburgh Courier* All-American Banquet in January 1968, Jake Gaither hinted at the Black Power aspects of HBCU athletes. He delivered a keynote address that surrounded the audience in a "hushed solemnity." Gaither's message returned to the theme of the Spirit of Excellence. He reminded the audience that it was this spirit that allowed African Americans to survive "decades of darkness." This spirit had served the Black community and had been a "major motivation . . . in winning football games."

Gaither's speech was met with uproarious applause at the end.[81] Despite a night of affirmation, social change swirled around Gaither's football team.

The Rattler program was beset on multiple fronts. Off the field, desegregation threatened to close off the program's access to the top African American players in Florida. Although the signing of the Rattlers' first white player signaled that Gaither's goals were aligned with the broader civil rights movement, he was still skeptical of the effects. He watched politicians who had once fought tooth and nail to keep Blacks out of the University of Florida Law School now move to close FAMU's law school in 1963 in favor of creating a new law school at FSU. The Board of Regents stopped enrolling new students at the FAMU law school in 1966, effectively closing it in 1968. Gaither kept a keen eye on these developments, knowing that FAMU would be targeted for a merger with FSU. He stated, "Now some educators want to integrate Florida A&M but what they really mean is to make it another predominately white school."[82] There was a deep vein of conservative suspicion in Gaither that questioned the impact of desegregation on Black institutions. This suspicion of the white power structure's sudden embrace of integration reflected a line of thinking in Black Nationalism.[83] The commonalities between Gaither's institution-oriented integrationism and Black Power notwithstanding, he opposed what he saw as a lack of discipline in the rebelling youth of the late 1960s. The rise of Black Power further exposed Gaither's hidebound position, especially his unwillingness to contest white politicians and his opposition to violence anywhere but on the gridiron. His failure to clarify his nuanced position and to publicly align himself with student criticisms of the status quo ultimately put him on the wrong side of Black Power.

Gaither's position vis-à-vis Black Power became clearer after Martin Luther King's assassination. On the night of King's murder, FAMU students' growing frustrations erupted into a violent protest. They threw bottles at passing cars, firebombed downtown businesses, lit small car fires, and even shot at officers with bows and arrows stolen from the physical education department. Tragically, a local white teenager died in a fire that investigators said was caused by a Molotov cocktail. The death further tied Black Power to antiwhite violence in the minds of many. A week before the uprising, Adam Clayton Powell spoke on FAMU's campus, calling for a "revolution to remake America" and declaring, "The day of nonviolence is over."[84] King's death and the rise of Black Power instilled students with a radical imagination. The call for Black Power hardened the sixty-five-year-old Gaither's conservatism. He told reporters, "I'm old fashioned, but I guess I just don't understand today's youth. I get a little tired of all this racism talk. These young guys keep calling for change but they don't offer any solutions except, 'burn, baby, burn' ones."[85] Gaither's tried-and-true solution to racism was demonstrated excellence.

Beginning in May 1968, Gaither convened with Grambling's Eddie Robinson and Morgan State's Earl Banks to come up with a different way for sports to contribute to the Black community. William Curtis, a marketing manager at Ballantine and Sons brewing company, invited the coaches to a private meeting to discuss the future of HBCU football. Curtis pitched a new classic game to open the season in New York City. He believed that in the wake of Martin Luther King's assassination, a single football game could accomplish two goals: demonstrate the greatness of HBCU teams and raise money for education. Curtis was fully aware of the potential of HBCU classics because he had worked as a corporate sponsor for the OBC. Inspired by Curtis's pitch, Gaither, Robinson, and Banks created the Football Coaches Foundation, which later added judge A. Leon Higginbotham and Ballantine and Sons president Richard H. Griebel to its board of directors. Curtis convinced Gaither, Robinson, and Banks that a game between two of their programs would sell out Yankee Stadium. Grambling and Morgan State were slated to play in the inaugural matchup. Although FAMU could not play because its schedule was full, Gaither was instrumental in getting the game off the ground. Curtis was so convinced that he persuaded his company to underwrite the costs. Curtis knew what he was doing. Gaither, Robinson, and Banks had rarely failed.[86] The game between Grambling and Morgan State netted $200,000 in profits, some of which was donated to the Urban League's Street Academy, an education program aimed at high school dropouts in northern cities. The game's earnings could have allowed the football programs to endure the changes spawned by desegregation through an improvement of each school's athletic resources. Still, the coaches chose to donate the money to the Urban League to help predominately Black high school dropouts get their high school diplomas, to change the outlook of their lives. A fraternity of leading Black college football coaches put the needs of the community above their programs.[87] This reflected the ethos of Black Power even without its rhetoric.

As Gaither focused on the Rattlers' 1968 season, he worried about "too many vacancies, too many injuries," and "too little time."[88] He faced, perhaps, the most significant rebuilding effort in his career. Fifteen members of the 1967 team were drafted or signed professional football contracts. The only solution was for Gaither to rely on freshmen. Despite Gaither's annual worries about his team, his desire to play predominately white schools was beginning to gain traction. There were discussions about playing UF. In a report about these preliminary meetings, the Gators' head coach stunningly admitted that Gaither's teams "would have beaten the Gators, FSU, and Miami," but he reassured his fan base that the earliest the two programs could play would be in twelve years.[89] Facing off against the Gators was not the only game against an in-state white opponent that Gaither had in the works. He finally broke the scheduling barrier against white teams when he got the University of Tampa for the 1969 season.[90]

For the 1968 season, Gaither entrusted quarterback Ken Riley to lead the program back to elite status on the field. FAMU won its first 5 games. The fifth game was the most satisfying because the Rattlers exorcised their demons against TSU. The Rattlers recovered a Tiger fumble on the opening kickoff and never looked back on the way to a 32 to 13 victory. Quarterback Ken Riley threw three touchdown passes, giving TSU some of its own medicine. With Eldridge Dickey in the NFL learning a new position for the Oakland Raiders, TSU did not have enough answers for FAMU.[91] However, the following week the Rattlers were upset at home by the North Carolina A&T Aggies 9 to 6. It was an impressive two weeks for the Aggies, who had ended Morgan State's 31-game win streak one week earlier.[92] Despite the loss, the Rattlers were still in the title hunt, as the other leading teams in Black college football—Morgan State, Acorn State, North Carolina A&T, and Grambling—had all lost at least 1 game.[93] Essential for the Rattlers was winning the remaining games on the schedule, including the always-tough OBC opponent.

Although a game against the University of Tampa was scheduled for the 1969 season, the Spartans emerged as a surprise candidate for the 1968 OBC. The University of Tampa's access to affluent boosters, athletic ambitions, civic initiatives, and a new stadium were a combination that posed immediate and long-term threats to FAMU football. After Tampa had begun football in 1933, the university was a nonfactor in the football world after more than three decades. The 1967 season was particularly bad, as the Spartans won just 2 games. To revive the program, the school hired Fran Curci, a former All-American quarterback at the University of Miami. The Spartans' football program ambitions were fueled by the post–World War II growth of the Sunbelt region. The Tampa Bay metropolitan region that included St. Petersburg and surrounding counties surpassed 1 million people in the mid-1960s. The civic competition was particularly intense in Florida, as Orlando, Tampa, St. Petersburg, Jacksonville, and

Miami all vied for regional influence and reputation. Tampa officials believed that they needed a new athletic stadium in the hopes of luring a professional football team—a sign of a big city. Beginning in 1965, the Tampa Sports Authority began plans for a new stadium that culminated in the construction of Tampa Stadium in 1967. The University of Tampa football team was the primary tenant. Curci remade the roster quickly by signing transfers from larger schools and taking talented but academically marginal student-athletes. In Curci's first season, Tampa went 5 and 1 before the calendar turned to November, with notable victories over big college programs Tulane and Mississippi State.[94]

The Spartans' hot start led Gaither to consider them as the Rattlers opponent for the OBC. Gaither announced that he was "seriously thinking about inviting the University of Tampa," while Frank Curci believed that the matchup "would be a natural" fit.[95] The Spartans were the highest-ranking among five teams—Morgan State, Alabama State, Maryland State, and Alcorn State—being evaluated for the game.[96] During a Rattler bye week on the first Saturday in November, Gaither traveled to Tampa to watch the Spartans play. He was one of more than 20,000 fans in the crowd as Tampa prevailed against Northern Michigan 22 to 19.[97] The Spartans win pushed the highly anticipated game closer to reality.

Each program had its reasons for considering the historic matchup. For Tampa, a game (and victory) against FAMU would quickly solidify it as the leading small college program in the state. Curci told reporters as much: "We think the new [47,000-seat] stadium, improved facilities at school, a new attitude, and stronger schedules will help us attract the best Florida high school players." The University of Tampa was a part of the new era in the city. "Somehow the new Tampa stadium seemed . . . to signify a slight change in the ingredients of the Tampa atmosphere—cigars, garbanzas [sic], and now football."[98] Although FAMU was going to play Tampa during the 1969 regular season, scheduling the Spartans for the OBC would indicate a massive change in the Black college football world, and Tampa supporters called on Gaither to name the University of Tampa to the OBC.[99] Playing a predominately white team in the premier HBCU football game meant that FAMU would be taking the moral high ground. Gaither's consideration of Tampa was more magnanimous than any PWI program had been toward the Rattlers. Sports editor Buddy Martin recognized the generosity, writing, "Jake Gaither never begged for a 'break' in putting Florida A&M on their schedule. . . . And now suddenly everybody expects Gaither to play Good Fairy and invite Tampa to the Orange Blossom Classic . . .

just because the Spartans won't get a bowl bid anywhere else."[100] In his competitiveness, Gaither wanted to show the world what HBCU programs could do when given the opportunity. There was an economic incentive for FAMU as well. Gaither anticipated that the OBC's declining attendance numbers would turn around with the first interracial game in the state. Yet Gaither refused simply to select Tampa because it was a PWI.[101]

A Spartans' loss to Southern Illinois made Gaither's decision not to invite Tampa easier. FAMU selected Alcorn State for the OBC based on its 7 and 1 record, which included dominant victories over OBC regulars Grambling, Jackson State, and Southern. Gaither also understood that it was the HBCU sporting congregation that had made the OBC great, and a game against Tampa, which had only three African American players, was a rejection of that tradition. After Gaither passed over Tampa for the OBC, Curci lashed out. He suggested that Gaither never seriously considered the Spartans. Curci further decried the snub by announcing, "I never heard of Alcorn." His dismissal of Alcorn implied a repudiation of HBCU football. Curci noted the University of Tampa would play FAMU the following season and announced, "We'll still recruit colored boys."[102] His use of the anachronistic "colored" also reminded many of his detachment from African American communities and the exploitative nature of college football.[103]

The thirty-sixth OBC would again determine the Black college champion. The Alcorn State Braves' rise to prominence echoed the University of Tampa's. Marino H. Casem, a former player at Xavier University in New Orleans, led the Braves' rapid ascension. Under Casem, the Braves boasted the best defense in Black college football, holding all opponents to less than 100 yards of offense all season. The 1968 offense also averaged more than 30 points per game.[104] The Braves' dominant regular season was not enough to warrant an invitation to the NCAA Small College Regional Championship games, confirming for longtime sportswriter Ric Roberts that the NCAA had "perpetuated a fraud on the national public."[105] Gaither's Rattlers, also snubbed by the NCAA, had the opportunity to win another Black college title with a victory. The intrigue leading up to the game was better than the product on the field for FAMU. Alcorn's defense held the Rattlers to minus 51 yards rushing and 6 yards passing in front of nearly 38,000 fans en route to a 36 to 9 win. The lopsided loss was FAMU's worst in OBC history, and the Braves' victory secured their first title.[106]

Despite the disappointing loss, Gaither viewed the season as a success. The Rattlers finished fourth in the *Pittsburgh Courier* poll and twentieth in the final small college poll.[107] Alcorn's win silenced critics of the selection who saw FAMU as picking an easy opponent. "I guess the results of the game proved I made a pretty good choice," said Gaither.[108]

While the effects of desegregation were still devastating to the Black sporting community, Gaither seemed to have stemmed the tide by adding the school's first white player and by scheduling the University of Tampa for the following season. The OBC again determined the Black college national title. All in all, Gaither's twenty-fourth season reminded everyone of his legacy and that he had no plans to retire. Gaither quipped that he would retire when his "losses catch up with my wins."[109] For twenty-four seasons Gaither had directed the Rattlers to the apex of Black college football. Now the question was whether he would be able to guide the program in a fully desegregated world.

8
JAKE GAITHER'S LAST SEASON AND THE END OF AN ERA

The 1969 season marked the centennial of college football and the semicentennial of professional football. Sportswriters rushed to name all-century teams of coaches and players to honor the occasion. A common thread in many of these celebratory lists was the absence of the great stars of Black college football.[1] The omission of Jazz Byrd, Willie Galimore, and the other HBCU stars, however, indicated that the white sports media failed to take Black college football seriously.

Occasionally, unimpeachable data allowed the accolades of Black college coaches to break through the media silence. When columnists evaluated the objective coaching variables—wins, winning percentage, and alumni in professional football—that defined excellence, Black college football programs were at or near the top of the list. One California sports columnist declared, "Negro Teams Best." Other sports columns debated whether Alabama's Paul "Bear" Bryant, the active white coach with the most wins, or Nebraska's Bob Devaney, the active white coach with the highest winning percentage, was the best active coach. California columnist Breard Snellings came to a different conclusion. He noted that Jake Gaither had more wins than Bryant (195 to 187) and a substantially higher winning percentage than Devaney (0.845 to 0.722). The columnist recognized that Gaither was mere percentage points from the 0.881 winning percentage of Notre Dame's Knute Rockne, the benchmark for coaching greatness according to most observers. Gaither was not the only Black college coach to best Devaney. Morgan State's Earl Banks (0.826) and Grambling's Eddie Robinson (0.724) also had a better winning percentage than the Cornhusker head coach.[2] Many sportswriters excluded Gaither, Banks, and Robinson from the "best coach" discussion because of their small school status, believing that their excellent records were a result of playing less-talented teams when compared with big PWI programs.

In the wake of professional football's semicentennial, the ability of college programs to produce successful pros became a convenient metric to compare talent among college teams—big and small, PWI and HBCU—that did not play on the field regularly. In 1968 more than 300 African Americans played professional football for twenty-six teams; 150 were from HBCUs. Black players from HBCUs produced more Pro Bowlers (23) than the total number of Black players who attended southern PWIs (17) the previous season. The success of African American players from the South in professional football put added pressures on southern PWIs and forced a recalculation of program success. As one columnist remarked, "There are facts to prove that Southern schools in general—and Florida colleges in particular—are letting good Negro players get away." The article identified twenty-one African American professional football players from Florida who did not receive a scholarship from UF, FSU, or Miami, and most had attended FAMU.[3] Gaither had sixteen former players on NFL rosters during the 1968 season—more than Miami (14), UF (11), and FSU (5). Grambling led all HBCUs in producing pro players with twenty-one alumni on rosters, trailing only Notre Dame (33), the University of Southern California (24), and Michigan State (22).[4] Despite many sportswriters excluding HBCU football coaches and programs from all-centennial lists, "pro Scouts know where the best college football is played even if nobody else does."[5] This analysis was never more valid than in the last three NFL drafts of the 1960s. Between 1967 and 1969 (the first three years of the combined AFL and NFL draft), HBCUs produced eight of the nineteen Black future Hall of Famers.[6]

Despite Black college football's apparent parity with its PWI counterparts regarding professional talent, there were ominous signs that many programs would struggle to replicate past successes as integration progressed. The very NFL draft process that signaled the caliber of HBCU football also foreshadowed looming changes. Namely, some of the first African American players to integrate southern PWIs were being drafted. Bracketing the Atlanta Falcons' selection of TSU's Claude Humphrey with the third pick in the 1968 NFL draft, fans watched teams draft Gene Upshaw (Texas A&M–Kingsville University) in 1967, and Joe Greene (University of North Texas) and Jerry LeVias (Southern Methodist University) in 1969 during the first two rounds.[7] The collegiate and professional success of these racial pioneers provided coaches at southern PWIs another selling point in the recruitment of African American players. Despite the racism at these schools, coaches could promote the logic of integration, ostentatious athletic facilities, and now professional football opportunities to potential African American prep athletes. Moreover, southern PWI coaches would be aided by the lack of athletic revolts in the South, which had plagued schools in the North and West, such as Syracuse and Wyoming in the late 1960s.[8]

The year 1969 marked the end of three eras. First, it signaled the end of the dual secondary education system throughout the South. The network of segregated schools had been a main recruiting mechanism for identifying talented Black athletes for Black college football. Second, the scheduled FAMU versus Tampa game ended a form of segregated athletics. Finally, the last season of the 1960s marked Jake Gaither's final year on the sidelines as the Rattler head coach. The cumulative effect was the beginning of the end of the golden age of HBCU football.

THE END OF THE DUAL EDUCATION SYSTEM

The final push in the desegregation of southern elementary and secondary schools further diminished the traditional recruiting pipelines to HBCUs. The size and complexity of Florida's dual system of education had once provided FAMU with distinct personnel advantages; now the vestiges of segregated education faced extinction because of stronger enforcement of desegregation laws. The intricate sporting congregation that FAMU had spent more than three decades developing was to be sacrificed in the name of racial progress. FAMU, as much as any HBCU football program, felt the contradictory sting of integration. Florida had made great strides; 71 percent of students attended integrated schools by 1968.[9] The statistic, however, obscured the variability of the quality of integration across the state. The positive data belied schemes such as "freedom of choice" plans that counties used to initiate the least amount and the slowest rate of desegregation. The May 1968 U.S. Supreme Court decision in *Green v. New Kent County, Virginia* ruled against the freedom-of-choice plans used to delay integrated schools. Thus, fifteen years after *Brown v. Board of Education* the federal government's Department of Health, Education, and Welfare increased its pressure on counties across Florida and the South to achieve school desegregation by withholding money as a means to bring recalcitrant districts into compliance.[10] The outcome of the department's new aggressive stance was clear: the 1968–69 school year was the end of the dual school system in Florida, and a unitary system of education would begin the following school year. The *Green* and *Alexandria v. Holmes County* (October 1969) rulings, plus the enhanced enforcement by the federal government, hastened the closing or recategorizing of many formerly all-black schools, permanently disrupting the sporting congregation that FAMU had created.[11]

The creation of a unitary school system affected the employment of Black teachers who served as coaches and mentors. County plans for desegregation included faculty mergers. For instance, Hillsborough County (Tampa) planned a 50:50 ratio of Black and white teachers at majority–African American schools and a 10:90 ratio in predominately white schools.[12] Black teachers and administrators failed to keep their positions and stature in newly desegregated schools despite the merger plans. African Americans in Tallahassee expressed frustration over the lack of Black head coaches at the newly integrated high schools.[13] Despite the material inequalities of segregated Black high schools, these schools were the community, cultural, and athletic pillars. For more than a quarter of a century, the vast network of FAMU alumni and coaches identified the top Black players in the state and ushered student-athletes to Tallahassee. In the mid-1960s, Gaither noted that fewer talented players were becoming Rattlers. "We don't get the best blacks anymore. . . . We get black leftovers." When FAMU's much-celebrated white recruit did not return for the 1969 season, Gaither surmised, "We're a black team that's being done in by integration."[14]

Facing the permanent loss of Black high schools, the recruiting battles before the 1969 season took on added significance. The competition for two recruits portended FAMU's future ability to sign the best Black players in Florida.

The recruitment of Eddie McAshan (pronounced Mc-Shan) symbolized the growing difficulty Black colleges would face in signing the best players from integrated schools. McAshan was a prep All-American quarterback from Gainesville. A decade earlier there would have been little doubt that the star quarterback would have signed with FAMU or another HBCU. By 1969, Lincoln High, the city's Black high school, was being converted to a vocational school, and integration had begun at Gainesville High School. Lincoln High had been an example of the sporting congregation. The school opened in 1923 under the leadership of FAMU graduate A. Quinn Jones. Football was central to the school and its community identity. T. B. McPherson, a FAMU alumnus, won the national high school Negro Championship in 1939. Jesse Heard, who played for Gaither at FAMU and made it to the NFL, was the head coach in the decade before the school closed. The school's demotion and citywide integration severed these athletic connections, thereby limiting the chances that McAshan would play for Gaither.

McAshan was a starter at integrated Gainesville High since his sophomore year, and his story demonstrated the role sports had to play in the process of integration. His high school coach noted he "charms his white teammates." McAshan's success on the field and in an integrated classroom resulted in more than 100 scholarship offers, many from leading PWIs in the South, including UF and Georgia Tech.[15] McAshan signed with Georgia Tech because of the opportunity to play quarterback and was the second African American player to sign with the program.[16] Although there is no evidence that McAshan strongly considered FAMU or any other HBCU, Gaither believed that the sporting congregation would deliver another talented athlete to FAMU. He recalled, "I thought I had Eddie McAshan . . . all set up to come to FAMU; then the coaches from Tech swayed him into going to their school. And what gets me is that McAshan's uncle graduated from FAMU!"[17] Gaither also explained the changing terrain of college football recruiting. "I once had my pick of Negro football players," Gaither lamented. "Now they go off to schools with more famous names." Gaither identified a lack of material resources as one problem. "My coaches are all on the field. The big schools have folks out looking [for players] all year. We just stay home and play during the season. We don't have any rich booster program or no airplanes to borrow from rich alumni. The big guys do it all—wine and dine the prospects [and give] cars to ride around in. Not us. Our budget isn't that fat."[18] For decades, FAMU and other HBCUs relied on the assistance of high school coaches and teachers that were alumni to offset the financial barriers to recruiting. The closing or repurposing of formerly segregated Black high schools gutted this network. McAshan's recruitment increasingly became the norm.

While McAshan's recruitment was disappointing to the Rattlers' coaches and fans, Clarence Burgess Owens's rejection of FAMU stung supporters to the core. Owens's father was an agriculture professor at FAMU. Owens knew of FAMU's history and legacy, yet he chose to be the third African American recruit at the University of Miami. His decision caught Gaither by surprise. Owens recalled, "There is no doubt I would have gone to Florida A and M or Grambling. . . . But the other schools worked so hard at trying to sell me what they have to offer, and assuring me the kind of exposure I would need for a lucrative professional offer, that I was compelled to think the whole thing out. . . . [I] made up my mind to go further south for my education."[19] Southern PWIs' ability to sell Black recruits better professional football opportunities was, in 1968, a lie. The only University of Miami alumni with any measurable success in the NFL was linebacker Dan Conners, who had been a three-time Pro Bowler. FAMU alumni Bob Hayes, Al

Denson, and Hewritt Dixon had all been multiyear Pro Bowl players in the NFL. These facts did not trump the logic of desegregation that presented predominately white spaces as universally better. Future African American recruits would go through a similar thought process, leading them from the sporting congregation of Black colleges and to the PWIs in the South. Gaither later lamented the changing recruiting environment. "It wasn't so bad when the northern schools took the Negro, but now I'm competing against Florida, Florida State, Tampa and Miami in my own state. I used to have many boys coaching [at] Negro schools, but most of the schools have been phased out and all the head coaches now are whites."[20]

Sometimes it took racial strife at the high school level for FAMU to secure a top recruit. Henry Lawrence played for Eddie Shannon at segregated Lincoln High School in Palmetto, Florida. In 1968, Lawrence was third-team all-state as a 225-pound defensive end.[21] The following year all-Black Lincoln and all-white Manatee High School merged. Lawrence should have been a star at the new school. In the third game of his senior season, the Manatee coach pulled him from the game. Lawrence and several other Black teammates thought the Black players were getting benched despite being better than their white counterparts. Lawrence spoke to the coach and the principal about the situation. He was benched for the remainder of the season, punished for his outspokenness against the racism. FAMU's sporting congregation provided him an opportunity. Eddie Shannon informed the FAMU coaching staff about Lawrence's ability. In 1972, Lawrence switched positions from defensive line to offensive line. Although FAMU didn't win much, Lawrence wowed NFL scouts with his blocking of Tampa's John Matuszak, the first pick in the 1973 draft, and Tennessee State's Ed "Too Tall" Jones, the first pick in the 1974 draft. In 1974, Lawrence became FAMU's last first-round draft pick when the Oakland Raiders selected him with the nineteenth pick. Lawrence played thirteen seasons for the Raiders, winning three Super Bowls. Racism meant that white coaches still overlooked Black players and that some of these players, like Lawrence, starred at HBCUs.[22]

Heading into his twenty-fifth season, Gaither witnessed the crumbling of the Black sporting congregation that had buttressed FAMU athletics. In this rapidly changing environment, HBCUs urgently needed to prove themselves against PWI teams or risk being permanently marginalized in integrated college football. Or worse, Black programs could be disbanded like Edward Waters College (Fla.) and Allen University (S.C.).[23] While TSU,

Grambling, and Morgan State had already played PWI teams, the 1969 season presented FAMU with its first opportunity to do so. The stakes for the program were never higher. The game against the University of Tampa came at a critical juncture for FAMU and HBCU football more generally. The question remained: would a victory be enough to keep FAMU and HBCU football relevant? The coming seasons were a stony road for Black athletic institutions. Some wondered if Gaither, after three decades in Tallahassee as an assistant and then as head coach, was the person to lead the program against its greatest challenge: the future.

GAITHER'S LAST SEASON

At sixty-six, Gaither's age added to the questions surrounding FAMU's program. Rumors abounded that his twenty-fifth season as the Rattlers' head coach would be his last.[24] The speculations about Gaither's future were fueled by the abrupt retirement of FAMU president George W. Gore a year earlier. Gore had navigated the school through the turbulent civil rights protests of the 1950s and 1960s. His final battle was against the state's merger plans that threatened the school's academic and athletic existence.

After politicians successfully closed the FAMU law school and opened the FSU law school, state legislators introduced new proposals that called for the consolidation of the smaller FAMU with the growing FSU or turning FAMU into a junior college.[25] Both plans functioned to end FAMU. State representative Robert Graham from Miami supported the merger because "we're still treating A&M as if the events of the past 15 years—racial integration—hadn't happened." The logic of integration called for the erasure of an "academic symbol of Negro culture." Implicit in Graham's and other merger supporters' arguments was the belief in FAMU's inferiority compared with the state's white institutions of higher education. State officials reflected this assumption by proposing the merger of FAMU while opening four new colleges in the previous decade—University of South Florida (1956), Florida Atlantic University (1961), University of Central Florida (1963), and Florida International University (1965). In response to the racist presumption of FAMU's poor quality, Gore mobilized the entire Rattler community—students, faculty, and alumni—to stave off threats of merger or a demotion to junior college status. In response to the proposed legislation, FAMU supporters countered by suggesting that integration "ought to be a two-way street, and not mean that all the Negro institutions ought to be abolished."[26] Gore announced his retirement shortly after the initial threat of merger subsided. The ordeal mirrored similar challenges facing the football program—the nearness in age between Gore and Gaither, the presumption of institutional inferiority, and the question of relevance after civil rights legislation. Now fans wondered if Gaither would soon announce his retirement, given that he, too, had steered the Rattlers through the choppy waters of the initial years of athletic integration. The state no longer prevented FAMU from playing white teams. Thus, the stage was set for the Rattlers to strike or be defanged.

In an interview with the *Palm Beach Post*, Gaither further hinted at retirement. He told the reporter that his "health was good now" but that he did not want "to press it." He hoped to stay around the game after he retired. When asked whether anyone could follow his tremendous legacy, Gaither replied, "Oh, there will be someone to come along and do a better job."[27] Missing from the interview was a firm statement about when Gaither would retire, but it was clear that it was on his mind before the pivotal 1969 season started.

Gaither's twenty-fifth season coincided with his longest national-title drought. It had been seven seasons since the Rattlers finished at the top of the polls. Signs pointed to the Rattlers having difficulty in reversing that trend in 1969. Gaither admitted that he was "quite concerned about the quarterback situation," knowing that he had to replace Ken Riley.[28] He turned over the offense to the left-handed Steve Scruggs and planned to rely on running back Hubert Ginn, the previous season's leading rusher and an honorable-mention All-American. During the last season, the Rattlers' offense only averaged 23 points per game, despite the 8 and 2 record. The FAMU defense, however, was dominant in 1968 under defensive coordinator Pete Griffin. The longtime defensive coach had prowled the sidelines for Gaither's entire career and had been a two-time All-American in 1938 and 1939. His defense allowed only 12 points per game and surrendered only 490 yards rushing during the 1968 season. In Gaither's silver anniversary season, Griffin's defense, with its ten returning starters, was again expected to carry the Rattlers to victory. Sportswriters were more optimistic about FAMU's title chances. "It is time for the Rattlers to roam and fang 'em dead, again."[29]

The preseason confidence was never more imperative, as FAMU had another difficult schedule that would test the team's mettle. Aside from FAMU's historic game against Tampa in the penultimate matchup, the Rattlers' schedule had the usual mix of SIAC opponents, plus they had to play intersectional rivals North Carolina A&T, TSU, and Southern. The push for another national title would also cumulate in Gaither reaching the 200-win plateau. More significant than Gaither's historic achievement, the 1969 season would be decisive in shaping the future of the program.

Wearing helmet decals that celebrated college football's 100th season, FAMU started strong, winning its first 3 games by an average of 26 points. The fourth game was against John Merritt's TSU Tigers. The Tigers had opened the season 3–0–1 with a victory over Grambling and a hard-fought tie against Texas Southern in Houston. The two teams' records told only part of the story. No coach had as much success against Gaither as Merritt. He had won five of the previous 8 games while coaching at Jackson State and TSU. The game would require each coach to summon a high degree of coaching acumen. Gaither "woke up at 4 A.M. . . . and started doodling with ways to stop [TSU's] passing attack."[30] Merritt worried about Gaither "bringing the fastest team in America to town."[31]

Twenty-thousand fans and scouts from every NFL team poured into TSU's W. J. Hale Stadium to watch the grid rivals. Local sophomore quarterback "Jefferson Street" Joe Gilliam led TSU's attack. Although the game had been close at the half, the Tigers dominated the Rattlers after intermission. Little went right in the 33 to 20 loss. FAMU's offensive line consistently failed to block TSU's six-foot six-inch, 240-pound defensive end Joe Jones, who regularly disrupted the Rattlers' offensive plays. Jones recorded five sacks and hurried Scruggs at least a half-dozen other times.[32] In addition to the deflating defeat, the officiating upset Gaither. He believed that TSU's use of referees from the defunct MAA smacked of favoritism. The loss left a sour taste in the venerable coach's mouth. "We had to play against 15 men," complained Gaither.[33] He was unusually bitter about the defeat, griping to the media well into the next week. "I am not a coach who alibis for losing," Gaither said, "but the spirit of football is one where one team does not have an unfair advantage over the other. There was an advantage in Nashville."[34] Gaither told reporters that he would not play in Nashville again. His uncertain future as head coach lay behind the surly response to the defeat.

The drubbing also ended any hope for a national championship. Despite the loss, there was still a considerable amount to play for: Gaither's 200th win, the Tampa game, and the OBC. The Rattlers rebounded from the loss to rout North Carolina A&T 26 to 9. The win against the Aggies was Gaither's 199th. His 200th win would have to come against Southern.

Gaither told reporters, "I think the 200th [win] might be a jinx." His fear was warranted. FAMU led the series with a 14–9–1 record, but the Jaguars were the most consistent thorn in Gaither's side. Seven times in twenty-four seasons the Jaguars had handed FAMU its first loss of the season. Three times the loss to Southern was the only blemish on FAMU's record. Even FAMU victories were costly. Gaither broke his leg in a sideline collision two years earlier. It was appropriate that the chance to move into college football's coaching elite called for a win against Southern under the lights.[35]

The highly anticipated matchup was the first between Gaither and new Southern coach Alva Tabor, a former assistant for the Jaguars and a former scout for the New Orleans Saints. Tabor was the third attempt to replace Arnett Mumford, the school's best coach. Southern's coaching carousel anticipated the difficulties of Gaither's successor at FAMU. Not only did Mumford's replacements have the unenviable task of following his twenty-five years as head coach and five national titles, but they also faced the rise of Grambling, Southern's in-state rival. Although Mumford had lost to Grambling only once (1947), during the short tenures of Robert Henry Lee (1962–64) and Robert Smith (1965–68), the Jags had lost four times to the Tigers. Grambling's rise to the elite of Black college football and the national media attention, including an ABC documentary, *Grambling College: 100 Yards to Glory*, produced by Howard Cosell, fueled Southern's growing "inferiority complex."[36] Smith's final mistake came in the 1968 game against the Tigers in which he failed to go for two in the fourth quarter and the Jaguars lost 34 to 32. The alumni and fans called for a new coach.

Southern had started the 1969 season 6 and 1, including a win over TSU. A talented but initially undervalued roster aided in Tabor's fast start. The 1969 Jaguars featured ten future NFL players, including (All-Pro) linebacker Isiah Robertson, (Hall of Fame) corner Mel Blount on defense, and six-foot six-inch (All-Pro) wide receiver Harold Carmichael on offense. Gaither's assessment that "Southern has the best personnel of any team in our league. They run from the pro-offense and really throw a lot" was more than just coach-speak.[37]

On an unusually cold night in front of nearly 13,000 home fans, FAMU squeaked out a 10 to 7 victory. The Rattlers kicked a field goal in the second quarter, only to watch Southern return the subsequent kickoff for a touchdown. Trailing 7 to 3 at the half, FAMU drove the ball deep into Southern territory midway in the third quarter. All-American Hubert Ginn dove

Gaither receiving a trophy from the Tallahassee Quarterback Club for his 200th win, 1969. (Florida Memory, Florida State Archives)

toward the end zone when he fumbled. A Rattler lineman jumped on the loose ball in the end zone for the 10 to 7 lead. Late in the fourth quarter, Southern drove the ball deep into Rattler territory, but FAMU defense stopped the Jaguars 3 yards short of the winning score. Players and fans reveled in Gaither's accomplishment. Representatives of FAMU's student government presented him with a plaque honoring the 200th victory. Gaither's players put him on their shoulders and carried him to the locker room. The revelry for Gaither's monumental win was short-lived as he quickly turned to the looming historic matchup against Tampa.[38]

THE TAMPA GAME

There was tremendous anticipation about the historic in-state matchup. The University of Tampa Spartans entered the game with 6 wins and 1 loss and the no. 6 ranking in the AP Small College Poll. They had dispatched California State University–Los Angeles a week earlier 53 to 0. After an easy win over Bethune-Cookman, the Rattlers, too, had 1 loss and a no. 16 ranking. Both coaches tried to downplay the game's significance, describing it as "just another game." But everyone understood the racial and historical dynamics that loomed over the game. The contest was about the credit-ability of Black college football. One report outlined the stakes: "If Tampa . . . should whip A&M by a wide margin, a lot of people will be ready with I-told-you-so's." However, "if the Rattlers win, or at least make it close," poll voters and fans "will have no choice but to admit that football in black colleges is on a par with football anywhere else."[39] Football fans could not wait for the opening kickoff to see the answers to these pressing questions.

Not only was the game the first between an HBCU and a PWI in Florida, but it was also a contrast in coaching styles. Gaither explained to report-ers his coaching philosophy of "mobile, agile, and hostile." He wanted his players to be mobile like an unfed hunting dog, to be as agile as a cat that is tossed into the air and lands on its feet, and to have a controlled hos-tility that reflected a mean streak. Despite a coaching philosophy laced with southern idioms, Gaither emphasized the fundamentals. Tampa's Fran Curci practiced "tricky multiple offenses and even trickier pro-set de-fenses."[40] The game pitted the Rattlers' run-oriented offense against the Spartans' passing attack. Although the Rattlers' running game was led by the powerful 235-pound Jim Owens and speedy Hubert Ginn, quarterback Steve Scruggs was the catalyst. The left-handed Scruggs, a St. Petersburg native, wanted to showcase his talents in front of the hometown fans. He entered the game with more than 1,000 yards passing. The Spartans relied on the left arm of Jim "Ice Man" Del Gaizo, who entered the game with a chance to surpass 2,000 yards passing. The dynamic running of Leon Mc-Quay complemented Tampa's passing offense. McQuay had set the fresh-man rushing record in 1968 and improved on those numbers in 1969. As one of three African American players on the Spartans' roster, McQuay was also a reminder of FAMU's emerging recruiting challenges. In a twist of fate, Gaither had fully expected McQuay and Spartan starting defensive end Willie Lee Jones to be Rattlers.[41] Now he had to devise ways to keep the two African American players from destroying the Rattlers' chances. After reviewing the matchups, sportswriters picked the Spartans as favorites to win.[42]

A sellout crowd of more than 45,000 people jammed into the newly built Tampa Stadium. Gaither gathered his men in the locker room before the start of the game. He prepared to give the final pep talk.

"I want you to go out there and stretch that Leon McQuay!"
   "Hubba! Hubba!"
"I want you to tackle him high!"
   "Hubba! Hubba!"
"I want you to tackle him in the belly!"
   "Hubba! Hubba!"
"Stretch him!"
   "Hubba! Hubba!"[43]

The Rattlers roared out of the locker room for the most important game in Gaither's four decades as a coach.

The capacity crowd was treated to a tremendous seesaw battle. Tampa won the coin toss and sent its powerful offense on the field. Del Gaizo completed his first two passes for 58 total yards. After several more explosive Spartan plays, Tampa had the ball deep into Rattler territory. From the sidelines, Griffin urged his defense to keep the Spartans out of the end zone. The Rattlers' defense stiffened against the powerful Tampa offense, forcing a 23-yard field goal. The Spartans' kicker, however, missed the short field goal, and the Rattler fans rejoiced. On FAMU's second play, Scruggs scrambled for 47 yards to the Tampa 34. Five plays later, Scruggs found wide receiver Alfred Sykes for a 19-yard touchdown and a 7 to 0 lead. Tampa immediately responded. Del Gaizo engineered a 14-play, 80-yard drive on the next series. The drive ended with a short touchdown run by McQuay to tie the game at 7.

In the second quarter, Scruggs again got the Rattlers on the board. After completing two passes for 35 yards, he scored on a 15-yard bootleg run for the FAMU's second score. The Rattlers looked to go into the locker room for halftime with the lead when a Tampa punt bounced off a FAMU player's leg. Tampa recovered at the 7-yard line. Three plays later the Spartans evened the score. Del Gaizo found wide receiver Paul Orndorff for a 4-yard touchdown. The game was tied 14 to 14, as the Marching 100 high-stepped onto the field for the halftime show.

Gaither was pleased with this team's first-half effort. It withstood the early forays of the Spartans' dynamic offense while showing its speed. The third quarter started slowly, as both teams exchanged punts. The Rattlers had the ball on their 16-yard line. Backed up near their end zone, Gaither called on his power running game. Scruggs handed the ball to James Owens, the 235-pound running back from Lake City, Florida. The Rattler offensive line opened a seam in the middle allowing Owens to rumble 41 yards to the Tampa 39-yard line. Scruggs added a pass for a first down, and then FAMU went back to the power running game. Three Owens runs later, the Rattlers led 21 to 14. The FAMU fans were rocking as the Marching 100's horn and drum sections provided the rhythm. The Rattler defense quickly stopped the Spartans. On the next drive, Gaither turned to his other running back, Hubert Ginn. Two and half minutes after Owens scored, Ginn added to the Rattler lead with a 21-yard run around the left end and a 28 to 14 lead. The Spartans high-powered offense needed to respond. Del Gaizo fired a deep pass to wide receiver Joe Sliker for a 60-yard completion. Mc-Quay finished the drive with a short run. The three-play drive cut the lead to 28 to 21 heading into the fourth quarter.

On FAMU's first drive of the final quarter, Scruggs led the team down the field looking to put the Rattlers ahead by two scores. Scruggs again tried to hit Sykes for a score, but this time the Spartans were prepared, and they intercepted the pass in the end zone. Del Gaizo advanced the ball to their 36-yard line. On the next play, Tampa fooled the Rattlers with a screen pass to Orndorff, who deftly used his blockers to score a 64-yard touchdown. The game was tied at 28 to 28 with more than 11 minutes remaining.

After the teams exchanged punts, the Rattlers pushed for the go-ahead score. Scruggs led FAMU deep into Spartan territory, leading to a Ginn 4-yard touchdown with 4:35 left in the game. However, the Spartans blocked the extra point. FAMU led 34 to 28 in the game's final minutes. With the Rattlers clinging to a 6-point lead, the FAMU defense needed to stop the explosive Spartan offense. On the third play of the drive, Del Gaizo threw his first interception of the game. The Rattlers looked to have the game sealed, but Tampa used its remaining timeouts and forced the Rattlers to punt.

With 2:04 left in the game, the Spartans could win with a touchdown. Starting on the Tampa 20-yard line, Del Gaizo showed the crowd why he was nicknamed the "Ice Man." He completed five consecutive passes to move the ball down to the Rattler 14-yard line with 40 seconds remaining in the game. On first down, Del Gaizo targeted Joe Sliker, but the ball went in and out of his hands. On second down, Curci tried to fool the Rattlers with a halfback pass from Leon McQuay, but he overthrew the intended receiver. With 30 seconds left, Del Gaizo tossed a high spiral to Bobby Fernandez, who had already caught four passes on the potential game-winning drive. Fernandez dove, but the ball went off his fingertips. It was fourth down and only 25 seconds remained. The sold-out crowd was on its feet. The Spartans needed a touchdown but could get a first down at the 4-yard line. Del Gaizo dropped back to pass and looked for his most trusted receiver, his twin brother, John, who got open at the 5-yard line. Del Gaizo fired the pass. John leaped, but the bullet pass went through his hands and landed harmlessly on the Tampa Stadium turf.[44]

When the referees blew the final whistle, Rattler fans erupted with a joyous cheer. The Marching 100's rhythm section paced the waving green and orange pom-poms. Fran Curci sprinted across the field, hugged Gaither, telling him over deafening jubilation, "Congratulations, Jake, you deserved it."[45] The coaches had shared breakfast in anticipation of the big game. Although this had been their first meeting, both coaches held each other in high esteem. Rattler players carried Gaither off the field to a cacophony of cheers, horns, and applause.

In the postgame interviews, each coach complimented the other team and discussed the game's importance. Gaither described the Spartans as "the greatest team we've ever played against."[46] And Curci paid the Rattlers a similar tribute. Despite upsetting Mississippi State and Tulane, he called FAMU "the best team we've played in the two years I've been here."[47] Gaither stayed up all night talking to bleary-eyed reporters about the game's significance. He and others saw this matchup as a positive sign for future race relations. Despite a phalanx of police officers in the stands and around the perimeter of the field, there were no racial episodes. "There were no incidents, nothing but good, clean hard hitting," Gaither exclaimed.[48] Given the urban rebellions that more than a hundred cities experienced after Martin Luther King's assassination and the growth of Black Power in sports, the fact that there were no conflagrations at a game of such magnitude presented exciting possibilities for future HBCU versus PWI games. FAMU was not the first team to take on a PWI; TSU, Southern, and Morgan State had all taken on white opponents before, but this was the first game between two southern teams, a game that had the potential to grow into a "natural rivalry."[49] Grambling's Eddie Robinson attended the game to scout FAMU for the OBC and noted the importance for southern HBCUs. "If people in other states can see what happened here tonight, it won't be long, before we and other black schools will be able to play the best of our all-white neighbors," said Robinson.[50] Sportswriters immediately began dreaming of FAMU playing the University of Miami or Grambling taking on LSU.[51]

For Gaither, the win immediately became the "most satisfying" of his career because it "vindicated Negro college athletics." He believed that Black college football "should be better appreciated now."[52] The game confirmed the truthfulness of Gaither's recruiting pitches; the Rattlers were as good as or better than many white programs. The win was evidence of the power of Black college athletics' sporting congregation and embodied HBCU football's golden age. "Now you and everyone else can see what can be done with a contest like this," declared Eddie Robinson.[53]

The sellout crowd also justified future games. Ticket sales amounted to a staggering $160,000, and each team received more than $55,000 net profit from the game. The game's revenue was essential for FAMU, with the state facing a budget crisis. The lower tax revenues forced legislators to eliminate UF's football subsidy and reduce FSU's by $50,000. FAMU athletics was spared, keeping its $80,000 biannual allowance. However, Gaither knew that after FAMU had to fight for its very existence, it could not continue to rely on the benevolence of the state government no longer invested in segregation.[54]

As important as the game was historically and financially for FAMU, the Rattlers were still overshadowed by the state's larger institutions. Florida defeated the University of Miami in front of 70,000 fans the same evening as the Tampa–FAMU game. More vital in the long term was UF's massive athletic budget. UF anticipated a surplus of more than $630,000, including more than $350,000 from the Florida–Georgia game alone. Gaither's "tightly-constructed budget" allowed the Rattlers to turn a $97,000 profit on par with FSU and better than Miami. Still, the state's big-three schools each generated more than $650,000 in revenues, compared with FAMU's $230,000. The Rattlers needed to play and defeat these schools soon before the financial advantages were transferred to the field.[55]

The intersection between the athletic revenue and integrated games pointed to the precarious position that FAMU and other HBCUs inhabited in the NCAA Small College Division. Many small colleges wanted to avoid playing powerful HBCUs like FAMU, Grambling, or TSU, fearing an embarrassing loss. The small college voters that determined the rankings allowed this to continue, as Black colleges often had lower rankings than their records suggested. For instance, undefeated and no. 5–ranked Alcorn

State trailed twice-defeated Akron and 1-loss Louisiana Tech in 1969. There was too much risk for teams at the top of the rankings and too much fear for those programs at the bottom. Moreover, fans wanted to see Grambling against LSU, not Louisiana Tech. While HBCUs once had a monopoly on African American athletes, integration increased the significance of the gap in athletic revenues. Superior facilities, better budgets, and the best players were obstacles that would be difficult to overcome. For now, FAMU was well positioned because of the Tampa game and its annual OBC.

GAITHER AND ROBINSON BATTLE ONE LAST TIME

After the exhilarating victory over Tampa, Gaither turned his attention to Eddie Robinson's Grambling State Tigers. Robinson had attended FAMU's historic game against Tampa, as a show of support to his longtime friend and to scout the Rattlers. The thirty-seventh OBC would be Grambling's fourth appearance, with the Tigers winning two of the previous three. It was fitting that a contest between the two premier Black college football programs would follow the historic matchup.

The game almost didn't happen, however. Gaither wanted to break the color line at the OBC. State politics had denied Gaither the opportunity to play a PWI in 1965. "Now the atmosphere is a more favorable one," said Gaither. Throughout the fall, he contacted several leading small college programs—California State University–Hayward (now California State University–East Bay), Troy State, and Texas A&I. Gaither's search for a PWI opponent had two causes. First, it reflected a belief in the quality of Black college football and the need to show this quality on a high-profile stage. A second reason was the continual athletic jealousy among HBCUs. As Sam Lacy noted, "The players, the coaches and the schools of all the conferences are jealous of each other."[56] The source of the disagreement ahead of the 1969 OBC was the agreement between the CIAA and the SWAC to create a new game at the Houston Astrodome that pitted the two conference winners. The game would eliminate two of the best choices for the OBC. In addition, the game was to be played on the same day as the OBC. Gaither was incensed. "Members of the CIAA stood behind us when we first started the Classic in the bleak years. When it started to become a profitable game, I took the stand that we should continue to play predominately black schools from that conference. Now, I regret that decision."[57] After California State–Hayward started with a 5 and 1 record, Gaither had the Pioneers at the top of his list, but the NCAA's 10-game rule posed a problem. The OBC was technically not an NCAA-sanctioned bowl game. For decades, FAMU compared the OBC to the exhibition bowl games that defined the pageantry of college football. In the OBC's early years, Black college football treated it as a bowl game, even naming mythical title winners before the game was played. However, when FAMU joined the NCAA Small College Division, the game needed further clarification. Rather than having the NCAA certify the classic as a bowl, FAMU treated the game as its final regular-season game for financial reasons. Therefore, Gaither needed a team that had not played a 10-game regular-season schedule. When a reporter asked Gaither why he did not select Ohio State, which had only played 9 games in 1969, Gaither responded confidently, "I doubt if Woody Hayes would want to play my boys."[58]

Among Black colleges, Grambling was the obvious choice. The Tigers entered the game with 2 losses; thus, the NCAA did not pick Grambling for one of its small college regional bowl games. Grambling was the most popular team in Black college football. Over the course of the 1968 and 1969 seasons, the Tigers played before more than 400,000 fans, playing in some of the largest stadiums in the country—the Houston Astrodome, the Los Angeles Coliseum, and New York's Yankee Stadium. Bringing the Tigers to the Orange Bowl was low-risk.

On a warm evening when wind gusts reached twenty miles per hour, FAMU and Grambling played another highly contested OBC. After Grambling scored the game's first touchdown, FAMU answered with two touchdowns of its own. Scruggs set up the Rattlers' first score with a 42-yard run. Ginn broke two tackles to finish the drive. Scruggs scored FAMU's second touchdown of the first half on a short 4-yard run. As the members of the Marching 100 made their way to the field, the Rattlers led 14 to 6 at the half.

During halftime, FAMU's band paid tribute to the Apollo 11 moon landing. Both coaches made adjustments and encouraged their players to play harder in the last game of the season. The Rattlers' opening drive of the third quarter stalled. FAMU added a short field goal to lead 17 to 6. Eddie Robinson unveiled his surprise adjustment for the second half. He substituted "freshman terror" Matthew Reed at quarterback. The six-foot five-inch, 225-pound Reed looked physically similar to James "Shack" Harris, who was on his way to becoming the first regular starting Black quarterback in the NFL. Both Harris and Reed were from Monroe, Louisiana. While Harris was the prototypical drop-back quarterback, Reed was among the first great dual-threat quarterbacks. Harris later described Reed as "the best high school quarterback I've ever seen."[59] Against the Rattlers, he showed why. On his first drive, he completed several passes in a 66-yard drive that ended with an 8-yard touchdown run. With its lead trimmed to 17 to 12, FAMU looked to retake control of the game. Three plays into the drive, Scruggs threw an interception. Grambling had the ball on the Rattler side of midfield and looked to take the lead. A fired-up Reed overthrew receivers on consecutive passes and then threw an interception. The third quarter ended after a FAMU punt pinned the Tigers deep in their end.

The Tigers opened the fourth quarter with the ball on their 8-yard line. Robinson knew his team couldn't afford another turnover, so he turned to his running game to give the offense some room to operate. Two runs on first and second down gained 7 yards. On third and three, Robinson surprised the Rattler defense by calling a pass play. Reed threw a bomb to Frank Lewis, Grambling leading receiver and rusher. The 85-yard touchdown quieted the Rattler fans and emboldened the smaller Grambling contingent of fans. The Tigers added an extra point, their first successful conversion of the evening, for a 19 to 17 lead. Gaither had just less than 14 minutes to find an answer.

The Rattlers had the ball with 6:39 remaining in the game. Gaither turned to the power running game. Jim Owens bulldozed through a tired Tigers' defense. On second down and six at the Grambling 22-yard line, the Rattlers ran a pitchout to the left. Ginn took the toss, cut back to the middle, and eluded three tacklers for the touchdown and a 23 to 19 lead. The senior running back spiked the ball after he scored. The spike or "busting the ball" had spread throughout high school, college, and professional football. FAMU's Willie Galimore started the spike in the 1950s, and the move had become a FAMU trademark. Integration at all levels spread "busting the ball" throughout the game. Black athletic joy could not be contained. However, the NCAA saw Blacks' stylish expression as taunting, an infraction needing to be punished. Before the season, Gaither explained his displeasure at the new penalty for spiking the football. "The new rule makes no sense at all."[60] After the touchdown and the penalty, the Rattlers kicked off from the 25-yard line, needing their defense to make one last stop.[61]

For the third time this season, it was up to the Rattler defense to stop a premier opponent. The Tigers started their drive at their 34-yard line. Sixty-six yards separated the Tigers from victory. Freshman quarterback Reed moved the ball over midfield with a couple of completions. The Rattler defense increased its intensity, forcing Reed into incomplete passes. On fourth down, defensive pressure led Reed to overthrow his receiver. The

Rattlers' defense held again. More than 36,000 fans cheered as the FAMU offense ran out the clock in the 23 to 19 victory.[62]

It was a fitting conclusion to a pathbreaking season. Gaither defeated old and new foes on his way to 203 career wins. The era of segregated football, for FAMU, was over. Gaither announced, "From now on, we're going after the best competition around. I'll schedule any team. I don't care if they're black, white, yellow, orange or green."[63] The victory over Tampa meant that Gaither had brought the Rattlers football program from the shadow of World War II to the new world of integrated football in the South. Only Grambling's Eddie Robinson had a similar career arc in Black college football.

Gaither's supporters demanded that he be honored on an equal plane with white coaches. When Clemson's Frank Howard retired in December 1969 with 165 wins, sportswriters noted that he was among the three winningest coaches with Alabama's Paul "Bear" Bryant (193) and Ole Miss's Johnny Vaught (177). Florida congressman Don Fuqua wanted the inaccuracy corrected on Capitol Hill. He declared, "In this centennial year of college football, let us get one thing straight. The winningest coach in football—and he has held the title for some time—is 'Jake' Gaither of Florida A. & M. University of Tallahassee, Florida."[64] Few expected Gaither to retire after his best season in five years.

GAITHER RETIRES

"Now that the pressures of the football season are over, I wish to make several recommendations involving personnel in athletics," wrote Gaither ten days after the season-ending victory over Grambling. In his letter to new FAMU president Benjamin L. Perry, Gaither informed the school's leader that "I want to be relieved of head coaching duties at the end of the 1969 football season" while keeping his positions as athletic director and professor of physical education. He explained the bittersweet feelings associated with his decision. "Coaching football at FAMU has brought me much happiness," but "the three positions [head coach, athletic director, and professor] are very heavy and demanding and I feel that it is time now to relinquish the coaching duties and responsibilities to a young man."

Gaither knew he had been lucky. The brain tumors should have killed him, yet he had survived and coached for twenty-five years. In the last few years, however, his age had begun to show. The broken leg suffered in 1967 had relegated him to a golf cart at practice. In 1969, he struggled with his eyesight and had to rely on his assistant coaches to relay key plays verbally.[65] His family perhaps remembered that Henry Arthur Kean had suffered a heart attack after a game in 1954 and died a year later. Sadie and his brothers had urged Gaither after the 1969 season to retire while he still had his health. "As I say often, Florida and the Almighty have been good to me as I have labored for Florida A&M" were the final words in his resignation letter. President Perry gave Gaither the holidays to contemplate the decision before accepting the resignation.[66]

In the weeks between Gaither submitting the letter and the New Year, he continued to pile up awards. The Washington, D.C., Touchdown Club announced that Gaither was receiving the Board of Governors Award for outstanding football contributions. The 100% Wrong Club named him SIAC Coach of the Year. The honors did not lure him back to the sidelines. As Christmas and New Year's passed, Gaither never wavered on retiring.[67]

"It is with much ambivalence that I reluctantly accept your resignation as head coach," wrote President Perry five days into the new year. Perry's letter noted that Gaither helped FAMU rise "from oblivion to notoriety" and he was a "legend in its development." More important, Gaither had given "youth the opportunity to attend college" and "inspired them to achieve and become leaders."[68] As Gaither attended awards banquets and spoke at football banquets, word spread of his impending retirement.[69] At the end of January, FAMU made it official by sending a press release announcing Gaither's retirement. Gaither told reporters, "The reason is simply this: I don't want to press my luck too long." He added, "Since being coach at Florida A&M I have survived a brain operation, I have survived blindness and I have survived a broken leg." For Gaither, God had been good. Now the team was in the hands of longtime defensive coordinator Pete Griffin.

The news of Gaither's retirement spurred organizations, universities, and sportswriters to recognize his legacy of greatness. The NAIA named him Coach of the Year.[70] Florida congressman Don Fuqua honored him as a "living legend" on Capitol Hill.[71] The Florida state legislators gave Gaither a standing ovation.[72] UF and the city of Miami made plans for Jake Gaither Day in the spring and summer.[73] Sports editor Buddy Martin of *Florida Today* described Gaither as a man of character and "the best-respected football coach" in Florida history.[74] Longtime *Atlanta Daily World* columnist Marion Jackson detailed their relationship. Jackson wrote, "I have publicly and privately disagreed with retired Coach A. S. (Jake) Gaither for years," but their friendship never wavered. Jackson admitted that Gaither's questioning of his articles made him a better writer. Despite the "fallouts,"

Jackson was always welcomed in Jake and Sadie's home "with dinner and goodwill."[75]

Gaither retired as the NCAA's active leader in wins with 203, including three undefeated seasons and a remarkable twelve 1-loss seasons. He won six Black college national titles. He won 83.5 percent of his games. He lost only 3 SIAC games in twenty-five years. He produced a *Pittsburgh Courier* All-American every season. More than thirty-five players made it to the NFL, and dozens more played in the Canadian Football League. Gaither was a profoundly religious southerner who molded young men into community leaders by preaching the "Spirit of Excellence." His postretirement speeches revealed that his winning coaching philosophy was tethered to a deeply held social conservatism. For instance, he warned high school graduates in West Palm Beach to avoid the social upheavals led by students—Black Power, antiwar protests, and hippies—that had led to "a new breed of American youth." He called on the new graduates to resist "a youth who is critical of the status quo . . . one who rebels against his heritage, one who taunts his parents." This radical youth of the 1970s, explained Gaither, requires law and order to return to cities and campuses. By parroting a component of President Richard Nixon's southern strategy, Gaither publicized his opposition to the 1960s push for social justice. Gaither called for uncritical "trust" of American leaders.[76] Given the revelations of Gaither's problematic political positions, he had been rightly criticized for not becoming more involved in the civil rights movement and for opposing the substance of Black Power. Nonetheless, he believed in Black people and Black institutions.

Journalist Ric Roberts perhaps best captured Gaither's significance. The venerable sportswriter was the historian of Black college football, having participated in and watched the game for nearly fifty years. As a former player at Clark College, Roberts had played against Gaither in the 1920s. Roberts contextualized Gaither's achievements against the other great Black college coaches. In Roberts's estimation, Gaither had surpassed Morgan State's Eddie Hurt and TSU's Henry Arthur Kean. The FAMU head coach's six national titles matched those of Tuskegee's Cleveland Abbott and Prairie View's Billy Nicks and were one better than Southern's Arnett Mumford's. Roberts also witnessed the reasons so many young men wanted to play for Gaither. Roberts described that Gaither's happiness "comes from seeing the many young lives he influenced blossom into useful productive elements of society, displaying the quality of leadership, patience, perseverance and a willingness to pay the price for a just cause."[77]

Gaither's retirement also coincided with a decline in circulation and influence in the Black press. Black newspapers such as the *Pittsburgh Courier* and the *Chicago Defender* were essential in making HBCU football national news. Just as integration undermined the recruiting networks of Black colleges, social change weakened many Black newspapers. All the leading Black newspapers saw a decline in circulation from the heights of post–World War II. By 1970, the *Defender* declined in circulation from 257,000 to 33,000, and the *Courier* fell from 202,000 to 20,000. The drop in circulation meant fewer readers about Black college football. Additionally, the total number of Black newspapers fell from 213 to 165 between 1974 and 1979.[78] Simultaneously, the mainstream media normalized athletic integration at PWIs, while often making HBCU football an afterthought on its pages. When combined with the elimination of Black high schools and the rise of television, HBCU football was barely visible for many up-and-coming high school athletes. The end of critical variables of the sporting congregation also marked the end of the golden age of Black college football.

Gaither's retirement signaled the end of FAMU's role as a leader in the golden age of Black college football. There was only one Jake Gaither, and FAMU struggled to find a coach who could replicate his winning ways and his larger-than-life influence in the state of Florida. The Rattlers quickly became a mediocre program, playing .500 ball in the first five seasons of the 1970s.

Beyond the matter of replacing Gaither, FAMU faced a changing landscape in which the Black sporting congregation could no longer overcome the material disadvantages. The end of Black high schools disrupted the recruiting pipeline, the influence of the Black press began to wane, and the OBC was beset by a weakened FAMU team and competition from professional football. Black colleges' limited budgets, buttressed by classics, were no match for the growing impact of television money. Athletic budgets soared to well over $1 million per year for Division I programs. Having a good team now meant being on television, which guaranteed more than $100,000 in revenue per appearance. The NCAA controlled the televised game schedule, meaning all small colleges were at the mercy of the NCAA TV committee that scheduled games. Black colleges were twice affected, as racism and size combined to keep the most compelling HBCU matchups off television. While Grambling and TSU carried the golden age into the 1970s, the Rattlers' decline served as the canary in the coal mine for what was to come.

EPILOGUE: CHASING GHOSTS
HBCU Football at the End of the Century

n February 1994, Gaither was buried in his green blazer. Two thousand people, many dressed in green or orange instead of traditional black, filled the gymnasium that bore his name to pay their respects. Three hundred of his former players, Gaither's "boys," including Bob Hayes, huddled one last time around their mentor. Lawton Chiles attended, representing four decades of Florida governors who respected Gaither. Chiles commanded that the flags across the state be lowered out of respect. FSU's Bobby Bowden and the Orange Bowl Committee were present on behalf of the fraternity of college football. No one was more heartbroken than Sadie, who had lost her husband of sixty-three years.[1]

Gaither's lessons infused the two-hour home-going ceremony. Ernest Fears Jr. noted the spirit of excellence. "If you're going to be a lawyer, win all your cases. If you're going to be a ditch-digger, then you dig that ditch deeper, wider, longer and faster than any ditch has ever been dug!" A teary-eyed Bob Hayes told the audience, "He was my friend, my coach, my mentor, but most of all he was my father." Mario Casem spoke for the HBCU coaching community: "Jake Gaither was the standard by which all coaches in our time were judged." He added, "Standing here today, I'm proud of Florida A&M."[2] Gaither was the gold standard of HBCU football, and the Rattlers were among the best of the golden age. By 1994, however, FAMU had struggled to replace Gaither, and HBCU football no longer threatened to upset the status quo of college football.

FOLLOWING A LEGEND

FAMU went through four coaches in five seasons in its attempts to find a quality replacement for Gaither. The soft-spoken Robert "Pete" Griffin had the unenviable task of succeeding a football coaching legend. The Columbus, Ohio, native, rarely seen on the sidelines without a fedora, well understood the magnitude of his task. Griffin was a member of FAMU's first national title team in 1938 and was an All-American center in 1939.[3] He showed his coaching acumen while still playing. When Gaither, then an assistant coach, was felled by his brain tumor, Griffin assisted Bill Bell during spring football practice.[4] He returned to Tallahassee in 1944, becoming a full-time assistant football coach. Like all of FAMU's football coaches, he directed other teams as well, serving as the track, baseball, and swimming coach at various times in his twenty-six years in Tallahassee. After earning his master's degree from Ohio State University, he became a professor of physical education. His thesis on the history of football at FAMU from 1887 to 1946 gave him a historical perspective on the enormity of his task.[5]

Griffin did not necessarily want the job, since he "knew it was a tough act to follow." Nevertheless, he accepted the position out of respect to Gaither.[6] Despite Griffin's reluctance, he was the right choice for the job. The longtime assistant had produced high-quality defenses annually. Griffin's hard-hitting, physical defenses had allowed only about 11 points per game in twenty-six seasons. His defenses had two remarkable seasons. In the undefeated 1957 season, the Rattler defense allowed only 41 points total. The defensive record was broken four seasons later when the Rattlers gave up 33 points on the way to another national title. In 1969, Griffin's unit marshaled the defensive stands to defeat Southern, Tampa, and Grambling. He had earned the job with service and production and planned on keeping "the winning tradition" Gaither had built.[7]

Unfortunately, the Rattlers struggled in Griffin's first season. FAMU won its first 3 games but was upset by Morris Brown in the fourth game of the season. Griffin's first loss highlighted the difficulties of integration. The Rattlers gave up an 88-yard kickoff return, had an extra point blocked, and had a punt blocked that was returned for a touchdown. Before the game, FAMU's placekicker Joseph Jewett announced that he had quit the team. Jewett, the first white player to score at FAMU, said he was harassed by a small group of students at FAMU, telling him, "Whitey, you should go home while you still can." The freshman reported that he was supported by the team and most of the student body, but he could not take the harassment. With no higher moral purpose, white students at FAMU refused to accept any mistreatment for the cause of integration—even when on an athletic scholarship.[8] The season only went downhill after the first loss. The Rattlers lost to TSU and Southern. However, the last 2 games were the most disappointing.

FAMU faced Tampa in a rematch of the previous season's historic game. Tampa entered the game as the no. 1–ranked small college team in the country, and the Spartans routed FAMU 49 to 7.[9] The following week FAMU faced the Jacksonville State University Gamecocks in the OBC. The Gamecocks become the first PWI to compete in the OBC. "It's a time of change," said Gaither, "and we went after the best available team."[10] Jacksonville State relied on the running of five-foot seven-inch, 157-pound Boyce Callahan to control the game in a 21 to 7 Gamecocks win. The freshman running back ran for 222 yards, finishing the season with more than 2,000 yards. The Rattlers again hurt themselves. FAMU fumbled four times. The turnovers led to two fourth-quarter scores for the Gamecocks.[11] One supporter told a reporter, "This is the first time since I can remember seeing a FAMU team outreached this bad."[12] Former player Nathaniel "Traz" Powell said, "The Jacksonville State game was the last straw."[13] Alumni who watched the losses to Tampa and Jacksonville State recognized a growing chasm in the talent between FAMU and the PWIs. The lopsided results showed how quickly integration had changed the Rattlers' ability to recruit. The end of the dual education system, which had been in motion since 1966, had gutted the sporting congregations that had supported the program. FAMU alumnus Traz Powell exemplified the changing network. He had coached for seventeen years at George Washington Carver in Miami and won six Black high school titles, but as part of Miami's desegregation plan, the school became a junior high. By 1970, he had retired, ending the coaching career of the best high school recruiter for FAMU in Miami. FAMU's recruiting was not only affected by the loss of high school coaches like Powell but failed in comparison with the material, and sometimes illegal, resources of big colleges. "You can talk to a boy all you want about being loyal to black schools, but when someone offers to help mama with payments for the house, a bright red car, or a charge account, that gives the boy a little something else to think about," said Powell. He spearheaded a fundraising effort that would allow FAMU to recruit the "blue chip" Black athletes to play football and get their degrees.[14] For the first time since 1944, FAMU failed to put a player on the *Pittsburgh Courier* All-American team.

Following the disappointing season, Griffin resigned. "I didn't take the job to become a mediocre coach," he said.[15] Two coaches—Clarence Montgomery and James Williams—followed with similar results. Both were alumni and understood the expectations. Yet both had similar results. Montgomery went 6–5, including a 56 to 14 loss to Tampa. Already a slight 140 pounds when he was hired, he fell ill with a "stomach ailment" during the season. The affliction forced Montgomery to miss the last 3 games of the season. There was little alarm about the coach's health. In January 1972, however, a FAMU press release somberly announced Montgomery's sudden death. Few realized he had been hospitalized since November. He had surgery, and most assumed he was on the road to recovery when he passed away. In hindsight, it appears that Montgomery's insistence on the "interim" head coach title was based on the illness. The tragedy forced FAMU to search for its third coach since Gaither's retirement.[16]

Williams lasted only two seasons. The Rattlers finished with a losing record both years. In 1972, Williams's first season, the OBC was a shadow of its former glory. The *Chicago Defender*'s A. S. "Doc" Young called the game "the Forgotten Bowl." He added, "It used to be a great big bowl. But, today it's just a small saucer in the footballic [sic] scheme of things."[17] FAMU administrators seriously debated moving the OBC from Miami back to Tampa after the poor attendance in 1971 and 1973. "We are happy to be working with Miami. We are not going to leave," said Gaither. "My greatest concern," he added, "is that we do a better job of getting people into the stands."[18] Gaither retired as athletic director in the fall of 1973. In March 1974, President Perry fired the entire coaching staff. The new coach would be the fourth since Gaither's retirement. Sportswriter Bill Nunn Jr. expected the next coach not to be a former Rattler. The program needed to move in a new direction and away from Gaither's shadow. The legendary coach's retirement as athletic director gave the administration the necessary space to move in a new direction.[19]

RUDY'S RENAISSANCE

After an exhaustive coaching search, FAMU announced that it had hired Rudy Hubbard, a former Ohio State University running back and an assistant coach. He became the first coach since Bill Bell who was not an HBCU graduate. At first glance, it seemed that new FAMU athletic director Hansel Tookes had decided to hire a coach outside Gaither's orbit. The twenty-eight-year-old Hubbard was an Ohio native who attended integrated elementary and secondary schools before playing running back for the Ohio State Buckeyes and head coach Woody Hayes. After his graduation, Hubbard joined Hayes's staff as an assistant coach, making a name for himself as a sharp recruiter of African American players. He was credited with recruiting Archie Griffin, then a highly touted freshman running back who would go on to win two Heisman Trophies, to Columbus, and John Hicks, the 1973 Outland Trophy and Lombardi Award winner, two awards for college football's best lineman. The Buckeyes won two national titles and five conference championships while Hubbard was an assistant under Hayes. Despite Hubbard appearing far removed from Black college football, his selection reflected the relationship between Gaither and Ohio State University. Gaither and Griffin had earned their master's degrees from the

Big Ten institution, and Hayes was a regular at the FAMU coaching clinic in the summer. It was no surprise, then, that Gaither supported the hire. "We made a great move when we hired Hubbard away from Ohio State," said Gaither.[20] The retired coach understood that Hubbard's coaching ethos of hard work, discipline, and fundamentals would be similar to Hayes's. "I think a lot like Woody," except for the controversial outbursts, stated Hubbard.[21] For Gaither, these principles were the foundation of winning. Rattler fans and alumni anticipated victories. Hubbard was not intimidated by the expectations. "I'm not worried about alumni pressure because I intend to win," he declared.[22]

Integration had made it difficult to get the best players to FAMU, thereby making wins scarcer. By the mid-1970s, many colleges in the South had moved beyond token desegregation. For instance, between 1973 and 1977 the percentage of Black lettermen in SEC football jumped from 11.6 percent to 27.3 percent.[23] UF exemplified the change. Under Florida head coach Doug Dickey, the 1974 Gators started an all-Black backfield, led by Don Gaffney at quarterback. The team won 9 games that season and appeared in the Gator Bowl. Sportswriters expected sixteen of the twenty-two Gator starters to be African American in 1975.[24] No longer able to rely on the FAMU sporting congregation that had powered Gaither's success, Hubbard reshaped the roster each off-season with undervalued but talented players. He also positioned FAMU to compete against leading PWIs. The Rattlers announced that they had signed a 2-game agreement to play the University of Miami in 1979 and 1980. The Rattlers' coach challenged the notion that "a black school won't do well against a white school." He added, "I don't believe in the superiority of a predominately white school over a predominately black one or a division one school over a division two. That's one of the things I'm trying to dispel. . . . I don't see how people can take it for granted that [UF's] Doug Dickey is a better coach than I am. . . . The University of Florida doesn't want to play us. I'd like to play them."[25]

The 1977 season proved Hubbard's expectations were correct. The Rattlers completed the school's first perfect season since 1961. The key game of the season was against TSU. Hubbard had rekindled the rivalry with a win in 1975. He raised questions about the officials and the eligibility of TSU's starting quarterback. The Rattlers won a seesaw battle 31 to 28.[26] After the no. 1–ranked University of Texas was upset in the Cotton Bowl on New Year's Day, the Rattlers were the only undefeated college football team in the country. Hubbard reminded anyone who would listen that HBCUs could contend against any school. "People from large schools say we [Black colleges] couldn't compete. Well I've been on both sides and I believe we could play anybody in the country and expect to win," declared Hubbard.[27]

FAMU's undefeated season came amid discussions among the NCAA's leading schools to reorganize the top level of football. FAMU and other HBCUs wanted to be members of the upper echelon—Division I football. There were 144 Division I teams at the end of the 1977 season. For some programs, there were far too many teams. During the 1976 and 1977 NCAA convention large football schools sought to form a "super division" of big-time institutions. Many universities from the leading conferences demanded larger revenues from television. Moreover, the schools believed their larger stadiums, which often seated more than 50,000 fans, should distance them from smaller institutions. The larger schools had tried to relegate about 100 institutions from Division I to Division II at earlier NCAA conventions. The smaller football schools and basketball schools, like Villanova, joined together to thwart the 1976 and 1977 reorganization plans.[28] Although plans for a super conference were initially foiled, schools from the Atlantic Coast Conference, SEC, Southwest Conference, Big-8, and leading independents, including Notre Dame, Miami, FSU, and Penn State, helped to form the College Football Association.[29]

HBCU football programs were categorized as small schools. However, the success of Grambling, TSU, and FAMU on the field and at the turnstiles during the OBC or the Bayou Classic signaled big-time football status. HBCUs' underfunded facilities, however, supported football on a much smaller scale. As one reporter described Grambling University, it "is an enigma in the sports world. It really doesn't belong in either Division 1 or Division 2. If the idea is to put all the schools with similar programs and problems in the same division, Grambling belongs in division 1-G, all by itself."[30]

Therefore, it was no surprise that when HBCUs jumped to Division I in 1977, Grambling led an octet that included TSU, Southern, Jackson State, Alcorn State, Texas Southern, Norfolk State, and South Carolina State.[31] For HBCU football after integration, Grambling was at the top of the mountain. Its Bayou Classic against Southern University outdrew the 1977 Sugar Bowl, featuring Heisman Trophy winner Tony Dorsett and an undefeated University of Pittsburgh team battling a 10 and 1 University of Georgia squad.[32] Eddie Robinson's Tigers had traveled to Tokyo twice, and Doug Williams finished fourth in the 1978 Heisman Trophy race. The move to the top division in football could potentially add hundreds of thousands of dollars to their athletic budgets. These schools were enticed by the opportunity to play on the highest level. FAMU, on the other hand, worried about the expanded costs and remained in Division II.

In 1978, the NCAA reorganized the football divisions, creating I-A and I-AA tiers.[33] In I-A were the elite large football schools, like Ohio State University. At the I-AA level were smaller schools with ambitions for the highest levels of football or a legacy of competing at that level. The NCAA guaranteed television appearances to entice teams to move to the lower tier. In total, the NCAA offered a pool of $750,000 in TV money to be distributed among I-AA teams, including those that participated in the subdivision's playoff. The television appearances and the chance to become an authentic, and not mythical, national champion was enough to get Alcorn, Grambling, Jackson State, and other HBCUs to move to I-AA.[34] FAMU decided to move up to the I-AA level from Division II. FAMU president Walter Smith stated, Division I "will afford us the opportunity to compete for bowl bids, TV appearances, and project our players into better positions for professional football draft possibilities."[35] In moving to I-AA, FAMU also severed its fifty-year relationship with the SIAC. FAMU's leap to I-AA also made the Rattlers eligible for the playoffs in 1978.[36]

In 1978, the Rattlers were holders of the nation's longest winning streak (12 games), but the program was still underestimated. FAMU pushed the win streak to 17 games before losing to TSU. Hubbard righted the ship, and the Rattlers finished the season with 1 loss and an invitation to the inaugural I-AA football playoff. In their first game, the Rattlers dispatched Jackson State University 15 to 10. The following week, FAMU headed to Wichita Falls for the championship game against the University of Massachusetts. The Rattlers' defense limited the damage of its mistakes, while the offense took advantage of its opponents. Behind three rushing touchdowns from Mike Solomon and the leadership of quarterback Albert Chester, FAMU defeated UMass 35 to 28.[37] Despite a slow start, Chester had orchestrated a masterful game. Chester did not complete a single pass and threw two interceptions, but his reads on the FAMU option attack led to 470 yards rushing on seventy-six attempts against a defense that had allowed one touchdown or less in 8 of its 12 games.[38] Solomon finished the game with 207 yards and three touchdowns, and running back Melvin McFayden added 177 yards and two touchdowns. One UMass defender said, "I knew from the [game] films that they'd be tough, but I never thought they'd be this tough." Head coach Bob Pickett was surprised by FAMU's ability to run the football. "They had real big splits in the line," he said, unaware of Gaither's innovative legacy.[39] Gaither had watched nearly every play during the Rattlers championship season. He told reporters, "I don't think Florida A&M has any better booster than me. I watched all but one game." The Rattlers wide splits and the prolific running game brought back memories.[40]

As noted in the introduction, Hubbard fulfilled his goal of FAMU becoming a big-time program by beating the University of Miami. The victory was Hubbard's last great moment as FAMU's head coach. In 1979, the Rattlers stumbled to a 7 and 4 record after beating Miami. After going 30 and 5 between 1977 and 1979, Hubbard won only 32 games over the next six seasons (with 34 loses). The Rattlers, despite a spectacular three seasons, had not regained their former dominance. The program continued to be plagued by problems into the 1980s. Hubbard's wins did not translate into a larger, more competitive budget. Before Hubbard resigned in 1985, he explained, "The missing ingredient [for success] is money."[41] The move to I-AA had increased the program's costs by adding an additional fifteen scholarships that ballooned the budget by $42,000.[42] Although the championship run in 1978 added $500,000 because of televised games, the Rattlers were not regularly on TV after 1979. Ahead of the 1981 season, Donn Bernstein, director of media relations for ABC Sports, explained, "We'll just look at I-AA games like we look at everything else. If we see a game that is hot and would be good for that market we'll consider it."[43] HBCU observers were dubious that Black college teams would be attractive enough for consistent television.

Cable television, though a boon for televised college sports, had little to offer HBCUs. In 1979, ESPN, the twenty-four-hour sports television network, was founded. Two years after its launch, only the FAMU versus Miami game had been broadcasted.[44] The differences in televised appearances between big-time college football and I-AA teams, especially Black college teams, meant a tremendous difference in revenue. For instance, a rare televised game on ABC against TSU in October 1983 brought in a much needed $334,000.[45] Rudy Hubbard explained, "We balanced our books with the television money. When the possibility of television money and exposure disappeared we had hard times. We have not been able to generate enough revenue to build the program and keep up with the times."[46] The 1984 NCAA v. *University of Oklahoma* Supreme Court decision ruled that athletic conferences, and not the NCAA, could negotiate their television deals. The ruling ended any chance of FAMU or any other Black college football program relying on television revenue. The free market of televised college football was a harsh terrain for HBCUs. In 1984 and 1985, no

Black college team appeared on television. Not even Grambling's victory over Oregon State University, in which Eddie Robinson tied Paul "Bear" Bryant with 322 career victories, warranted television coverage. According to Donn Bernstein, ABC's college sports publicist, "Showing [HBCU] games was a matter of symbolism, more or less, it was a good thing. But this is business, and a cold business at that and when the Supreme Court's decision came down, a lot of little people got hurt."[47] The absence of TV revenue combined with growing costs meant that most HBCU's bled money on athletics.

The decline of the OBC signaled that there would not be a return to the dominance of Gaither's era. In the early 1980s, the OBC was marred by irregularity, as locations and dates shifted constantly. In 1980, the University of Miami refused to name its home game against FAMU the "Orange Blossom Classic," and there were no other open dates at the Orange Bowl. The forty-eighth OBC was held away from Miami for the first time in thirty-three years.[48] With the Rattlers amid a losing season and Bragg Stadium being repaired, only 7,117 fans attended the 1980 OBC in Tallahassee. The game that had annually balanced the athletic budget lost money. The game returned to Miami in 1981 and 1982 but had lower than expected crowds. In an attempt to revive the game, FAMU officials moved it to Tampa in 1983 and 1984. Finally, the OBC returned to Miami in Hubbard's final season. No longer was the OBC played the first weekend in December in Miami, no longer marking the end of the Rattlers' regular-season schedule. The game was moved around on the Rattlers' schedule. With the I-AA playoffs beginning the first week in December, FAMU played the OBC three times in November and three times in October. The game's changing host city and revolving spot on the Rattlers' schedule depressed attendance and hurt the athletic department's budget. In order for the Rattlers to not lose money on the game, the OBC, excluding the 1980 game in Tallahassee, needed 19,000 fans.[49] The average attendance for the OBC from 1981 to 1985 was 19,319. The game was no longer guaranteed to put the Rattlers' budget in the black.

The informal sporting congregation that had sustained Gaither's program was transformed into a booster club under Hubbard. But there were key differences that were never reconciled. Teaching opportunities, information about recruits, and Florida's Black communities were the currency of exchange for the sporting congregation of a segregated educational system. The modern booster club, especially under Hubbard, only had to raise money. He minimized the ethos that had sustained Black college football under segregation and focused on the money it needed to compete on the national stage. Hubbard appreciated the recommendations on players but needed donations for his ambitious plans for big-time football. Boosters countered by withdrawing their support.

The 1982 homecoming weekend highlighted the growing divide between Hubbard and the school's alumni. The weekend damaged Hubbard in the eyes of the alumni. In front of a sellout crowd of 25,000, the Rattlers played an uninspired game against the 2–5 Alcorn State Braves, losing 23 to 13. The Rattlers led at halftime but only managed 30 yards of offense and a single first down in the second half. Hubbard admitted, "We were blah. Even at halftime, we were blah."[50] The FAMU Hall of Fame ceremonies at halftime contributed to alumni anger. The celebration highlighted for fans and alumni the difference between the past and the present. Six former football players that all played for Gaither were inducted, led by Ken Riley.

The rifts continued after the game. Hubbard's younger supporters gathered at his house in an integrated community in northwest Tallahassee. The "ole-timers" that ate and slept FAMU football went to Gaither's home blocks from campus. Gaither's home was filled with former players and coaches, such as Riley, Hansel Tookes, Howard Gentry, and Robert Paremore. Alumni at Gaither's home even queried Riley if he would be interested in coaching the Rattlers.[51] The divisions were clear to anyone who observed the program.

Black college booster programs made little to no financial impact. Plagued by the legacy of segregation and economic discrimination, few African Americans had the disposable income to donate to athletic programs.[52] FAMU's football rosters never raised more than $60,000 and averaged $52,000 between 1980 and 1983. Despite the boosters' small donations, the alumni organization was near the top in Black college football. TSU, Jackson State, and Grambling all raised less than $5,000 per year, choosing to rely on state funds.[53] Prairie View's booster club raised about $20,000 per year. Winston-Salem State's Clarence "Bighouse" Gaines, who led the Rams to the 1967 NCAA Division II national basketball championship, captured the budgetary challenges facing Black college sports. "We don't get $15,000 in gifts from blacks." The alumni "want to save black schools on faith. You need money," he stated.[54]

Athletic giving symbolized the growing separation between HBCU football and its PWI counterpart. The amount raised by FAMU boosters paled in comparison with the $2.5 million raised by FSU. In another case, the University of Richmond, which was winless in 1982, raised $7.5 million to endow its football scholarships by 1985.[55] Even Montana State boosters had raised $325,000 per year.[56] These donations stimulated championship ambitions.

Boosters and supporters let their displeasure with Hubbard and the Rattlers' program be known, however. Representative Al Lawson was among the most vocal. He told the *Tallahassee Democrat*, "There needs to be a major reshuffling. Are you going to just blame it on money and not find out what is really wrong?"[57] Frederick S. Humphries took over as the school's eighth president in June 1985. He was a FAMU alumnus who looked to revive the athletic department, especially after the football team went a combined 3–7–1 in 1984. Hubbard said, "There's a very strong possibility this could be my last year here. We're in a new situation all around with a new administration and new leadership. . . . I don't expect any loyalty."[58] Gaither did not publicly support Hubbard. "I've had my day, . . . I have horror [stories] about older coaches coming in and telling younger coaches what to do," he said.[59] Gaither's silence was deafening. Hubbard's 1985 squad went 4–7, and he resigned at season's end.[60]

Ken Riley, a former quarterback under Gaither, was hired as head coach. He had little coaching experience but had a successful NFL career. Riley lasted eight seasons but never could return the Rattlers to the heights of Gaither, nor could he match Hubbard's run in the late 1970s. Jake Gaither could do little to save his former quarterback's job. The elderly coach was in his ninetieth year. His legacy was an albatross around the program. Five head coaches had tried and failed to meet the expectations created by Gaither. The sixth head coach would have to forge a path without the celebrated mentor. Gaither had suffered several strokes in the 1990s, which left him bedridden for several months. Two months after FAMU had named Billy Joe as its next coach, Gaither passed away.

FAMU spent the last three decades of the twentieth century chasing Gaither's coaching legend. The inability for Hubbard to maintain his success or other coaches to win at a high rate reveals the ways that the structural disadvantages facing Black colleges in terms of athletic funding, facilities, and the logic of integration have proven difficult to overcome. These structural problems have always existed, but the sporting congregation allowed HBCU football to use its material resources in overcoming these weaknesses.

In the twenty-five years after World War II, FAMU was the best football program in Florida and among the very best in the country, Black or white. The golden age of Black college football was a result of Black sporting communities turning segregation into congregation. A belief in self-determination supported the creation of Black college football and other HBCU sports. This ethos reflected Black communities' ability to thrive in spite of white supremacy. HBCUs produced greatness because of the belief in their human resources—administrators, professors, coaches, staff members, and students. The confluence of support and inequitable but substantial resources allowed for Black college football programs like FAMU's to be among the very best in the nation.

Integration was necessary, but it came at a cost. The sporting congregation crumbled, especially for Black coaches. Lost in the rightful celebration of *Brown v. Board of Education* is the fact that thousands of teachers and coaches lost their jobs. The human resources that had guided young African American students to HBCUs dramatically declined. HBCUs' golden age of football waned. What still exists in Black college football is the ethos of the southern Black community. This community is exemplified in the tailgates, the classics, and most importantly, the marching bands. In the decades after the golden age, the community ethos in the stands, parking lots, and after-parties has become more important than the game on the field. The continued community support for FAMU and other HBCU programs signals that Black communities still support the teams even if the era of Gaither, Merritt, Mumford, or Robinson never returns. HBCU football is still a location for self-determination and culture.

ACKNOWLEDGMENTS

I have received tremendous support for this project from colleagues, friends, and family. The seeds for this project grew from my classes at Florida Atlantic University. I'd like to thank my former colleagues Evan Bennett, Sika Dagbovie, Stephen Engle, Clevis Headley, Talitha LeFlouria, and Chris Strain for their advice and support for this project. This project could not have been completed without the support from Robert Bonner, Carolyn Dever, Annelise Orleck, and Rashauna Johnson at Dartmouth College. Thank you for your continued support. I'd like to thank Donald and Shevie Brooks, Winston Bodrick, and Vincent Wilson for helping to make a community in the Upper Valley.

A number of scholars have read drafts, listened to presentations, and provided sage advice. Sports historians Brad Austin, Amira Rose Davis, Louis Moore, and Johnny Smith have welcomed me into their tribe. Thank you. The number of scholars of African American history that have influenced, inspired, and encouraged me is too long to list. But I'd like to especially thank Leslie Alexander, Scot Brown, Khalilah Brown-Dean, Pero Dagbovie, Reena Goldthree, Maurice Hobson, Hasan Jeffries, Anna Lawrence, Charles McKinney, Leonard Moore, Paul Ortiz, Kerry Pimblott, and Sherie Randolph for listening to my ideas or allowing me an opportunity to present my work at your campuses. I need to shout out my line brothers, especially Jelani Favors and Danny Hoey. Thank you for your scholarly contributions and your support—'06. I know I have forgotten some folks. Please blame it on the head and not the heart.

This project required extensive research in Tallahassee and Atlanta, and I want to thank key people in these two cities. This project could not have been completed without the help of Elizabeth Dawson in the Black Archives at Florida A&M University. I'd like to thank FAMU scholars Kwasi Densu, Reginald K. Ellis, Will Guzman, David Jackson Jr., Ameenah Shakir, and Darius Young. I would like to especially thank Kimberlyn Elliott for helping conduct research in Tallahassee. At Florida State University, I would like to thank Andrew Frank, a former colleague and friend. My debts to folks based in Atlanta are numerous. I'd like to thank Andrea Jackson, formerly of Atlanta University Center's Woodruff Library.

I also want to thank Dartmouth's football coaches and staff for allowing me to gain a better understanding of the inner workings of college football. My conversations with head coach Eugene "Buddy" Teevens; assistant coaches Cheston Blackshear, Duane Brooks, Kyle Cavanaugh, Keith Clark, Kevin Daft, Don Dobes, Sammy McCorkle, and Danny O'Dea; former coaches Jerry Taylor and Steve Thames; and current and former football staff members Callie Brownson, Dino Cauteruccio, Vaughn Johnson, Dion King, and Seitu Smith have provided insights into how coaches recruit players and prepare game plans. I would also like to thank Dartmouth's athletic administrators for showing me the business side of Division I college sports, especially athletic director Harry Sheehy, associate athletic director Richard Whitmore, and former associate athletic directors Donald Brooks and Drew Galbraith.

I couldn't have finished this project without my family's support. To my parents, H. E. and Joyce White, thanks for your love. Jerome, Jenell, Nicholas, and Avery, thanks for letting me crash at your house for "research." I love you guys. To my wife, Stephanie, you've been a rock. You've been my biggest cheerleader and critic. Thank you for pushing me to finish this book. I love you. To Douglass and Langston, Daddy loves you.

NOTES

ABBREVIATIONS IN THE NOTES
FSA
Florida State Archives, Tallahassee
Gaither Papers
Jake Gaither Papers, Black Archives, Florida A&M University, Tallahassee

INTRODUCTION
1. Tom Archdeacon, "Jake Gaither's Still a Part of FAMU's Football Success," *Miami News*, October 3, 1979, 6C; Bob Cohn, "Little Guy Savors Big Win," *Tallahassee Democrat*, October 7, 1979, 1A, 5A.

2. "FAMU, Miami in Historic Meeting at Tallahassee," *Ocala Star-Banner*, October 5, 1979, 4B.

3. "Florida A&M Ready for Miami," *Montgomery Advertiser*, October 6, 1979, 2B.

4. Schnellenberger, "Oral History."

5. Herschel Nissenson, "Will Wichita Shock Tide? Don't Bet on It," *Owensboro Messenger-Inquirer*, October 5, 1979, 3B; Will Grimsley, "Southern Cal Predicted to Win Again," *Staunton News Leader*, October 4, 1979, 12.

6. Tom Archdeacon, "Jake Gaither's Still a Part of FAMU's Football Success," *Miami News*, October 4, 1979, 6C; Bill Beck, "College Football," *St. Louis Post-Dispatch*, October 4, 1979, 2E.

7. Tom McEwen, "The Morning After: Like the Bucs, FSU, Rattlers, Unblemished Beat Goes On," *Tampa Tribune*, October 5, 1979, 1C, 4C; "Joyce's Choices, Weekly Football Picker," *Pensacola News Journal*, October 5, 1979, 12.

8. "Beat the Experts," *Ft. Lauderdale News*, October 4, 1979, 6D.

9. Bob Cohn, "Little Guy Savors Big Win," *Tallahassee Democrat*, October 7, 1979, 1A, 5A.

10. Bernie Daley, "Florida A&M Discriminated Against in Polls?," *Wilkes-Barre Times Leader*, October 6, 1979, 26A.

11. Bob Cohn, "Little Guy Savors Big Win," *Tallahassee Democrat*, October 7, 1979, 1A, 5A.

12. "Locker Room Quotes," *FAMUAN*, October 11, 1979, 11. Vince Coleman was better known for his baseball talent. He played thirteen seasons in the Major Leagues and was the 1985 National League Rookie of the Year. He led the National League in stolen bases for six consecutive seasons (1985–90).

13. Barry Cooper, "Rattlers Can Play with Big Boys," *Tallahassee Democrat*, October 7,

1979, F1, F10; Bob Cohn, "Hurricanes Find Loss a Bitter One," *Tallahassee Democrat*, October 7, 1979, F1, F5; Jim Martz, "FAMU Rattles Hurricanes, 16–13," *Miami Herald*, October 7, 1979, C1, C7; Bob Rubin, "Rattlers Dance to Hubbard's Hip Tune," *Miami Herald*, October 7, 1979, C6; Laura Weiss, "Blood, Sweat, and Tears," *Miami Hurricane*, October 9, 1979, 10.

14. Tom Archdeacon, "It's So Easy to Get Rattled," *Sports Illustrated*, October 15, 1979, 73–74.

15. Bob Cohn, "Hurricanes Find Loss a Bitter One," *Tallahassee Democrat*, October 7, 1979, F1; Bob Rubin, "Rattlers Dance to Hubbard's Hip Tune," *Miami Herald*, October 7, 1979, C6; Kellen Kress, "Miller Not to Blame; Is Kelly the Answer," *Miami Hurricane*, October 9, 1979, 10.

16. Tom Archdeacon, "It's So Easy to Get Rattled," *Sports Illustrated*, October 15, 1979, 74; Dave Scheiber, "FAMU Just Proved What It Already Knew," *St. Petersburg Times*, October 8, 1979, C11.

17. Tom Archdeacon, "Gaither's Still a Part of FAMU's Football Success," *Miami News*, October 4, 1979, 6C.

18. Scott Rabalais, "LSU Should Host Southern, Grambling if It Plays Other Louisiana Schools," *Baton Rouge Advocate*, September 7, 2018, https://www.theadvocate.com/baton_rouge/sports/lsu/article_091643aa-b242-11e8-8df4-9f26f1a2d4b9.html (accessed October 26, 2018).

19. Lewis, *In Their Own Interests*, 90.

20. Alexander, *African or American?*, xvii–xviii.

21. Foner, *Short History of Reconstruction*, 36.

22. Williams, *They Left Great Marks on Me*.

23. Jeffries, *Bloody Lowndes*, 7–37.

24. Wiggins, *Glory Bound*, 222.

25. Ellison, "American Dilemma," 315–16.

26. In order of induction: Alonzo Gaither, Earl Banks, John Merritt, Eddie Robinson, William Nicks, Arnett Mumford, Marino Casem, Billy Joe, William Gorden, Willie Jeffries. See "College Football Hall of Fame," https://www.cfbhall.com/about/inductees/ (accessed June 6, 2018).

27. Rodgers, "'It's HBCU Classic Time!,'" 149–50.

28. Wiggins and Miller, *Unlevel Playing Field*, 85.

29. Rhoden, *Forty Million Dollar Slaves*, 138.

CHAPTER 1

1. "Summary of Football Scores of Southern School [*sic*]," *Chicago Defender*, January 1, 1916, 7.

2. Eric Roberts, "Southern Sportsdom," *Chicago Defender*, December 25, 1926, 11.

3. Quoted in Curry, *Jake Gaither*, 11.

4. Ibid.

5. Ibid.; "Morehouse, 25; Knoxville, 0," *Chicago Defender*, December 2, 1922, 10.

6. Swanson, "Cleveland Abbott," 2; Willey A. Johnson Jr., "From the Press Box," *Norfolk Journal and Guide*, December 26, 1925, 4.

7. "*Courier*'s Mythical 'All-America' Team Selected," *Pittsburgh Courier*, December 19, 1925, 12; "Afro Offers First Authentic All-American Football Team," *Baltimore Afro-American*, December 19, 1925, 7.

8. Wilson, *Agile, Mobile, Hostile*, 62.

9. "Tuskegee's Game with Army Off," *Pittsburgh Courier*, October 2, 1926, 15.

10. "Knoxville Beaten by Tuskegee," *Pittsburgh Courier*, October 9, 1926, 15.

11. Booker, *And There Was Light*, 83.

12. Logan, *Betrayal of the Negro*, xxii.

13. Foner, *Short History of Reconstruction*, 36.

14. Jeffries, *Bloody Lowndes*, 4.

15. Lewis, *In Their Own Interests*, 90.

16. Anderson, *Education of Blacks in the South*, 5.

17. Gasman, *Envisioning Black Colleges*, 11–15.

18. Parker, *Rise and Decline*, 13–27.

19. The 1890 Morrill Act, *U.S. Congress Statutes at Large*, 26, 417–18, https://www.loc.gov/law/help/statutes-at-large/51st-congress/session-1/c51s1ch841.pdf (accessed December 20, 2018).

20. Du Bois, *Souls of Black Folk*, 89–90.

21. Booker, *And There Was Light*, 10–45; Savitt, "Money Versus Mission."

22. Parker, *Rise and Decline*, 230.

23. Lovett, *Touch of Greatness*, 1–12.

24. Neyland, *Florida Agricultural and Mechanical University*, 1–47.

25. Adams, "History of Public Higher Education in Florida," 132–42.

26. Quoted in Ortiz, *Emancipation Betrayed*, 65–66.

27. For a summary of this debate and the history of vocational and liberal arts education at Black colleges, see Anderson, *Education of Blacks in the South*, 33–109.

28. Fairclough, *Teaching Equality*, 1–19.

29. Du Bois, *Souls of Black Folk*, 28.

30. Washington, *Up from Slavery*, 144.

31. Neyland, *Florida Agricultural and Mechanical University*, 35–47.

32. Favors, *Shelter in the Time of Storm*, 5.

33. Ibid.

34. Oriard, *Reading Football*, 3.

35. Rader, *American Sports*, 84–89.

36. Des Jardins, *Walter Camp*, 76–77.

37. Roosevelt, *Strenuous Life*, 1.

38. Chalk, *Black College Sport*, 140–60.

39. "Color Line Drawn on the Gridiron," *Raleigh Morning Post*, November 8, 1903, 1.

40. Martin, "Color Line in Midwestern College Sports"; Matthews, "Negro Foot-Ball Players on New England Teams."

41. "Salisbury, NC," *Charlotte Observer*, December 29, 1892, 2; Davis, "History of Livingstone College," 117.

42. Hornsby-Gutting, *Black Manhood and Community Building in North Carolina*.

43. Nelson, *Anatomy of a Game*, 45–48.

44. "College Football National Championship History," *NCAA.com*, April 9, 2018, https://www.ncaa.com/news/football/article/college-football-national-championship-history.

45. Watterson, *College Football*, 39–48.

46. Miller, "The Manly, the Moral, and the Proficient," 293.

47. Patrick B. Miller describes the process of football being spread from the Northeast to the South as "cultural diffusion." His analysis, however, fails to include Black colleges. See Miller, "The Manly, the Moral, and the Proficient," 286–87.

48. Davis, *Clashing of the Soul*, 74.

49. Smith and Horton, *Historical Statistics of Black America*, 2:1738.

50. Du Bois and Dill, *College Bred Negro*, 66.

51. Fairclough, *Class of Their Own*, 63.

52. Albright, "William Henry Lewis"; Lindholm, "Vita."

53. Walter Camp, "The American Game of Football," *Harper's Weekly*, November 10, 1888, 858; Walter Camp, "Football of '94: A Forecast of the Season," *Outing*, November 1894, 169–74; Walter Camp, "Football: Review of Season of 1894," *Outing*, October 1895, 81–88; Walter Camp, "The Substitute," *Los Angeles Times*, November 3, 1895, 21.

54. Camp, *American Football*.

55. Davis, *Football*, 72; "'Twas a Physical Cyclone," *New York Times*, November 25, 1888; "Yale Again Triumphant," *New York Times*, November 25, 1894, 1; "The Yale-Princeton Football Game: A Big Crowd Will See the Collegians Battle on the Gridiron," *New York Times*, November 21, 1895.

56. Wiggins, "Edwin Bancroft Henderson, African American Athletes, and the Writing of Sports History," in *Glory Bound*, 221–40.

57. Henderson, *Negro in Sports*, 123.

58. See Runstedtler, *Jack Johnson, Rebel Sojourner*; Moore, *I Fight for A Living*.

59. Michaeli, *The Defender*, 22, 54–56; Frank A. Young, "In the World of Sports," *Chicago Defender*, April 24, 1915, 7.

60. Willey A. Johnson, "From the Press Box," *Norfolk Journal and Guide*, November 29, 1924.

61. "*Courier*'s Mythical 'All America' Team Selected," *Pittsburgh Courier*, December 19, 1925, 12.

62. Bill Gibson, "Hear Me Talkin' to Ya," *Baltimore Afro-American*, September 28, 1929, 14.

63. William L. Gibson, "The Old Football Rulers Pass," *Crisis*, December 1934, 363.

64. Eric Roberts, "Dixie Doings," *Chicago Defender*, October 29, 1927, 11.

65. "Legendary Sportswriter Ric Roberts Says He's a Historian by Choice," *Atlanta Daily World*, January 11, 1985, 6.

66. "Constitution and By-laws: 100 Per Cent Wrong Club of the Atlanta Daily World," box 1, folder 8, 100% Wrong Club Papers, Auburn Avenue Research Library on African American Culture and History.

67. Interview with Ric Roberts, July 2, 1971, Black Journalist Project, Columbia University.

68. Ibid.

69. Between 1889 and World War I, Camp named only three African Americans: William Henry Lewis (Harvard) in 1892, Robert Marshall (Minnesota) in 1905, and Fritz Pollard (Brown) in 1916.

70. Miller, "The Manly, the Moral, and the Proficient"; Doyle, "'Causes Won, Not Lost.'"

71. Oriard, *Reading Football*, 189–276.

72. Wiggins, "Biggest 'Classic' of Them All"; Aiello, "Black Heart of Dixie"; Aiello, *Bayou Classic*.

73. Quoted in Wiggins, "Biggest 'Classic' of Them All," 36.

74. Rodgers, "It's HBCU Classic Time!," 149.

75. McQuilkin and Smith, "Rise and Fall of the Flying Wedge."

76. Watterson, *College Football*, 401.

77. Ibid., 54–55.

78. Rader, *American Sports*, 182–88; Oriard, *Reading Football*, 142–88.

79. Kuska, *Hot Potato*, 41–46.

80. Ibid., 43–44; Drewry and Doermann, *Stand and Prosper*, 127–59; Jones, *Negro Education*, 171, 553; Fairclough, *Class of Their Own*, 11.

81. Hawkins, *History of the Southern Intercollegiate Athletic Conference*, 1–2; J. B. Bragg, "A Brief History of the SIAC Conference," in *Silver Jubilee: SIAC Anniversary Program, 1913–1938*, 4, box 10, folder 10, Gaither Papers.

82. W. H. Kindle, "A Brief Survey of the Development of the Southern Intercollegiate Athletic Conference from the College Year 1923–24 to the Present," in *Silver Jubilee: SIAC Anniversary Program, 1913–1938*, 5, box 10, folder 10, Gaither Papers.

83. Hawkins, *History of the Southern Intercollegiate Athletic Conference*, 2; Wiggins, *Glory Bound*, 221–42.

84. Dickerson, *Militant Mediator*, 27.

85. "SWAC History," http://www.swac.org/ViewArticle.dbml?ATCLID=205246152 (accessed January 24, 2017).

86. Curry, *Jake Gaither*, 13–14.

87. Neyland, *Twelve Black Floridians*, 67.

88. Wilson, *Agile, Mobile, Hostile*, 44.

89. "Interview with Jake Gaither," April 4, 1975, M77-164, box 2, Junior League of Tallahassee, FSA.

90. Curry, *Jake Gaither*, 7.

91. Ibid.

92. Arthur Evans, "Knoxville Trounces Tennessee 21–0," *Baltimore Afro-American*, November 6, 1926, 15.

93. Neyland, *Twelve Black Floridians*, 69.

94. State of Tennessee Certificate of Death for J. D. Gaither, November 5, 1926, Ancestry.com, Tennessee, Death Records, 1908–1958, https://search.ancestry.com/cgi -bin/sse.dll?indiv=1&dbid=2376&h=519957&tid=&pid=&usePUB=true&_phsrc=Ex 02&_phstart=successSource (accessed May 17, 2018).

95. "Interview with Jake Gaither," April 4, 1975, M77-164, box 2, Junior League of Tallahassee, FSA.

96. "Program of the Fifty-First Annual Session of the Old North State Medical, Dental and Pharmaceutical Society, Inc.," May 17–19, 1938, North Carolina History of Health Digital Collection, http://archives.hsl.unc.edu/nchh/nchh-27/nchh-27-051.pdf (accessed January 28, 2017).

97. Parker, *Rise and Decline*, 135–37.

98. Grundy, *Learning to Win*, 165.

99. "Jake Gaither Winning Wide Renown for Coaching Ability by His Results at Henderson," *Norfolk Journal and Guide*, December 2, 1933, 16.

100. Pruter, *Rise of American High School Sports*, 273–91.

101. "Interview with Jake Gaither," April 4, 1975, M77-164, box 2, Junior League of Tallahassee, FSA.

102. Wilson, *Agile, Mobile, Hostile*, 62.

103. Ibid., 62–63.

104. "Interview with Jake Gaither," April 4, 1975, M77-164, box 2, Junior League of Tallahassee, FSA.

105. Gaither and Wade shared a stage at the opening of the College Football Hall of Fame. Neither mentioned the letter but talked for the first time. See Bill McGrotha, "Wade, a Football Pioneer, Demanded More Than the Best," *Tallahassee Democrat*, October 15, 1986, 1B, and John Bansch, "College Grid Gather Dedicates Hall of Fame," *Indianapolis Star*, August 4, 1978, 38.

106. "Summer Coaching School Launched," *New Philadelphia Daily Times*, June 24, 1932, 6.

107. Oriard, *King Football*, 3; Wakefield, *Playing to Win*, 35–78.

108. Sabock, "History of Physical Education at the Ohio State University."

109. Gaither, "System for Recording the Health Conditions of Athletes in College."

110. "Jake Gaither Winning Wide Renown for Coaching Ability by His Results at Henderson," *Norfolk Journal and Guide*, December 2, 1933, 16.

111. "Henderson Wins 48–0," *Baltimore Afro-American*, October 11, 1930, 14A; "Coach Uses 26 Men Still Wins, 52–0," *Baltimore Afro-American*, November 22, 1930, 15; "N.C. Preps in Fast Contest," *Baltimore Afro-American*, October 18, 1930, 15.

112. Booker, *And There Was Light*, 83; Charles Edwards, "Students Said 'Big Jake' Was

'Nuts' When He Started Basketball at Henderson Inst.—But What a Coach," *Norfolk Journal and Guide*, March 31, 1994, A12.

113. E. B. Rea, "From the Pressbox," *Norfolk Journal and Guide*, March 24, 1934, A13; "National Cage Tournament Begins at Gary Friday," *Chicago Defender*, March 31, 1934, 16; "Gary Wins Prep Cage Title," *Chicago Defender*, April 7, 1934, 16; Pruter, "National Interscholastic Basketball Tournament."

114. "Jake Gaither Winning Wide Renown for Coaching Ability by His Results at Henderson," *Norfolk Journal and Guide*, December 2, 1933, 16.

115. "Henderson Teams Can't Be Beaten So N.C. Conference Solves It, Puts 'Em Outside," *Norfolk Journal and Guide*, January 19, 1935, 18.

116. Ibid.

117. "Says Conference Was Justified in Action against Two Schools," *Norfolk Journal and Guide*, February 2, 1935, 18.

118. Charles C. Edwards, "Former Henderson Student Defends Coach, School's Athletic Set-Up," *Norfolk Journal and Guide*, February 16, 1935, 14; "Dr. Cotton Defends Henderson Institute's Athletic Set-Up," *Norfolk Journal and Guide*, February 9, 1935, 14, 18.

119. E. B. Rea, "North Carolina Athletic Conference Puts Ban on Two Coaches, Principal for Reporting Deliberation at Meet," *Norfolk Journal and Guide*, March 16, 1935, 1, 10.

120. E. B. Rea, "Henderson and Winchester Cop NC State Flags," *Norfolk Journal and Guide*, March 23, 1935, 14.

121. "Interview with Jake Gaither," April 4, 1975, M77-164, box 2, Junior League of Tallahassee, FSA.

122. E. B. Rea, "From the Press Box," *Norfolk Journal and Guide*, July 6, 1935, 13.

123. E. B. Rea, "From the Press Box," *Norfolk Journal and Guide*, September 19, 1936, 15.

124. E. B. Rea, "From the Press Box," *Norfolk Journal and Guide*, November 14, 1936, 15; E. Wm. Gilbert, "Tigers Beat St. Aug.; Meet Trojans Next," *Norfolk Journal and Guide*, November 14, 1936, 14.

125. "Interview with Jake Gaither," April 4, 1975, M77-164, box 2, Junior League of Tallahassee, FSA.

126. Gaither's two wins at St. Paul's have not been counted in Gaither's career win totals. His record at St. Paul's was 2–5–1.

CHAPTER 2

1. "Foot Ball at Howard," *University Journal*, December 1, 1903, 1–3, 6, http://dh .howard.edu/cgi/viewcontent.cgi?article=1001&context=huj_v1 (accessed June 18, 2018).

2. Hurd, *Black College Football*, 164.

3. "Howard Has Best Record," *Baltimore Afro-American*, November 26, 1920, 7.

4. Schmidt, *Shaping College Football*, 137–41; Louis Lautier, "Paid Athletes in Colleges Must Go, Says Howard Head," *Baltimore Afro-American*, October 19, 1929, 3; "Howard to Invade Florida Rattlers' Stronghold," *Pittsburgh Courier*, December 2, 1933, A4; Chester Washington, "Ches Sez," *Pittsburgh Courier*, December 9, 1933, A5; W. Rollo Wilson, "Howard Bison Gore Lincoln Lions in 13–7 Defeat," *Pittsburgh Courier*, December 9, 1933, A4.

5. "Howard–Fla. Outfits in Post Season Contest," *Philadelphia Tribune*, November 20, 1933, 10.

6. Wiggins, "Biggest 'Classic' of Them All"; Aiello, "Black Heart of Dixie."

7. "Negro Football Game Scheduled for Fair," *Shreveport Times*, October 12, 1922, 8; "Wiley and Langston Battle to 0–0 Tie," *Marshall News Messenger*, 8.

8. "Atlanta University 11 Defeats Prairie View in Thrilling Contest," *New York Age*, January 12, 1929, 6.

9. Hurd, *Black College Football*, 131–35.

10. Jackson, "'Industrious, Thrifty and Ambitious'"; Phelts, *American Beach for African Americans*, 3–9.

11. "Howard to Invade Florida Rattlers' Stronghold," *Pittsburgh Courier*, December 2, 1933, A4; Bunie, *Robert L. Vann of the* Pittsburgh Courier, 143–44.

12. A. L. Kidd, "Florida Rattlers Down Bison by Score of 9–6," *Norfolk Journal and Guide*, December 9, 1933, 17; "Special to Wait for Howard," *Pittsburgh Courier*, December 2, 1933.

13. "Howard to Invade Florida Rattlers' Stronghold," *Pittsburgh Courier*, December 2, 1933, A4.

14. Chester Washington, "Sez Ches," *Pittsburgh Courier*, December 2, 1933, A5.

15. Chester Washington, "Florida A. & M. Upsets Howard, 9–6, in Thriller," *Pittsburgh Courier*, December 9, 1933, A5.

16. "College Prexy Is Host to Leaders of Secret Order," *Chicago Defender*, August 22, 1931, 2.

17. Alma Lucille Johnson, "The Famcee Digest," *Atlanta Daily World*, October 4, 1934, 2.

18. "An Adelbert Graduate Honored," *Cleveland Plain Dealer*, September 19, 1899, 4.

19. Neyland, *Florida Agricultural and Mechanical University*, 124–27.

20. Little, "Extra-Curricular Activities of Black College Students."

21. Neyland, *Florida Agricultural and Mechanical University*, 113.

22. Holland, *Nathan B. Young and the Struggle over Black Higher Education*, 1–70.

23. Neyland, *Florida Agricultural and Mechanical University*, 123.

24. Brandt, *When Oberlin Was King of the Gridiron*, 22–36.

25. Bragg, "Story of a Blacksmith," 281.

26. Neyland, *Florida Agricultural and Mechanical University*, 59–60.

27. *Bulletin of the Academic Department*, ed. Florida A&M College (Tallahassee: A&M College Press, 1910), 17, FAMU Digital Resource Center, https://famu.digital.flvc.org

/islandora/object/famu%3A18457#page/Front+cover/mode/2up (accessed November 25, 2009).

28. Ibid.

29. There appears to have been a South Georgia and Florida Athletic conference, but there is only intangible evidence. See "Edward Waters College Defeats St. Augustine," *Chicago Defender*, November 18, 1916, 7.

30. Bartley, *Brief History of the Division of Health, Physical Education, and Recreation*, 4–5.

31. Neyland, *Florida Agricultural and Mechanical University*, 76–77.

32. Ibid., 124.

33. Ibid.

34. Neyland, *Florida Agricultural and Mechanical University*, 127–28; "Spectacular Runs by Byrd Figure in Win," *Pittsburgh Courier*, October 25, 1924, 7; Frank Young, "Lincoln Tramples Howard," *Chicago Defender*, December 6, 1924, 1; "*Courier* Scribe Picks All-Time All-American Teams," *Pittsburgh Courier*, December 26, 1925, 12.

35. Quoted in Neyland, *Florida Agricultural and Mechanical University*, 125.

36. Eric Roberts, "Southern Sportsdom," *Chicago Defender*, December 11, 1926, 11.

37. Tebeau and Marina, *History of Florida*, 361–95; Vickers, *Panic in Paradise*; Kleinberg, *Black Cloud*.

38. Newkirk, "Edward Waters College," 28.

39. Gasman, *Envisioning Black Colleges*, 17–18.

40. Blose and Caliver, *Statistics of the Education of Negroes*, 27.

41. Anderson, *Education of Blacks in the South*, 239.

42. Neyland, *Florida Agricultural and Mechanical University*, 147–70.

43. Ibid., 77–112, 151, 158, 171–72; Calvin J. Floyd, "The Non-Bragging President Plugs on to Greater Things," *Pittsburgh Courier*, December 1, 1928, 10; Calvin J. Floyd, "Florida Governor Praises A. & M.," *Pittsburgh Courier*, December 1, 1928, 10; Calvin J. Floyd, "Improve the School the Slogan at Fla. A. & M.," *Pittsburgh Courier*, December 30, 1933, A8; Calvin J. Floyd, "Increased Recreational Facilities Reduce Discipline Problem Among Fla. College Boys," *Pittsburgh Courier*, January 13, 1934, A3; "Negro Team Has Financial Trouble," *Palm Beach Post*, December 15, 1939, 21.

44. "Florida Plans Huge Stadium: President Tigert Sanctions Monstrous Grid Bowl; to Seat 75,000," *St. Petersburg Times*, October 25, 1928, 6.

45. Ossie Jefferson, "Florida Official Reviews Grid Year in Alligator State," *Pittsburgh Courier*, January 5, 1929, B3; A. I. Saunders, "Edward Waters College Beats Florida, 13 to 12," *Chicago Defender*, January 11, 1930, 9; Cleve L. Abbott, "Cleve Abbott Gives Review of 1930 Football in South," *Chicago Defender*, January 31, 1931, 8; "Edward Waters College Is Florida's Champion Eleven," *Chicago Defender*, January 2, 1932, 9.

46. J. C. Chunn, "Spotlighting Southern Colleges," *Pittsburgh Courier*, September 7, 1929, A4; J. C. Chunn, "The Southern Grid Situation," *Pittsburgh Courier*, September 14, 1929, A4; W. H. Kindle, "A Brief Survey of the Development of the Southern Inter-

collegiate Athletic Conference from the College year 1923–24 to the Present," in *Silver Jubilee: SIAC Anniversary Program, 1913–1938*, 5, box 10, folder 10, Gaither Papers; "FAMU Laments about Loss of Candidates," *Atlanta Daily World*, October 5, 1932, 5A; Chief Aiken, "Ineligibility Heat Grips Dixie Coaches," *Atlanta Daily World*, October 30, 1932, 7A.

47. Calvin J. Floyd, "Florida Governor Praises A. & M.," *Pittsburgh Courier*, 10.

48. Calvin J. Floyd, "Florida Approves Edward Waters College," *Pittsburgh Courier*, December 7, 1929, 14; "Enrollment at Bethune-Cookman Up," *Atlanta Daily World*, November 13, 1934, 5.

49. Neyland, Estaras, and Alexander, *History of the Florida Interscholastic Athletic Association*, 11.

50. Lansbury, *Spectacular Leap*, 46–48.

51. Ric Roberts, "Four Year Standards Tough on Super Grid Ensembles," *Atlanta Daily World*, November 29, 1937, 5.

52. Wilson, *Agile, Mobile, Hostile*, 71.

53. The four coaches were W. McKinley King (1929), Jubie B. Bragg (1930), Ted Wright (1931–33), and Eugene Bragg (1934–35). There is an apparent discrepancy between FAMU sports information and the evidence. FAMU currently lists J. B. Bragg as head coach from 1930 to 1932 and Ted Wright's only season as 1933. However, all reports of the 1931 and 1932 season mention Wright as the head coach. See Frank A. Young, "Fay Says," *Pittsburgh Courier*, September 5, 1931; "Florida Wins from Claflin," *New York Amsterdam News*, October 21, 1931, 12; Cleve L. Abbot, "Abbott Writes Annual Review of Southern Grid Campaign," *Atlanta Daily World*, January 13, 1932, 5; "Bragg Expecting Ted Wright to 'Go' This Year," *Atlanta Daily World*, September 9, 1932, A5.

54. J. C. Chunn, "Spotlighting Southern College: All-Southern Squads," *Pittsburgh Courier*, December 24, 1927, 17.

55. J. C. Chunn, "Bragg-Boss Coaching Set-Up Has Brought Glory to Famcee," *Atlanta Daily World*, November 22, 1935, 5; Ric Roberts, "Famcee's Men in Orange Upset 'Bama Hornet Eleven, 7–6," *Atlanta Daily World*, October 29, 1934, 5.

56. Ric Roberts, "Juby Bragg, Jr., Dies Enroute to Hospital," *Atlanta Daily World*, January 25, 1936, 6.

57. "Bell of Ohio Leaves East for School," *Chicago Defender*, September 19, 1931, 9.

58. "Bell on Bench as Ohio State Loses to Dixie 11," *Pittsburgh Courier*, October 17, 1931, 14; Martin, *Benching Jim Crow*, xvii, 29–30.

59. Quoted in Neyland, *Florida Agricultural and Mechanical University*, 200–201.

60. Ric Roberts, "Florida's Orange '11' Holds Alabama, 0–0," *Atlanta Daily World*, October 25, 1936.

61. Wilson, *Agile, Mobile, Hostile*, 71.

62. "Coaching School June 7 to June 11," *Bulletin of the Florida Agricultural and Mechanical College*, Summer Series, 1937, 23, FAMU Digital Resource Center, http://famu.digital.flvc.org/islandora/object/famu%3A16061#page/Cover/mode/2up (accessed May 22, 2018).

63. "All-Master's Quartet at Florida A. and M.," *Norfolk Journal and Guide*, September 11, 1937, 16.

64. David Lee Simmons, "Founding a Tradition," *Tallahassee Democrat*, November 5, 1988, 13D, 14D, 22D.

65. A. L. Kidd, "Florida Wins Opener under Bill Bell–Jake Gaither Rule," *Norfolk Journal and Guide*, October 9, 1937, 17.

66. A. L. Kidd, "Florida A. and M. Eleven Wrecks Hampton 25–20," *Chicago Defender*, December 11, 1937, 9; F. A. Jackson, "Prairie View Beats Florida in New Year's Tilt," *Pittsburgh Courier*, January 8, 1938, 17; Lucius Jones, "Slant on Sports," *Atlanta Daily World*, September 20, 1938, 5.

67. J. C. Chunn, "Fans Await One of the Greatest Spectacles in SIAC History," *Atlanta Daily World*, October 26, 1938, 5.

68. Ric Roberts, "Morris Brown Faces Best SIAC Backfield I've Seen . . . Lockhart," *Atlanta Daily World*, October 28, 1938, 5; Ric Roberts, "Tom Jones Dashes 64 Years, Hank Butler 79; Florida Tags MBC, 16–0," *Atlanta Daily World*, October 30, 1938, 8.

69. "Kean Cries; Must Build a New Team," *Chicago Defender*, September 3, 1938, 8; Lucius Jones, "Slants on Sports," *Atlanta Daily World*, October 18, 1938, 5.

70. Russell Kay, "Too Late to Classify," *Fort Myers News-Press*, November 27, 1938, 6.

71. David Lee Simmons, "Founding a Tradition," *Tallahassee Democrat*, November 5, 1988, 13D, 14D, 22D.

72. Ric Roberts, "Florida Hard Pressed to Whip Ky. State, 9–7," *Atlanta Daily World*, December 4, 1938, 8; Ric Roberts, "Florida Fans Dizzy at End of Game; Kean's Great Chance," *Atlanta Daily World*, December 6, 1938, 5; A. L. Kidd, "Florida Defeats Kentucky State: Cops Orange Blossom Classic and National Grid Title Game 9–7," *Chicago Defender*, December 10, 1938, 8.

73. "Florida's 'Men in Orange' End as National, SIAC Champions," *Atlanta Daily World*, December 19, 1938.

CHAPTER 3

1. A. L. Kidd, "Florida Upsets Tuskegee Quint," *Chicago Defender*, February 21, 1942, 24.

2. J. C. Chunn, "Morris Brown, Florida in Renewal of Age-Old Hate," *Atlanta Daily World*, January 22, 1942, 5.

3. Melancholy Jones, "Sports Slants," *Atlanta Daily World*, March 6, 1942, 5.

4. Lucius Jones, "Florida Trips 'Skegee in Thrilling Contest," *Atlanta Daily World*, March 1, 1942, 8.

5. Wilson, *Agile, Mobile, Hostile*, 18.

6. Curry, *Jake Gaither*, 18–24.

7. "Leon's Third Draft Registration Arranged in Order Number Sequence," *Tallahassee Democrat*, April 5, 1942, 5.

8. Donna Britt, "From Layups to Bricklaying, a Special Hero," *Washington Post*, January 19, 1993, https://www.washingtonpost.com/archive/local/1993/01/19/from-layups

-to-bricklaying-a-special-hero/c7d85ef7–71c9–4cd0–8d4a-2c2c536e8d49/?utm_term=
.a34424e6c321 (accessed February 8, 2017).

9. The Associated Negro Press (ANP) and the *Pittsburgh Courier* determined the champion after all bowl exhibition games, while the *Atlanta Daily World*/100% Wrong Club gave its title at the end of the regular season.

10. "Junior Chamber Seeks Football Games for City," *Tallahassee Democrat*, December 20, 1938.

11. "Orange Blossom Classic on Pathé News Releases," *Chicago Defender*, December 21, 1940, 22.

12. A. L. Kidd, "21 Lettermen End Fourth Week's Drill at Florida," *Chicago Defender*, September 30, 1939, 9.

13. "The Great Betrayal," *Crisis*, October 1939, 305.

14. A. L. Kidd, "Florida Opens with N.C. Aggies on Oct. 7," *Chicago Defender*, October 7, 1939, 9; A. L. Kidd, "Florida Rolls Over Tuskegee for First Victory of Season," *Baltimore Afro-American*, October 28, 1939, 20; A. L. Kidd, "Orange Blossom Classic Battle of Wits by Brother Coaches," *Atlanta Daily World*, December 7, 1939, 5.

15. Ric Roberts, "Florida's Brilliant Football Empire May Recede," *Atlanta Daily World*, September 2, 1940, 5.

16. *Crisis*, July 1940.

17. "Florida Football Coach Joins *Courier* Army Drive; Asks F.D.R. for More Race Soldiers," *Pittsburgh Courier*, July 16, 1940, 16.

18. Wynn, *The Afro-American and the Second World War*, 22–23.

19. "Joe Louis Leads Negro Sports Starts in Draft," *New York Amsterdam News*, October 26, 1940, 19; Sklaroff, "Constructing G.I. Joe Louis."

20. Thompson, "Editorial Comment," 547.

21. "3,768 Register to 1:30 Today in Leon County," *Tallahassee Democrat*, October 16, 1940, 1.

22. J. Archie Hargraves, "Florida Stuns Nation with 7–0 Defeat of Mighty A&T," *Atlanta Daily World*, October 8, 1940, 5.

23. A. L. Kidd, "Florida Bids for Second National Title in Week End Wilberforce Battle," *Atlanta Daily World*, December 2, 1940, 5.

24. "Dickinson Rating System," *Atlanta Daily World*, November 27, 1935, 5.

25. "Florida Claims National Title," *Norfolk Journal and Guide*, December 7, 1940, 18. FAMU's official records claim this as a national title, but it is not supported by a review of the Black press.

26. Lucius Jones, "Morris Brown Finishes as No. 1 Grid Eleven of Nation," *Atlanta Daily World*, December 10, 1940, 5; J. C. Chunn, "Morris Brown Claims National Title," *New York Amsterdam News*, December 14, 1940, 19.

27. Ric Roberts, "Florida and Wilberforce in Brutal 0–0 Battle," *Atlanta Daily World*, December 8, 1940, 8.

28. Lucius Jones, "Slants on Sports," *Atlanta Daily World*, January 4, 1941, 5.

29. George S. Schuyler, "Views and News," *Pittsburgh Courier*, January 25, 1941, 6.

30. Bates, *Pullman Porters and the Rise of Protest Politics in Black America*, 148–88.

31. James G. Thompson, "Should I Sacrifice to Live 'Half-American'?," *Pittsburgh Courier*, January 31, 1942, 3.

32. "The *Courier's* Double 'V' for a Double Victory Campaign Gets Country-Wide Support," *Pittsburgh Courier*, February 14, 1942, 1.

33. Lucius Jones, "Florida Leads Nation on Final Figures Afforded by Dickinson Rating System: Men in Orange Rated 27.50, MBC 27.00, Langston 25.50," *Atlanta Daily World*, January 4, 1942, 8; "Florida A. & M. Lays Claim on National Grid Diadem," *New York Amsterdam News*, January 10, 1942, 14.

34. "Florida Rattlers Feted; Seven Sing Swan Songs," *Atlanta Daily World*, December 19, 1941, 5.

35. Ibid.

36. Hare, *Tallahassee*, 114–15.

37. Curry, *Jake Gaither*, 18–21.

38. Flexner, *Medical Education in the United States and Canada*, 180–81.

39. Ibid., 308–9.

40. Rose, *Psychology and Selfhood in the Segregated South*, 69–72.

41. Savitt, "Abraham Flexner and the Black Medical Schools"; Jacobson, *Making Medical Doctors*; Summerville, *Educating Black Doctors*.

42. Riley and Meachem, "Cobb Pilcher, MD," 78.

43. Ibid., 77–86; Rish, "Vanderbilt University Neurosurgical Heritage."

44. Thomas, *Partners of the Heart*, 16; "51st Convention–N.M.A."

45. Dandy, "Radiography in the Diagnosis of Brain Conditions"; Kilgore and Elster, "Walter Dandy and the History of Ventriculography."

46. Curry, *Jake Gaither*, 20–21.

47. Ibid., 20.

48. Wilson, *Agile, Mobile, Hostile*, 29.

49. Curry, *Jake Gaither*, 20–21.

50. "Football in Dixie Aids U.S. War Effort: Southeastern Conference Has Contributed 200 Players," *New York Times*, August 2, 1942, S4.

51. "ODT Curbs Travel to Big Games in a Move to Conserve Facilities," *New York Times*, September 13, 1942, 1, 29.

52. Harold Claassen, "Moving Football to Fans Is Colleges' Answer to Transportation Problem," *Gettysburg Times*, August 19, 1942, 3.

53. A. L. Kidd, "War Cuts Florida A. & M. Chances with Team Facing Tough Schedule," *New York Amsterdam News*, October 10, 1942, 15.

54. "Gators to Start Practice Sept. 1," *St. Petersburg Evening Independent*, August 14, 1942, 11.

55. Lem Graves Jr., "From the Press Box: Big Bill Bell Says He'll Do All Right," *Norfolk New Journal and Guide*, April 11, 1942, C23.

56. Joel W. Smith, "Six SIAC Teams Play Nine-Game Schedules," *Atlanta Daily World*, September 21, 1942, 5; "War Ends Football at Bishop College," *New York Amsterdam*

News, September 26, 1942, 15; "Livingston Drops Football for Duration," *Atlanta Daily World*, October 24, 1942, 5.

57. A. L. Kidd, "War Cuts Florida A. & M. Chances with Team Facing Tough Schedule," *New York Amsterdam News*, October 10, 1942, 15; Lucius Jones, "Florida, Tuskegee, Cream of the Dixie Grid Crop," *Pittsburgh Courier*, September 26, 1942, 17.

58. Joel W. Smith, "Surveying the Sports Front," *Atlanta Daily World*, November 16, 1942, 5.

59. "Florida Rattlers Maintain Grid Pace," *Pittsburgh Courier*, November 28, 1942, 16; "Dream Game in Florida Today," *Atlanta Daily World*, December 12, 1942, 5.

60. Joel W. Smith, "Florida Cops Nation's Gridiron Title By Turning Back Texas, 12 to 6, before 5,000," *Atlanta Daily World*, December 13, 1942, 8; Joel W. Smith, "Surveying the Sports Front," *Atlanta Daily World*, December 14, 1942, 5.

61. Wynn, *The Afro-American and the Second World War*, 24–26.

62. A. L. Kidd, "Florida A. & M. Coach and 28 Men Join Army," *Chicago Defender*, April 10, 1943, 20; Enoc P. Waters, "Girls Take Over Florida A&M as Men Depart to Join Army," *Chicago Defender*, April 10, 1943, 8.

63. "'Bill' Bell, Ex-Florida Mentor, Stationed at 'Skegee Air Field," *Atlanta Daily World*, May 24, 1943, 5.

64. "William M. Bell Sr.: World War II Enlistment Records," Ancestry.com., *U.S., World War II Army Enlistment Records, 1938–1946*, Provo, Utah, USA: Ancestry.com Operations, Inc., 2005 (database online).

65. Jess Duncan, "Racial Sacrifices Deserve Reward," *Philadelphia Tribune*, April 10, 1943, 9.

66. "Near Riot Results as MPs Mar Football Homecoming," *Pittsburgh Courier*, November 7, 1942, 23; Enoc P. Waters, "Racial Flare-ups in Tallahassee Follow Florida A&M Jim Crow," *Chicago Defender*, April 24, 1943, 8; Mormino, "GI Joe Meets Jim Crow."

67. A. L. Kidd, "Florida A. & M. Coach and 28 Men Join Army," *Chicago Defender*, April 10, 1943, 20; Lucius Jones, "The Sports Roundup," *Pittsburgh Courier*, October 9, 1943, 17.

68. Eastman, "Office of Defense Transportation"; "Induction Statistics," http://www.sss.gov/induct.htm (accessed December 14, 2010).

69. "Football Attendance Down 19%; 419 Games Attracted 7,025,560," *New York Times*, December 1, 1942, 29.

70. "Football Dropped by 189 Colleges," *New York Times*, July 14, 1943, 26.

71. "SIAC Football Is Uncertain," *Cleveland Call and Post*, July 17, 1943, 11-A.

72. Nelson, "Organized Labor and the Struggle for Black Equality in Mobile during World War II"; Johnson, "Gender, Race, and Rumours"; White, *What Caused the Detroit Riots*.

73. Johnson, "Gender, Race, and Rumours," 263.

74. Hobbs, *Democracy Abroad, Lynching at Home*, 68–120.

75. John McCray, "The Need for Changing," *Atlanta Daily World*, July 8, 1943, 6.

76. Rominger, "From Playing Field to Battleground"; MacCambridge, *ESPN College Football Encyclopedia*, 1191.

77. Wakefield, *Playing to Win*, 126–32; "White and Colored Grid Team Defeats Marines in N.C." *New York Amsterdam News*, October 23, 1943, 9.

78. Alvin E. White, "Why No Negro Army Football Teams? Wouldn't They Aid Morale?," *Atlanta Daily World*, September 19, 1942, 5; "Writer Reviews Activities of Ft. Benning Serving 'Bn,'" *Atlanta Daily World*, September 10, 1943, 5; "Ex-College Stars on Fort Benning Grid Team," *Pittsburgh Courier*, October 9, 1943, 17; Wakefield, *Playing to Win*, 95–110, 126–32.

79. Ric Roberts, "Morgan Nips Florida in Washington, 50–0, before 14,000 Fans," *Pittsburgh Courier*, November 13, 1943, 16.

80. A. L. Kidd, "Hampton Slugs Rattlers via Air in Classic," *Atlanta Daily World*, December 7, 1943, 5.

81. John Rembert Jr., "Florida A. and M. Grid Hopes High," *Chicago Defender*, September 9, 1944, 7; Spike Washington, "Florida's Clever Rattlers Overpower Morris Brown Wolverines Saturday 19–0," *Atlanta Daily World*, October 22, 1944, 8; "Tennessee State Upsets Dope, Trims Florida, 19–7," *Chicago Defender*, November 11, 1944, 7; "Florida Loses to Tenn. State," *Chicago Defender*, December 2, 1944, 9; "Florida Is New Southern Champ," *Atlanta Daily World*, December 3, 1944, 7; "Florida Bows to Virginia, 15–7," *Atlanta Daily World*, December 10, 1944, 7.

82. "Education," *New York Amsterdam News*, October 21, 1944, 6A.

83. Van West, "Tennessee State Tigerbelles."

84. "Kean Quits Ky. State for Tennessee," *Pittsburgh Courier*, September 9, 1944, 12; Fay Young, "Through the Years," *Chicago Defender*, September 9, 1944, 7.

85. Robinson and Lapchick, *Never Before, Never Again*, 47–71.

CHAPTER 4

1. "Bell, Jefferson to Instruct at Coaching School," *Norfolk Journal and Guide*, May 19, 1945, B15.

2. John W. Rembert, "Asthma Wrecks Florida's Football Hopes," box 6, folder 10, Gaither Papers; "Weather Causes Florida College to Lose Coaches," *New York Amsterdam News*, July 7, 1945, B6.

3. Noell Barnidge, "Gaither Is Synonymous with FAMU and Success," *Tallahassee Democrat*, December 5, 1993, 1D, 12D.

4. Wilson, *Agile, Mobile, Hostile*, 37.

5. "Negro Colleges Open Peak Year," *Chicago Defender*, September 28, 1946, 3; Herbold, "Never a Level Playing Field"; Bartley, *Brief History of the Division of Health, Physical Education, and Recreation*, 14.

6. AP, "College Favor Tightening Athletic Eligibility Rules," *Akron Beacon Journal*, September 16, 1945, 2C.

7. "'Country' Lewis Gets 2 Assistants," *Chicago Defender*, September 15, 1945, 9; Wen-

dell Smith, "Florida Topples Wilberforce in Thriller, 26–20," *Pittsburgh Courier*, October 13, 1945, 16.

8. Joel W. Smith, "Surveying the Sports Front," *Atlanta Daily World*, October 28, 1945, 7.

9. "Florida's Cromartie Defeats Tennessee, 20–18," *Chicago Defender*, November 10, 1945, 9.

10. Spike Washington, "Florida Rattlers Shade Tennessee State, 20–18," *Atlanta Daily World*, November 8, 1945, 5.

11. "Wiley Wins Orange Blossom Classic," *Atlanta Daily World*, December 9, 1945, 5.

12. C. B. Lindsay, "Coach Gaither Elevated at Florida A&M College," *Atlanta Daily World*, 5.

13. Fay Young, "Through the Years," *Chicago Defender*, March 2, 1946; C. B. Lindsay, "Florida Rattlers to Play Nine-Game Grid Schedule," *Atlanta Daily World*, August 16, 1946, 5.

14. "Tuskegee Is Beaten, 21–12," *Chicago Defender*, November 16, 1946, 11; "Lincoln Takes 20–14 Triumph from Florida," *New York Amsterdam News*, December 14, 1946, 12.

15. Edward Robinson, "Abie's Corner," *Los Angeles Sentinel*, January 9, 1947, 22.

16. Taylor, *In Search of the Racial Frontier*, 223, 254.

17. Edward Robinson, "Abie's Corner," *Los Angeles Sentinel*, January 9, 1947, 22; Fay Young, "Through the Years," *Chicago Defender*, December 7, 1946, 10.

18. George, "Colored Town"; Dunn, *Black Miami*, 51–73.

19. Dunn, *Black Miami*, 151, 163; Connolly, *World More Concrete*, 90.

20. Mohl, "Clowning Around."

21. Davis, "Baseball's Reluctant Challenge"; Adelson, *Brushing Back Jim Crow*.

22. The January 1939 game was a matchup of no. 2–ranked University of Tennessee against no. 4–ranked University of Oklahoma. Tennessee won 17–0.

23. Martin, "Integrating New Year's Day," 367–68.

24. "Miami Balks on Negroes, Penn State Cancels Game: Southern School Fears 'Unfortunate Incidents,' Lions Are Informed," *Pittsburgh Post-Gazette*, November 5, 1946, 15.

25. "Penn State Game with Miami Is Off," *New York Times*, November 6, 1946, 40; Martin, *Benching Jim Crow*, 27–54.

26. Richard Frontman, "From Reliable Sources . . . ," *Daily Collegian*, November 1, 1946, 2.

27. Ross, *Outside the Lines*, 44–47.

28. Wendell Smith, "The Sports Beat," *Pittsburgh Courier*, January 12, 1946, 16; Coenen, *From Sandlots to the Super Bowl*, 115–25.

29. Ross, *Outside the Lines*, 94–95; Piascik, *Best Show in Football*, 58.

30. Dunn, *Black Miami*, 173.

31. Miami City Commission Meeting Minutes, December 18, 1946, Miami-Dade Public Library, Florida Room. For information on Culmer, see Dunn, *Black Miami*, 177–81; Taylor, *Black Religious Intellectuals*, 79–93; and "Poor Miami," *Chicago Defender*, May 18, 1946, 14.

32. "Play Orange Blossom Tilt in Miami Stadium," *New York Amsterdam News*, May 24, 1947, 12.

33. "OBC Correspondence 1947–1953," box 7, folder 1, Gaither Papers.

34. "Play Orange Blossom Tilt in Miami Stadium," *New York Amsterdam News*, May 24, 1947, 12.

35. Moore, *We Will Win the Day*, 51–72.

36. "Rattlers Grid Squad Going thru Tough Drill, Hot Sun," *Atlanta Daily World*, September 12, 1947, 4.

37. "Leroy Cromartie to Add Punch to Florida's Offensive Attack," *Atlanta Daily World*, September 20, 1947, 7.

38. "Alert Ball Wins for Shaw over Florida Rams, 19–0," *Baltimore Afro-American*, October 11, 1947, 15.

39. Lem Graves, "Griffin Returns as Hampton Coach," *Pittsburgh Courier*, September 13, 1947, 15; Lucius Jones, "Tennessee No. 1 in Nat'l Grid Ratings," *Pittsburgh Courier*, December 6, 1947, 14.

40. W. Anthony Gaines, "Sports Figures Pay Final Tribute to J. B. Bragg," *Atlanta Daily World*, December 4, 1947, 5; Calvin E. Adams, "Thousands Mourn Dean J. B. Bragg, Sr.," *Pittsburgh Courier*, December 6, 1947, 1, 5.

41. Calvin Adams, "Florida Picked to Beat Hampton," *Pittsburgh Courier*, December 6, 1947, 15.

42. Ric Roberts, "Florida Defeats Hampton in Thriller," *Pittsburgh Courier*, December 13, 1947, 15.

43. Marion E. Jackson, "Marion Jackson's Sports News Reel," *Atlanta Daily World*, December 9, 1947, 5.

44. Fay Young, "Through the Years," *Chicago Defender*, December 20, 1947, 6.

45. MacCambridge, *ESPN College Football Encyclopedia*, 278, 294, 485; "Battered Florida Elevens Have No Rest Ahead," *Miami Times*, November 11, 1947, 3-B; "Harding Drops Coaching Chores," *St. Petersburg Times*, February 17, 1948, 19.

46. Marion E. Jackson, "Southern, Florida, Force Seek National Grid Title," *Atlanta Daily World*, November 16, 1948, 5.

47. Marion E. Jackson, "Union Beats Florida 39–18 in Orange Blossom Classic," *Atlanta Daily World*, December 7, 1948, 5.

48. "Southern Cats Curst Florida Bubble, 31–13," *Chicago Defender*, November 26, 1949, 15.

49. Marion E. Jackson, "A&T Beats Florida in the Orange Blossom Classic," *Atlanta Daily World*, December 13, 1949, 5.

50. "A. S. Gaither Builds Champions at Florida," *Atlanta Daily World*, July 23, 1950, 6.

51. Ibid.

52. Marion E. Jackson, "'Trouble Ahead' for Florida A&M in Tough '50 Football Title Bid," *Atlanta Daily World*, August 13, 1950, 7.

53. Lucius Jones, "Morgan, Southern Early Picks in Nat'l Grid Derby," *Pittsburgh Courier*, September 23, 1950, 22.

54. "Florida Rattlers Strike Down M'Brown, 20–0," *Atlanta Daily World*, October 15, 1950, 1, 7.

55. Marion E. Jackson, "Florida Rattlers Overpower Unbeaten A&T Aggies, 14–9," *Atlanta Daily World*, October 22, 1950, 7.

56. Lucius Jones, "Florida, Southern U. Battle Ends in 0–0 Stalemate," *Pittsburgh Courier*, November 25, 1950, 19; Marion E. Jackson, "Florida A&M Looms as National Grid Champions," *Atlanta Daily World*, November 22, 1950, 5.

57. An integrated baseball game between the Brooklyn Dodgers and the Boston Braves was played in 1949. See "Breaking the Ice: Iowa's Tan Gridders Play against Miami," *Washington Afro-American*, December 2, 1950, 17.

58. Turnbull, *Stadium Stories*, 74.

59. "Hawks Fall to Miami in the Finale, 14–6," *Daily Iowan*, November 25, 1950, 1.

60. J. D. Marshall Jr., "Coach Gaither Has No Excuse in Team Loss," *Chicago Defender*, December 16, 1950, 16.

61. Marion E. Jackson, "Wilberforce Upsets Florida A&M, 13–7," *Atlanta Daily World*, December 5, 1950, 5.

62. "The Final Dickinson Rating Standings of Grid Season," *Pittsburgh Courier*, December 2, 1950, 15.

63. John Rembert, "Fla. A. and M. to Hold Coaching Clinic June 11–16," *Atlanta Daily World*, April 20, 1945, 5.

64. Wilson, *Agile, Mobile, Hostile*, 72–73.

65. "Annual Coaching Clinic Set for Florida A. & M., June 21–26," *Atlanta Daily World*, May 12, 1948, 5.

66. "Jefferson, Wade, Snavely to Lecture at North Carolina College Coaching Clinic," *Norfolk New Journal and Guide*, July 13, 1946, 20; "Southern Sets Coaching Clinic," *Norfolk New Journal and Guide*, May 29, 1948, 20.

67. "'Coaching Clinic Needed in Georgia.' Ralph Long," *Atlanta Daily World*, July 9, 1948, 5.

68. "Florida A&M's 5th Coaching Clinic Ends," *Atlanta Daily World*, June 19, 1949, 7.

69. Gorr, *Bear Memories*, 40–41.

70. Bill Peterson, "Cincinnati's Connection to Football's 'West Coast Offense,'" *Cincinnati City Beat*, August 16, 2006, http://www.citybeat.com/cincinnati/article-1446 -cincinnatis_connection_to_footballs_west_coast_offense.html (accessed September 20, 2012); John Bach, "Sid Gillman Transformed Football with Film," *UC Magazine*, January 2001, http://magazine.uc.edu/issues/0101/sports.html (accessed September 20, 2012); Lewis, *The Blind Side*, 117–18; Josh Katzowitz, *Sid Gillman*.

71. Johnson, *The Wow Boys*, 1–6.

72. W. C. Miles, "Florida's 1948 Grid Machine to Be Loaded with Lettermen," *Atlanta Daily World*, September 16, 1948, 5.

73. "Florida Fetes Tallahassee Quarterback," *Atlanta Daily World*, November 22, 1951, 7; "8th Annual Florida A&M Coaching Clinic June 16–21," *Atlanta Daily World*, June 3, 1952.

74. Faurot, *Football*, 4.

75. Gaither, *Split-Line T Offense*, 20–31.

76. Marion E. Jackson, "Sports of the World," *Atlanta Daily World*, December 16, 1952, 5.

77. Marion E. Jackson, "Sports of the World," *Atlanta Daily World*, December 19, 1952, 5.

78. Roosevelt Wilson, "Alonzo Gaither: Elder Statesman," in *Alonzo Smith "Jake" Gaither Celebrity Roast Souvenir Journal*, May 31, 1986, box 1, folder 2, Gaither Papers.

79. Jake Gaither memo to President George W. Gore, March 27, 1956, box 1, folder 9, Gaither Papers.

80. Quoted in Griffin, "Historical Development of Athletics at Florida Agricultural and Mechanical College," 22.

81. Curry, *Jake Gaither*, 29–30; *Guide to Teaching Physical Education in Secondary Schools*, 86.

82. Gaither correspondence with Charles Mather, May 8, 1953, box 6, folder 2, Gaither Papers; Curry, *Jake Gaither*, 30.

83. Neyland, Estaras, and Alexander, *History of the Florida Interscholastic Athletic Association*, 112–13.

84. Marion E. Jackson, "Sports of the World," *Atlanta Daily World*, December 8, 1949, 5.

85. Marion E. Jackson, "Sports of the World," *Atlanta Daily World*, May 8, 1954, 5.

86. Curry, *Jake Gaither*, 32.

87. Jake Gaither, "Florida A&M Seeks to Instill the 'Spirit of Excellence' in Athletes," *Atlanta Daily World*, July 29, 1951, 7–8; "Florida A. & M. Fetes Gridders at Annual Banquet," *Atlanta Daily World*, December 27, 1951, 5.

88. Marion E. Jackson, "Sports of the World," *Atlanta Daily World*, December 28, 1949, 5.

89. John McLendon, "Sportsdust," *Philadelphia Tribune*, February 28, 1950, 11; John McLendon, "Sportsdust," *Philadelphia Tribune*, March 11, 1950, 10.

90. Wilson, *Agile, Mobile, Hostile*, 175.

91. Curry, *Jake Gaither*, 78.

92. Ron Bliss, "Jake Gaither Liked Mobile, Agile, Hostile Winners," *Kingsport News*, October 18, 1977, 6A.

93. Fred Girard, "Jake Pits A&M Philosophy against Spartan Class," *St. Petersburg Times*, November 27, 1969, 5C.

94. Wilson, *Agile, Mobile, Hostile*, 154–58.

95. Ibid., 148.

96. Jake Gaither, "Florida A&M Seeks to Instill the 'Spirit of Excellence' in Athletes," *Atlanta Daily World*, July 29, 1951, 7–8.

97. Wilson, *Agile, Mobile, Hostile*, 158.

98. "Alonzo 'Jake' Gaither: Florida A&M Coaching Boss Is the Winningest in Negro College Football," *Ebony*, November 1960, 169.

99. Charles J. Smith, III, "Florida A. & M. Backfield Loaded with Hard Running Sprint Aces," *Atlanta Daily World*, September 25, 1953, 7; Richard Prior, "Local Hero Was an NFL Champion," *St. Augustine.com*, http://staugustine.com/stories/020605/new _2870907.shtml (accessed October 29, 2012).

100. Committee on Regulated Industries, *Legalized Gambling in Florida*, 1–11; McIver, *Dreamers, Schemers, and Scalawags*, 252–59; Crittenden, *Hialeah Park*.

101. "$6,824,268 State's Take from Racing," *St. Petersburg Evening Independent*, June 1, 1944, 13.

102. "Warren Gives First Campaign Address," *Palm Beach Post*, January 31, 1940, 5.

103. "Extra Day of Racing Proposed to Provide Scholarship Fund," *St. Petersburg Times*, May 26, 1949, 3; "Dogs to Run Tonight to Aid Gator Athletic Program," *Daytona Beach Morning Journal*, August 25, 1949, 9.

104. "Board of Controls Athletic Allocation, 1953–54—Race Track Scholarship Committee Meeting—June 24, 1953," box 1, folder 3, Gaither Papers; "Board of Control Meeting—June 16, 1958 Race Track Allocation," box 1, folder 4, Gaither Papers.

105. "Board of Controls Athletic Allocation, 1953–54—Race Track Scholarship Committee Meeting—June 24, 1953," box 1, folder 3, Gaither Papers.

106. Gordon B. Hancock, "Between the Lines: Athletics," *Atlanta Daily World*, February 1, 1948, 4; see also Gavins, *Perils and Prospects of Southern Black Leadership*.

107. "Coach 'Jake' Gaither Defends Athletics in Address at Forum," *Atlanta Daily World*, February 16, 1952, 5.

108. Watterson, *College Football*, 219–40; Joe Goldstein, "Explosion: 1951 Scandals Threaten College Hoops," November 19, 2003, *ESPN.com*, http://espn.go.com/classic/s /basketball_scandals_explosion.html (accessed November 18, 2012); Clair Bee, "I Know Why They Sold Out to the Gamblers," *Saturday Evening Post*, February 2, 1952, 26–27, 76–80.

109. Watterson, *College Football*, 202–3.

110. Hurd, *Black College Football*, 164–65. According to Hurd's records, this can be extended until 1992. See also Marion E. Jackson, "Sports of the World," *Atlanta Daily World*, October 16, 1949, 7.

111. Watterson, *College Football*, 241–59.

112. "LeMoyne College Quits Football," *Atlanta Daily World*, June 27, 1951, 5.

113. "Tillotson Quits Grid," *Pittsburgh Courier*, July 7, 1951, 14; "Is the Southwest Dodging Tillotson?," *Pittsburgh Courier*, February 4, 1950, 23; Marion E. Jackson, "Sports of the World," *Atlanta Daily World*, July 5, 1951, 5.

114. Cleve L. Abbott, "Private Colleges Beginning to Feel Pinch of Big Time Athletics," *Atlanta Daily World*, August 19, 1951, 7.

115. Allison Danzig, "New N.C.A.A. Code Puts Teeth in Move to Correct Abuses," *New York Times*, January 13, 1952, S1; "SIAC Winter Meeting Set for Miami, Florida, December 3–4," *Atlanta Daily World*, November 13, 1951, 5.

116. Arthur Daley, "Sports of the Times: Down with the Platoons," *New York Times*,

January 9, 1953, 26; Allison Danzig, "N.C.A.A. Council 'Strongly' Urges End of Two-Platoon System," *New York Times*, January 8, 1953.

117. Russ J. Cowan, "Coaches Divided on New Rule," *Chicago Defender*, January 24, 1953, 16.

118. "Jake Gaither Hits Ban on Grid Platoons," *Atlanta Daily World*, January 18, 1953, 6.

119. Russ J. Cowan, "Coaches Divided on New Rule," *Chicago Defender*, January 24, 1953, 16; A. M. Riveria Jr., "Grid Mentors Ready to Junk One Platoon Play," *Pittsburgh Courier*, December 26, 1953, 16; Nelson, *Anatomy of a Game*, 253–63.

120. "Jake Gaither Hits Ban on Grid Platoons," *Atlanta Daily World*, January 18, 1953, 6.

121. Nelson, *Anatomy of a Game*, 262–63.

122. Gaither mentioned to *Ebony* that he developed the idea from watching the LSU 1958 championship team that eliminated the distinctions between starters and re-serves. However, his comments following the rule change suggest that he had the idea earlier. See "Alonzo 'Jake' Gaither: Florida A&M Coaching Boss Is the Winningest in Negro College Football," *Ebony*, November 1960, 165.

123. Marion E. Jackson, "Sports of the World," *Atlanta Daily World*, November 5, 1953, 7.

124. Ric Roberts, "Sal Hall Eyes Hall of Fame," *Pittsburgh Courier*, December 6, 1952, 25.

125. Ibid.

126. Ric Roberts, "Famcee Grabs Top Spot in National Gridiron Ratings," *Pittsburgh Courier*, December 13, 1952, 19.

127. "Negroes Assured on Segregation," *Tallahassee Democrat*, May 11, 1949, 2; "Communism Probers Say: Negro Profs Not Required to Endorse Segregation," *St. Petersburg Times*, May 11, 1949, 1.

128. "Florida Check on Teachers' Loyalty Stirs Up Racial Issue," *Atlanta Daily World*, May 29, 1949, 1.

129. Woods, *Black Struggle*; Gilmore, *Defying Dixie*, 414–20.

130. "Reveal Background of Dr. Gray's Resignation," *Atlanta Daily World*, July 13, 1949, 1, 6.

131. "College President 'Forced to Quit,'" *Pittsburgh Courier*, July 16, 1949, 1, 4.

132. C. Blythe Andrews, "So They Tell Me," *Florida Sentinel*, June 11, 1949, 1, 4. See also Andrews's columns on February 12 and February 19, 1949.

133. Letter from C. Blythe Andrews to Fuller Warren, July 11, 1949, box 30, folder 5, Warren Papers, FSA.

134. Letter from Mary McLeod Bethune to Fuller Warren, August 2, 1949, box 30, folder 5, Warren Papers, FSA.

135. Quoted in Samuels, *Is Separate Unequal?*, 55.

136. Ibid., 27–59.

CHAPTER 5

1. Pompey, *More Rivers to Cross*, 386–87.

2. Delray Beach City Council Meeting Minutes, September 26, 1950, http://weblink.mydelraybeach.com/LFExternal/0/doc/11776/Page1.aspx (accessed May 24, 2018).

3. Delray Beach City Council Meeting Minutes, January 25, 1955, http://weblink.mydelraybeach.com/LFExternal/0/doc/11508/Page1.aspx (accessed May 24, 2018).

4. Francis Mitchell, "3000 Negroes in Florida Face Exile," *Jet*, June 28, 1956, 8–12.

5. Jack Ledden, "Race Clash on Beach Is Averted at Delray," *Palm Beach Post*, May 21, 1956, 1.

6. Haines Colbert, "Teen-Agers Cause 'Incident' at Delray," *Miami News*, May 21, 1956, 2A; "Delray Beach In [*sic*] Banned to Negroes," *Atlanta Daily World*, May 24, 1956, 1.

7. Delray Beach City Commission Minutes, May 25, 1956, http://weblink.mydelraybeach.com/LFExternal/0/doc/11470/Page1.aspx (accessed May 24, 2018).

8. Pompey, *More Rivers to Cross*, 385.

9. Ibid., 388–91.

10. Samuels, *Is Separate Unequal?*, 56.

11. Neyland, *History of Florida Agricultural and Mechanical University*, 237–42.

12. Marion E. Jackson, "Sports of the World," *Atlanta Daily World*, April 19, 1950, 5.

13. Tomberlin, "Florida Whites and the *Brown* Decision of 1954"; Wagy, *Governor LeRoy Collins of Florida*, 60.

14. Quoted in Tomberlin, "Florida Whites and the *Brown* Decision," 24; "Johns Considers Legislature Call to Study Segregation Ban," *Orlando Sentinel*, May 18, 1954, 1.

15. Cal Adams, "Gaither Tells Grads to Strive for Best," *St. Petersburg Times*, June 11, 1954, 29.

16. James A. Bond, "A Negro Looks at Supreme Court Ruling," *St. Petersburg Times*, May 23, 1954, 13-E.

17. Quoted in Kluger, *Simple Justice*, 316.

18. Fairclough, *Class of Their Own*, 357.

19. Ric Roberts, "What Will Our Coaches Do?," *Pittsburgh Courier*, December 5, 1953, 26.

20. William Nunn Jr., "FAMU Gains Revenge, Beats Prairie View, 19–7," *Pittsburgh Courier*, October 30, 1954, 23; Marion E. Jackson, "Sports of the World," *Atlanta Daily World*, November 9, 1954, 5.

21. Chuck Smith, "Florida A&M Out to 'Show' Writers," *Tallahassee Democrat*, November 19, 1954, 10.

22. Robert M. Ratcliffe, "Behind the Headlines," *Pittsburgh Courier*, December 20, 1954, 20; Marion E. Jackson, "Sports of the World," *Atlanta Daily World*, November 23, 1954, 7.

23. Chuck Smith, "Penalties Stymied Rattlers—Gaither," *Tallahassee Democrat*, November 22, 1954, 10.

24. Marion E. Jackson, "Sports of the World," *Atlanta Daily World*, October 31, 1954, 8.

25. Marion E. Jackson, "Sports of the World," *Atlanta Daily World*, November 4, 1956, 7.

26. Marion E. Jackson, "Sports of the World," *Atlanta Daily World*, November 11, 1954, 5.

27. Wilson, *Agile, Mobile, Hostile*, 163–64.

28. Marion E. Jackson, "FAMU Plays Maryland State in Orange Blossom Classic: Rattlers Favored over Hawks," *Atlanta Daily World*, December 4, 1954, 5; Marion E. Jackson, "Florida Routs Maryland State in Orange Blossom Classic," *Atlanta Daily World*, December 4, 1954, 7; "Wrangle over Mythical Grid Champs Title: 4 Schools Lay Claim to Crown," *Chicago Defender*, December 18, 1954, 11.

29. Hurd, *Black College Football*, 164.

30. Marion E. Jackson, "Florida A&M, Grambling Lead Nation's Unbeaten Elevens," *Atlanta Daily World*, October 12, 1955, 7.

31. "Florida A&M Comes from Behind to Tie A&T 28–28," *Atlanta Daily World*, November 8, 1955, 5; "Maryland State Takes Over No. 1 Sport in ANP Ratings," *Atlanta Daily World*, November 9, 1955, 5.

32. "Florida A&M Takes Over Top Spot in Grid Rating: Rattlers Shellack Southern Cats to Move to No. 1 Rating," *Atlanta Daily World*, November 23, 1955, 7.

33. Marion E. Jackson, "Sports of the World," *Atlanta Daily World*, November 15, 1955, 5.

34. Collie J. Nicholson, "Grambling Sizzles over Fla. A&M Slur," *Atlanta Daily World*, November 23, 1955, 7; Davis, Martyka, and Davis, *Closing the Gap*, 36–40.

35. Russ Cowans, "Russ' Corner," *Chicago Defender*, December 3, 1955, 10.

36. "Grambling Stuns Fla. A&M 28–21 for National Title," *Atlanta Daily World*, December 6, 1955, 7; Luix Virgil Overbea, "Grambling College Acclaimed '56 National Champs by ANP," *Atlanta Daily World*, December 7, 1955, 5.

37. For a history of Rosa Parks's activism, see Theoharis, *Rebellious Life of Mrs. Rosa Parks*, and McGuire, *At the Dark End of the Street*, 3–110.

38. Emory O. Jackson, "Leaders Continue Protests against Montgomery Bus Co.," *Atlanta Daily World*, December 11, 1955, 1.

39. Rabby, *The Pain and the Promise*, 9–23.

40. Wagy, *Governor LeRoy Collins of Florida*, 72.

41. Rabby, *The Pain and the Promise*, 13, 34–35; Braukman, *Communists and Perverts under the Palms*, 16–40.

42. Killian and Smith, "Negro Protest Leaders in a Southern Community"; Rabby, *The Pain and the Promise*, 26–27; Hobbs, *Democracy Abroad, Lynching at Home*.

43. Rabby, *The Pain and the Promise*, 21.

44. "Bus Boycotters Rap Fla. A&M President: Charge Gore Made Threats to Staff," *Chicago Defender*, September 29, 1956, 1; Rabby, *The Pain and the Promise*, 38–40.

45. "Boycott Unit Regrets Attack on Fla. Prexy," *Chicago Defender*, October 6, 1956, 1.

46. Eason, "Philosophy, Impact, and Contributions of Alonzo Smith 'Jake' Gaither," 95–96.

47. Curry, *Jake Gaither*, 161.

48. Ibid., 161.

49. Robinson and Lapchick, *Never Before, Never Again*, 111–12.

50. "Integration: A Two Way Street," *Chicago Defender*, November 13, 1954, 12; "White Boy Plays Center Position for Lincoln U.! Paradox of Sports Places German-Irish Lad on Colored Eleven," *New York Amsterdam News*, October 21, 1939, 18.

51. Katz, *Breaking Through*, 40–46; Ellsworth, *Secret Game*.

52. Katz, *Breaking Through*, 79–82.

53. Robinson and Lapchick, *Never Before, Never Again*, 83.

54. John McLendon, Frank Broyles, Tom Nugent, and Sid Gilman all attended the 1954 Coaching Clinic. See "Florida A&M Coaching Clinic a Hugh Success," *Atlanta Daily World*, June 25, 1954, 7.

55. D. C. Collington, "Gaither Has Troubles in the Future," *Chicago Defender*, August 18, 1956, 18.

56. "Willie Galimore Vote Back of Week by Florida Writers," *Atlanta Daily World*, October 25, 1956, 4; Ric Roberts, "Galimore, Frazier Spark FAMU Route [*sic*]," *Pittsburgh Courier*, October 27, 1956, 24.

57. "N.C. Eagles Turn Back Tenn. State 19–6 in National Classic," *Atlanta Daily World*, December 8, 1954, 6.

58. Earl S. Clanton III, "Gentry New Top Coach at Tennessee State U.," *Chicago Defender*, August 4, 1956, 17; Marion E. Jackson, "Fla. A&M to Play Tenn. State in 24th Orange Blossom Classic," *Atlanta Daily World*, November 8, 1956, 6.

59. Bill Nunn Jr., "Tenn. State Edges Fam-U, 41–39," *Pittsburgh Courier*, December 8, 1956, A24; Marion E. Jackson, "Tenn. State Nips Florida A&M 41–39 for U.S. Grid Title," *Atlanta Daily World*, December 4, 1956, 5; Marion E. Jackson, "Sports of the World," *Atlanta Daily World*, December 4, 1956, 5.

60. Bill Nunn Jr., "Change of Pace," *Pittsburgh Courier*, September 28, 1957, 19.

61. "Galimore Signs with Ch. Bears," *Chicago Defender*, February 2, 1957, 18; "Jake Gaither Makes NCAA Grid Report," *Atlanta Daily World*, January 23, 1957, 5.

62. "Control Board Sells $500,000 Stadium Issue," *St. Petersburg Times*, March 17, 1950, 13.

63. "Rattlers, Eyes on U.S. Title Face Texas Team," *Sarasota Herald-Tribune*, October 25, 1952, 5.

64. Board of Control of Florida, "The Support of Negro Public Higher Education in Florida," July 9, 1956, box 33, folder 2, Collins Papers, FSA.

65. "A Rivalry Is Decreed: Florida and Florida State Are Ordered to Meet in Football," *New York Times*, November 19, 1955, 14.

66. "Florida State Quietly Plans to Enter SEC," *Sarasota Herald-Tribune*, November 22, 1955, 12.

67. Letter from A. S. "Jake" Gaither to Governor LeRoy Collins, November 29, 1955, box 9, folder 7, Gaither Papers; Florida Board of Regents Minutes, 1905–1997, vol. 19, November 18, 1955, 278, FSA.

68. Notes on FAMU's Stadium Needs, box 9, folder 7, Gaither Papers.

69. Letter from A. S. "Jake" Gaither to Governor LeRoy Collins, November 29, 1955, box 9, folder 7, Gaither Papers.

70. Board of County Commissioners of Leon County Resolution, November 29, 1955, box 9, folder 7, Gaither Papers.

71. Letter to Guy C. Fulton, Architect to the Board of Control, August 20, 1956, box 9, folder 7, Gaither Papers.

72. Letter to President George W. Gore from A. S. Gaither, box 9, folder 7, Gaither Papers.

73. Florida Board of Regents Minutes, 1905–1997, vol. 19, December 8, 1955, 279, FSA.

74. Russ J. Cowans, "Russ' Corner," *Chicago Defender*, December 15, 1956, 18.

75. "Spring Grid Sessions Open for Rattlers," *St. Petersburg Times*, February 20, 1957, 37.

76. Marion E. Jackson, "Sports of the World," *Atlanta Daily World*, September 5, 1957, 7.

77. Marion E. Jackson, "Sports of the World," *Atlanta Daily World*, October 18, 1957, 7.

78. D. C. Collington, "Maryland State to Play in 25th Orange Blossom Classic," *Atlanta Daily World*, December 1, 1957, 6.

79. Marion E. Jackson, "Florida A&M Edges Maryland State 27 to 21 for U.S. Title," *Atlanta Daily World*, December 17, 1957, 5; "Fla. A&M Downs Maryland St., 27–21," *Chicago Defender*, December 21, 1957, 24; "1957 *Courier* All-American Team," *Pittsburgh Courier*, December 28, 1957, 16–17.

80. The rule stated that "a player withdrawn from the game during either the first or third period may not return during that period." Thus once a player is inserted into the game in either of these quarters, he must remain for the rest of that quarter. See "NCAA Rules Committee Bans Two Platoon System," *Daily Princetonian*, January 15, 1953, 1.

81. Dietzel, *Call Me Coach*, 73–93; "Ace Coaches Top Clinic at Florida," *Chicago Defender*, April 7, 1956, 17.

82. Ned West, "West Wind Blows," *Tallahassee Democrat*, October 12, 1945, 8. The motto stems from Winston Churchill's first speech as prime minister in 1940, http://www.winstonchurchill.org/resources/speeches/1940-the-finest-hour/blood-toil-tears-and-sweat (accessed March 2, 2017).

83. "Florida A&M Football Coach Sets Precedent," *Chicago Defender*, October 15, 1960, 24.

84. Marion E. Jackson, "Sports of the World," *Atlanta Daily World*, February 4, 1958, 5.

85. "A&M Champions Receive Honors," *Tallahassee Democrat*, January 18, 1958, 8.

86. "Rattlers to Open Spring Grid Drills," *Tallahassee Democrat*, February 5, 1958, 13.

87. "Nat'l Grid Title . . . Where Does It Go from Here," *Pittsburgh Courier Magazine*, September 27, 1958, 4.

88. "Southern Univ. Cats Roll Over Florida A. & M. Rattlers 35–6," *Atlanta Daily*

World, November 26, 1958, 6; Ric Roberts, "Prairie View '58 Nat'l Champs," *Pittsburgh Courier*, December 20, 1958, 28.

89. Aiello, *Bayou Classic*, 42–43; MacCambridge, *ESPN College Football Encyclopedia*, 1253.

90. Collie J. Nicholson, "Prairie View Rips Grambling 44–6 in Southeast Showdown," *Atlanta Daily World*, October 28, 1958, 4; "Prairie View Jars Fla. A&M 26–8," *Chicago Defender*, December 20, 1958, 2.

91. "Same Story: FAMU Is Favored in the SIAC," *Pittsburgh Courier*, October 3, 1959, B3.

92. D. C. Collington, "Same Old Story: FAMU '11' Loaded," *Pittsburgh Courier*, September 12, 1959, 17.

93. Marion E. Jackson, "Sports of the World," *Atlanta Daily World*, October 13, 1959, 7; D. C. Collington, "Florida A. & M. Runs Over Benedict, 74–0," *Chicago Defender*, October 17, 1959, 24; Marion E. Jackson, "Fla. A&M, Morehouse Pace Torrid SIAC Football Race," *Atlanta Daily World*, October 28, 1959, 5.

94. Marion E. Jackson, "Florida A&M Leads SIAC Standings with 5-0-0 Mark," *Atlanta Daily World*, November 3, 1959, 5.

95. "Fla. A&M Frosh QB in Grave Condition," *Atlanta Daily World*, October 24, 1959, 5; Gaither letter to Dr. George W. Gore, November 12, 1959, box 7, folder 2, Gaither Papers; "$3,026 Fund Aids Family of Fatally Injured Gridder," *Baltimore Afro-American*, March 12, 1960, 15.

96. AP, "Gus, Perry, Bob—Hung, Burned and Buried; Tampa Coach Also 'Victim,'" *Miami News*, November 3, 1959, 23; "Moss Hails (1) Hanging (2) Woodruff (3) Staff Job," *Tallahassee Democrat*, November 5, 1959, 22; "Huerta 'Hung' Right in Front of Newspaper," *Tallahassee Democrat*, November 5, 1959, 22.

97. Bill McGrotha, "From the Sidelines," *Tallahassee Democrat*, November 5, 1959, 22.

98. Bill Nunn Jr., "FAMU Defeats Southern; Asks Prairie View to Classic," *Pittsburgh Courier*, November 28, 1959, 23.

99. Marion E. Jackson, "Sports of the World," *Atlanta Daily World*, October 12, 1959, 7.

100. Marion E. Jackson, "Florida A&M Risks Perfect Slate against Prairie View," *Atlanta Daily World*, December 5, 1959, 7.

101. Bill McGrotha, "From the Sidelines," *Tallahassee Democrat*, December 8, 1959, 12.

102. Bill Nunn Jr., "Change of Pace," *Pittsburgh Courier*, December 16, 1959, 23.

103. Ric Roberts, "Gaither's Mark of 73-9-2 Paces Decade Begun in '51," *Pittsburgh Courier*, January 9, 1960, 19.

104. "The Sit-In Movement," International Civil Rights Center & Museum, https://www.sitinmovement.org/history/sit-in-movement.asp (accessed May 7, 2018).

105. Due and Due, *Freedom in the Family*, 46–50; Fendrich, *Ideal Citizens*, 14–21; "Negroes in Dixie Sing: 'Sit Down and Fight a Little While,'" *New York Amsterdam News*, February 27, 1960, 1.

106. Due and Due, *Freedom in the Family*, 7–18; Rabby, *The Pain and the Promise*, 83–84.

107. Ford, "SNCC Women, Denim, and the Politics of Dress."

108. Due and Due, *Freedom in the Family*, 47.

109. Ibid.

110. Rabby, *The Pain and the Promise*, 86–88.

111. Ibid., 88.

112. Due and Due, *Freedom in the Family*, 49.

113. "Break Up Florida Sit-Down 11 Deny Police Charge," *Chicago Defender*, February 23, 1960, 2.

114. Rabby, *The Pain and the Promise*, 88–89; Due and Due, *Freedom in the Family*, 48–50. The other students arrested were John and Barbara Boxton, William Larkins, Angelina Nance, Merritt Spaulding, and Clement Carney.

115. Rabby, *The Pain and the Promise*, 91–9; Due and Due, *Freedom in the Family*, 54–55; "80 Florida Students in Protest," *Chicago Defender*, March 7, 1960, 28; "Tear Gas Routs Florida Negroes," *New York Times*, March 13, 1960, 50.

116. "8 Negroes Choose Jail in 'Sacrifice,'" *New York Times*, March 19, 1960, 8.

117. "Dr. King Praises Students Who Stay in Jail," *Atlanta Daily World*, March 22, 1960, 6.

118. Curry, *Jake Gaither*, 158.

119. "Alton White Oral History Interview by Andy Huse, July 10, 2006," *Digital Collection—Florida Studies Center Oral Histories—University of South Florida*, http://scholarcommons.usf.edu/cgi/viewcontent.cgi?article=1162&context=flstud_oh (accessed May 24, 2018).

120. "Interview with Jake Gaither," April 4, 1975, M77-164, box 2, Junior League of Tallahassee, FSA.

121. Due and Due, *Freedom in the Family*, 45; Rabby, *The Pain and the Promise*, 121.

122. Marion E. Jackson, "Sports of the World," *Atlanta Daily World*, December 3, 1957, 5.

123. Anders Walker describes Gaither as an agent for Governor Collins. This description does not account for Gaither's firm belief in Black institutions, his willingness to preserve them, and his fear of violent reprisals for civil rights activity. To suggest that Gaither was only working for the state and not for his own beliefs is misleading. See Walker, *Ghost of Jim Crow*, 103–5, and Curry, *Jake Gaither*, 157–87.

124. Marion E. Jackson, "Sports of the World," *Atlanta Daily World*, February 28, 1960, 8.

125. Box 139, folder 14, Collins Papers, FSA.

126. MacCambridge, *ESPN College Football Encyclopedia*, 276, 294.

127. "Peterson Faces No. 1 Problem—Personnel," *Sarasota Herald-Tribune*, December 8, 1959, 15.

128. "State Cabinet Approves $17,000 Salary for Florida Coach Graves," *Ocala Star-Banner*, January 20, 1960, 11.

129. "Fla. A&M Coaching Clinic, June 13–18," *Atlanta Daily World*, May 14, 1955, 5.

130. "Mentors Praise 13th Annual Florida A&M Coaching Clinic," *Atlanta Daily World*, June 26, 1957; "FAM Clinic Offers Top Coaches," *Chicago Defender*, June 4, 1960, 24.

131. Bell, "Serving Two Masters," 477–78.

132. George B. Brady, "Fruit Bowl Won by Southern U. 30–0: San Francisco State Fails to Stem Tide," *Los Angeles Sentinel*, December 9, 1948, 23.

133. Spivey, *"If You Were Only White,"* 205.

134. "Florida A&M Opens Spring Grid Practice," *Atlanta Daily World*, March 4, 1960, 7.

135. "Sport: A Hard-Nosed Game," *Time*, October 17, 1960.

136. Bill McGrotha, "From the Sidelines," *Tallahassee Democrat*, August 21, 1960, 9.

137. "FAM Heads 3 NAIA Categories," *Chicago Defender*, November 12, 1960, 24.

138. "NAIA Names Four Coaches to Key Posts," *St. Petersburg Times*, November 16, 1955, 30.

139. Martin, *Benching Jim Crow*, 70–71; Katz, *Breaking Through*, 65–77.

140. "Memphis May Get NAIA Bowl Contest," *Spartanburg Herald-Journal*, November 5, 1957, 12. For the international view on the Little Rock Nine, see Dudziak, *Cold War Civil Rights*, 115–51.

141. "Holiday Bowl, Students' Hop Slated Today," *St. Petersburg Times*, December 21, 1957, 5-C.

142. "Integration Hits NAIA Bowl Game," *Owosso Argus-Press*, December 24, 1957, 7.

143. The class division among southern whites is often an underexamined feature of the process of desegregation. See Eskew, *But for Birmingham*, 153–92, and Connolly, *World More Concrete*, 1–18.

144. "Integration Hits NAIA Bowl Game," *Owosso Argus-Press*, December 24, 1957, 7.

145. "Holiday Bowl Game Signed for This City," *St. Petersburg Independent*, February 25, 1958, 10A.

146. Bob Boyson, "Sports Showcase: NAIA to Establish System of Playoffs for Holiday Bowl," *St. Petersburg Independent*, July 27, 1958, 8A.

147. Martin, "Integrating New Year's Day."

148. Marion E. Jackson, "Sports of the World," *Atlanta Daily World*, November 4, 1960, 7; "FAM Heads 3 NAIA Categories," *Chicago Defender*, November 12, 1960, 24.

149. Boy Boyson, "NAIA Defenses Rattlers: Club Can't Prove It in Holiday Bowl," *St. Petersburg Independent*, November 1, 1960, 6A.

150. Jack Ellison, "Rattlers Not out of Holiday Bowl," *St. Petersburg Times*, November 3, 1960, 1C.

151. Sam Adams Maestro, "Sam's Song," *St. Petersburg Times*, November 14, 1960, 10D.

152. Marion E. Jackson, "Sports of the World," *Atlanta Daily World*, November 20, 1960, 8.

153. Bill Nunn Jr., "Southern Claws FAMU 14–6; Becomes Champs," *Pittsburgh Courier*, November 26, 1960, 16.

154. Southern won the 1960 HBCU football title. See Marion E. Jackson, "Southern University Cats Win W. A. Scott II Memorial Trophy," *Atlanta Daily World*, December 9, 1960, 7; Lux Virgil Overbea, "ANP Picks Southern No. 1," *Los Angeles Sentinel*, December 29, 1960, A11.

155. Ric Roberts, "A New Challenge," *Pittsburgh Courier*, January 7, 1961, 13.

156. Bill Nunn Jr., "Change of Pace," *Pittsburgh Courier*, January 21, 1961, 17; Mac-Cambridge, *ESPN College Football Encyclopedia*, 1259, 735.

157. Bill Nunn Jr., "Change of Pace: Just How Good Is Negro College Football Today?," *Pittsburgh Courier*, September 30, 1961, A29.

158. Ibid. The Southwest Conference included Arkansas, Baylor, Texas, Rice, Texas Christian University, Texas Tech, Texas A&M, and Southern Methodist University in 1960.

159. Bill Nunn Jr., "Change of Pace: Just How Good Is Negro College Football Today?," *Pittsburgh Courier*, September 30, 1961, A29.

160. "Humboldt State Prexy Blacks Team Jim Crow: Asks Bowl Removal," *Chicago Defender*, December 17, 1960, 24.

161. "Segregation, Stadium End Stay of Holiday Bowl in St. Pete," *Atlanta Daily World*, March 18, 1961, 5; "NAIA Playoff Game Sell-Out," *Chicago Defender*, November 30, 1960, 31; Bob Boyson, "Sports Showcase," *St. Petersburg Independent*, December 11, 1961, F1.

162. "44 FAMU Athletes Cited at Annual Football Fete," *Atlanta Daily World*, February, 1, 1961, 5.

163. "FAMU Coach Is Fired; He Plans Appeal," *Tallahassee Democrat*, March 18, 1961, 7; "'Body Builder' Out on 'Moral Issue,'" *Pittsburgh Courier*, March 25, 1961, A2.

164. Marion E. Jackson, "Sports of the World," *Atlanta Daily World*, March 26, 1961, 8.

165. "Gaither Appraises Florida A&M Prospects," *St. Petersburg Independent*, 4-D.

166. D. C. Collington, "Florida A&M Expects 26 Returning Lettermen," *Atlanta Daily World*, August 23, 1961, 5; D. C. Collington, "FAMU Rattlers Getting Ready for Grid Season," *Atlanta Daily World*, September 14, 1961, 8.

167. Ric Roberts, "1921–1960 and Now: A New Challenge!," *Pittsburgh Courier*, September 30, 1961, A30.

168. Ric Roberts, "S. Conn. State Eager to Give Our Football a 3rd 'Shiner,'" *Pittsburgh Courier*, September 16, 1961, A28.

169. Ric Roberts, "Maryland State's Rally Nips South Conn., 7–6," *Pittsburgh Courier*, October 7, 1961, A29.

170. "Florida A-M in Top 10 Small College Rating," *Chicago Daily Defender*, November 1, 1961, 22; "Pittsburgh [sic], Kansas Leads NAIA Small College Rankings," *Atlanta Daily World*, November 18, 1961, 5.

171. "FAMU against the Field: Gaither Would Jet Team to Calif. Dec. 2 or 16 for 'Camellia Bowl,'" *Pittsburgh Courier*, November 25, 1961, A27.

172. "N.A.I.A. Picks Bowl Teams," *New York Times*, November 21, 1961, 51. The semifinal teams were Pittsburg State (Kans.), Northern State (S.Dak.), Whittier (Calif.), and Linfield (Oreg.).

173. Bennie Thomas, "Our Colleges Chained to Middle Ground," *Pittsburgh Courier*, December 2, 1961, A27.

174. Ric Roberts, "In National Derby: FAMU, Southern, Texas Southern, Jackson 'Alive,'" *Pittsburgh Courier*, November 4, 1961, A28.

175. "Florida A&M Rattlers Power over N.C. A&T Aggies, 32–12," *Atlanta Daily World*, November 7, 1961, 5.

176. Bill Nunn Jr., "Rattlers Humiliate Southern U., 46–0," *Pittsburgh Courier*, November 25, 1961, A25.

177. "FAMU Rattlers Win W. A. Scott National Championship Trophy," *Atlanta Daily World*, November 28, 1961, 5.

178. "Jake Gaither Awarded Small College Coach of the Year Trophy," *Atlanta Daily World*, January 17, 1962, 5.

179. Tommy Picou, "Tommy's Corner," *Chicago Daily Defender*, January 16, 1962, 22.

180. Martin, *Benching Jim Crow*, 123–24; White, "From Desegregation to Integration."

181. "Fla. Flash Runs Record 9.2 in 100," *Baltimore Afro-American*, February 24, 1962, 13.

182. D. C. Collington, "Robert Hayes: 'My Ambition Is Run 100-Yard Dash in 9 Seconds Flat,'" *Atlanta Daily World*, February 28, 1962, 4.

183. "Florida A. & M. Gets Many Bids for Robert Hayes," *Atlanta Daily World*, March 13, 1962, 5.

184. Quoted in Marion E. Jackson, "Sports of the World," *Atlanta Daily World*, May 11, 1962, 7; Mike Gora, "The Sports Hub: Don't Throw Stones," *Alligator*, April 3, 1962.

185. "Coach Hurt Quits Post at Morgan," *Baltimore Afro-American*, October 17, 1959, 14.

186. Bill Nunn Jr., "Change of Pace: Mumford's Death Marks End of a Sports Era," *Pittsburgh Courier*, May 12, 1962, A28.

187. Walsh, *Who's #1?*, 15–16.

188. Mary Eddy, "Florida A&M Heads Small College Football Teams," *Philadelphia Tribune*, October 9, 1962, 13.

189. "Florida A. and M. Retains Lead in Small-College Poll," *New York Times*, November 1, 1962, 39.

190. Martin Lader, "Fla. A&M Holds UPI First Place Rating for Fifth Straight Week," *Atlanta Daily World*, November 2, 1962, 7.

191. Dick Joyce, "Florida A&M Clings to Top Spot in UPI Football Poll," *Atlanta Daily World*, November 9, 1962, 7.

192. D. C. Collington, "Florida A&M Wins No. 20 Defeating Southern, 25–0," *Atlanta Daily World*, November 20, 1962, 6.

193. Dick Joyce, "Mississippi Southern Leads Small College Football Poll," *Atlanta Daily World*, November 23, 1962, 7.

194. "Wittenberg, Florida A. & M. Share First in Writers' Poll," *New York Times*, November 22, 1962, 58.

195. Ric Roberts, "FAMU, May Be First Repeat Champ in 15 Years, Underrated by UPI, NAIA," *Pittsburgh Courier*, December 8, 1962, 40.

196. AP, "Rattlers Top AP Poll," *Washington Spokesman-Review*, November 30, 1962, 18.

197. "Fla. Hotels Host Grid Fans: Miami Hotels Will Open Doors to Football Fans," *Chicago Defender*, October 30, 1962, 24; "Hotels Drop Classic Bias," *Chicago Defender*, November 27, 1962, 21; Marion E. Jackson, "Sports of the World," *Atlanta Daily World*, December 4, 1962, 5.

198. "Orange Blossom Classic Means $ to Miami Business," *Atlanta Daily World*, December 27, 1962, 5.

199. Connolly, *World More Concrete*, 202–10.

200. Sam Lacy, "Rattlers Stopping 'Blossom' Tilt: Jackson Humbles A&M at Miami," *Baltimore Afro-American*, December 15, 1962, 9.

201. Brad Pye Jr., "Who Will Be Rams Next Coach? Why Not Florida A&M's Jake Gaither," *Los Angeles Sentinel*, November 8, 1962, A21; "Florida A&M Grid King," *Cleveland Call and Post*, November 10, 1962, 7C.

202. Rabby, *The Pain and the Promise*, 141–43.

203. "Negro Grid Star Helps South Rise to Victory," *Cleveland Call and Post*, December 28, 1962, 1A.

CHAPTER 6

1. Hayes and Pack, *Run, Bullet, Run*, 66.

2. "Stars Fell on Atlanta," *Atlanta Daily World*, February 20, 1963, 2; Marion E. Jackson, "1913—A Salute to the 50th Anniversary of the SIAC—1963," *Atlanta Daily World*, February 2, 1963, 5.

3. Marion E. Jackson, "Sports of the World," *Atlanta Daily World*, March 3, 1963, A5.

4. "FAMU Rattlers May Be Sitting on a Powder Keg," *Atlanta Daily World*, September 26, 1963.

5. "8 Football Coaches Relieved of Duties by President Davis," *Atlanta Daily World*, April 4, 1963, 8.

6. Marion E. Jackson, "Sports of the World," *Atlanta Daily World*, May 12, 1963, 8; "Merritt Lands $15,000 Gridiron Post at Tenn. A&I," *Pittsburgh Courier*, May 18, 1963, 22.

7. "Tennessee State Upsets Florida Rattlers, 14–12," *Norfolk Journal and Guide*, November 2, 1963, 16; "Rattlers Third in National Poll," *Norfolk Journal and Guide*, November 9, 1963, 15.

8. "SWAC Football Teams Won 15 of 18 Non-League Games," *Atlanta Daily World*, December 8, 1963, A7.

9. Bill Nunn Jr., "Change of Pace," *Pittsburgh Courier*, November 30, 1963, 23.

10. Ibid.

11. Tommy Devine, "Price Is Right, but Game Switch Brings Problems," *Miami Times*, November 15, 1963, 2B.

12. Hochberg and Horowitz, "Broadcasting and CATV"; AP, "Miami's Gustafson Says All Sorts Problems Involved in Contest Shift," *Florence Times*, November 27, 1963, 21; AP, "Miami-'Bama Delayed: School Officials Bow to TV Request," *Daytona Beach Morning Journal*, November 30, 1963, 9; AP, "Miami to Pay Difference in Florida's Aggies' Loss," *Washington Spokesman-Review*, February 11, 1964, 14.

13. Marion E. Jackson, "Sports of the World," *Atlanta Daily World*, December 18, 1963, 5.

14. "Prairie View Is Bowl Bound Following, 20–7 Victory," *Pittsburgh Courier*, December 14, 1963, 22.

15. George Skelton, "Prairie View Falls to St. John's, 33–27," *Atlanta Daily World*, December 15, 1963, 8.

16. Sheep Jackson, "From the Sidelines," *Cleveland Call and Post*, August 17, 1963, 15C.

17. "South Carolina Prep Star South by Three Southern Universities," *Philadelphia Tribune*, March 9, 1963, 12; Marion E. Jackson, "Sports of the World," *Atlanta Daily World*, April 10, 1963, 5; "Entire Program Desegregated: Wake Forest Rolls Out Red Carpet for Athletes," *Norfolk Journal and Guide*, February 9, 1963, 12; Trezzvant W. Anderson, "Dixie Colleges Ready to Open Sports Doors," *Pittsburgh Courier*, February 9, 1963, 23.

18. Hayes and Pack, *Run, Bullet, Run*, 68.

19. Ibid., 93; "Rattlers' Hayes Does It Again," *Cleveland Call and Post*, January 11, 1964, 7B; "Robert Hayes Eyes Olympics," *Atlanta Daily World*, January 26, 1964.

20. "Hayes May Rebuild Image of Negro Runners," *Pittsburgh Courier*, June 20, 1964, 22.

21. Hayes and Pack, *Run, Bullet, Run*, 4.

22. Ibid., 22; Cooper Rollow, "2 Bear Stars Die in Auto Crash," *Chicago Tribune*, July 27, 1964, 1; "Gaither Calls Galimore 'Finest I Ever Coached,'" *Baltimore Afro-American*, August 8, 1964, 10; "Black Highway Sign in Death of 2 Chi Bears Stars," *Philadelphia Tribune*, July 28, 1964, 1; "Car Kills Galimore and Farrington," *Jet*, August 13, 1964, 54.

23. "FAMU Eleven Begins Fall Workouts," *Norfolk Journal and Guide*, August 29, 1964, 27; "'Small' Title Again Goal," *Baltimore Afro-American*, September 26, 1964, 10.

24. Ric Roberts, "FAMU–Tennessee State Tops Crucial Week," *Pittsburgh Courier*, October 24, 1964, 26.

25. "*Courier*–RC Cola: Player of the Week — Eldridge Dickey," *Pittsburgh Courier*, October 24, 1964, 25; Curry, *Jake Gaither*, 99–101.

26. Bill Nunn Jr., "Rhubarb Marks FAMU's 22–20 Win over Tenn. State," *Pittsburgh Courier*, October 31, 1964, 14.

27. Ibid.; Bill Nunn Jr., "Change of Pace," *Pittsburgh Courier*, November 7, 1964, 23.

28. Hayes and Pack, *Run, Bullet, Run*, 20–25.

29. Ibid., 26–31.

30. D. C. Collington, "Hayes Hailed! Benedict Raided by FAMU," *Pittsburgh Courier*, November 7, 1964, 22.

31. "Aggies Feel Sting of Rattlers," *Baltimore Afro-American*, November 14, 1964, 10.

32. "Southern Upsets Fla. A&M, 45–20," *Baltimore Afro-American*, November 21, 1964, 10.

33. "Was NCAA Grid Ban of Prairie View Slap at NAIA? National Negro Grid Champs Penalized," *Pittsburgh Courier*, May 2, 1964, 22.

34. Ric Roberts, "Nicksmen Clinch Honors for '64," *Pittsburgh Courier*, November 28, 1964, 22.

35. Ric Roberts, "More Than 40,000 Expected, Orange Blossom Classic," *Pittsburgh Courier*, December 5, 1964, 23.

36. Bill Nunn Jr., "FAMU Ignores Rain to Chop Down Grambling, 42–15," *Pittsburgh Courier*, December 12, 1964, 23.

37. "Hayes in Senior Bowl: Tan Players Integrate South in Senior Bowl," *Chicago Defender*, January 7, 1965.

38. "Bob Hayes Signs Pact with Dallas Cowboys," *Chicago Defender*, December 9, 1964, 30.

39. "North Pins Hopes on Halting Hayes: Namath also Poses Problem in Senior Bowl Today," *New York Times*, January 9, 1965, 19.

40. "North, South Play 7–7 Tie in Senior Bowl," *New York Times*, January 10, 1065, S1.

41. William N. Wallace, "Left Tackle: The Story of a Lineman—Roosevelt Brown—and What It Takes to Be One," *New York Times*, November 8, 1964, SM137.

42. Ross, *Outside the Lines*, 140, 167–73.

43. MacCambridge, *Lamar Hunt*, 89–107.

44. Ross, *Outside the Lines*, 167–73.

45. "More Pros from Florida A&M Than Any Other," *Chicago Defender*, August 8, 1961, 24; "Fifty Pro Gridders Up from Tan Colleges," *Pittsburgh Courier*, August 5, 1961, A32.

46. Marion E. Jackson, "Sports of the World," *Atlanta Daily World*, December 10 1961, 8.

47. Ibid.

48. "N.Y. Giants Sign Fla. A&M Center," *Philadelphia Tribune*, January 2, 1962, 6.

49. July 11, 1955, letter from Eddie Kotal, LA Rams Head Scout, to Gaither, box 5, folder 13, Gaither Papers.

50. Sheep Jackson, "From the Sidelines," *Cleveland Call and Post*, December 26, 1964, 7C.

51. William N. Wallace, "Left Tackle: The Story of a Lineman—Roosevelt Brown—and What It Takes to Be One," *New York Times*, November 8, 1964, SM137.

52. Sam Lacy, "Buddy Young Retires, Colts' New Job Makes Him 'Happy,'" *Baltimore Afro-American*, September 29, 1956, 16.

53. "Tunnell to Retire: Halfback Says He Will Scout for Packers and Giants," *New York Times*, March 29, 1962, 39; William N. Wallace, "Weary Tunnell Ends Talent Trip," *New York Times*, May 10, 1964, S3; Wendell Smith, "Sports Beat: Young, Tunnell Pick Aces," *Pittsburgh Courier*, December 15, 1962, 26.

54. William N. Wallace, "Weary Tunnell Ends Talent Trip," *New York Times*, May 10, 1964, S3.

55. Al Monroe, "So They Say," *Chicago Defender*, December 10, 1964, 36.

56. Collie J. Nicholson, "'Best Player in Country,' Says AFL Draftee's Coach," *Baltimore Afro-American*, December 22, 1963, 8.

57. Gruver, *American Football League*, 142–43.

58. Ibid., 143–44; Taylor and Stallard, *Need to Win*, 41–52.

59. Bill Nunn Jr., "Change of Pace," *Pittsburgh Courier*, January 2, 1965, 15; Claude E. Harrison Jr., "Pro Grid Squads Discriminate against Tan QBs," *Philadelphia Tribune*, September 15, 1964, 13.

60. "'Negroes Were Justified' Says Joe Foss," *Chicago Defender*, January 12, 1965, 21. The eight players from HBCUs were Mack Lee Hill (Southern University), Buck Buchanan (Grambling University), Ernie Ladd (Grambling University), Dick Westmoreland (North Carolina A&T University), Willie Brown (Grambling University), Ernie Warlick (North Carolina Central University), Sherman Plunkett (University of Maryland–Eastern Shore), and Winston Hill (Texas Southern University).

61. "Tan Colleges Boast 48 Graduate-AFL Stars: Grambling Has 12, FAMU 5 in the League," *Pittsburgh Courier*, November 19, 1966, 10A.

CHAPTER 7

1. Luther Golden, "Florida A&M Coach Doesn't Understand Everything, but Gaither Knows Youth of Today Are Rebellion," *Pensacola News*, October 23, 1968, 13.

2. "FAMU Coaching Clinic Big Hit," *Pittsburgh Courier*, July 10, 1965; "Record 131 Attend Fla. Coaching Clinic," *Norfolk Journal and Guide*, July 10, 1965, 12.

3. "Rattlers Open Grid Practice," *Chicago Defender*, August 21, 1965, 17.

4. Ric Roberts, "Only Fla. A&M in Every Top-Ten of Last 20 Years," *Pittsburgh Courier*, September 25, 1965, 15.

5. Bill Nunn Jr., "Change of Pace," *Pittsburgh Courier*, October 16, 1965, 23.

6. Earl S. Clanton III, "Tennessee State Wallops Fla. A&M, 45–6," *Chicago Defender*, October 30, 1965, 17.

7. D. C. Collington, "Defeat Second of the Year: Texas Southern Upsets Fla. Rattlers, 34–21," *Norfolk Journal and Guide*, December 4, 1965, 17.

8. A. S. Doc Young, "Good Morning Sports: The Thundering Herd," *Chicago Defender*, December 15, 1965.

9. "Nicks Ends 36-Yr. Stint as Coach; 20 at Pr. View," *Pittsburgh Courier*, January 29, 1965, 11A.

10. Ric Roberts, "Change of Pace: Sam Taylor Loses 8-Weeks Struggle," *Pittsburgh Courier*, April 16, 1966, 14A; Ric Roberts, "Fred Long Oldest Active Coach, Heart Victim," *Pittsburgh Courier*, April 2, 1966, 10A.

11. Ric Roberts, "Banks Closes in on 'Name' Coaches," *Pittsburgh Courier*, February 5, 1966, 10A; "Only 3 National Grid Title Coaches Active: Gaither, Robinson, Merritt," *Pittsburgh Courier*, April 30, 1966, 10A.

12. "Rattlers on Grid," *Pittsburgh Courier*, March 19, 1966, 10A.

13. "Grid Outlook at FAMU Filled with ?? Marks," *Pittsburgh Courier*, August 20, 1966, 10A.

14. "Tenn. State Batters Fla. A. and M., 29–0," *Pittsburgh Courier*, October 29, 1966, 10A.

15. Brad Pye Jr., "SU Bops Florida A&M 17–13," *Los Angeles Sentinel*, November 17,

1966, B4; Bennie Thomas, "Southern Rally Trips Fla. Rattlers, 17–13," *Norfolk Journal and Guide*, November 19, 1966, 13.

16. Bill McGrotha, "From the Sidelines," *Tallahassee Democrat*, September 1, 1967, 14.

17. Bill Nunn Jr., "Change of Pace," *Pittsburgh Courier*, December 3, 1966, 10A.

18. "Florida A&M Converts Two Alabama A&M Fumbles into Touchdowns," *Philadelphia Tribune*, December 6, 1966, 12.

19. Cal Jacox, "From the Press Box," *Norfolk Journal and Guide*, December 17, 1966, 22.

20. Bill Nunn Jr., "Change of Pace," *Pittsburgh Courier*, December 4, 1966, 10A; Bill McGrotha, "From the Sidelines," *Tallahassee Democrat*, September 1, 1967, 14.

21. Xavier Athletics Hall of Fame, http://goxavier.com/hof.aspx?hof=54&path=&kiosk= (accessed August 25, 2015); "Carroll Williams Signs Grant with Xavier U.," *Miami News*, August 27, 1963, 4B.

22. Al Levine, "Yes, There Is One Pro Negro Quarterback," *Miami News*, August 13, 1968, C1; Claude Harrison, "Sports Roundup: Number of Negro QBs in Major Colleges Increases," *Philadelphia Tribune*, October 15, 1966, 20; John Hansen, "Scramble at TU: Xavier's Williams One of Nation's Best," *Toledo Blade*, September 15, 1966, 41.

23. "Negro Quarterback from Florida to Play at Toledo U," *Cleveland Call and Post*, January 15, 1966, 6C.

24. Jack Houghteling, "County Athletics Integrate in Peace," *Miami News*, February 1, 1963, 2C; Robert Sherrill, "Negro Progress in Florida: Confederate Flag Said an Integration Sign," *St. Petersburg Times*, February 23, 1966, 1B.

25. Chris Anderson, "Breaking Through: A Young Black Man's Groundbreaking Path from the Migrant Field to the Football Field," *Sarasota Herald-Tribune*, February 1, 2002, 1A, 14A; "U-M ready to Sign Negro Football Players," *Miami News*, December 8, 1966, 3-D.

26. White, "From Desegregation to Integration," 486.

27. Dunnavant, *Missing Ring*.

28. David M. Moffit, "Race No Longer a Question in South," *Chicago Defender*, April 3, 1967, 30.

29. Baker, "Paradoxes of Desegregation."

30. Leon W. Lindsay, "Blacks in the SEC," *Christian Science Monitor*, September 1, 1970, 11.

31. "Memo from Hobe Hooser to Ray Graves," January 29, 1969, box 25, folder "Athletics, Intercollegiate, Recruiting Negro Athletes," series P12, Office of the President: Stephen O'Connell, Presidential Collection, University of Florida Archives; White, "From Desegregation to Integration," 487–88.

32. *Staff Report on Public Education Submitted to United States Commission on Civil Rights*, October 1964, https://www.law.umaryland.edu/marshall/usccr/documents/cr12ed82964.pdf (accessed May 25, 2018).

33. United States Commission on Civil Rights, *Survey of School Desegregation in the*

Southern and Border States, 1965–66, February 1966, https://www.law.umaryland.edu /marshall/usccr/documents/cr12sch611.pdf (accessed May 25, 2018).

34. Campbell, *University in Transition*, 103.

35. Ibid., 108–10.

36. Mark Schlabach, "Teammates Work to Restore Patterson's Place in History," *ESPN.com*, February 15, 2008, http://www.espn.com/espn/blackhistory2008/news /story?id=3246138 (accessed October 27, 2017).

37. "FSU Gets Two Stars," *Pittsburgh Courier*, May 6, 1967, 27; Marion Jackson, "Negro Cagers Win Raves at FSU," *Atlanta Daily World*, January 10, 1971, 10.

38. Miller, "Psychological Characteristics of the Negro," 23.

39. Jim Henry, "Honoring History," *Tallahassee Democrat*, October 14, 2015, 1D–2D.

40. Hayes and Pack, *Run, Bullet, Run*, 53–56; "Hayes Released from Probation on Theft Charge," *Chicago Defender*, June 24, 1965, 37.

41. Ben Funk, "And I Know Some White Boys I'd Like to Get — Gaither," *Miami Times*, February 1, 1963, 2C.

42. Claude E. Harrison Jr., "Sports Roundup: Morgan State College's Recruiting System on Par with Big 10 Teams," *Philadelphia Tribune*, September 16, 1969, 17.

43. Piascik, *Gridiron Gauntlet*, 77.

44. "Proposals by the Florida State University Black Student Union Presented to the Florida State Faculty Senate, February 2, 1970" (emphasis in original), http://fsu sixties.omeka.net/exhibits/show/student-unrest-at-florida-stat/item/62 (accessed November 10, 2015).

45. Jonathan White, "Ralph Oves, White Gridder at Lincoln, Has Set a Precedent," *Pittsburgh Courier*, December 19, 1942, 16.

46. "VA. Union May Be Next: Spartans Third College in CIAA to Integrate," *Norfolk Journal and Guide*, September 3, 1966, 25.

47. A. S. Doc Young, "Good Morning Sports: The Thundering Herd," *Chicago Defender*, December 15, 1965, 26.

48. *Grambling's White Tiger* (1981) starred Harry Belafonte as Eddie Robinson, LeVar Burton as Charles "Tank" Smith, Dennis Haysbert as James "Shack" Harris, and Caitlyn Jenner as Jim Gregory, http://www.imdb.com/title/tt0082468/?ref_=nm_flmg_act_13 (accessed March 6, 2017).

49. Jimmy Mann, "Gaither Signs White Gridder: A&M Opportunity Knocks for Rufus," *St. Petersburg Times*, March 20, 1968, 3C.

50. Thomas Fazio, "Southerner Is Rattlers' Pioneering Grid Player: Florida's First White Recruit," *Norfolk Journal and Guide*, March 30, 1968, 12. There were two other white athletes at FAMU before Brown. Both Boden Logan and Herb Hoyt were on the track and field team.

51. Ibid.

52. Ibid.; "Grambling–Morgan Clash a Sellout," *Chicago Defender*, September 25, 1968, 30.

53. David. M. Moffit, "Sports Integration in South Slow but Sure," *Chicago Defender*, April 4, 1967, 26.

54. A. S. Doc Young, "Good Morning Sports: The Thundering Herd," *Chicago Defender*, December 15, 1965, 26.

55. Rex Newman, "Rattlers Should Be Allowed to Play Anyone—Adams," *Palm Beach Post*, October 15, 1965, 1.

56. "Rattlers Should Be Allowed to Play Any Team: Dyson," *Palm Beach Post*, October 28, 1965, A4.

57. Ibid.

58. "NCAA Axed Bi-racial Classic: Conference and National Titles Remain Top Lures," *Pittsburgh Courier*, September 25, 1965, 14.

59. "No. Dakota State Beats Grambling," *New York Times*, December 12, 1965.

60. Brad Pye Jr., "14–14 Tie: Dickey Dazzles for Tenn. State," *Los Angeles Sentinel*, December 16, 1965, B2.

61. Sam Lacy, "Bears Achieve Double Victory in Tangerine Bowl," *Baltimore Afro-American*, December 17, 1966, 9; "Bears Find West Chester Eleven No Pushover in Fla.," *Baltimore Afro-American*, December 17, 1966, 9; Ronald James, "A Man Concerned: Negro Athletes Can Look Better Playing, Not Bowing and Scraping," *Philadelphia Tribune*, December 17, 1966, 7.

62. "Dickey Passes, Runs for Five TDs as Tennessee State Wins Bowl Game," *Philadelphia Tribune*, December 13, 1966, 12.

63. "Tenn. St.–San Diego to Meet: Top Ranked Grid Teams to Open the Season," *Chicago Defender*, February 18, 1967, 14.

64. "EWC, Pr. View, NCC Stun Biggies," *Pittsburgh Courier*, December 3, 1966, 10A.

65. "South Losing Smith and Farrs: Big Colleges Raiding Fla., Texas Areas," *Pittsburgh Courier*, January 28, 1967, 11; "FAMU Grabs Jacksonville QB," *Pittsburgh Courier*, February 4, 1967, 18.

66. "FAMU's 5 Plays Miami," *Los Angeles Sentinel*, May 18, 1967, B2.

67. Charles Nobles, "Exposure In U-M Game Helps A&M Recruiting," *Miami News*, February 12, 1968, 1C, 5C.

68. Cal Jacox, "From the Press Box," *Norfolk Journal and Guide*, September 16, 1967, 12.

69. "FAMU Rattlers Sharpening for Combat," *Pittsburgh Courier*, September 16, 1967, 10.

70. Earl Clanton III, "Tennessee State Tigers End Losing Streak, 32–8," *Norfolk Journal and Guide*, October 28, 1967, 14.

71. Cal Jacox, "From the Press Box," *Norfolk Journal and Guide*, November 4, 1967, 13.

72. "A&M Toils on Errors with Open Date Due," *Tallahassee Democrat*, October 24, 1967, 10.

73. "FAMU Downs Southern U. 36–25: Rattlers Get Sixth Win in 7 Games," *Pittsburgh Courier*, November 18, 1967, 10; "Hard Week on Coaches," *St. Petersburg Times*, November 15, 1967, 1C.

74. Freedman, *Breaking the Line*.

75. Carmichael and Hamilton, *Black Power*, 34–57.

76. Biondi, *Black Revolution on Campus*, 142–73; White, *Challenge of Blackness*, 19–58.

77. Larry Nichols, "A&M Campus Said 'Normal' Following Carmichael Talk," *Tallahassee Democrat*, April 17, 1967, 9.

78. "Gaither Fights to Keep Athletics," *Florida Today*, October 29, 1970, 1C.

79. Quoted in Roosevelt Wilson, "Alonzo Gaither: Elder Statesman," in *Alonzo Smith "Jake" Gaither Celebrity Roast Souvenir Journal*, May 31, 1986, box 1, folder 2, Gaither Papers.

80. Edwards, *Revolt of the Black Athlete*, 4–9.

81. Ric Roberts, "All-America Banquet Greatest Ever," *Pittsburgh Courier*, January 20, 1968, 1, 4.

82. Ed Plaisted, "Gaither Tells It as It Is . . . ," *Palm Beach Post*, November 27, 1968, 21.

83. Scott, *Contempt and Pity*, 161–85.

84. "Powell Declares Nonviolent Days Have Come to End," *Chicago Defender*, April 2, 1968, 9; Rabby, *The Pain and the Promise*, 190–96.

85. Ed Plaisted, "Gaither Tells It as It Is . . . ," *Palm Beach Post*, November 27, 1968, 21.

86. Pat Putnam, "'A Man Has Got to Go with What He Believes,'" *Sports Illustrated*, October 7, 1968, 60–61, http://www.si.com/vault/1968/10/07/550864/a-man-has-got -to-go-with-what-he-believes (accessed May 25, 2018).

87. Rhoden, *Forty Million Dollar Slaves*, 18–31; Bill Nunn Jr., "Change of Pace," *Pittsburgh Courier*, October 12, 1968, 14; Jonathan Black, "Street Academies: One Step off the Sidewalk," *Saturday Review*, November 15, 1969, 88–89, 100.

88. "Florida A&M Releases 1968 Football Slate," *Atlanta Daily World*, March 23, 1968, 5.

89. Jack Harper, "Gator Tilt Pleases Gaither," *Palm Beach Post*, September 25, 1968, 21.

90. Ric Roberts, "Grid Vista in NYC," *Pittsburgh Courier*, August 28, 1968, 15; Bob Balfe, "Column," *Palm Beach Post*, August 11, 1968, E1.

91. "Rattlers Roll for 4-0," *Palm Beach Post*, October 28, 1968, 23; "Florida A&M Breezes 32–13 by Tenn. A&I," *Tennessean*, October 27, 1968, 7-G; "Dickey Pro Spot Up To Raiders," *Chicago Defender*, March 2, 1968, 15.

92. Dick Moore, "Aggies Doom Florida A&M in Surprise Victory," *Pittsburgh Courier*, November 16, 1968, 14; "*Courier* RC Cola Player of the Week," *Pittsburgh Courier*, November 16, 1968, 14.

93. Ric Roberts, "FAMU, A&T, Morgan Led Lack-Luster 'Twelve,'" *Pittsburgh Courier*, November 16, 1968, 14.

94. Fred Girard, "New Coach, Fresh Money, Fueled Tampa Blastoff," *St. Petersburg Times*, November 6, 1968, 1C, 2C; Fred Girard, "Curci Theory: Think Big, Act Big, Play Big," *St. Petersburg Times*, November 7, 1968, 1C, 4C; Fred Girard, "Spartans Resemble Foreign Legion," *St. Petersburg Times*, November 8, 1968, 1C, 2C; Buddy Martin, "Fight-

ing with a Short Stick," *Florida Today*, November 27, 1968, 1B, 4B; "Tampa 5th in AP Poll," *St. Petersburg Times*, November 8, 1968, 1C.

95. "Tampa, Rattlers in Classic?," *Florida Today*, October 23, 1968, 1B.

96. "Five Foes Considered for Rattlers in Bowl," *Palm Beach Post*, November 1, 1968, 31.

97. Bob Smith, "Tampa Edges N. Michigan," *Florida Today*, November 3, 1968, 2B.

98. Bob Balfe, "Column," *Palm Beach Post*, August 11, 1968, E1.

99. "Fla. A&M, Alcorn Blossom Foes," *Chicago Defender*, November 23, 1968, 16.

100. Buddy Martin, "Graves Sticks His Neck Out," *Florida Today*, November 1, 1968, 1B.

101. "Tampa, Rattlers in Classic?," *Florida Today*, October, 23, 1968, 1B.

102. "Curci Raps Gaither's Choice," *Florida Today*, November 21, 1968, 6B.

103. Lerone Bennett Jr., "What's in a Name? Negro vs. Afro-American vs. Black," *Ebony*, November 1967, 46–48, 50–52, 54.

104. "Fla. A&M, Alcorn Blossom Foes," *Chicago Defender*, November 23, 1968, 16.

105. Ric Roberts, "NCAA Lays an Egg," *Pittsburgh Courier*, December 21, 1968, 15.

106. Ibid.; Ric Roberts, "Alcorn A&M Champs, Destroy FAMU 36–9," *Pittsburgh Courier*, December 14, 1968, 14.

107. "Bears Finish 6th in Nation," *Baltimore Afro-American*, December 21, 1968, 16.

108. Buddy Martin, "Huggins Leans toward FSU," *Florida Today*, December 12, 1968, 1B.

109. Buddy Martin, "NCAA Rules Hinders Scholar," *Florida Today*, December 20, 1968, 1B.

CHAPTER 8

1. Dan Jenkins, "The First 100 Years," *Sports Illustrated*, September 15, 1969, 46–54.

2. Breard Snellings, "Shootin' the Breeze: Negro Teams Best," *San Bernardino County Sun*, September 19, 1969, 49.

3. Buddy Martin, "Time to Keep Good Boys Home," *Florida Today*, February 8, 1969, 1B.

4. Information gathered from "Pro Football Roundup," *Ebony*, November 1968, 185–95, and www.pro-football-reference.com.

5. Breard Snellings, "Shootin' the Breeze: Negro Teams Best," *San Bernardino County Sun*, September 19, 1969, 49.

6. 1967 Pro Football Draft: Lem Barney (Jackson State University), Ken Houston (Prairie View State University), Willie Lanier (Morgan State University), Rayfield Wright (Fort Valley State University).

1968 Pro Football Draft: Art Shell (University of Maryland–Eastern Shore [Maryland State]), Claude Humphrey (Tennessee State University), Elvin Bethea (North Carolina A&T University).

1969 Pro Football Draft: Charlie Joiner (Grambling State University).

African American Hall of Famers in these drafts not from HBCUs (6): 1967—Alan Page (Notre Dame), Gene Upshaw (Texas A&M–Kingsville University), Floyd Little (Syracuse University); 1968—Curley Culp (Arizona State University); 1969—Joe Greene (North Texas University), O. J. Simpson (University of Southern California).

7. Gene Upshaw followed Sid Blanks, who desegregated then Texas A&I in 1960. Joe Greene arrived at the University of North Texas a decade after Abner Haynes had desegregated the team. Jerry LeVias was the first African American in the Southwestern Conference. See Martin, *Benching Jim Crow*, 180–214; Marcello, "Integration of Intercollegiate Athletics in Texas"; and Fink, "Black College Football in Texas."

8. Henderson, *Sidelined*, 149–77.

9. Rabby, *The Pain and the Promise*, 247.

10. Jane Apre, "Schools Lose Suit in Integration Fight," *Palm Beach Post*, June 4, 1969, 1, 2.

11. United States Commission on Civil Rights, *Diminishing Barrier*, 4–5.

12. Shircliffe, *Best of That World*, 128.

13. Ibid., 45.

14. Associated Press, "Jake Gaither Loves Violence," *Asbury Park Press*, November 13, 1969, 26.

15. "Fla. Prep QB Prodigy Eagerly Sought by Ga. Tech, UCLA, 54 Other Biggies," *Pittsburgh Courier*, December 21, 1968, 15; "Georgia Tech Signs Gainesville Grid Star," *Palm Beach Post*, February 19, 1969, 16.

16. Dave Larimer, "Georgia Tech Gets State's Top Gridder," *Florida Today*, February 19, 1969, 1B.

17. "The Man: Jake Gaither," *Black Sports*, June 1971, 72.

18. "Gaither Is Caught Up in Trend of Times," *Panama City News-Herald*, September 7, 1969, 27.

19. Sam Lacy, "Catch an Attitude by the Tail," *Baltimore Afro-American*, April 28, 1973, 7.

20. Tom Powell, "Great Coaches Mastermind Tiger–Rattler Grid Tilt," *Tennessean*, October 25, 1969, 18.

21. Bill Buchalter, "Place in the Stars for Area Quartet," *Orlando Sentinel*, December 15, 1968, 2-D.

22. Jim Murray, "Lawrence More Than Holds His Own," *Los Angeles Times*, December 7, 1986, CC-1.

23. "At Edward Waters College 400 Students Protest Loss of Grid Program," *Norfolk Journal and Guide*, May 18, 1968, 12; "Casualty List of Tan College Grid Elevens Soars Up to 21: Costs Soar to $35,000 per Eleven," *Pittsburgh Courier*, July 5, 1968, 14.

24. Bill Nunn Jr., "Change of Pace," *Pittsburgh Courier*, March 15, 1969, 19.

25. Jack Harper, "Future Role for A&M at Issue," *Palm Beach Post*, March 17, 1968, A9.

26. "FAMU Phase-Out Idea Seen Losing Ground," *Palm Beach Post*, June 10, 1968, 20.

27. Don Boykin, "Gaither Talks About Quitting Football Post," *Palm Beach Post*, May 21, 1969, 21.

28. "All Jake Needs Is QB," *Florida Today*, September 12, 1969, 6E.

29. "'Hungry' FAMU off Crest 7 Years: Longest Stay off Top in Gaither Era," *Pittsburgh Courier*, September 6, 1969, 18.

30. "Gaither Losing Sleep over Next Foe," *Florida Today*, October 23, 1969, 3C.

31. Tom Powell, "Great Coaches Mastermind Tiger–Rattler Grid Tilt," *Tennessean*, October 25, 1969, 18.

32. Tom Powell, "Tigers' Destroyer Wrecks the Rattlers," *Tennessean*, October 27, 1969, 28.

33. Tom Powell, "TSU Rattles A&M," *Tennessean*, October 26, 1969, 33.

34. "Out-of-Character Gaither Sounds Off," *Palm Beach Post*, October 30, 1969, 29.

35. "Gaither Fears Jinx May Prevent 200th Win," *Florida Today*, November 13, 1969, 13C.

36. Aiello, *Bayou Classic*, 74; "Grambling Has Reached Lofty Heights," *Pittsburgh Courier*, November 22, 1969, 14.

37. "Gaither Fears Jinx May Prevent 200th Win," *Florida Today*, November 13, 1969, 13C; "Southern Football's Unique 1969 Team Produced Some of the School's Greatest Players," *New Orleans Times-Picayune*, August 4, 2014, http://www.nola.com/southern -university/index.ssf/2014/08/southern_universitys_unique_19.html (accessed June 16, 2016).

38. Jim Chitwood, "Gaither Gets No. 200," *Tallahassee Democrat*, November 16, 1969, D1.

39. Fred Girard, "FAMU–Tampa Isn't 'Just Another Game,'" *St. Petersburg Times*, November 28, 1969, 2C.

40. Fred Girard, "Jake Pits A&M Philosophy Spartan Class," *St. Petersburg Times*, November 27, 1969, 5C; Wilson, *Agile, Mobile, Hostile*, 149–50.

41. UPI, "A&M and Tampa Meet for State Title," *San Bernardino County Sun*, November 27, 1969, 62.

42. "Beat the Today Experts," *Florida Today*, November 26, 1969, 4C; Bill McGrotha, "From the Sidelines," *Tallahassee Democrat*, November 27, 1969, 45.

43. Edwin Pope, "Gaither the Talker Big on Listening, Too," *Tallahassee Democrat*, February 1, 1970, 38.

44. Bill Sargent, "Rattlers Hold Off Late Tampa Rally, 34–28," *Florida Today*, November 30, 1969, 4C; Fred Girard, "Curci Faces Spartan Task," *St. Petersburg Times*, November 27, 1969, 5C; "13 Seniors Gone," *St. Petersburg Times*, December 1, 1969, 4C.

45. Jim O'Brien, "Jake Gaither Elated," *Decatur Daily Review*, December 2, 1969, 11.

46. Bill Sargent, "Rattlers Find Happiness," *Florida Today*, December 1, 1969, 3C.

47. Don Boykin, "Tampa, Rattlers: No Problems in Initial Meeting," *Palm Beach Post*, December 1, 1969, 23.

48. Ibid.

49. Jim O'Brien, "Jake Gaither Elated," *Decatur Daily Review*, December 2, 1969, 11.

50. Bill Sargent, "Rattlers Find Happiness," *Florida Today*, December 1, 1969, 3C.

51. "New Era Opened by Tampa–FAMU Gross?," *Pittsburgh Courier*, December 27,

1969, 10; Neil Amdur, "College Football Meets an Issue," *New York Times*, December 14, 1969, S4.

52. Jim O'Brien, "Jake Gaither Elated," *Decatur Daily Review*, December 2, 1969, 11.

53. Bill Sargent, "Rattlers Find Happiness," *Florida Today*, December 1, 1969, 3C.

54. Florida A. & M. University Athletic Association, "Financial Report of the Tampa Classic," box 6, folder 14, Gaither Papers; "Subsidy of Athletics in Question," *St. Petersburg Times*, October 13, 1969, 1B.

55. "Gators Find Big Fortune from Football," *Florida Today*, November 18, 1969, 3C.

56. Sam Lacy, "College Football in Giant Stride," *Baltimore Afro-American*, August 30, 1969, 8.

57. Will Parrish, "Gaither Turns against CIAA," *Palm Beach Post*, December 2, 1969, 19.

58. Ibid.

59. Adam Hudsucker, "Dual Threat Pioneer Enjoyed Great Run," *Monroe News-Star*, July 15, 2014, C1, C4.

60. Lloyd Hogan, "Playin' the Game," *Chicago Defender*, October 1, 1969, 34.

61. On "Black style" in sports, see Rhoden, *Forty Million Dollar Slaves*, 147–70.

62. Glen Barnes, "Rattlers Edge Grambling," *FAMUAN*, December 11, 1969, 6, 8; Stanley B. Brown, "Rattlers Edge Grambling in Blossom Tilt," *Baltimore Afro-American*, December 13, 1969, 8.

63. Will Parrish, "Gaither Turns against the CIAA," *Palm Beach Post*, December 2, 1969, C1.

64. *Congressional Record*, December 11, 1969, 38484.

65. Marion Jackson, "Views Sports of the World," *Atlanta Daily World*, February 3, 1970, 5.

66. "Jake Gaither Ends an Era at Florida A&M," *Los Angeles Sentinel*, February 5, 1970, B2.

67. "TD Club Names Dell, Gaither Award Winners," *Washington Post*, December 31, 1969, D4; "'100' Club Will Honor McCovey," *Atlanta Constitution*, January 7, 1970, 4C.

68. "Jake Gaither Ends an Era at Florida A&M," *Los Angeles Sentinel*, February 5, 1970, B2.

69. Buddy Martin, "Jake: Man of Character," *Florida Today*, January 30, 1970, 1C.

70. "Gaither Wins NAIA Coach Honor," *Atlanta Constitution*, March 8, 1970, 5C.

71. "Jake Gaither in Congressional Records Now," *Atlanta Daily World*, February 22, 1970, 6.

72. "Lawmakers Cheer for Jake Gaither," *Florida Today*, April 24, 1970, 6B.

73. "Gaither Honored Today," *Palm Beach Post*, March 31, 1970, B4; "Gaither Day Proclaimed," *Palm Beach Post*, June 26, 1971, C4.

74. Buddy Martin, "Jake: Man of Character," *Florida Today*, January 30, 1970, 1C.

75. Marion Jackson, "Views Sports of the World," *Atlanta Daily World*, February 22, 1970, 6.

76. "Graduates Hear Gaither," *Palm Beach Post*, June 1, 1970, D3.

77. Ric Roberts, "Jake Joins Hurt, Nicks, Mumford, Kean, Abbott," *Pittsburgh Courier*, February 14, 1970, 12.

78. Emery, Emery, and Roberts, *The Press and America*, 425–28.

EPILOGUE

1. Barry Cooper, "In Death, Gaither Gathers His Team One More Time," *Orlando Sentinel*, February 27, 1994, A1, A14.

2. David Lee Simmons, "Memories of Gaither Soothe Ache of His Loss," *Tallahassee Democrat*, February 27, 1994, 1A, 12A.

3. "Fay Young's All-Americans," *Chicago Defender*, December 30, 1939, 20.

4. Drape Davis, "Florida in Spring Grid Activities," *Atlanta Daily World*, February 13, 1939, 5.

5. Griffin, "Historical Development of Athletics at Florida Agricultural and Mechanical College."

6. "Fla. Mentor Promises No Miracles: Tough Act to Follow for Griffin as Rattler Coach," *Norfolk Journal and Guide*, April 18, 1970, 12.

7. "Robert P. Griffin Named Head Football Coach at Fla. A&M," *Atlanta Daily World*, February 3, 1970, 5.

8. "FAMU White Quits," *Palm Beach Post*, October 31, 1970, B5.

9. Lamar Thames, "Rattlers Rally for 20–9 Win," *Florida Today*, November 22, 1970, 3C.

10. John A. Diaz, "Color Barrier to Be Broken in Football Tilt," *Pittsburgh Courier*, December 5, 1970, 14.

11. Will Parrish, "Rattlers Fall, 21–7," *Palm Beach Post*, December 13, 1970, E3.

12. "Gaither a Tough Act to Follow," *Palm Beach Post*, December 14, 1970, C3.

13. "Losing to Whites Angers A&M," *Florida Today*, December 28, 1970, 2C.

14. Ibid.

15. "Griffin's Only Critic Was Himself," *Florida Today*, February 26, 1971, 3C.

16. "Florida A&M's Montgomery Dies of Stomach Ailment," *Palm Beach Post*, January 8, 1972, C1.

17. A. S. "Doc" Young, "Good Morning Sports," *Chicago Defender*, December 18, 1972, 26.

18. Marion Jackson, "World Sports," *Atlanta Daily World*, February 25, 1973, 7.

19. Bill Nunn Jr., "Change of Pace," *Pittsburgh Courier*, April 13, 1974, 9.

20. "Can Ohio State's Hubbard Fill Gaiter's [sic] Shoes?," *Cleveland Call and Post*, August 24, 1974, 24.

21. "Hubbard to Fashion A&M Squad after Hayes," *Chicago Defender*, June 15, 1974, 22.

22. "Ohio State Assistant Named Florida A&M Coach," *Palm Beach Post*, June 5, 1974, D1.

23. Paul, McGhee, and Fant, "Arrival and Ascendence of Black Athletes in the Southeastern Conference," 290.

24. Bob Bassine, "Hubbard Facing Facts Recruiting Athletes," *Palm Beach Post*, August 22, 1975, D1–D2.

25. "Rattlers' Hubbard Seeks Big School Competition," *Naples Daily News*, October 7, 1976.

26. John Bibb, "A&M Wins in Unbeatens' Duel," *Tennessean*, October 23, 1977, D1, D7.

27. "At Florida A&M Hubbard Proud, Thinking Big," *Jackson Clarion-Ledger*, January 15, 1978, D12.

28. Paul Attner, "Big Schools Try Again to Form Super Division," *Washington Post*, January 9, 1977, D4.

29. Oriard, *Bowled Over*, 145–58.

30. Jerry Bryd, "Grambling University Tigers Join Division One of Power NCAA," *Atlanta Daily World*, February 15, 1977, 8.

31. "Grambling, State in NCAA," *Memphis Tri-State Defender*, January 22, 1977, 14.

32. Collie J. Nicholson, "Grambling–Southern Game Top Bowls in Attendance," *Pittsburgh Courier*, January 22, 1977, 22.

33. Watterson, *College Football*, 332–42; David Davison, "Reorganization the Big Issue Again," *Atlanta Constitution*, January 8, 1978, 3D.

34. Bob Oates, "And Now Football Has a Super Conference—Sort Of," *Los Angeles Times*, February 4, 1978, D1.

35. Horace W. Gosier, "Florida A&M to Put in Bid to Attain Division 1 Status," *Atlanta Daily World*, January 17, 1978, 2.

36. "Rattlers to Appeal NCAA Division Status," *Palm Beach Post*, August 5, 1978, B5; "NCAA Elevates Rattlers to Division I-AA Status," *Palm Beach Post*, August 31, 1978, D8; "News Was Good for A&M," *Florida Today*, September 1, 1978, 4C.

37. Barry Cooper, "FAMU Captures a National Title," *Tallahassee Democrat*, December 17, 1978, 1A, 7A.

38. Bob Cohn, "Minutemen Come Battle-Toughened," *Tallahassee Democrat*, December 13, 1978, 1B, 2B.

39. Bob Cohn, "Stunned Silence Filled UMass Dressing Room," *Tallahassee Democrat*, December 17, 1978, 4D.

40. Barry Cooper, "Gaither Watched with Pride," *Tallahassee Democrat*, January 4, 1979, 2.

41. David Whitley, "The Puzzle of FAMU's Woes," *Tallahassee Democrat*, November 25, 1984.

42. Barry Cooper, "Growing Pains Put Tookes in Squeeze," *Tallahassee Democrat*, April 22, 1979, 1D, 8D.

43. Barry Cooper, "TV Blackout for Black Colleges," *New York Amsterdam News*, September 1, 1979, 76.

44. "ESPN Blacks Out Black Colleges," *Pittsburgh Courier*, November 7, 1981, 9.

45. Pamela R. Porter, "TV Revenue Pays Off," *FAMUAN*, October 13, 1983, 6.

46. John Eisenberg, "High-Cost Programs, Low-End Budgets," *Baltimore Sun*, November 3, 1985, 13G, 14G.

47. Ibid.

48. Barry Cooper, "Orange Blossom Classic Squeezed out of Miami," *Tallahassee Democrat*, July 12, 1980, 4B.

49. Andy Cohen, "Orange Blossom's Wilting Image Puts Future 'Classics' in Doubt," *Ft. Lauderdale News*, November 6, 1982, 6C.

50. Barry Cooper, "FAMU Snoozes to 23–13 Defeat," *Tallahassee Democrat*, October 31, 1982, 1F.

51. Chico Renfroe, "This and That in Sports," *Atlanta Daily World*, November 4, 1982, 6.

52. Oliver and Shapiro, *Black Wealth/White Wealth*.

53. David Whitley, "The Puzzle of FAMU's Woes," *Tallahassee Democrat*, November 25, 1F, 2F.

54. Allen Johnson, "What Ails Black College Athletics," *Norfolk Journal and Guide*, January 30, 1985, A3.

55. John Eisenberg, "High-Cost Programs, Low-End Budgets," *Baltimore Sun*, 13G, 14G.

56. Ibid.

57. David Whitley, "The Puzzle of FAMU's Woes," *Tallahassee Democrat*, November 25, 1984, 1F, 2F.

58. "Hubbard Hints Changes May Include Him," *Pensacola News Journal*, August 23, 1985, 1D.

59. David Whitley, "The Puzzle of FAMU's Woes," *Tallahassee Democrat*, November 25, 1984, 1F, 2F.

60. David Whitley, "Rudy Hubbard Ends His Struggles at FAMU," *Tallahassee Democrat*, November 28, 1985, 1E.

BIBLIOGRAPHY

ARCHIVES AND SPECIAL COLLECTIONS

Florida
    Florida A&M University, Black Archives, Tallahassee
        Jake Gaither Papers
    Florida Atlantic University, Special Collections, Boca Raton
        Howard Schnellenberger, "An Oral History." Interview by Eric P. Salzman, 2013,
            session 2.
    Florida State Archives, Tallahassee
        Leroy Collins Papers
        Florida Board of Regents, Minutes, 1905–1997
        Junior League of Tallahassee, Oral Histories, 1976–1977
        Fuller Warren Papers
    Miami-Dade Public Library, Miami
        Florida Room, Miami City Commission Minutes
    University of Florida Archives, Gainesville
        Presidential Collection, Stephen O'Connell
    University of South Florida, Tampa
        Florida Studies Center Oral Histories, Digital Collection
Georgia
    Auburn Avenue Research Library on African American Culture
           and History, Atlanta
        100% Wrong Club Papers
New York
    Columbia University, New York
        Black Journalist Project

NEWSPAPERS AND PERIODICALS

Akron Beacon Journal

Atlanta Constitution

Atlanta Daily World

Baltimore Afro-American

Baltimore Sun

Black Sports

Charlotte Observer

Chicago Defender

Christian Science Monitor

Cleveland Call and Post

Cleveland Plain Dealer

The Crisis

Daily Princetonian

Daytona Beach Morning Journal

Decatur Daily Review

Ebony

FAMUAN

Florence Times

Florida Today

Fort Lauderdale News

Fort Myers News-Press

Gettysburg Times

Harper's Weekly

Howard University Journal

Indianapolis Star

Jackson Clarion-Ledger

Jet

Kingsport News

Los Angeles Sentinel

Los Angeles Times

Marshall News Messenger

Miami Herald

Miami Hurricane

Miami Times

Monroe News-Star

Naples Daily News

New Orleans Times-Picayune

New Philadelphia Daily Times

New York Age

New York Amsterdam News

New York Times

Norfolk Journal and Guide

Orlando Sentinel

Outing: An Illustrated Monthly
 Magazine of Recreation

Owosso Argus-Press

Palm Beach Post

Panama City News-Herald

Penn State Daily Collegian

Pensacola News

Philadelphia Tribune

Pittsburgh Courier

Pittsburgh Post-Gazette

Raleigh Morning Post

San Bernardino County Sun

Sarasota Herald-Tribune

Saturday Evening Post

Saturday Review

Shreveport Times

Spartanburg Herald-Journal

Sports Illustrated

St. Petersburg Evening Independent

St. Petersburg Times

Tallahassee Democrat

Tennessean

Time

Toledo Blade

University of Florida Alligator

Washington Post

Washington Spokesman-Review

BOOKS, ARTICLES, ESSAYS, DISSERTATIONS, AND THESES

"51st Convention–N.M.A." *Journal of the National Medical Association* 38, no. 4 (July 1946): 143.

Adams, Alfred Hugh. "A History of Public Higher Education in Florida, 1821–1961." Ph.D. diss., Florida State University, 1962.

Adelson, Bruce. *Brushing Back Jim Crow: The Integration of Minor League Baseball in the American South*. Charlottesville: University of Virginia Press, 2007.

Aiello, Thomas. *Bayou Classic: The Grambling-Southern Football Rivalry*. Baton Rouge: LSU Press, 2010.

———. "The Black Heart of Dixie: The Turkey Day Classic and Race in Twentieth-Century Alabama." In *Separate Games: African American Sport behind the Walls of Segregation*, edited by David K. Wiggins and Ryan Swanson, 93–108. Fayetteville: University of Arkansas Press, 2016.

Albright, Evan J. "Blazing the Trail." *Amherst Magazine*, Winter 2007, https://www
    .amherst.edu/amherst-story/magazine/issues/2007_winter/blazing.
———. "Three Lives of an African American Pioneer: William Henry Lewis (1868–
    1949)." *Massachusetts Historical Society* 13 (2011): 127–63.
———. "William Henry Lewis: Brief Life of a Football Pioneer." *Harvard Magazine*,
    November–December 2005, https://harvardmagazine.com/2005/11/william
    -henry-lewis-html.
Alexander, Leslie M. *African or American? Black Identity and Political Activism in New
    York City, 1784–1861*. Urbana: University of Illinois Press, 2008.
"Alonzo 'Jake' Gaither: Florida A&M Coaching Boss Is the Winningest in Negro
    College Football." *Ebony*, November 1960.
Anderson, James D. *The Education of Blacks in the South, 1860–1935*. Chapel Hill:
    University of North Carolina Press, 1988.
Arsenault, Raymond. *Freedom Riders: 1961 and the Struggle for Racial Justice*. New York:
    Oxford University Press, 2006.
Atwood, R. B. "The Public Negro College in a Racially Integrated System of Higher
    Education." *Journal of Negro Education* 21, no. 3 (1952): 352–63, https://doi.org
    /10.2307/2293376.
Baker, R. Scott. "The Paradoxes of Desegregation: Race, Class, and Education, 1935–
    1975." *American Journal of Education* 109, no. 3 (2001): 320–43.
Bartley, Lua S. *A Brief History of the Division of Health, Physical Education, and
    Recreation at Florida Agricultural and Mechanical University from 1918 through 1978*.
    Tallahassee: Florida A&M Press, 1978.
Bates, Beth Thompkins. *Pullman Porters and the Rise of Protest Politics in Black America,
    1925–1945*. Chapel Hill: University of North Carolina Press, 2001.
Bee, Clair. "I Know Why They Sold Out to the Gamblers." *Saturday Evening Post*,
    February 2, 1952.
Bell, Derrick A. "Serving Two Masters: Integration Ideals and Client Interests in
    School Desegregation Litigation." *Yale Law Journal* 85, no. 4 (1976): 470–516,
    https://doi.org/10.2307/795339.
Bennett, Lerone, Jr. "What's in a Name? Negro vs. Afro-American vs. Black." *Ebony*,
    November 1967.
Biondi, Martha. *The Black Revolution on Campus*. Berkeley: University of California
    Press, 2014.
Blight, David. *Race and Reunion: The Civil War in American Memory*. Cambridge:
    Harvard University Press, 2001.
Blose, David T., and Ambrose Caliver. *Statistics of the Education of Negroes, 1929–30
    and 1931–32*. Washington, D.C.: U.S. Office of Education, 1936.
Bond, Horace Mann. "The Origin and Development of the Negro Church." *Journal of
    Negro Education* 29, no. 3 (n.d.): 217–26.
Booker, Robert J. *And There Was Light: The 120-Year History of Knoxville College, 1875–
    1995*. Virginia Beach: Donning Company, 1994.

Bragg, Jubie B. "The Story of a Blacksmith." In *Tuskegee and Its People: Their Ideals and Achievements*, edited by Booker T. Washington. New York: D. Appleton, 1905.

Branch, Taylor. *Parting the Waters: America in the King Years, 1954–63*. New York: Simon and Schuster, 1988.

Brandt, Nat. *When Oberlin Was King of the Gridiron: The Heisman Years*. Kent, Ohio: Kent State University Pres, 2001.

Braukman, Stacy. *Communists and Perverts under the Palms: The Johns Committee in Florida, 1956–1965*. Gainesville: University Press of Florida, 2013.

Brawley, Benjamin. *History of Morehouse College*. Atlanta: Morehouse College Press, 1917.

Bunie, Andrew. *Robert L. Vann of the* Pittsburgh Courier: *Politics and Black Journalism*. Pittsburgh: University of Pittsburgh Press, 1974.

Camp, Walter. *American Football*. New York: Harper and Brothers, 1891.

Campbell, Doak S. *A University in Transition*. Tallahassee: Florida State University Press, 1964.

Carmichael, Stokely, and Charles V. Hamilton. *Black Power: The Politics of Liberation in America*. New York: Vintage, 1967.

Chafe, William H. *The Rise and Fall of the American Century: The United States from 1890–2009*. New York: Oxford University Press, 2009.

Chafe, William H., and William Henry Chafe. *Civilities and Civil Rights: Greensboro, North Carolina, and the Black Struggle for Freedom*. New York: Oxford University Press, 1981.

Chalk, Ocania. *Black College Sport*. New York: Dodd, Mead, 1976.

Christy, Ralph D., Lionel Williamson, and Handy Williamson Jr. "Introduction: A Century of Service: The Past, Present, and Future Roles of 1890 Land-Grant Colleges and Institutions." In *A Century of Service: Land-Grant Colleges and Universities, 1890–1990*, edited by Ralph D. Christy and Lionel Williamson, xvii–xxi. New Brunswick, N.J.: Transaction, 1992.

Coenen, Craig R. *From Sandlots to the Super Bowl: The National Football League, 1920–1967*. Knoxville: University of Tennessee Press, 2005.

Committee on Regulated Industries. *Legalized Gambling in Florida: The Competition in the Marketplace*. Tallahassee: Florida State Senate, 2004.

Connolly, N. D. B. *A World More Concrete: Real Estate and the Remaking of Jim Crow South Florida*. Chicago: University of Chicago Press, 2014.

Cooper, Algia R. "*Brown v. Board of Education* and Virgil Darnell Hawkins: Twenty-Eight Years and Six Petitions to Justice." *Journal of Negro History* 64, no. 1 (1979): 1–20, https://doi.org/10.2307/2717122.

Crittenden, John. *Hialeah Park: A Racing Legend*. Miami: Pickering Press, 1989.

Curry, George E. *Jake Gaither: America's Most Famous Coach*. New York: Dodd, Mead, 1977.

Dandy, Walter. "The Radiography in the Diagnosis of Brain Conditions—

Ventriculography." *Medical Record: A Weekly Journal of Medicine and Surgery* 101, no. 10 (March 11, 1922): 434.

Davis, Jack E. "Baseball's Reluctant Challenge: Desegregating Major League Spring Training Sites, 1961–1964." *Journal of Sport History* 19, no. 2 (1992): 144–62.

Davis, Lenwood G. "A History of Livingstone College, 1879–1957." Ph.D. diss., Carnegie-Mellon University, 1979.

Davis, Leroy. *Clashing of the Soul: John Hope and the Dilemma of African American Leadership and Black Higher Education in the Early Twentieth Century.* Athens: University of Georgia Press, 1998.

Davis, Park H. *Football: The American Intercollegiate Game.* New York: Charles Scribner's Sons, 1912.

Davis, Willie, Jim Martyka, and Andrea Erickson Davis. *Closing the Gap: Lombardi, the Packers Dynasty, and the Pursuit of Excellence.* Chicago: Triumph Books, 2012.

Demas, Lane. *Integrating the Gridiron: Black Civil Rights and American College Football.* New Brunswick, N.J.: Rutgers University Press, 2010.

D'Emilio, John. *Lost Prophet: The Life and Times of Bayard Rustin.* New York: Simon and Schuster, 2010.

Des Jardins, Julie. *Walter Camp: Football and the Modern Man.* New York: Oxford University Press, 2015.

Diaz, Jamie. "He's the Catch of the Year: Mississippi Valley State's Jerry Rice Is a Record-Breaking Wide Receiver." *Sports Illustrated,* November 14, 1983.

Dickerson, Dennis C. *Militant Mediator: Whitney M. Young Jr.* Lexington: University of Kentucky Press, 1998.

Dietzel, Paul F. *Call Me Coach: A Life in College Football.* Baton Rouge: LSU Press, 2008.

Douglass, Frederick. *The Narrative of Frederick Douglass, an American Slave.* New York: Signet, 1845.

Doyle, Andrew. "'Causes Won, Not Lost': College Football and the Modernization of the American South." *International Journal of the History of Sport* 11, no. 2 (1994): 231–51.

Drewry, Henry N., and Humphrey Doermann. *Stand and Prosper: Private Black Colleges and Their Students.* Princeton: Princeton University Press, 2001.

Du Bois, W. E. B. *The College Bred Negro.* Atlanta: Atlanta University Press, 1900.

———. *The Souls of Black Folk.* Boston: Bedford St. Martin's, 1903.

Du Bois, W. E. B., and Granville Dill, eds. *The College Bred Negro.* Vol. 2. Atlanta: Atlanta University Press, 1910.

Dudziak, Mary L. *Cold War Civil Rights: Race and The Image of American Democracy.* Princeton: Princeton University Press, 2000.

Due, Tananarive, and Patricia Stephens Due. *Freedom in the Family: A Mother-Daughter Memoir of the Fight for Civil Rights.* New York: Ballantine, 2003.

Dunn, Marvin. *Black Miami in the Twentieth Century.* Gainesville: University Press of Florida, 1997.

Dunnavant, Keith. *The Missing Ring: How Bear Bryant and the 1966 Alabama Crimson Tide Were Denied College Football's Most Elusive Prize*. New York: Thomas Dunne Books, 2006.

Dyckman, Martin A. *Floridian of His Century: The Courage of Governor LeRoy Collins*. Gainesville: University Press of Florida, 2006.

Eason, Arcenouis John. "The Philosophy, Impact, and Contributions of Alonzo Smith 'Jake' Gaither to Black Athletes, Football, and Florida Agricultural and Mechanical University." Ph.D. diss., Florida State University, 1987.

Eastman, Joseph B. "The Office of Defense Transportation." *Annals of the American Academy of Political and Social Science* 230 (November 1943): 1–4.

Edwards, Harry. *The Revolt of the Black Athlete*. Urbana: University of Illinois Press, 2017.

Ellison, Ralph. "An American Dilemma: A Review." In *Shadow and Act*, 303–17. New York: Vintage, 1995.

Ellsworth, Scott. *The Secret Game: A Wartime Story of Courage, Change, and Basketball's Lost Triumph*. New York: Little, Brown, 2015.

Emery, Michael, Edwin Emery, and Nancy L. Roberts. *The Press and America: An Interpretative History of the Mass Media*. 9th ed. Boston: Alyn and Bacon, 2000.

Emmons, Caroline. "'Somebody Has Got to Do That Work': Harry T. Moore and the Struggle for African-American Voting Rights in Florida." *Journal of Negro History* 82, no. 2 (1997): 232–43, https://doi.org/10.2307/2717518.

Eskew, Glenn T. *But for Birmingham: The Local and National Movements in the Civil Rights Struggle*. Chapel Hill: University of North Carolina Press, 1997.

Fairclough, Adam. *A Class of Their Own: Black Teachers in the Segregated South*. Cambridge: Harvard University Press, 2007.

———. *Teaching Equality: Black Schools in the Age of Jim Crow*. Athens: University of Georgia Press, 2001.

Faurot, Don. *Football: Secrets of the "Split T" Formation*. New York: Prentice-Hall, 1950.

Favors, Jelani. *Shelter in the Time of Storm*. Chapel Hill: University of North Carolina Press, 2019.

Fendrich, James Max. *Ideal Citizens: The Legacy of the Civil Rights Movement*. Albany: SUNY Press, 1993.

Fields, Sarah K. "Title IX and African American Female Athletes." In *Sports and the Racial Divide: African American and Latin Experience in an Era of Change*, edited by Michael E. Lomax, 126–43. Jackson: University Press of Mississippi, 2008.

Fink, Robert Christopher. "Black College Football in Texas." Ph.D. diss., Texas Tech University, 2003.

Flemming, Cynthia Griggs. "The Effect of Higher Education on Black Tennesseans after the Civil War." *Phylon* 44, no. 3 (1983): 209–16.

Flexner, Abraham. *Medical Education in the United States and Canada*. New York: Carnegie Foundation, 1910.

Foner, Eric. *A Short History of Reconstruction*. New York: Harper & Row, 1990.

Ford, Tanisha C. "SNCC Women, Denim, and the Politics of Dress." *Journal of Southern History* 79, no. 3 (2013): 625–58.

Franklin, John Hope. *The Free Negro in North Carolina, 1790–1860*. Chapel Hill: University of North Carolina Press, 1971.

Freedman, Samuel G. *Breaking the Line: The Season in Black College Football That Transformed the Sport and Changed the Course of Civil Rights*. New York: Simon and Schuster, 2013.

Gaines, Kevin. *Uplifting the Race: Black Leadership, Politics, and Culture in the Twentieth Century*. Chapel Hill: University of North Carolina Press, 1996.

Gaither, Alonzo S. *The Split-Line T Offense*. New York: Prentice-Hall, 1963.

———. "A System for Recording the Health Conditions of Athletes in College." M.A. thesis, Ohio State University, 1937.

Gasman, Marybeth. *Envisioning Black Colleges: A History of the United Negro College Fund*. Baltimore: Johns Hopkins University Press, 2007.

Gavins, Raymond. *The Perils and Prospects of Southern Black Leadership: Gordon Blaine Hancock, 1884–1970*. Durham: Duke University Press, 1993.

George, Paul S. "Colored Town: Miami's Black Community, 1896–1930." *Florida Historical Quarterly* 56, no. 4 (1978): 432–47.

Gibson, William L. "The Old Football Rulers Pass." *Crisis*, December 1934, 363.

Gilmore, Glenda Elizabeth. *Defying Dixie: The Radical Roots of Civil Rights, 1919–1950*. New York: Norton, 2008.

Gorr, Beth. *Bear Memories: The Chicago–Green Bay Rivalry*. Charleston: Arcadia, 2005.

Green, Ben. *Before His Time: The Untold Story of Harry T. Moore, America's First Civil Rights Martyr*. New York: Free Press, 1999, https://books.google.com/books?id=wNOOVHxzDUoC&printsec=frontcover&dq=harry+t.+moore&hl=en&sa=X&ved=0ahUKEwig7PDVlI_YAhWK30MKHXsBDX4Q6AEIKTAA#v=onepage&q=harry%20t.%20moore&f=false.

Greene, Linda S. "The New NCAA Rules of the Game: Academic Integrity or Racism?" *Saint Louis University Law Journal* 28 (1984): 101–51.

Griffin, Robert Pete. "The Historical Development of Athletics at Florida Agricultural and Mechanical College." Master's thesis, Ohio State University, 1946.

Grundy, Pamela. *Learning to Win: Sports, Education, and Social Change in Twentieth-Century North Carolina*. Chapel Hill: University of North Carolina Press, 2001.

Gruver, Ed. *The American Football League: A Year-by-Year History, 1960–1969*. Jefferson, N.C.: McFarland, 1997.

A Guide to Teaching Physical Education in Secondary Schools: Bulletin No. 3. Tallahassee: State Board of Control, 1948.

Hare, Julianne. *Tallahassee: A Capital City History*. Charleston: Arcadia, 2002.

Harlan, Louis R., and Raymond W. Smock, eds. *The Booker T. Washington Papers, 1899–1900*. Vol. 5. Urbana: University of Illinois Press, 1976.

Harper, Shaun R., Collin D. Williams Jr., and Horatio W. Blackman. *Black Male Student-Athletes and Racial Inequities in NCAA Division I College Sports*.

Philadelphia: University of Pennsylvania, Center for the Study of Race and Equity in Education, 2013.

Hawkins, Billy, Joseph Cooper, Akilah Carter-Francique, and J. Kenyatta Cavil, eds. *The Athletic Experience at Historically Black Colleges and Universities: Past, Present, and Persistence*. Lanham, Md.: Rowman and Littlefield, 2015.

Hawkins, James E. *History of the Southern Intercollegiate Athletic Conference, 1913–1990*. Butler, Ga.: Benns Printing, 1994.

Hayes, Bob, and Robert Pack. *Run, Bullet, Run: The Rise, Fall, and Recovery of Bob Hayes*. New York: Harper & Row, 1990.

Henderson, Edwin Bancroft. "The Colored College Athlete." *Crisis*, July 1911.

———. *The Negro in Sports*. Washington, D.C.: ASALH Publishers, 1939.

Henderson, Simon. *Sidelined: How American Sports Challenged the Black Freedom Struggle*. Lexington: University Press of Kentucky, 2013.

Herbold, Hilary. "Never a Level Playing Field: Blacks and the GI Bill." *Journal of Blacks in Higher Education*, no. 6 (1994): 104–8, https://doi.org/10.2307/2962479.

Hobbs, Tamara Bradley. *Democracy Abroad, Lynching at Home: Racial Violence in Florida*. Gainesville: University Press of Florida, 2015.

Hochberg, Philip, and Ira Horowitz. "Broadcasting and CATV: The Beauty and the Bane of Major College Football." *Law and Contemporary Problems* 38, no. 1 (1973): 112–28.

Holland, Nathan B. *Nathan B. Young and the Struggle over Black Higher Education*. Columbia: University of Missouri Press, 2006.

Hornsby-Gutting, Angela. *Black Manhood and Community Building in North Carolina, 1900–1930*. Gainesville: University Press of Florida, 2009.

Hurd, Michael. *Black College Football, 1892–1992: One Hundred Years of History, Education, and Pride*. Virginia Beach: Donning Co., 1998.

Jackson, David H., Jr. "'Industrious, Thrifty and Ambitious': Jacksonville's African American Businesspeople during the Jim Crow Era." *Florida Historical Quarterly* 90, no. 4 (Spring 2012): 453–87.

Jacobson, Timothy C. *Making Medical Doctors: Science and Medicine at Vanderbilt since Flexner*. Tuscaloosa: University of Alabama Press, 1987.

Jeffries, Hasan Kwame. *Bloody Lowndes: Civil Rights and Black Power in Alabama's Black Belt*. New York: New York University Press, 2009.

Jenkins, Dan. "The First 100 Years." *Sports Illustrated*, September 15, 1969.

Johnson, James W. *The Wow Boys: A Coach, a Team, and a Turning Point in College Football*. Lincoln: University of Nebraska Press, 2006.

Johnson, Marilynn S. "Gender, Race, and Rumours: Re-Examining the 1943 Race Riots." *Gender & History* 10, no. 2 (July 1, 1998): 252–77, https://doi.org/10.1111/1468-0424.00099.

Johnston, V. D., and Edwin Bancroft Henderson. "Debating and Athletics in Colored Colleges." *Crisis*, July 1917.

Jones, Maxine D., and Joe M. Richardson. *Talladega College: The First Century*. Tuscaloosa: University of Alabama Press, 1990.

Jones, Thomas Jesse. *Negro Education: A Study of the Private and Higher Schools for Colored People in the United States*. Vol. 2. Washington, D.C.: Department of Interior, Bureau of Education, 1916.

Kaplan, Amy. *The Anarchy of Empire in the Making of U.S. Culture*. Cambridge: Harvard University Press, 2002.

Kaplan, Carla, ed. *Zora Neale Hurston: A Life in Letters*. New York: Knopf Doubleday, 2007.

Katz, Milton S. *Breaking Through: John B. McLendon, Basketball Legend and Civil Rights Pioneer*. Fayetteville: University of Arkansas Press, 2010.

Katzowitz, Josh. *Sid Gillman: Father of the Passing Game*. Covington, Ky.: Clerisy Press, 2012.

Kelley, Robin D. G., and Earl Lewis, eds. *To Make Our World Anew: A History of African Americans*. Vol. 2. New York: Oxford University Press, 2005.

Kemper, Kurt Edward. *College Football and American Culture in the Cold War Era*. Urbana: University of Illinois Press, 2009.

Kilgore, E. J., and A. D. Elster. "Walter Dandy and the History of Ventriculography." *Radiology* 194, no. 3 (March 1995): 657–60, https://doi.org/10.1148/radiology.194.3.7862959.

Killian, Lewis M., and Charles U. Smith. "Negro Protest Leaders in a Southern Community." *Social Forces* 38, no. 3 (1960): 253–57, https://doi.org/10.2307/2574089.

King, Gilbert. *Devil in the Grove: Thurgood Marshall, the Groveland Boys, and the Dawn of a New America*. New York: Harper Collins, 2012.

King, Dr. Martin Luther, Jr. *Stride toward Freedom: The Montgomery Story*. Boston: Beacon Press, 2010.

Klarman, Michael J. *From Jim Crow to Civil Rights: The Supreme Court and the Struggle for Racial Equality*. New York: Oxford University Press, 2006.

Kleinberg, Eliot. *Black Cloud: The Deadly Hurricane of 1928*. New York: Carroll and Graf, 2004.

Kluger, Richard. *Simple Justice: The History of* Brown v. Board of Education *and Black America's Struggle for Equality*. New York: Knopf Doubleday, 1975.

Kuska, Bob. *Hot Potato: How Washington and New York Gave Birth to Black Basketball and Changed America's Game Forever*. Charlottesville: University of Virginia Press, 2004.

Lanctot, Neil. *Negro League Baseball: The Rise and Ruin of a Black Institution*. Philadelphia: University of Pennsylvania Press, 2004.

Lansbury, Jennifer H. *A Spectacular Leap: Black Women Athletes in Twentieth-Century America*. Fayetteville: University of Arkansas Press, 2014.

Lawson, Steven F., David R. Colburn, and Darryl Paulson. "Groveland: Florida's Little Scottsboro." *Florida Historical Quarterly* 65, no. 1 (1986): 1–26.

Lester, Robin. *Stagg's University: The Rise, Decline, and Fall of Big-Time Football at Chicago*. Urbana: University of Illinois Press, 1995.

Lewis, Earl. *In Their Own Interests: Race, Class, and Power in Twentieth-Century Norfolk, Virginia*. Berkeley: University of California Press, 1991.

Lewis, Michael. *The Blind Side: Evolution of a Game*. New York: Norton, 2007.

Lidz, Franz. "The Day the Godfather Did in the Gunslinger." *Sports Illustrated*, November 12, 1984.

Lindholm, Karl. "Vita: William Clarence Matthews." *Harvard Magazine*, September 1998, https://harvardmagazine.com/1998/09/vita.html.

Lindsay, Leon W. "Blacks in the SEC." *Christian Science Monitor*, September 1, 1970.

Little, Monroe H. "The Extra-Curricular Activities of Black College Students, 1868–1940." *Journal of African American History* 87 (Winter 2002): 43–55.

Litwack, Leon F. *Trouble in Mind: Black Southerners in the Age of Jim Crow*. New York: Knopf, 1998.

Logan, Rayford. *Betrayal of the Negro: From Rutherford B. Hayes to Woodrow Wilson*. New York: Da Capo Press, 1965.

Longa, Ernesto. "Lawson Edward Thompson and Miami's Negro Municipal Court." *St. Thomas Law Review* 18 (2005): 125–38.

Looney, Douglas S. "The Rattlers Are Rolling." *Sports Illustrated*, October 9, 1978.

Lovett, Bobby L. *The Civil Rights Movement in Tennessee: A Narrative History*. Knoxville: University of Tennessee Press, 2005.

———. *A Touch of Greatness: A History of Tennessee State University*. Macon, Ga.: Mercer University Press, 2012.

MacCambridge, Michael. *America's Game: The Epic Story of How Pro Football Captured a Nation*. New York: Random House, 2004.

———. *Lamar Hunt: A Life in Sports*. Kansas City: Andrews McMeel, 2012.

———, ed. *ESPN College Football Encyclopedia: The Complete History of the Game*. New York: ESPN Books, 2005.

"The Man: Jake Gaither." *Black Sports*, June 1971.

Marcello, Ronald E. "The Integration of Intercollegiate Athletics in Texas: North Texas State College as a Test Case, 1956." *Journal of Sport History* 14, no. 3 (1987): 286–316.

Martin, Charles H. *Benching Jim Crow: The Rise and Fall of the Color Line in Southern College Sports, 1890—1980*. Urbana: University of Illinois Press, 2010.

———. "The Color Line in Midwestern College Sports, 1890–1960." *Indiana Magazine of History* 98, no. 2 (June 2002): 85–112.

———. "Integrating New Year's Day: The Racial Politics of College Bowl Games in the American South." *Journal of Sport History* 24, no. 3 (1997): 358–77.

Matthews, William Clarence. "Negro Foot-Ball Players on New England Teams." In *Unlevel Playing Field: A Documentary History of the African American Experience in Sport*, edited by David K. Wiggins and Patrick B. Miller, 46–50. Urbana: University of Illinois Press, 2003.

McGuire, Danielle L. *At the Dark End of the Street: Black Women, Rape, and Resistance — a New History of the Civil Rights Movement from Rosa Parks to the Rise of Black Power*. New York: Vintage, 2011.

McIver, Stuart. *Dreamers, Schemers, and Scalawags: Florida Chronicles*. Sarasota: Pineapple Press, 1994.

McQuilkin, Scott A., and Ronald A. Smith. "The Rise and Fall of the Flying Wedge: Football's Most Controversial Play." *Journal of Sport History* 20, no. 1 (1993): 57–64.

Meier, August, and Elliott M. Rudwick. *CORE, a Study in the Civil Rights Movement, 1942–1968*. New York: Oxford University Press, 1973.

Michaeli, Ethan. *The Defender: How the Legendary Black Newspaper Changed America*. Boston: Houghton Mifflin Harcourt, 2016.

Miller, Kent. "Psychological Characteristics of the Negro." In *The Negro in American Society*, edited by the Research Council of the Florida State University. Tallahassee: Florida State University Press, 1958.

Miller, Patrick B. "The Manly, the Moral, and the Proficient: College Sport in the New South." *Journal of Sport History* 24, no. 3 (1997): 285–316.

———. "To 'Bring the Race Along Rapidly': Sport, Student Culture, and Educational Mission at Historically Black Colleges during the Interwar Years." *History of Education Quarterly* 35, no. 2 (1995): 111–35.

Mohl, Raymond A. "Clowning Around: The Miami Ethiopian Clowns and Cultural Conflict in Black Baseball." *Tequesta* 62 (2002): 40–67.

Moody, Anne. *Coming of Age in Mississippi: The Classic Autobiography of Growing Up Poor and Black in the Rural South*. New York: Random House, 2011.

Moore, Louis. *I Fight for A Living: Boxing and the Battle for Black Manhood, 1880–1915*. Urbana: University of Illinois Press, 2017.

———. *We Will Win the Day: The Civil Rights Movement, the Black Athlete, and the Quest for Equality*. Santa Barbara: Praeger, 2017.

Mormino, Gary R. "GI Joe Meets Jim Crow: Racial Violence and Reform in World War II Florida." *Florida Historical Quarterly* 73, no. 1 (July 1994): 23–42.

Morris, Aldon D. *The Origins of the Civil Rights Movement: Black Communities Organizing for Change*. New York: Free Press, 1986.

Myrdal, Gunnar. *An American Dilemma: The Negro Problem and Modern Democracy*. New York: Harper and Brothers, 1944.

Nelson, Bruce. "Organized Labor and the Struggle for Black Equality in Mobile during World War II." *Journal of American History* 80, no. 3 (1993): 952–88, https://doi.org/10.2307/2080410.

Nelson, David M. *The Anatomy of a Game: Football, the Rules, and the Men Who Made the Game*. Newark: University of Delaware Press, 1994.

Newkirk, Vann R., "Edward Waters College." In *New Life for Historically Black Colleges and Universities: A Twenty-First Century Perspective*, edited by Vann R. Newkirk, 26–32. Jefferson, N.C.: McFarland, 2012.

Neyland, Leedell W. *Florida Agricultural and Mechanical University: A Centennial History, 1887–1987*. Tallahassee: Florida A&M Press, 1987.

———. *Twelve Black Floridians*. Tallahassee: Florida A&M Press, 1970.

Neyland, Leedell W., Matthew H. Estaras, and Wilts C. Alexander. *The History of the Florida Interscholastic Athletic Association, 1932–1968*. Tallahassee: Florida A&M Press, 1982.

Nieves, Angel David. "Cultural Landscapes of Resistance and Self-Definition for the Race: Interdisciplinary Approaches to a Socio-Spacial Race History." In *"We Shall Independent Be": African American Place Making and the Struggle to Claim Space in the United States*, edited by Angel David Nieves and Leslie M. Alexander, 1–20. Boulder: University Press of Colorado, 2009.

Nunley, Vorris L. *Keepin' It Hushed: The Barbershop and African American Hush Harbor Rhetoric*. Detroit: Wayne State University Press, 2011.

Oliver, Melvin L., and Thomas M. Shapiro. *Black Wealth/White Wealth: A New Perspective on Racial Inequality*. New York: Routledge, 1995.

Olsen, Jack. "The Black Athlete—A Shameful Story." Pt. 1. *Sports Illustrated*, July 1, 1968.

Oriard, Michael. *Bowled Over: Big-Time College Football from the Sixties to the BCS Era*. Chapel Hill: University of North Carolina Press, 2009.

———. *King Football: Sport and Spectacle in the Golden Age of Radio and Newsreels, Movies and Magazines, the Weekly and the Daily Press*. Chapel Hill: University of North Carolina Press, 2001.

———. *Reading Football: How the Popular Press Created an American Spectacle*. Chapel Hill: University of North Carolina Press, 1993.

Ortiz, Paul. *Emancipation Betrayed: The Hidden History of Black Organizing and White Violence in Florida from Reconstruction to the Bloody Election of 1920*. Berkeley: University of California Press, 2005.

Paolantonio, Sal. *How Football Explains America*. Chicago: Triumph Books, 2008.

Parker, Inez Moore. *The Rise and Decline of the Program of Education for Black Presbyterians of the United Presbyterian Church U.S.A., 1865–1970*. San Antonio: Trinity University Press, 1977.

Paul, Joan, Richard V. McGhee, and Helen Fant. "The Arrival and Ascendence of Black Athletes in the Southeastern Conference, 1966–1980." *Phylon* 45, no. 4 (1984): 284–97, https://doi.org/10.2307/274909.

Peterson, Robert. *Only the Ball Was White: A History of Legendary Black Players and All-Black Professional Teams*. New York: Oxford University Press, 1992.

Phelts, Marsha Dean. *An American Beach for African Americans*. Gainesville: University Press of Florida, 1997.

Piascik, Andy. *Gridiron Gauntlet: The Story of the Men Who Integrated Pro Football in Their Own Words*. Lanham, Md.: Taylor Trade, 2011.

———. *The Best Show in Football: The 1946–1955 Cleveland Browns—Pro Football's Greatest Dynasty*. Lanham, Md.: Taylor Trade, 2010.

Pleasants, Julian M. "Claude Pepper, Strom Thurmond, and the 1948 Presidential Election in Florida." *Florida Historical Quarterly* 76, no. 4 (1998): 439–73.

———, ed. *Gator Tales: An Oral History of the University of Florida.* Gainesville: University Press of Florida, 2006.

Pompey, C. Spencer. *More Rivers to Cross: A Forty-Year Look at the Quest for Fair and Equitable Fulfillment of the "American Dream."* West Palm Beach, Fla.: Star Group, 2003.

Price, Hugh Douglas. "The Negro and Florida Politics, 1944–1954." *Journal of Politics* 17, no. 2 (1955): 198–220.

Pruter, Robert. "The National Interscholastic Basketball Tournament: The Crown Jewel of African American High School Sports during the Era of Segregation." In *Separate Games: African American Sport behind the Walls of Segregation*, edited by David K. Wiggins and Ryan Swanson, 75–92. Fayetteville: University of Arkansas Press, 2016.

———. *The Rise of American High School Sports and the Search for Control.* Syracuse: Syracuse University Press, 2013.

Rabby, Glenda Alice. *The Pain and the Promise: The Struggle for Civil Rights in Tallahassee, Florida.* Athens: University of Georgia Press, 1999.

Rader, Benjamin G. *American Sports: From the Age of Folk Games to the Age of Televised Sports.* 5th ed. Upper Saddle River, N.J.: Prentice Hall, 2004.

Rahim, Raja Z. "King of the Court: John B. McClendon and the Origins of Black Basketball at North Carolina College during Jim Crow Segregation, 1937–1952." Master's thesis, North Carolina Central University, 2015.

Rhoden, William C. *Forty Million Dollar Slaves: The Rise, Fall, and Redemption of the Black Athlete.* New York: Three Rivers Press, 2006.

Richardson, Joe M., and Maxine D. Jones. *Education for Liberation: The American Missionary Association and African Americans, 1890 to the Civil Rights Movement.* Tuscaloosa: University of Alabama Press, 2009.

Riley, Harris D., and William F. Meachem. "Cobb Pilcher, MD: A Remarkable Neurologic Surgeon." *Southern Medical Journal* 84, no. 1 (1991): 77–86.

Rish, Berkley L. "The Vanderbilt University Neurosurgical Heritage." *Journal of Neurosurgery* 79, no. 3 (September 1993): 464–66.

Robinson, Eddie, and Richard Lapchick. *Never Before, Never Again: The Autobiography of Eddie Robinson.* New York: Macmillan, 1999.

Robinson, Jo Ann Gibson. *The Montgomery Bus Boycott and the Women Who Started It: The Memoir of Jo Ann Gibson Robinson.* Knoxville: University of Tennessee Press, 1987.

Rodgers, R. Pierre. "'It's HBCU Classic Time!': Origins and the Perseverance of Historically Black College and University Football Classic Games." In *The Athletic Experience at Historically Black Colleges and Universities: Past, Present, and Persistence*, edited by Billy Hawkins, Joseph Cooper, Akilah Carter-Francique, and J. Kenyatta Cavil, 145–65. Lanham, Md.: Rowman and Littlefield, 2015.

Rominger, Donald W. "From Playing Field to Battleground: The United States Navy
V-5 Preflight Program in World War II." *Journal of Sport History* 12, no. 3 (1985):
252–64.

Roosevelt, Theodore. *The Strenuous Life: Essays and Addresses*. New York: Century,
1902.

Rose, Anne C. *Psychology and Selfhood in the Segregated South*. Chapel Hill: University
of North Carolina Press, 2009.

Ross, Charles K. *Outside the Lines: African Americans and the Integration of the National
Football League*. New York: NYU Press, 2001.

Runstedtler, Theresa. *Jack Johnson, Rebel Sojourner: Boxing in the Shadow of the Global
Color Line*. Berkeley: University of California Press, 2012.

Sabock, Ralph J. "A History of Physical Education at the Ohio State University—
Men and Women's Divisions, 1898–1969." Ph.D. diss., Ohio State University, 1969,
https://search.proquest.com/pqdtglobal/docview/302432785/citation/1C798DC9
EFD247AFPQ/3.

Samuels, Albert L. *Is Separate Unequal? Black Colleges and the Challenge to
Desegregation*. Lawrence: University Press of Kansas, 2004.

Sarratt, Reed. *The Ordeal of Desegregation: The First Decade*. New York: Harper & Row,
1966.

Sasscer, Amy. "Justice Delayed Is Justice Denied: Florida's 'Public Mischief' Defense
and Virgil Hawkins's Protracted Legal Struggle for Racial Equality." In *Old South,
New South, or Down South? Florida and the Modern Civil Rights Movement*, edited by
Irvin D. S. Winsboro, 134–54. Morgantown: West Virginia University Press, 2009.

Savitt, Todd L. "Abraham Flexner and the Black Medical Schools." *Journal of the
National Medical Association* 98, no. 9 (2006): 1415–26.

———. "Money Versus Mission at an African-American Medical School: Knoxville
College Medical Department, 1895–1900." *Bulletin of the History of Medicine* 74,
no. 4 (2000): 680–716.

Schmidt, Raymond. *Shaping College Football: The Transformation of an American Sport,
1919–1930*. Syracuse: Syracuse University Press, 2007.

Scott, Daryl Michael. *Contempt and Pity: Social Policy and the Image of the Damaged
Black Psyche, 1880–1996*. Chapel Hill: University of North Carolina Press, 1997.

Sellers, Cleveland, and Robert L. Terrell. *The River of No Return: The Autobiography
of a Black Militant and the Life and Death of SNCC*. Jackson: University Press of
Mississippi, 1973.

Shircliffe, Barbara J. *The Best of That World: Historically Black High Schools and the Crisis
of Desegregation in a Southern Metropolis*. Cresskill, N.J.: Hampton Press, 2006.

Shropshire, Kenneth L. *In Black and White: Race and Sports in America*. New York: New
York University Press, 1996.

"The Sit-in Movement." International Civil Rights Center & Museum, https://www
.sitinmovement.org/history/sit-in-movement.asp. Accessed May 7, 2018.

Sklaroff, Rebecca. "Constructing G.I. Joe Louis: Cultural Solutions to the 'Negro Problem' during World War II." *Journal of American History* 89, no. 3 (2002): 958–83.

Smith, Jessie Carney, and Carrell Horton, eds. *Historical Statistics of Black America*. New York: Gale Group, 1994.

Smith, Ronald A. "Far More Than Commercialism: Stadium Building from Harvard's Innovations to Stanford's 'Dirt Bowl.'" *International Journal of the History of Sport* 25, no. 11 (2008): 1453–74.

———. *Play-by-Play: Radio, Television, and Big-Time College Sport*. Baltimore: Johns Hopkins University Press, 2001.

———. *Sports and Freedom: The Rise of Big-Time College Athletics*. New York: Oxford University Press, 1988.

Smith, Ronald Austin. *Pay for Play: A History of Big-Time College Athletic Reform*. Urbana: University of Illinois Press, 2011.

Spivey, Donald. *"If You Were Only White": The Life of Leroy "Satchel" Paige*. Columbia: University of Missouri Press, 2012.

Strain, Christopher B. *Pure Fire: Self-Defense as Activism in the Civil Rights Era*. Athens: University of Georgia Press, 2005.

Suggs, Henry Lewis. "P. B. Young and the Norfolk 'Journal and Guide,' 1910–1954." Ph.D. diss., University of Virginia, 1976, https://search.proquest.com/pqdtglobal/docview/302838511/citation/401B4DDDDD348AFPQ/2.

Summerville, James. *Educating Black Doctors: A History of Meharry Medical College*. Tuscaloosa: University of Alabama Press, 1983.

Swanson, Richard A. "Cleveland Abbott." In *African Americans in Sports*, edited by David K. Wiggins, 2. London: Routledge, 2015.

Taylor, Clarence. *Black Religious Intellectuals: The Fight for Equality from Jim Crow to the Twenty-First Century*. New York: Routledge, 2013.

Taylor, Otis, and Mark Stallard. *Otis Taylor: The Need to Win*. Champaign, Ill.: Sports Publishing, 2003.

Taylor, Quintard. *In Search of the Racial Frontier: African Americans and the American West*. New York: Norton, 1999.

Tebeau, Charlton W., and William Marina. *A History of Florida*. 3rd ed. Miami: University of Miami Press, 1999.

Theoharis, Jeanne. *The Rebellious Life of Mrs. Rosa Parks*. Boston: Beacon Press, 2015.

Thomas, Vivien T. *Partners of the Heart: Vivien Thomas and His Work with Alfred Blalock*. Philadelphia: University of Pennsylvania Press, 1998.

Thompson, Chas. H. "Editorial Comment: The American Negro and National Defense." *Journal of Negro History* 9, no. 4 (1940): 547.

———. "Editorial Comment: Negro Teachers and the Elimination of Segregated Schools." *Journal of Negro Education* 20, no. 2 (1951): 135–39.

Toma, J. Douglas. *Football U.: Spectator Sports in the Life of the American University*. Ann Arbor: University of Michigan Press, 2003.

Tomberlin, Joseph A. "Florida Whites and the *Brown* Decision of 1954." *Florida Historical Quarterly* 51, no. 1 (1972): 22–36.

Turnbull, Jack E. *Stadium Stories: Iowa Hawkeyes*. Guilford, Conn.: Globe Pequot Press, 2004.

Tyson, Timothy B. *Radio Free Dixie: Robert F. Williams and the Roots of Black Power*. Chapel Hill: University of North Carolina Press, 1999.

Umoja, Akinyele Omowale. *We Will Shoot Back: Armed Resistance in the Mississippi Freedom Movement*. New York: New York University Press, 2013.

United States Commission on Civil Rights. *The Diminishing Barrier: A Report on School Desegregation in Nine Communities*. Washington, D.C.: U.S. Government Printing Office, 1972.

U.S. Department of Commerce. *Social Indicators, 1976*. Washington, D.C.: U.S. Government Printing Office, 1977.

Van West, Carroll. "The Tennessee State Tigerbelles: Cold Warriors on the Track." In *Separate Games: African American Sport behind the Walls of Segregation*, edited by David K. Wiggins and Ryan Swanson, 61–71. Fayetteville: University of Arkansas Press, 2016.

Vickers, Raymond B. *Panic in Paradise: Florida's Banking Crash of 1926*. Tuscaloosa: University of Alabama Press, 1994.

Von Eschen, Penny M. *Race against Empire: Black Americans and Anticolonialism, 1937–1957*. Ithaca: Cornell University Press, 1997.

Wagy, Tom. *Governor LeRoy Collins of Florida: Spokesman of the New South*. Tuscaloosa: University of Alabama Press, 1985.

Wakefield, Wanda Ellen. *Playing to Win: Sports and the American Military, 1898–1945*. Albany: SUNY Press, 1997.

Walker, Anders. *The Ghost of Jim Crow: How Southern Moderates Used* Brown v. Board of Education *to Stall Civil Rights*. New York: Oxford University Press, 2009.

Walsh, Christopher J. *Who's #1? 100-Plus Years of Controversial National Champions in College Football*. Lanham, Md.: Rowman and Littlefield, 2007.

Ware, Susan. *Game, Set, Match: Billie Jean King and the Revolution in Women's Sports*. Chapel Hill: University of North Carolina Press, 2011.

Washington, Booker T. *The Story of the Negro: The Rise of the Race from Slavery*. Vol. 1. New York: Doubleday, 1909.

———. *Up from Slavery*. New York: Bedford St. Martin's Books, 1901.

Watkins, William H. *The White Architects of Black Education: Ideology and Power in America, 1865–1954*. New York: Teacher's College Press, 2001.

Watterson, John Sayle. *College Football: History, Spectacle, Controversy*. Baltimore: Johns Hopkins University Press, 2000.

Wesley, Charles H. "John W. Davis." *Journal of Negro History* 66, no. 1 (1981): 76–78.

White, Arthur O. "State Leadership and Black Education in Florida, 1876–1976." *Phylon* 42, no. 2 (1981): 168–79.

White, Derrick E. *The Challenge of Blackness: The Institute of the Black World and Political Activism in the 1970s*. Gainesville: University Press of Florida, 2011.

———. "From Desegregation to Integration: Race, Football, and 'Dixie' at the University of Florida." *Florida Historical Quarterly* 88, no. 4 (2010): 469–96.

White, Sol, and Jerry Malloy. *Sol White's History of Colored Base Ball with Other Documents on the Early Black Game, 1886–1936*. Lincoln: University of Nebraska Press, 1996.

White, Walter. *What Caused the Detroit Riots*. New York: NAACP, 1943.

Whitfield, Stephen J. *A Death in the Delta: The Story of Emmett Till*. Baltimore: Johns Hopkins University Press, 1991.

Wiggins, David K. "The Biggest 'Classic' of Them All: The Howard University and Lincoln University Thanksgiving Day Football Games, 1919–1929." In *Rooting for the Home Team: Sport, Community, and Identity*, edited by Daniel A. Nathan, 36–53. Urbana: University of Illinois Press, 2013.

———. "'The Future of College Athletics Is at Stake': Black Athletes and Racial Turmoil on Three Predominately White University Campuses, 1968–1972." *Journal of Sport History* 15, no. 3 (1988): 304–33.

———. *Glory Bound: Black Athletes in a White America*. Syracuse: Syracuse University Press, 1997.

Wiggins, David K., and Patrick B. Miller. *The Unlevel Playing Field: A Documentary History of the African American Experience in Sport*. Urbana: University of Illinois Press, 2003.

Williams, Kidada E. *They Left Great Marks on Me: African American Testimonies of Racial Violence from Emancipation to World War I*. New York: New York University Press, 2012.

Wilson, Roosevelt. *Agile, Mobile, Hostile: The Biography of Jake Gaither*. Tallahassee: Roosevelt Wilson, 2017.

Woods, Jeff R. *Black Struggle, Red Scare: Segregation and Anti-Communism in the South, 1948–1968*. Baton Rouge: LSU Press, 2003.

Woodward, C. Vann. *The Strange Career of Jim Crow*. New York: Oxford University Press, 1955.

Wynn, Neil A. *The Afro-American and the Second World War*. 2nd ed. New York: Holmes & Meier, 1993.

INDEX

Note: In this index JG stands for Jake Gaither. *Page numbers in italics indicate illustrative material.*

Boston, Ralph, 154

Bowden, Bobby, 212

Boxton, John and Barbara, 253n114

Braddock, Joe Mills, 43

Bragg, Eugene, 53, 236n53

Bragg, Jubie B., 44–48, 51–52, 53, 63, 73, 81, 236n53

Britt, Elwood "Duck," 59

Brodsky, Larry, 4

Brooks, Barney, 65

Brooks, David, 111

Brown, Paul, 80, 86

Brown, Roosevelt, 159

Brown, Rufus, 173–74

Brown, Willie, 260n60

Browne, Edgar S., 77–78

Browns. *See* Cleveland Browns

Brown v. Board of Education, 101, 102, 104

Broyles, Frank, 112

Bryant, Paul "Bear," 67, 70, 88, 135, *136*, 189, 208

Buchanan, Buck, 161, 163, 179, 260n60

Bullock, Matthew, 24

Burns, Haydon, 172

Burt, Jim, 3

bus boycotts, 102, 108–11, 114

Butkus, Dick, 161

Butler, Henry, 55, 60

Byrd, Frantz "Jazz," 48, 53, 189

Caldwell, Millard, 81

Calhoun, Lee, 154

Calhoun, Solomon, 91

Callahan, Boyce, 214

Camp, Walter C., 25, 27–28, 29, 231n69

Campbell, Doak, 116, 171

Carlos, John, 165, 181

Carmichael, Harold, 198

Carmichael, Stokely, 180, *181*

Carney, Clement, 253n114

Cartwright, Seth, 162

Casem, Marino H., 187, 212

character development, 23, 24–25, 30, 33, 52, 91, 94, 180

Cheney State University, 19

Chester, Albert, 218

Chicago Bears, 114–15, 154, 159, 161–62

Chicago Defender (newspaper), 48, 211

Chiefs. *See* Kansas City Chiefs

Childs, Clarence, 128

Chiles, Lawton, 212

Chunn, J. C., 62

Churchill, Winston, 70

CIAA (Colored/Central Intercollegiate Athletic Association), 32, 38, 106

Civic League, 101–2

Civil Rights Act (1964), 175

civil rights movement: Black Power movement, 180–84; bus boycotts, 102, 108–11, 114; Delray Beach campaign, 101–2; emergence of in Florida, 98–100; JG's pragmatic approach to, 110–11, 124–27, 133, 140–41, 165, 181–84, 210, 253n123; sit-in movement, 123–26, 140, 253n114. *See also* desegregation and integration

Clark, Kenneth and Mamie, 104

Clark College, 21

Clay, Cassius, 151

Clemons, Edward "Ox," 98, 123

Cleveland Browns, 80

Coaches and Officials Conference, 33

coaching clinics, 36–37, 54, 73, 85–87, 89, 126

Coachman, Alice, 154

Cofield, May Frances, 69

Coleman, A. M., 170

Coleman, Vince, 4, 227n12

college football. *See* HBCU football; PWI football

Collins, LeRoy, 102, 109, 116, 126, 131

Colts. *See* Baltimore Colts

Columbia University, 23

Communism, 98–99, 109

ing for, 49–51, 92–93, 100, 115–17, 126, 204, 219, 221–22; Galimore funeral at, 154–55; under Hubbard, 2–6, 215–22; and institutional challenges of desegregation, 183, 191–92, 195, 211; involvement of in SIAC, 21; NAIA championship prospects of, 130–31, 133, 134–35, 148–49, 151–52; postwar enrollment at, 75; recruitment efforts of, 51–52, 88–89, 168–74, 177, 192–94, 214; rivalry with TSU, 149, 155–56, 166–67, 178–79, 197; and search for quality coaching, 52–55, 73–74, 212–15, 236n53; significance of Tampa game for, 200–204; small college championship prospects of, 138–39, 155–56, 157; and tension caused by civil rights movement, 98–100, 110–11, 123–26, 133, 180–82, 183–84; track and field at, 136–37; university title of, 103–4; during World War II, 60–64, 67–71. *See also* OBC

Farrington, Bo, 154

Faubus, Orval, 129

Faurot, Don, 71, 87

Favors, Jelani, 22

Fears, Ernest, Jr., 212

Felts, Bob, 149, 157–58

Fernandez, Bobby, 203

Fisk University, 16, 20, 32, 94

Flexner, Abraham, 64

Florida A&M University. *See* FAMU

Florida Interscholastic Athletic Association, 52

Florida Sentinel (newspaper), 100

football. *See* HBCU football; PWI football

Football Coaches Foundation, 184

Forte, Calvin, 4

Foss, Joe, 163

Four Ghosts, 55

four-platoon system, 96

Fowles, Raymond, 16

Frazier, Al, 90, 105, 108, 111, 112, 114

free substitutions, 94–96, 119–20, 251n80

FSU (Florida State University), 82, 92, 93, 115–17, 121, 126, 170–72, 173

Fuqua, Don, 208, 209

Gaffney, Don, 216

Gaines, Clarence "Bighouse," 221

Gaines, Mary Ola, 124

Gaither, A. D. (brother of JG), 75

Gaither, Alonzo "Jake" (JG), *38*, *97*, *113*, *118*, *125*, *136*, *142*, *143*, *160*, *199*

—awards and honors of: 200th win, 199–200; Board of Governors Award, 209; coach of the decade (1950s), 123; SIAC Coach of the Year (1969), 209; Small College Coach of the Year (1961), 135; W. A. Scott Memorial Trophies, 120, 135, 148

—career of, 1920s–30s: as coach at Henderson Institute, 35–38; as coach at St. Paul's College, 38, 38–39, 233n126; as football player at KC, 16, 32, 33, 34–35

—career of, 1937–44: coaching during World War II, 71; as FAMU basketball coach, 58–59; first season at FAMU, 54–55; and health concerns, 58, 59, 64, 65–66

—career of, 1945–53: coaching style and philosophy, 90–91, 96–98; development of FAMU coaching clinic, 85–87, 89; first national title, 85; offensive strategy, 87–88; opposition to substitution and platoon reforms, 96; promotion to and early seasons as FAMU head coach, 74, 75–78, 81–85; recruitment efforts, 88–90; second national title, 98

—career of, 1954–64: early attempts at perfect season, 105–8, 112–14; on

Harris, James "Shack," 179, 206

Harris, John D. "Grose," 55

Harrison, Cecile, 54

Harrison, Cellos, 70

Harvard University, 23, 24, 95

Harvey, B. T., 77

Hawkins, G. W., 80

Hawkins, Virgil, 99

Hayes, Bob, *146, 153, 158, 160*; accused of
robbery, 172; on JG, 212; Merritt on,
149; in NFL, 162, 174, 179, 193–94; in
Olympics, 152–54, 155, 156–57; reputation and success of at FAMU, 133, 134,
135, 136, 138, 147, 157–58

Hayes, Tony, 5

Hayes, Woody, 70, 206, 215

Haynes, Abner, 266n7

Hazelton, Major, 178, 179

HBCU football (historically Black colleges and universities): and athletic
eligibility, 31–32; campaigns of to play
against PWIs, 6–7, 174–77, 184–87,
204–5, 216–17; coaching role in development of, 25–27; community role in
development of, 29–30; and competition with PWIs for Black athletes, 152,
166, 168–74, 190–94, 214; economics
of, 92–96; founding of, 18–22; institutional challenges of desegregation at,
104, 183, 191–92, 195, 211; and movement for integrated college sports,
128–33, 134–41, 152; press role in development of, 27–29; reforming role in
development of, 31–33; representation
of in Olympics, 154; representation of
in professional sports, 114–15, 159–
63, 174, 190, 193–94, 260n60, 265n6;
scholarship on, 9–10; significance of
Tampa game, 200–204; student role in
development of, 23–25; viewed as inferior, 127, 140, 175. *See also* FAMU

Heard, Jesse, 192

Henderson, Edwin B., 9, 28

Henderson Institute, 35–38

Hendrieth, Algie, 5

Hicks, John, 215

Hicks, Vernon, 76

Higginbotham, A. Leon, 184

Hill, Darryl, 137, 140

Hill, Mack Lee, 260n60

Hill, Winston, 260n60

Holiday Bowl. *See* NAIA

Holmes, Robert, 163

Hooser, Hobe, 170

Hope, John, 26, 32

Houston, Ken, 265n6

Howard, Frank, 208

Howard University, 32, 40–41, 43–44

Hubbard, Rudy, 2–6, 215–22

Huerta, Marcelino, 121

Humphrey, Claude, 190, 265n6

Hunt, Lamar, 159

Hurt, Edward, 52, 72, 83, 86, 98, 122, 137,
154, 210

ICC (Inter Civic Council), 109–11, 114

industrial education, 21–22, 31–32

integration. *See* desegregation and
integration

Intercollegiate Football Association, 23,
25, 31. *See also* NCAA

Ivy League, 95

Jackson, Edward, 148

Jackson, Marion E., 84, 89, 90, 106, 117–
18, 122, 133, 148, 159–60, 209–10

Jackson, Sheep, 152, 160–61

Jackson, William, 23–24

Jackson, Willie, 171

Jackson State University, 32, 135, 139

jail-in movement, 124

Jakes, Wilhelmina, 102, 109

Jefferson, Dennis, 114

Jefferson, Harry, 86, 98, 129

157, 175; and television contracts, 150, 219–20

NCAA v. University of Oklahoma, 219–20

Neely, Jess, 178

Negro Civic League, 101–2

Neilson, Herman "Buck," 69, 71, 73

New York Giants, 159, 161

Neyland, Bob, 67

NFL (National Football League), 76–77, 112, 128, 158–63, 190

Nicholson, Collie J., 107

Nicks, Billy, 11, 120, 123, 162–63, 167, 210

Norfolk Journal and Guide (newspaper), 28, 37

North Carolina A&T University, 73, 84

North Carolina Central University, 106, 107

North Carolina Negro High School Athletic Association, 37

Nugent, Tom, 112

Nunn, Bill, Jr., 132, 150, 168, 215

OBC (Orange Blossom Classic), 83; decline of, 220; as de facto national championship game, 2, 11, 60, 76, 82; Pioneer Award for, 148; profits from, 50–51, 93, 150; relocation of to Miami, 80–82; scheduling overlap with National Classic, 106; scouting at, 159–60; vs. Howard University (1933), 40, 41–44; vs. Virginia State (1934), 53; vs. Hampton University (1937), 54; vs. Kentucky State (1938), 56–57; vs. Wilberforce (1940), 62, 238n25; vs. Texas College (1942), 67–68; vs. Wiley College (1945), 76; vs. Lincoln (1946), 77; vs. Virginia Union (1948), 84; vs. North Carolina A&T (1949), 84; vs. Wilberforce (1950), 84; vs. Virginia State (1952), 98; vs. Maryland State (1954), 106–7; vs. Grambling (1955), 107–8; vs. TSU (1956), 112–14;

vs. Maryland State (1957), 118–19; vs. Prairie View (1958), 120; vs. Prairie View (1959), 121–22; vs. Langston College (1960), 131; vs. Jackson State (1961), 135; vs. Jackson State (1962), 139; vs. Morgan State (1963), 150–51; vs. Grambling (1964), 157; vs. Morgan State (1965), 167, 173; vs. Alabama A&M (1966), 168; vs. Grambling (1967), 179; vs. Alcorn State (1968), 187–88; vs. Grambling (1969), 205–8; vs. Hampton University (1947), 81–82

Odom, Earl, 64, 65–66

offensive strategies (football), 87–88, 119–20, 166, 167

Oglesby, Edward, 60, 177

Ohio State University, 36, 53, 54, 215–16

Oliver, Harrell, 4

Olympics, 152–54, 155, 156–57, 180–81

one-platoon system, 96, 119

Orange Bowl, 79, 85

Oriard, Michael, 23

Orndorff, Paul, 201

Oves, Ralph, 112, 173

Owens, Clarence Burgess, 193

Owens, Jesse, 152–54

Owens, Jim, 200, 202, 207

Packers. *See* Green Bay Packers

Page, Alan, 266n6

Paige, Satchel, 127

Paremore, Robert, 121, 136, 138, 140–41, 144, 148

Parker, Buddy, 162

Parker, Richard A., 130

Parks, Rosa, 108

Patterson, Calvin, 171

Patterson, Carrie, 102, 109

Penn State University, 79

Perry, Benjamin L., 208–9, 215

Peterson, Bill, 126

Pickett, Bob, 218

Pilcher, Cobb, 65–66, 111, 126
Pioneer Awards, 148
Pitts, Frank, 163
Pittsburgh Courier (newspaper), 28, 40, 48, 60, 63, 84, 85, 91, 119, 120, 139, 162, 211, 238n9
platoon systems, 94–96, 119
Plessy v. Ferguson (1896), 18, 104
Plunkett, Sherman, 260n60
politics. *See* civil rights movement
Pollack, Syd, 77
Pollard, Fritz, 48, 231n69
Pompey, C. Spencer, 101, 102
Powell, Adam Clayton, 183
Powell, Nathaniel "Traz," 75, 81, 214
Prairie View A&M University, 120, 121–22, 151–52, 157
press: coverage of JG's coaching, 37, 52, 84, 89, 96–98, 105, 117–18, 120, 128, 160–61, 189, 209–10; coverage of OBC, 43–44, 81–82, 108, 122, 150, 157; coverage of sporting regulations, 77, 90; declining influence of, 211; determining national champions, 60, 238n9; promotion of civil rights movement and integrated sports, 80–81, 105, 130, 132, 133, 134, 137, 138–39, 141, 152, 174, 176; role in development of football, 27–29; white press, 27–28, 56–57
Price, Hollis F., 95
Princeton University, 23, 24
Principles of Conduct of Intercollegiate Athletics, 90
private/public divide: and athletic economies of scale, 94–96; and athletic eligibility, 20–21; in founding of HBCUs, 20–21
professional sports: AFL, 159, 161–63; HBCU representation in, 114–15, 159–63, 174, 190, 193–94, 260n60, 265n6; integration in, 9, 79, 127, 128, 158–63, 244n57; NFL, 76–77, 112, 128, 158–63,

190; Olympics, 152–54, 155, 156–57, 180–81; and political integration, 9
protests, 102, 108–11, 114, 123–26, 140, 253n114
PWI football (predominately white institutions): factors in development of, 23–24, 25–26, 27–28, 29–30, 31; HBCU campaigns to play against, 6–7, 174–77, 184–87, 204–5, 216–17; recruitment of Black athletes in South, 152, 166, 168–74, 190–94, 214; significance of Tampa game, 200–204

Race riots, 69, 70
Race Track Allocation Fund, 92–93
racism. *See* civil rights movement; desegregation and integration; segregation
Randolph, A. Philip, 63
Ratcliffe, Robert M., 105
Rattlers. *See* FAMU
Rea, E. B., 38
recruitment (football): at FAMU, 51–52, 88–89, 168–74, 177, 192–94, 214; through coaching clinics, 89; regulation of, 90; of veterans, 75
Redskins. *See* Washington Redskins
Reed, Matthew, 206–8
regulations: in early football development, 31–33; at NCAA, 90, 94, 96, 205–6; of recruitment, 90; at SIAC, 51, 77, 95–96; of substitutions and platoons, 95–96, 251n80
religion: and cultural autonomy, 8; and JG's ministerial coaching style, 90; and missionary foundation of HBCUs, 19, 20; muscular Christianity movement, 45–46
The Revolt of the Black Athlete (Edwards), 182
Rice, Louis, 173
Richardson, Gloster, 163
Richardson, Willie, 140–41

Solomon, Mike, 218
South Carolina State University, 94
Southern University, 6–7, 72, 84, 94, 105–6, 120, 131, 198–99
Southwestern Classic, 42
Spaulding, Merritt, 253n114
Spirit of Excellence, 91, 93, 182
split-T formation, 87–88, 119–20, 128, 166, 168
sporting congregations, as concept, 8. *See also* HBCU football
Stagg, Amos Alonzo, 178
Stahl, Floyd, 54
State Normal College for Colored Students, 21. *See also* FAMU
Staubach, Roger, 151
Stebbins, Richard, 154, 156
Steele, Charles and Henry, 123–24
Steele, C. K., 109–10, 111, 124
Stephens, Pricilla and Patricia, 123–24, 125, *125*, 140
Stevenson, Ben, 17, 28, 32
St. Louis University, 95
St. Paul's College, *38*, 38–39, 233n126
Strachan, Stanley, 55, 57, 60
Strayhorn, Guy, 99
Stroud, Morris, 163
Student Nonviolent Coordinating Committee, 128
substitutions (football rules), 94–96, 119–20, 251n80
SWAC (Southwestern Athletic Conference), 33, 72, 132, 150, 255n158
Sweatt, Herman, 100
Swift Junior College, 16
Sykes, Alfred, 201

Tabor, Alva, 198
Talladega College, 32
Tallahassee bus boycott, 102, 109–11, 114
Tangerine Bowl, 176, 177, 178
Tanner, Oscar, 68

Tatum, Jim, 71
Taylor, Jim, 67
Taylor, Otis, 162, 163
Taylor, Pete, 3–4
Taylor, Sam, 167
televised games, 150, 219–20
Temple, Ed, 154
Texas State Fair Classic, 42
T-formation offense, 87–88, 119–20, 128, 166, 168
Thomas, Emmitt, 163
Thomas, James, 171–72
Thomas, Vivien, 65
Thompson, Chas. H., 62
Thompson, James, 68
Thomson, Lawson E., 80
Tillotson College, 95
Time (magazine), 128
Tolan, Eddie, 152–54
Toney, James, 99
Tookes, Hansel, 215
Tookes, Hansel E., 60, 111
tourism, 42–43
track and field, 37, 136–37, 152–54, 155, 156–57, 180–81
Trent, William J., 24
Truman, Harry, 95, 98
Truvillion, Eric, 3
TSU (Tennessee State University): athletics program improvement at, 71–72; founding and growth of, 21; involvement of in SIAC, 33; Merritt hired at, 149; in National Classic, 106, 107; in OBC, 112–14; reputation and dominance of, 6–7, 95, 176–77; rivalry with FAMU, 149, 155–56, 166–67, 178–79, 197; vs. white schools, 112
Tucker, Thomas De Saille, 21, 45
Tullis, Jim, 138, 149, 155
Tunnell, Emlen, 161
Turkey Day Classic, 42
Tuskegee University, 16–17, 40, 58–59, 76

two-platoon system, 94–96

Twyman, William A., 96

UF (University of Florida), 56, 82, 92, 93, 116, 121, 126, 170–71, 185, 216

University of Iowa, 84–85

University of Miami, 1–6, 82, 84–85, 121, 169–70, 177, 219

University of San Francisco, 95

University of Tampa, 121, 177, 185–87, 200–204

University of Tennessee, 6

UPI (United Press International), 138–39

Upshaw, Gene, 190, 266nn6–7

Vanderbilt University, 64–65

Vaught, Johnny, 208

Vickers, James, 172

violence, 21, 24, 69, 70

Virginia State University, 98

Virginia Union University, 32, 84

vocational education, 21–22, 31–32

Wade, Wallace, 36, 86, 232n105

Walker, Anders, 253n123

Walker, Moses Fleetwood, 45

Walker, Pat, 4

Wallace, George, 150

Ward, Charlie, 149

Warlick, Ernie, 163, 260n60

Warner, Glenn "Pop," 178

Warren, Fuller, 100

wartime industry, 61, 62–63

W. A. Scott Memorial Trophy, 120, 135, 148

Washington, Booker T., 17, 21–22, 31

Washington, Chester, 43–44

Washington Redskins, 128

Watts, Leon "Sunshade," 59

Wells, Lloyd, 162

Westmoreland, Dick, 163, 260n60

White, Alton, 124–25

White, Walter, 100

White, Willye, 154

white institutions. *See* PWI football

Whitfield, Mal, 152–54

Whitney, Caspar, 31

Widener, Joseph, 92

Wilberforce University, 19, 62, 75–76, 84

Wilder, Vernon, 119, 120

Wiley College, 76, 77–78, 95

Williams, Alton, 43

Williams, Carroll, 169, 175

Williams, Doug, 217

Williams, Hugh, 124

Williams, James, 214, 215

Williams, Jim, 81, 120

Williams, Macon "Bodybuilder," 62, 68, 71, 120, 133

Willis, Bill, 80

Winning High School Football (Mather), 87

Wolf, Raymond, 86

Women, in athletics, 35, 71, 154

Wooden, John, 129

Woodruff, Bob, 121

World War II: impact of on college football, 66–72; outbreak and escalation of, 60, 61; segregation in context of, 61–63

Wright, Rayfield, 265n6

Wright, Ted, 236n53

Xavier University, 94, 175

Yale University, 23, 24, 25, 95

YMCA (Young Men's Christian Association), 46

Young, A. S. Doc, 174, 215

Young, Buddy, 161–62

Young, Frank "Fay," 28, 30, 77, 81–82

Young, Nathan B., 44–46, 47

Younger, Paul "Tank," 107, 112